THE OTHER SIDE OF THE MOUNTAIN:
Mujahideen Tactics in the Soviet-Afghan War

by
Ali Ahmad Jalali and Lester W. Grau
Foreign Military Studies Office, Fort Leavenworth, Kansas

Introduction by

Lieutenant General John E. Rhodes
Commanding General
U.S. Marine Corps Combat Development Command

Courtesy of
The United States Marine Corps Studies and Analysis Division
Quantico, Virginia

CONTENTS

INTRODUCTION

As we have throughout our history—the Philippines, Haiti, Nicaragua, Lebanon, Vietnam and Somalia—Marines will encounter guerrilla forces in the 21st century. Marines must understand potential adversaries, and learn as much as possible about them. The mujahideen of the Soviet-Afghan War prevailed against a larger and decisively better equipped foe, the Soviet Army. *The Other Side of the Mountain* presents the story of the mujahideen's fight against that foe.

On 27 December 1979, Moscow ordered the Soviet Army into Afghanistan. Organized, equipped, and trained for the execution of combined arms operations, that force embodied the concept of blitzkrieg. Nine years later, it withdrew in defeat. *The Other Side of the Mountain* was written from the reports of mujahideen combat veterans and provides a tactical look at a decentralized army of foot-mobile guerrillas waging war against a technologically superior foe. Absolute supremacy of firepower did not guarantee victory. Native knowledge of terrain and detailed study of a known adversary offset that advantage. In particular, the chapter on urban combat will be of great interest to commanders concerned with force protection. This book and its companion volume, *The Bear Went Over the Mountain: Soviet Combat Tactics in Afghanistan*, published for the United States Marine Corps in 1996, offers a chronicle of the Afghan War by the warfighters.

The Marine Corps of the 21st century will have tremendous advantages over guerrilla forces. Our equipment, technology, training, and support are the best in the world. Yet, technological superiority is not in and of itself a guarantee of success. Insight into our adversary's capabilities, tactics and motivation will provide the decisive edge. *The Other Side of the Mountain* will help us gain this insight. I heartily recommend this book to all Marines.

J. E. RHODES
Commanding General
Marine Corps Combat
    Development Command

FOREWORD

When the Soviet Union invaded Afghanistan in 1979, few experts believed that the fledgling Mujahideen resistance movement had a chance of withstanding the modern, mechanized, technologically-advanced Soviet Army. Most stated that resistance was futile and that the Soviet Union had deliberately expanded their empire to the south. The Soviet Union had come to stay. Although some historians looked at the British experience fighting the Afghan mountain tribesmen, most experts discounted any parallels since the Soviet Union possessed an unprecedented advantage in fire power, technology and military might. Although Arab leaders and the West supplied arms and material to the Mujahideen, they did so with the hope of creating a permanent, bleeding ulcer on the Soviet flank, not defeating the Soviet Union. They did not predict that the Soviet Union would voluntarily withdraw from Afghanistan in 1989.

What caused the Soviet withdrawal? The Soviets realized that they were trapped in an unwinnable war where they were suffering "death from a thousand cuts" by an intractable enemy who had no hope of winning, but fought on because it was the right thing to do. After failing to achieve military victory, the Soviet Union cut its losses and withdrew. The Soviet Union lost 13,833 killed. Over 1.3 million Afghans died and over a third of the population became refugees. Most have not yet returned to war-torn Afghanistan.

There have been few studies of guerrilla warfare from the guerrilla's perspective. To capture this perspective and the tactical experience of the Mujahideen, the United States Marine Corps commissioned this study and sent two retired combat veterans to interview Mujahideen. The authors were well received and generously assisted by various Mujahideen who willingly talked about their long, bitter war. The authors have produced a unique book which tells the guerrillas' story as interpreted by military professionals. This is a book about small-unit guerrilla combat. This is a book about death and survival, adaptation and perseverance.

This is a book for the combat-arms company and field grade officer and NCO. It provides an understanding of guerrilla field craft, tactics, techniques and procedures. It has application in Basic and Advanced Officer and NCO courses as well as special warfare courses. Senior leaders will also find valuable insights for training and supporting guerrilla forces as well as defending against guerrilla forces. This book is a companion piece to *The Bear Went Over the Mountain: Soviet Combat Tactics in Afghanistan* which National Defense University press published in 1996.

ACKNOWLEDGMENTS

This book would not be possible without the open, friendly and willing support of the many Mujahideen we interviewed. We thank Mawlawi Abdul-Rahman, Haidar Ahmadi, Mohammad Akbar, Akhtarjhan, Doctor Abdul Qudus Alkozai, Assadullah Mohammad Asef, Assadullah, Mawlawi Mohayddin Baloch, Abdul Baqi Balots, Abdul Nasrin Baz, Commander Didar, Daoud, Gulaga Farid, Ghulam Farouq, Pir Syed Ahmad Gailani, Haji Zaman Ghamsharik, Abdul Ghani, Sofi Lal Gul, Wazir Gul, Tsaranwal Sher Habib, Haji Habibulah, Ghulam Haidar, Haji Sayed Mohammad Hanif, Mawlali Nezamuddin Haqani, Hedayatullah, Toryalai Hemat, Engineer Mohammad Ibrahim, Mohammad Shah Kako, Asef Khan, Asil Khan, Haji Badshah Khan, Nawaz Khan, Counsel General Haji Abdul Khaleq, Haji Badshah Khan, Major Sher Aqa Kochay, Lalai, Mulla Malang, Haji Malangyar, Akhtar Mohammad, Amir Mohammad, Haji Lal Mohammad, Haji Pir Mohammad, Engineer Sayed Mohammad, Qari Feda Mohammad, Sultan Mohammad, Mohammad Amin Mudaqeq, Haji Nematullah, Lieutenant Zabet Omar, Sher Padshah, Haji Abdul Qader, Akhund Zada Qasem, Mawlawi Qasem, LTC Haji Mohammad Rahim, Abdul Razek, Mohammad Saber, Abdul Sabur, Doctor Mohammad Sadeq, Amin Safi, Haji Aaquelshah Sahak, Abdul Sadiq Sahebzada, Sarshar, Haji Mohammad Seddiq, Shahabuddin, Haji Mohammad Shah, Mohammad Humayun Shahin, Mawlawi Abdul Shukur Yasini, Haji Sidiqullah, Qazi Guljan Tayeb, General Abdul Rahim Wardak, Doctor Mohammad Wakil, Doctor Mohammad Wali, Haji Mohammad Yakub, General Gulzarak Zadran and Zakari for generously sharing their time and experience. We can only hope that peace will finally come to Afghanistan so that they can start the long, difficult job of rebuilding their shattered country.

Our special thanks for the generous hospitality and support extended to us by Nancy Dupree of the Agency Coordinating Body for Afghan Relief, Pir Gailani, Mr. Kamaluddin of the Afghan Media Resource Center, Abdul Ahad Karzai, Ahmed Wali Karzai, General Counsel Haji Abdul Khaleq, Vice Counsel Muhammad Wali Naeemi and Abdul Ghani Wardak.

A special thanks to our colleague, Major Nasrullah Safi, who went into areas of Afghanistan to conduct interviews where we could not go. We contacted several major Mujahideen commanders such as Ismail

Khan, Masood, Abdul Haq, and Jalaluddin Haqani for interviews and material, but we were unable to meet with them before the book deadline. Our thanks in advance for the privilege of returning at a future time to conduct those interviews and to include them in a follow-on book.

Our special thanks to Colonel David O. Smith, Lieutenant Colonel Terry Cook, Captain Bob Hehl and TSGT Barry Cuthbertson of the United States Defense Attache Office in Islamabad and Principal Officer of the United States Consulate in Peshawar, Brad Hanson.

The United States Marine Corps funded the research, writing and publication of this book. Charlie Cutshaw, Karen Dolan and Dick Voltz of the USMC Studies and Analysis Division at Quantico, Virginia provided funding for printing *The Bear Went Over The Mountain: Soviet Combat Tactics in Afghanistan* and agreed to underwrite the production of this counterpart volume on Mujahideen tactics. Colonel Charles Johnston, the former Director of the U.S. Army Foreign Military Studies Office (FMSO) enthusiastically supported the research and production as did FMSO Director Dr. Graham Turbiville, and FMSO analysts Dr. Jacob Kipp, Tim Thomas and Major Ray Finch. Robert Love helped with translation support and Linda Pride and Al Lindman provided computer assistance. The Combined Arms Research Library and Command and General Staff College Map Library at Fort Leavenworth provided invaluable assistance. Alice Mink of FMSO kept the whole production on time and under budget.

A "band of brothers," skilled in tactics, read and provided commentary on the manuscript. Our special thanks to Colonel (Ret) David M. Glantz of Carlisle, Pennsylvania; Colonel (Ret.) Charles E. Johnston, former Director of FMSO; Colonel (Ret) William M. Mendel of FMSO; Allen E. Curtis, Director of Intelligence and Security at the National Training Center; former Marine Captain (Ret) Tim Leaf of Quantico, Virginia; Lieutenant Colonel John E. Sray of CENTCOM; Lieutenant Colonel Karl Prinslow of FMSO; and Major Darr Reimers of the 1st Cavalry Division.

Mary Ann Glantz graciously edited the manuscript. Jonathan Pierce was the book editor/designer, Rhonda Gross created the initial map graphics, and Emily Pierce did a superb job of finishing the maps and designing the cover.

Homaira Jalali and Gina Grau showed remarkably good humor and supported the efforts of their husbands as they gathered the material and worked on the book. We thank all of you for your help. Any mistakes are the authors.

PREFACE

Afghanistan, a multi-ethnic state in southwest Asia, is home to diverse social communities that share common experience through interaction with dominant states, empires, invading armies, trade and cultural movements that traversed the land during their thousands of years of history. The different ethnic groups in modern Afghanistan (Pashtuns, Tajiks, Uzbeks, Turkmans, Persian-speaking Hazaras, Balochis, etc.) straddle the boundries of the state. However, their national identity is mostly defined by their differences with their ethnic kinsmen across the borders rather than their national commonalities. About 99% of Afghanistan's over 17 million population are Muslim, of which 85% are followers of the Sunni sect while the rest are Shia. About 85% of Afghans live in rural communities in a land dominated by mountains and deserts. Modern travel is primarily restricted to a highway ring connecting the various cities. There is no railroad network.

Afghanistan has mostly been a loose collection of tribes and nationalities over which central governments had varying degrees of influence and control at different times. The country has been historically known for its remarkable Islamic and ethnic tolerence. However tribal rivalries and blood feuds, ambitions of local chieftains, and tribal defiance of pervasive interference by the central government have kept the different parts of the land at war at different times. In such cases the kinship-based identity has been the major means of the community's political and military mobilization. Such identity places far greater importance on kinship and extended family than ideology.

Afghanistan stands at a geographic crossroads that has seen the passage of many warring peoples. Each of these has left their imprint on the ancient land and involved the people of Afghanistan in conflict. Often this conflict got in the way of economic development. What has developed is a country composed of somewhat autonomous "village states" spread across the entire country.[1] Afghans identify themselves by Qawm—the basic subnational identity based on kinship, residence and sometimes occupation. Western people may refer to this as "tribe", but this instinctive social cohesiveness includes tribal clans, ethnic

[1] Ali A. Jalali, "Clashes of Ideas and Interests in Afghanistan", paper given at the Institute of World Politics, Washington, D.C., July 1995, page 4.

subgroups, religious sects, locality-based groups and groups united by interests.[2]   The Qawm, not Afghanistan, is the basic unit of social community and, outside the family, the most important focus on individual loyalty.   Afghanistan has, at times, been characterized as a disunited land riven by blood feuds.   The feuds center on family and Qawm. Yet, the leaders of the various Qawm have resolved feuds and held the land together.   Village elders can put feuds on hold for a decade or longer and then let them resume once the agreed-on time has expired and the matter is still unresolved. Afghanistan's ancient roots and strong ties of kinship provide an anchor against progress, but also the means to cope when central authority has collapsed.   Historically, the collapse of the central government of Afghanistan or the destruction of its standing armies has never resulted in the defeat of the nation by an invader.   The people, relying on their decentralized political, economic and military potential, have always taken over the resistance against the invaders.[3]   This was the case during two wars with Great Britain in the 19th Century (1839-1842, 1878-1880).   This happened again in the Soviet-Afghan War.

The tactics of the Mujahideen reflected this lack of central cohesion.   Their tactics were not standard, but differed from valley to valley and tribe to tribe.   No more than 15 percent of the guerrilla commanders were military professionals.   However, Afghanistan had a conscript army and virtually every 22-year-old male served his two year obligation.   This provided a basic military education which eased cooperation between the various Mujahideen groups.   The Mujahideen were true volunteers—unpaid warriors who fought to protect their faith and community first and their nation next.   As true volunteers, fighting for their Qawm and religion, the Mujahideen looked down on the professional soldier (asker) as a simple mercenary who was either the victim of a press gang or too stupid to ply any other trade.[4]   This disdain did not attach to the professional officer, who enjoyed a great deal of prestige.

Afghanistan was not a guerrilla war ala Mao Tse Tung or Vo Nguyen Giap.   The Mujahideen were not trying to force a new ideology and government on a land.   Rather, they fought to defend their Qawm and their religion against a hostile ideology, an atheistic value

---

[2] ibid,3.

[3] ibid,4.

[4] Oliver Roy, The Failure of Political Islam, Cambridge: Harvard University Press, 1994, page 158-159.

system, an oppressive central government and a foreign invader. It was a spontaneous defense of community values and a traditional way of life by individual groups initially unconnected to national or international political organizations.[5]

The Great Game [6]

Russian expansionism and empire building in Central Asia began in 1734 and Moscow's interest in Afghanistan was apparent by the late 1830s. The Great Game described the British and Russian struggle for influence along the unsettled northern frontier of British India and in the entire region between Russia and India. Afghanistan lay directly in this contested area between two empires. Russia described her motives in the Great Game as simply to abolish the slave trade and to establish order and control along her southern border. The British, however, viewing Russian absorption of the lands of the Caucasus, Georgia, Khirgiz, Turkmens, Khiva and Bukhara, claimed to feel threatened by the presence of a large, expanding empire near India and ascribed different Russian motives. The British stated that Russian motives were to weaken British power and to gain access to a warm-water port. Britain claimed that her own actions were to protect the frontiers of British India.

The Great Game spilled into Afghanistan when British forces invaded during the First Anglo-Afghan War (1839-1842). Britain claimed that the invasion was supposed to counter Russian influence. After hard fighting, the British withdrew. By 1869, the Russian empire reached the banks of the Amu Darya (Oxus) river—the northern border of Afghanistan. This caused additional British concern. In 1878, the arrival of a special Russian diplomatic mission to Kabul led to another British invasion and the Second Anglo-Afghan War. The British Army again withdrew. In the Anglo-Russian Treaty of 1907, the Russians agreed that Afghanistan lay outside its sphere of interest and agreed to confer with Britain on all matters relating to Russian-Afghan relations. In return, Britain agreed not to occupy or annex any part of Afghanistan nor interfere in the internal affairs of that country. Although the Amir of Afghanistan refused to recognize the treaty, Russia and Britain agreed to its terms and honored them

[5] Jalali,1
[6] Section derived from Richard F. Nyrop and Donald M. Seekins (editors), Afghanistan: A Country Study, Fifth edition, Washington: US Government Printing Office, 1986, 22-73 and Peter Hopkirk, The Great Game, New York: Kodansha International, 1994.

until 1919 when Afghan troops crossed into British India, seized a village and attempted to raise a popular revolt in the area. The British responded with yet another invasion and the Third Anglo-Afghan War. The political settlement resulted in Afghanistan's full independence from Great Britain.

Afghanistan's foreign policy from 1919 until 1978 balanced the demands of her immediate neighbors, and external powers such as the United States, Germany and Great Britain. Normal relations with her northern neighbor, the Soviet Union, led to increased Soviet investment and presence in Afghanistan.

In April 1978, a small leftist group of Soviet-trained Afghan officers seized control of the government and founded the Democratic Republic of Afghanistan, a client state of the Soviet Union. Civil war broke out in Afghanistan. The putsch installed President Nur M. Taraki, a Marxist who announced sweeping programs of land distribution, changed status for women and the destruction of the old Afghanistan social structure. Disregarding the national social structure and mores, the new government enjoyed little popular support. The wobbly Taraki government was almost immediately met by increased armed resistance as the Mujahideen ranks grew. In 1978, religious leaders, in response to popular uprisings across Afghanistan, issued statements of *jihad* (holy war) against the communist regime. This was an appeal to the supranational identity of all Afghans--a fight to defend the faith of Islam. The combat readiness of the Army of the Democratic Republic of Afghanistan plunged as government purges swept the officer corps. Soldiers, units and entire regiments deserted to the resistance and by the end of 1979, the actual strength of the Afghan Army was less than half of its authorized 90,000. In March 1979, the city of Herat revolted and most of the Afghan 17th Infantry Division mutinied and joined the rebellion. Forces loyal to Taraki reoccupied the city after the Afghan Air Force bombed the city and the 17th Division. Thousands of people reportedly died in the fighting, including some Soviet citizens.

Soviet Intervention

The Soviet-Afghan War began over the issue of control. The Democratic Republic of Afghanistan was nominally a socialist state governed by a communist party. However, the state only controlled some of the cities, while tribal elders and clan chiefs controlled the countryside. Furthermore, the communist party of Afghanistan was split into two hostile factions. The factions spent more time fighting each other than trying to establish socialism in Afghanistan. In September 1979, Taraki's Prime Minister, Hafizullah Amin, seized power and murdered Taraki. Amin's rule proved no better and the Soviet Union watched this new communist state spin out of control. Meanwhile, units of the army mutinied, civil war broke out, cities and villages rose in revolt and Afghanistan began to slip away from Moscow's control and influence. Leonid Brezhnev, the aged Soviet General Secretary, saw that direct military intervention was the only way to prevent his client state from disintegrating into complete chaos. He decided to intervene.

The obvious models for intervention were Hungary in 1956 and Czechoslovakia in 1968. The Soviet General Staff planned the Afghanistan invasion based on these models. However, there was a significant difference that the Soviet planners missed. Afghanistan was embroiled in a civil war and a coup de main would only gain control of the central government, not the countryside. Although participating military units were briefed at the last minute, the Soviet Christmas Eve invasion of 1979 was masterfully planned and well-executed. The Soviets seized the government, killed the president and put their own man in his place. According to some Russian sources, they planned to stabilize the situation, strengthen the army and then withdraw the majority of Soviet forces within three years. The Soviet General Staff planned to leave all fighting in the hands of the army of the Democratic Republic. But Afghanistan was in full revolt, the dispirited Afghan army was unable to cope, and the specter of defeat following a Soviet withdrawal haunted the Politburo. Invasion and overthrow of the government proved much easier than fighting the hundreds of ubiquitous guerrilla groups. The Soviet Army was trained for large-scale, rapid-tempo operations. They were not trained for the platoon leaders' war of finding and closing with small, indigenous forces which would only stand and fight when the terrain and circumstances were to their advantage.

Back in the Soviet Union, there was no one in charge and all decisions were committee decisions made by the collective leadership. General Secretary Brezhnev became incapacitated in 1980 but did not die until November 1982. He was succeeded by the ailing Yuri Andropov. General Secretary Andropov lasted less than two years and was succeeded by the faltering Konstantin Chernenko in February 1984. General Secretary Chernenko died in March 1985. Although the military leadership kept recommending withdrawal, during this

"twilight of the general secretaries" no one was making any major decisions as to the conduct and outcome of the war in Afghanistan. The
war bumped on at its own pace. Finally, Mikhail Gorbachev came to
power. His first instinct was to order military victory in Afghanistan
within a year. Following this bloodiest year of the war, Gorbachev realized that the Soviets could not win in Afghanistan without unaccept-
able international and internal repercussions and began to cast
about for a way to withdraw with dignity. United Nations negotiators
provided that avenue and by 15 October 1988, the first half of the
Soviet withdrawal was complete. On 15 February 1989, the last Soviet
forces withdrew from Afghanistan. Soviet force commitment, initially
assessed as requiring several months, lasted over nine years and
required increasing numbers of forces. The Soviet Union reportedly
killed 1.3 million people and forced 5.5 million Afghans (a third of the
prewar population) to leave the country as refugees. Another 2 million
Afghans were forced to migrate within the country. The country has
yet to recover.

Initially the Mujahideen were all local residents who took arms and
banded together into large, rather unwieldy, forces to seize the local
district capitols and loot their arms rooms. The DRA countered these
efforts where it could and Mujahideen began to coalesce into much
smaller groups centered around the rural village. These small groups
were armed with a variety of weapons from swords and flintlock mus-
kets to British bolt-action rifles and older Soviet and Soviet-bloc
weapons provided to Afghanistan over the years. The guerrilla
commanders were usually influential villagers who already had a
leadership role in the local area. Few had any professional military
experience. Rebellion was wide-spread, but uncoordinated since the
resistance was formed along tribal and ethnic lines.

The Soviet invasion changed the nature of the Mujahideen resistance. Afghanistan's neighbors, Pakistan and Iran, nervously regard-
ed the advance to the Soviet Army to their borders and began providing training and material support to the Mujahideen. The United
States, Peoples Republic of China, Britain, France, Italy, Saudi Arabia,
Egypt, and the United Arab Emirates began funneling military,
humanitarian and financial aid to the Mujahideen through Pakistan.
Pakistan's assessment was that the Soviet Union had come to
Afghanistan to stay and it was in Pakistan's best interests to support
those Mujahideen who would never accept the Soviet presence. The
Pakistan Inter-Services Intelligence Agency (ISI) began to funnel aid

through various Afghan political factions headquartered in Pakistan. Eventually there were seven major Afghan factions receiving aid. The politics of these factions were determined by their leaders' religious convictions—three of which were Islamic moderates and four of which were Islamic fundamentalists. Pakistan required that the various ethnic and tribal Mujahideen groups join one of the factions in order to receive aid. Over time, this provided the leaders of these factions with political power which they used to dominate the politics of post-communist Afghanistan. The Pakistani authorities favored the most-fundamentalist groups and rewarded them accordingly. This aid distribution gave the Afghan religious leaders unprecedented power in the conduct of the war. It also undermined the traditional authority of the tribal and village leaders.

The Mujahideen were unpaid volunteers with family responsibilities. This meant that they were part-time warriors and that spoils of war played a major role in military actions. Mujahideen sold mostly captured weapons and equipment in the bazaars to support their families. As the war progressed, mobile Mujahideen groups emerged. The mobile Mujahideen groups were larger and consisted of young (under 25), unmarried, better-trained warriors. Sometimes the mobile Mujahideen were paid. The mobile Mujahideen ranged over a much larger area of operations than the local Mujahideen and were more responsive to the plans and desires of the factions.

The strategic struggle for Afghanistan was a fight to strangle the other's logistics. The Mujahideen targeted the Soviet lines of communication—the crucial road net work over which the Soviet supplies had to travel. The Soviet attack on the Mujahideen logistics was two phased. From 1980 until 1985, the Soviets sought to eliminate Mujahideen support in the rural countryside. They bombed granaries and rural villages, destroyed crops and irrigation systems, mined pastures and fields, destroyed herds and launched sweeps through rural areas—conscripting young men and destroying the infrastructure. The Soviet leadership, believing Mao Tse Tung's dictum that the guerrilla lives in the population like a fish in water, decided to kill the fish by draining off the water.[7] As a result, Afghanistan became a nation of refugees as more than seven million rural residents fled to the relative safety of neighboring Pakistan and Iran or to the cities of Afghanistan. This Soviet effort denied rural support to the Mujahideen, since the villagers had left and most of the food now had

[7] Claude Malhauret, Afghan Alternative Seminar, Monterey, California, November 1993.

to be carried along with weapons and ammunition and materials of war. The Mujahideen responded by establishing logistics bases inside Afghanistan. The Soviet fight from 1985 to withdrawal was to find and destroy these bases.

Terrain, as any infantryman knows, is the ultimate shaper of the battlefield. Afghanistan's terrain is varied and challenging. It is dominated by towering mountains and forbidding desert. Yet it also has lush forests of larch, aspen and juniper. It has tangled "green zones"—irrigated areas thick with trees, vines, crops, irrigation ditches and tangled vegetation. It has flat plains full of wheat and swampy terraces which grow delicious long-grained rice. It is not ideal terrain for a mechanized force dependent on fire power, secure lines of communication and high-technology. It is terrain where the mountain warrior, using ambush sites inherited from his ancestors, can inflict "death from a thousand cuts". The terrain dictates different tactics, force structure and equipment from those of conventional war.

This book is not a complete history of the Soviet-Afghan War. Rather, it is a series of combat vignettes as recalled by the Mujahideen participants. It is not a book about right or wrong. Rather, it is a book about survival against the overwhelming firepower and technological might of a superpower. This is the story of combat from the guerrilla's perspective. It is the story of brave people who fought without hope of winning because it was the right thing to do.

About the Book

Author Les Grau, regularly travels back and forth to Russia. He received a book from the History of Military Art department at the Frunze Combined Arms Academy in Moscow. The book was intended for students' classroom use only and, as such, shows both the good and the bad. With Frunze Academy permission, Les translated this book and added commentary before it was published by NDU Press as *The Bear Went Over the Mountain: Soviet Combat Tactics in Afghanistan.* Author Ali Jalali, helped in the editing process. "The Bear" showed the tactics of the Soviets, but the Mujahideen tactics were absent. Charlie Cuthbertson and Dick Voltz of the USMC in Quantico agreed that both sides needed to be presented and sent Ali and Les to Pakistan and Afghanistan to interview Mujahideen commanders for a companion volume.

Author Ali Jalali has the perfect credentials to do this book. Ali was a Colonel in the Afghan Army and taught at the Afghan Military

Academy and Army Staff College. His foreign education included the Infantry Officer's Advanced Course at Fort Benning, Georgia; the British Army Staff College at Camberley; and the Soviet Frunze Academy. Many of Ali's officer students were key resistance figures. Ali was also a member of the resistance and an accredited journalist during the conflict. Now Ali works as a journalist and has covered Afghanistan and Central Asia over the last 15 years. Ali is respected by all the factions and has exceptional entre to the Mujahideen.

Ali and Les arrived in Pakistan in September 1996 and were preparing to go into Afghanistan when the Taliban advance on Kabul closed the borders to American citizens. Ali interviewed some 40 Mujahideen during a month in Peshawar, Quetta, and Islamabad, Pakistan. Our colleague, Major Nasrullah Safi, conducted interviews for another two months inside Afghanistan for this book. The interviews are the basis of this book. In those interviews where we have several sources for the same vignette or where we have lots of supporting written reports and material, we have written the vignette in the third person. In those cases where the person interviewed is the primary source, we have written the vignette in the first person. The vignettes are arranged chronologically by type of action. Occasionally, when the actions occur at the same place over time, we lump those actions together instead of chronologically. We have tried to make the book as accurate as possible, but realize that time and retelling may have altered some of the facts. We have limited the span of the book from the Soviet invasion until their withdrawal. The war started before the Soviet invasion and continued long after their departure. We plan to write about these battles in a future book.

We used edition 2-DMA series U611 1:100,000 maps from the U.S. Defense Mapping Agency for the final preparation of the material. For those who wish to consult the map sheets, map sheet numbers are given with each vignette. We have numbered each vignette within the chapter and started each chapter with a country map showing the rough location of each vignette. The interviews were long and exhaustive, so many details are available. Many of the interviews were conducted at different times and places, with different people who had been part of the same battle or operation. This allowed us to check and compare details and sequences of events. Map elevations are given in meters. Contour intervals are not consistent and merely show elevation. Place and name spelling is based on Ali Jalali's best transliteration efforts. Consistency in spelling is difficult when two alphabets are involved—some spellings are different than in other books on Afghanistan. Although the Mujahideen always say 'Russian' instead of 'Soviet', we have used 'Soviet' throughout unless it is a direct quote.

We use Russian map graphics on the maps. The Afghan Army used the Soviet graphics system and most Mujahideen were familiar with them. Russian graphics are more "user friendly" (flexible and illustrative) than Western graphics. The Russians can show the sequential development of an action by adding times or identifying lines to their graphics. These lines are explained in the legend. A table of Russian map graphics is located in the back of the book. Mujahideen forces are shown in blue and Soviet/DRA forces are shown in red.

THE OTHER SIDE OF THE MOUNTAIN:
Mujahideen Tactics in the Soviet-Afghan War

CHAPTER 1
AMBUSHES

The ambush is a favorite tactic of the guerrilla since it allows him to mass forces covertly, attack the enemy, seize needed supplies and retreat before the enemy can effectively react. The ambush has long been part of the Afghan warrior tradition and has been a key feature of historic Afghan warfare—whether fighting other tribes, the British or the government. The Mujahideen ambush served to attack the Soviet/DRA lines of communication, provided needed supplies, and forced the bulk of Soviet/DRA maneuver forces to perform security missions. Logistics were key to the conduct of the Soviet/Afghan War and Mujahideen ambushes threatened the resupply of Soviet and DRA forces and limited the number of Soviet troops that could be deployed into the country. The Mujahideen ambush was their most effective counter to Soviet/DRA military activity and threatened the ability of the Soviets and DRA to prosecute the war.

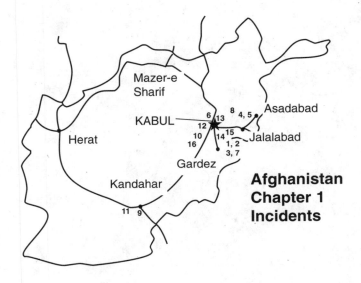

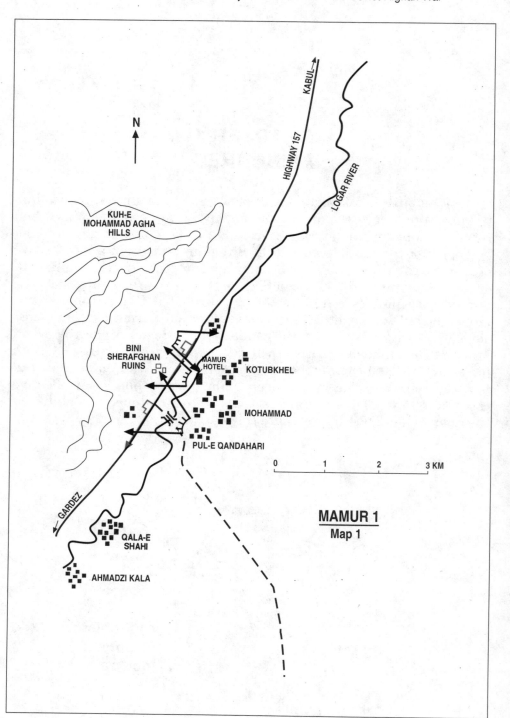

KABUL

HIGHWAY 157

LOGAR RIVER

N

KUH-E
MOHAMMAD AGHA
HILLS

BINI
SHERAFGHAN
RUINS

MAMUR
HOTEL

KOTUBKHEL

MOHAMMAD

PUL-E QANDAHARI

GARDEZ

QALA-E
SHAHI

AHMADZI KALA

0   1   2   3 KM

MAMUR 1
Map 1

VIGNETTE 1
AMBUSHES AT THE MAMUR HOTEL
by Commander Mohammad Akbar

A day seldom passed without a clash between the Mujahideen and the Soviets or DRA in Logar Province. In the summer of 1980, my group set an ambush to attack a supply column of Soviet and DRA forces moving from Kabul to Gardez on highway 157. At that time, the populace had not migrated from the area and it was full of people. The Mujahideen had contacts in the government who reported on the movement of columns along the main highway. This was to be our first attack on a major column on this highway following the Soviet invasion. The ambush site was located around the Pul-e Qandahari junction with the main highway. At this point, the Logar River comes within 200 meters of the highway to the east, and the Kuh-e Mohammad Agha hills rise some 700 meters over the highway to the west. Ten kilometers to the south, the road runs through a steep gorge where vehicles cannot easily turn back (Map 1 - Mamur 1). We had 50 Mujahideen armed with Mosin-Nagant carbines, Enfield rifles and two RPG-7s. Our leader, Commander Hayat, divided our men into three groups and put one group in the Bini Sherafghan ruins some 70 meters west of the road. He put the second group to the east of the road around the Mamur Hotel and put the third group to the east in Pul-e Qandahari facing the Mohammad Agha High School. Our ambush occupied a two-kilometer stretch. At this time, I was the late Commander Hayat's deputy commander, commanding the Pul-e Qandahari positions.

Commander Hayat ordered that the attack would start when the end of the column reached the Bini Shirafghan ruins. The DRA column came. It had about 100 vehicles carrying food, ammunition and fuel. There were quite a few POL tankers in the column. We let it pass and, as the end of the column reached the ruins, we started to attack at the end of the column. In those days, convoy escort was very weak and air support was insufficient. There was practically no resistance or reaction to our attack from the column. Even the APCs which were escorting the column were passive. We left our positions

Mohammad Akbar is from the village of Shahi Kala in Mohammad Agha District of Logar Province. He graduated from high school in the region and joined the resistance in 1979 and fought in Logar Province until the collapse of the DRA. He was a member of the Islamic Party (HIH - *Hezb-e Islami Gulbuddin*). [Map sheet 2885, vic grid 1086].

and started moving up the column, firing as we went, and damaged or destroyed almost all the vehicles. We had no casualties. I don't know how many DRA casualties there were, but we wounded many drivers who the government evacuated later. We left the area promptly after the ambush.

The area around the Mamur Hotel was ideal for an ambush and we, and other Mujahideen groups, used it often. In September 1981, we set an ambush at the Mamur Hotel and in Pule-e Qandahari facing the high school. The Mamur Hotel group was commanded by the noted HIH commander Doctor Abdul Wali Khayat and the Pule-Qandahari position was commanded by my commander, the late Commander Hayat. There were some 35 Mujahideen armed with AK-47 rifles and three RPG-7s. The ambush site occupied about one kilometer of roadway. When the column arrived, we destroyed twelve trucks and captured three intact. The three trucks were large, heavy-duty, eight-cylinder trucks and they were loaded with beans, rice and military boots. We needed all this gear. We also captured two 76mm field guns and a heavier gun that I don't know the type or caliber. We did not have any Mujahideen casualties.

In July 1982, the late Doctor Wali Khayat set an ambush near the Mamur Hotel. A Soviet column, moving supplies from Kabul to Gardez, entered the ambush kill zone. During the attack, one Mujahideen fired an RPG-7 at an escorting APC. It hit the APC and a Soviet officer jumped out of the damaged APC and took cover. The officer was wounded. While the fighting was going on, the column sped up and left the ambush area—and left the officer behind. Doctor Abdul Wali Khayat fired at the position where the Soviet officer was. The Soviet officer returned fire with his AK-74. Doctor Khayat fired again and wounded the Soviet officer a second time—this time in the hand. The Soviet officer dropped his AK-74 and took out his pistol. Doctor Khayat threw a hand grenade at the officer and killed him. Then he crossed the road and took his AK-74 and his Makarov pistol. He left the body where it lay and the Mujahideen left the ambush site.

The next day the Soviets returned in a column from Kabul. They cordoned off the area and searched the houses around Mohammad Agha District headquarters and the town of Kotubkhel. They went house to house looking for their missing officer. HIH commander Sameh Jan was in Kotubkhel at that time. He coordinated and organized the actions of all the Mujahideen factions which were caught in the cordon. There were about 150 Mujahideen caught in the cordon. The Mujahideen began attacking the searching Soviets. They

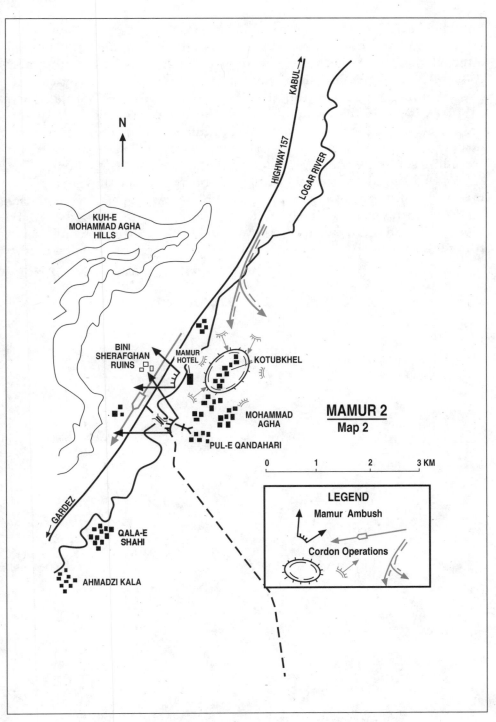

launched sudden, surprise attacks in the close streets and alleys of the villages and in the spaces between the villages. The fighting was often at point-blank range. The fighting began in the morning and continued until the late afternoon (Map 2 - Mamur 2). Soviet casualties are unknown but we think that they were heavy. The Mujahideen captured four AK-74s. Mujahideen casualties were seven KIA including Sameh Jan. Most of the dead Mujahideen had run out of ammunition. The Soviets captured the weapons of the dead Mujahideen including some AK-47s, a Goryunov machine gun, an RPG-7 and a few AK-74s captured from the Soviets in the past. As the Soviets got involved in fighting, they stopped searching. As daylight waned, the Soviets disengaged, took their dead and withdrew back to Kabul. They did find and evacuate the body of their officer who Doctor Khayat killed the day before. It was still lying where he was killed.

VIGNETTE 2
YET ANOTHER AMBUSH AT THE MAMUR HOTEL
by Toryalai Hemat

My mobile regiment fought in many provinces in Afghanistan during the war. One of our battles was in Mohammad Agha District of Logar Province. The Jihad began here attacking columns between Gardez and Kabul. This action occured on 8 July 1986. It was a joint action with the HIH Mujahideen commanded by Doctor Wali Khayat and was reported in the media. It was a small ambush involving 13 Mujahideen armed with two RPG-7s, one PK machine gun and 10 AK-47s. Seven of the Mujahideen were my men and six were HIH. We set the ambush in Kotubkhel near the Mamur Hotel which sits beside the main highway. I split the force into two groups. I put a six-man group on the east side of the road along the Logar River bank. At this point the river is some 40 meters from the road and some two meters lower than the surrounding ground. This site is by the hotel. I put my seven-man group on the west side of the road on high ground. This site is a little further to the south, about 150 meters from the hotel. The high ground is known as Gumbazo Mazogani by the locals. There was an RPG-7 at both sites. We had instructed the group that if the column came from Kabul the furthest group (the western group on the high ground) would fire first to get the column into the kill zone. That would be the river site's signal to fire. We prepared our high ground positions in a ditch which was not visible from the road. It is some 200 meters from the road. We camouflaged our positions well (Map 3 - Mamur 3).

Our base was three kilometers southeast of Mohamad Agha south of the village of Qala-e Shahi near Ahmadzi Kala. We moved from Ahmadzi Kala at midnight. It took us one hour to reach the ambush site. I was with the western group. We took our positions in the ditch. At that time, there was fighting in Paktia Province, Jajai District and the enemy was moving reinforcements to the area. In the morning, a reinforcing column came. We opened fire when it reached us and the eastern ambush site opened up as well. We destroyed or damaged two armored vehicles, three jeeps and eight trucks. Some trucks turned

Toryalai Hemat was a regimental commander of a Mujahideen Mobile Regiment belonging to the Etehad-e Islami (IUA) faction of Sayyaf. He fought in many provinces in Afghanistan during the war. [Map sheet 2885, vic grid 1086].

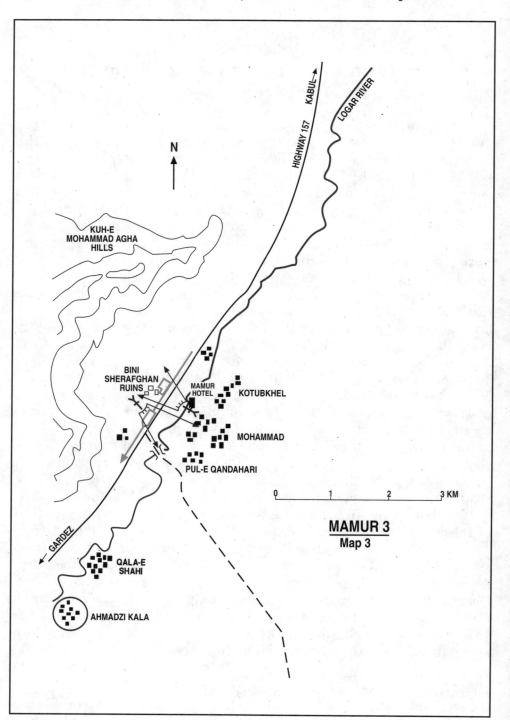

N

KUH-E
MOHAMMAD AGHA
HILLS

HIGHWAY 157

KABUL→

LOGAR RIVER

BINI
SHERAFGHAN
RUINS

MAMUR
HOTEL

KOTUBKHEL

MOHAMMAD

PUL-E QANDAHARI

GARDEZ

QALA-E
SHAHI

AHMADZI KALA

0   1   2   3 KM

MAMUR 3
Map 3

back to Kabul and others were abandoned. There were some intact abandoned trucks outside the kill zone. Dead and wounded lay on the ground. Only damaged vehicles were left in the kill zone. We had no casualties. In one of the jeeps we found some movie projectors. We also captured 11 AKs, two pistols and one heavy machine gun (which was mounted on an armored vehicle). We took what we could and split the spoils. HIH got all the projectors. We left and went to Wazir Kala some four kilometers away. Helicopter gunships came and fired at our old positions. Four Soviet helicopters came and took away their dead and wounded. We stayed in Wazir Kala for two or three hours. The helicopters were bombing and strafing the positions all of this time. In the late afternoon, when everything settled down, we returned to the area to search and see what was left. We removed the heavy machine gun and projectors at this time. We stopped a passing bus and asked the passengers for matches. At first they refused, not wanting to be accomplices, so we searched their pockets and got some matches and set fire to the damaged vehicles. Two days later, the Soviets sent a force to search our old positions. Of the 13 men in the ambush, only Baryali, Asef of HIH and I survived the war.

COMMENTARY: Both the Soviets and Mujahideen set patterns. The Mujahideen use the Mamur Hotel ambush site over and over again, yet apparently the Soviets or DRA seldom dismounted troops to search the area to spoil the ambush or to try to set a counterambush. This last example is from 1986, yet there seems to be no learning curve on the part of the Soviets. Air support is tardy, artillery fire is unavailable and there is no reserve to move against the ambush. Aggressive patrolling, specially-trained counter-ambush forces and priority counter-ambush intelligence are lacking. The standard Soviet/DRA counter-ambush techniques include an aerial patrol in front of the column, an engineer sweep in front of the column look-ing for mines, armored vehicles in the front of the column, occasion-al armored vehicles throughout the column and a robust rear guard. Once hit, the armored vehicles in the column would return fire while the soft-skin vehicles tried to drive out of the kill zone. Seldom would the ambushed force dismount forces to clear the ambush site and pursue the ambush party.

The Mujahideen did vary ambush positions in the same ambush site. Their primary concern was to hit the column where it was weak-est—usually in the middle or rear—unless the purpose was to bottle up the column. In most ambushes, a small number of highly-mobile

Mujahideen were able to move and attack with little logistic support, but were unable to conduct a sustained fight. The RPG-7 was probably the most effective weapon of the Mujahideen. When used at close quarters with the element of surprise, it was devastating.

In this region, Mujahideen ambushes occupied a very wide front. This was a function of the open terrain and the spacing between convoy vehicles. Convoy SOP was to maintain 100 meters or more between vehicles. In order to have enough vehicles in the kill zone to make the ambush worthwhile, the Mujahideen had to constitute a kill zone much bigger than that employed by most Western armies.

AMBUSH SOUTH OF THE TANGI WAGHJAN GORGE
by Haji Sayed Mohammad Hanif

In May 1981, we joined other Mujahideen for an ambush in Kolangar District, Logar Province (Map 4 - Kolangar). We were 11 Mujahideen with an RPG-7, seven Kalashnikovs and two Enfields. We moved into the area the night before, spent the night in a village and set up our ambush site the next morning north of Kolangar District Headquarters. We were told that a column was coming from Kabul to Gardez, and so we had time to set up during the daylight before the column arrived, since the convoys always left Kabul in the morning well after dawn. Kabul is about 50 kilometers north of the ambush site. We set our ambush just south of the Tangi Waghjan Gorge. There, the river continues to run parallel to the road and restricts maneuver while providing better firing positions for the ambush force. We had a collapsed electric pylon that we stretched across the road as a road block. We put in an RPG firing position for Mulla Latif,[1] our RPG gunner, and put two other Mujahideen on the edge of the river in positions. Then we set up the rest of our positions and went to some nearby houses for breakfast. At that time we were so popular with the population that we didn't have to worry about supplies and the people were always feeding us in their homes or sending us prepared food. Mulla Latif left his RPG at the ambush position since the people were moving about freely and would keep an eye on things.

As we were leisurely enjoying our breakfast, some people came into the house and said that the convoy was coming from the north. This was at about 1000 hours. While we were running to our positions, the lead tank in the column came to our road block. The tank driver stopped his tank, got out of the tank and moved the barrier. He had gotten back into his tank and driven past as we reached our positions. Mulla Latif was breathing heavily as he picked up his RPG-7 and fired at the next tank. His first shot missed. He reloaded, fired again and missed again. He was still breathing too heavily to aim accurately. He then reloaded, jumped out of position, and ran down to the road. He then sat down in the middle of road and fired at the tank from close range. He hit the tank this time and it burst into flames. The column

---

Haji Sayed Mohammad Hanif is from Logar Province. [Map sheet 2885, vic grid 0674].

[1] Mulla Latif was killed in fighting later in the war.

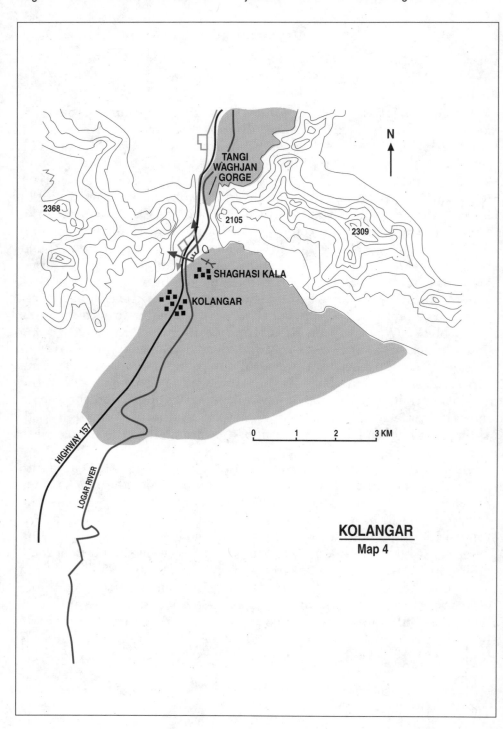

N

TANGI
WAGHJAN
GORGE

2368

2105

2309

SHAGHASI KALA

KOLANGAR

0   1   2   3 KM

HIGHWAY 157

LOGAR RIVER

KOLANGAR
Map 4

was just coming out of the narrow Tangi Waghjan Gorge. This burning tank stopped the convoy since there was no room to maneuver or pass. Other Mujahideen from other areas and groups ran to the area and moved up the gorge by the trapped column and started firing at the vehicles. There was not much resistance from this supply convoy. The column consisted of 150 to 200 trucks full of many things such as food and furniture. Whatever we could take away, we did. Hundreds of Mujahideen came and looted the column. We captured 15 trucks for my group which we eventually moved to our base in Durow canyon. We torched the vehicles we could not take and left the area around 1300 hours. After we had finished, helicopters and aircraft came and bombed some areas around the ambush site. Despite our lack of warning when the lead vehicle came toward our ambush site, the ambush turned out well.

There is a reason why we were not in our positions when the column came. Prior to any ambush, we would select and prepare our ambush positions, but we would not occupy them since helicopters would always overfly the route ahead of the convoy looking for ambushes and roadblocks. Normally, we would not put out the road block until after the flyover, but for some reason this time we did. The helicopter flyover was our usual tipoff that the convoy was coming, and our signal to put out the roadblock and occupy our positions. The helicopters did not do their road sweep in front of this particular convoy. I later learned why the helicopters were absent. DRA President Barbak Karmal was flying to Moscow that day and so the DRA had imposed a "no fly zone" over Kabul. This meant that helicopters were either grounded or had to refuel at Ghazni. The helicopters were not available to do the sweep.

COMMENTARY: The Mujahideen were quick to key on Soviet and DRA tactical patterns and procedures and came to rely on them. As a result, Mujahideen reactions to these patterns were often stereotyped, but the Soviets and DRA evidently did not always pick up on Mujahideen patterns or insure that the relevant tactical commanders got the word. In this case, the Tangi Waghjan Gorge is an obvious choke point and ambush area. The convoy commander needed to send reconnaissance/security elements ahead of the convoy to secure the gorge's entry, high ground and exit prior to moving the convoy into the gorge, but did not. His lead armored vehicle spotted the road block and removed it. This should have served as a warning, but the convoy commander already had the leading part of the convoy driving through the gorge.

Depending on initial vehicle interval and the commander's ability to stop the convoy from bunching up, some 70 to 150 vehicles may have been caught in the three-kilometer gorge. The drivers were dependent on firepower to rescue them, but the convoy was unable to bring firepower to bear to save their column.

Helicopters have an important role in convoy security, not only as scouts, but as a rapid reaction force and as a lift force to move security elements from one piece of dominant high ground to the next. The lack of helicopters deprived the convoy of needed warning and firepower.

The Mujahideen needed radios and early warning pickets to alert ambush forces about the approach of convoys and aircraft. At this point of the war, few Mujahideen had tactical radio communications

VIGNETTE 4
AMBUSH AT KANDAY
by Doctor Mohammad Sadeq

We fought the DRA and Soviets for control of the Kunar Valley. The area borders Pakistan and is very mountainous and forested. Many of the mountains are over 5,000 meters high and are permanently snow-capped. We operated in Shewa District along the Kunar River. There, the mountains are not as high and the key terrain feature is the Kunar River and the highway which parallels it. In September 1982, we ambushed a supply column which was traveling from Jalalabad to Kunar (Map 5 - Kanday). The column was about eight kilometers in length. I had 22 Mujahideen armed with two RPG-7s, four AK-47 Kalashnikovs and 16 bolt-action Enfield rifles.

I set up the ambush on the high ground north of the Kunar River at Kanday. I divided my force into a support group and an ambush and attack group. The support group was on the high ground, while the ambush and attack group was below them next to the road. When the column came, we let it pass. I wanted to attack near the end of the column. As the head of the column reached Ziraybaba, which is six kilometers northeast of Kanday, a contact signaled us. We then opened fire on the column with our RPGs. An armored vehicle turned off and left the road to fire at us. It hit an antitank mine that we had planted there. We also hit it with RPG-7 fire. We also hit a ZIL truck. Our action split the convoy. Half of the convoy went on to Kunar and the rest returned to Jalalabad. We didn't have enough fire power to continue the fight, so we withdrew. Besides taking out the armored vehicle and truck, we killed six enemy. I had one Mujahideen wounded.

COMMENTARY: Deciding where to ambush a long convoy is usually driven by geography, intent and escape routes. The Soviet/DRA convoy commander was primarily concerned with not being on the road at night and delivering the bulk of his cargo on time. He did not want to fight a long, involved battle with guerrillas. If the terrain at the ambush site is very constricted, the guerrilla may want to attack the head of the convoy and block the route with a combination of a road block and burning vehicles. If the convoy has armored vehicles and engineer vehicles concentrated to the front of the convoy, the guerrilla

---

Doctor Mohammad Sadeq was a commander with the HIH in Kunar Province. [Map sheet 3186, vic grid 5328].

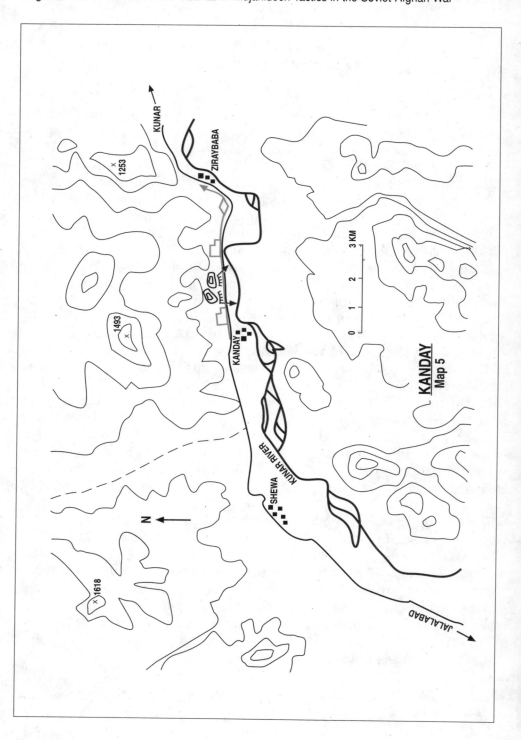

KANDAY
Map 5

may want to attack the middle or tail of the convoy with the hope that the convoy commander will not divert a great deal of combat power back to deal with his attack. If the guerrilla is after supplies, the middle of the convoy is best if he can isolate a piece of the middle, since most convoys have a rear guard. In this case, the purpose of the ambush was to harass, not to capture supplies. The ambush site was fairly constricted due to the proximity of the river and road to the high ground, but it still allowed armored vehicles to turn around in the area. The ambush commander decided to attack toward the rear of the convoy, but far enough forward to avoid the rear guard.

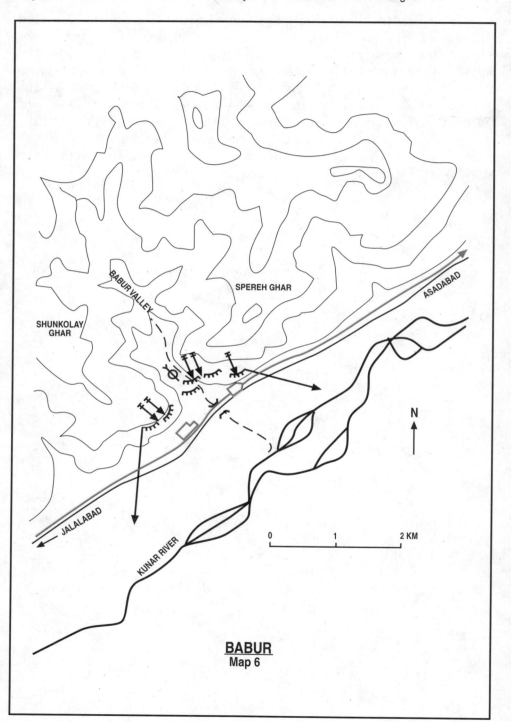

BABUR
Map 6

AMBUSH ON THE JALALABAD-ASADABAD ROAD
by LTC Haji Mohammad Rahim

The Jalalabad-Asadabad road runs right by the mouth of the Babur Valley (which we nicknamed Islamdara—the Valley of Islam). I had my base in the valley with 150 Mujahideen, one 82mm recoilless rifle, three DShK heavy machine guns, a Goryunov medium machine gun, five RPG-7s, some Kalashnikovs and some Enfields. I decided to set the ambush at the mouth of the valley. It was December 1984. The area is perfect for an ambush (Map 6 - Babur). The mouth of the valley allows a U-shaped ambush with a 1000-meter kill zone. The forested valley allows a quick escape into the forested mountains. I positioned the DShK machine guns on the high ground and put the five RPGs and the recoilless rifle close to the road. I had three positions for my force—the bottom of Spereh Ghar facing southwest, the valley floor and the ridge of Shunkolay Ghar facing south and southeast. I put myself in the center in the valley floor position where I could best control the ambush. I had good fields of fire to both sides of the ambush site. The terrain is close and prevented the enemy from massing fires against the ambush. The river prevented the enemy from maneuvering effectively against the site. The withdrawal routes are covered.

A supply convoy came from Jalalabad. We let part of it pass to attack the middle of the convoy. When we opened fire, the enemy was hit from three directions. We destroyed three armored vehicles and one truck fully loaded with melons and other fruit and one truck full of boxes of cash. Some enemy tried to flee, but were trapped by the river which has many channels in this area. The money truck caught on fire and some of the money was burned, but we took what we could and later I made it a payday for everyone. I still have some of those burnt notes and someday I will cash them in for some good ones. The enemy tried to fight back and maneuver against us, but he could not find any favorable positions. Eventually, enemy helicopter gunships came and forced us out of position. Our concealed withdrawal routes through the trees protected us from the gunships. Sameh Jan Hejran from Chakdara was killed. He was a teacher. I also had one WIA. The enemy losses are unknown since they evac-

---

LTC Haji Mohammad Rahim was an officer in the Afghan Army who became a Mujahideen and led a group in Kunar Province. [Map sheet 3186, vic grid 7842].

uated their dead. The following day, the DRA came and towed the damaged armored vehicles away.

COMMENTARY: The Mujahideen were unpaid volunteers, so the money truck was a real boon. Mujahideen still had to support their families, so normally all heavy weapons and 1/5th of the loot from an ambush or raid went to the commander. The other 4/5ths was divided among the Mujahideen combatants. Some Mujahideen would take their captured Kalashnikovs to Pakistan where they would sell them and give the money to their families to live on. Governments supporting the Mujahideen would buy the weapons in Pakistan's bazaars and give them to Mujahideen faction leaders for distribution.

LTC Rahim's military professionalism shows throughout this vignette. His ambush lay down is by the book and very effective. He might have blown the bridge in the middle of the kill zone, but that would have meant that a guarded bridge repair crew would be near his base camp for an indefinite period of time impeding his freedom of movement.

VIGNETTE 6
NO-PULA AMBUSH
by Commander Sofi Lal Gul

In December 1980, I led a group of 12 Mujahideen in an ambush on the Kabul-Charikar highway at No-Pula, near Qara Bagh. We were armed with Kalashnikov rifles and two RPG-7s. I selected the ambush site at a point where orchards and other vegetation provide covered approaches to the road and offered concealed positions for the ambush team.[2] We left our base at Farza, some ten kilometers to the west, long before daybreak to arrive at the ambush site before sunrise. I deployed my force into two ambush positions near the road and placed a three-man flank security team on the road which intersected with the main highway (Map 7 - No-Pula).

About 0900 hours, an enemy column of trucks, jeeps and armored vehicles arrived. As the head of the column passed our ambush position kill zone, we opened fire on the convoy and destroyed one of the leading tanks with a direct hit by RPG-7. As the convoy unsuccessfully scurried to take cover, our fire destroyed a jeep and an APC. Explosions in the disabled vehicles set some trucks on fire. The enemy returned fire but failed to use its infantry to attack us directly. The action continued for less than an hour. When enemy aircraft arrived over the ambush site, we broke contact and pulled out through the green zone. We had no casualties, while we destroyed or damaged one tank, one APC, one jeep and eight trucks.

COMMENTARY: The Mujahideen group achieved surprise by deploying in the dark and using the covered area close to the road for the ambush. The small number of the Mujahideen limited its action to one strike, after which they had to pull out. Failure to act decisively cost the convoy several vehicles and allowed the Mujahideen to slip away unscathed. The passive response of the Soviets caught in ambush often was due to the fact that they were carrying very few infantry in

---

Commander Sofi Lal Gul is from Farza village of Mir Bacha Kot District, about 25 kilometers north of Kabul. He was affiliated with Mojadeddi's Afghanistan National Liberation Front of Afghanistan (ANLF) during the war with the Soviet forces. Commander Sofi Lal Gul concentrated his efforts on the Kabul-Charikar highway. [Map sheet 2886, vic grid 1356].

[2] The green zone is an irrigated area thick with trees, crops, irrigation ditches and tangled vegetation. Green zones usually run parallel to rivers and are usually practically impassable for vehicles.

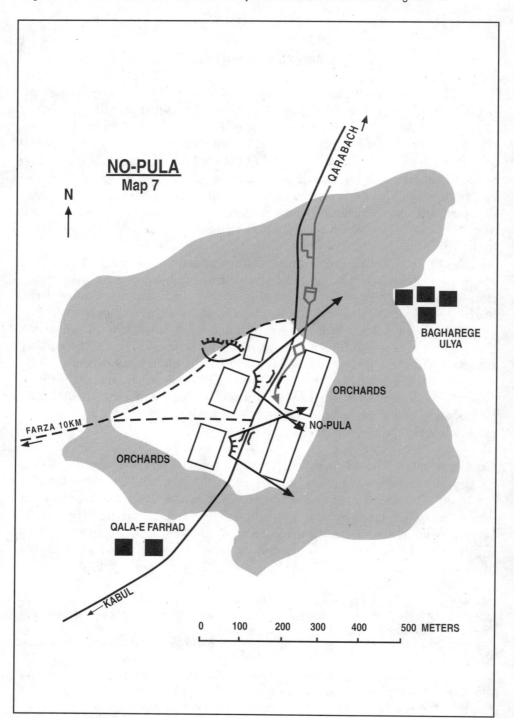

NO-PULA
Map 7

N

QARABACH

BAGHAREGE
ULYA

ORCHARDS

NO-PULA

FARZA 10KM

ORCHARDS

QALA-E FARHAD

KABUL

0   100   200   300   400   500 METERS

their escorting personnel carriers.

The cover provided by the orchards and vegetation that flanked both sides of the Kabul-Charikar highway helped the Mujahideen lay successful ambushes. Later in the war, the Soviets destroyed the roadside orchards and villages to prevent the Mujahideen from using them in their ambushes.

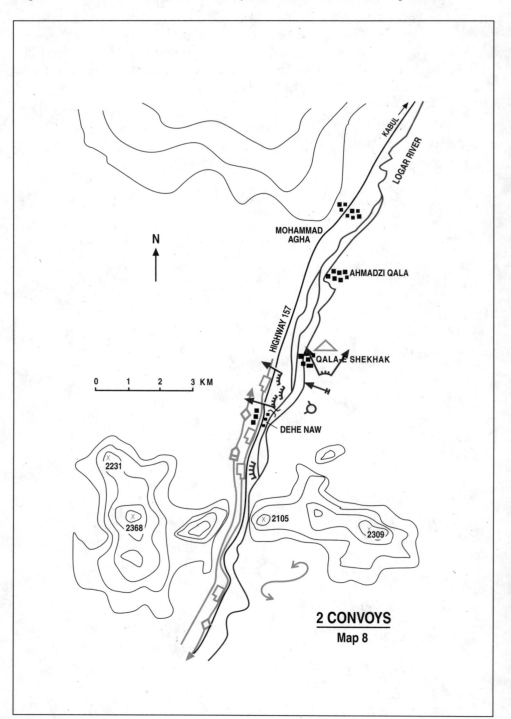

KABUL

LOGAR RIVER

MOHAMMAD
AGHA

AHMADZI QALA

HIGHWAY 157

N

QALA-E SHEKHAK

0   1   2   3 KM

DEHE NAW

X
2231

X
2368

X 2105

2309

2 CONVOYS
Map 8

TWO CONVOYS IN THE KILL ZONE
by Toryalai Hemat

In the summer of 1986, the Soviets and DRA were moving lots of reinforcements and supplies to Paktia Province. We set an ambush on Highway 157 south of Mohammad Agha District headquarters on the 12th of July. This was four days after an ambush at the Mamur Hotel. I sited the ambush along a two-kilometer stretch between Qala-e Shekhak and Dehe Naw. Qala-e Shekhak is six kilometers south of Mohammad Agha and Dehe Naw is three kilometers further south from Qala-e Shekhak. There was a DRA outpost at Qala-e Shekhak, so we started our ambush a kilometer south of the outpost. The outpost was surrounded by mines and the DRA seldom left the outpost. I felt that the DRA might shoot at us, but would not attack from the outpost (Map 8 - Two Convoys).

I had 35 Mujahideen in my group. I divided them into four groups—a northern containment group, an ambush group, a southern security group and a support group. The northern containment group was to fire on the DRA outpost to prevent them from interfering with our ambush. The ambush group would attack the convoy from close up. The southern security group would occupy a position at Dehe Naw to protect our southern flank and prevent the arrival of reinforcements from the south. These three groups were armed with AK-47s, PK machine guns and RPGs. The support group had one 82mm mortar and a Goryunov machine gun.[3] I positioned the support group on the east bank of the Logar River behind the ambush group. All the groups were on the east side of the road. We moved from Ahmadzi Qala before dawn and occupied our ambush positions.

We did not have any advance information on the movement of columns, but there were enough columns moving to Paktia. At this time, there was usually a daily column, so it was a free hunt. There were many petrol tankers in these convoys. They were easy to set on fire, and just firing at them would do the job. Once you set them on fire, it would demoralize the entire column as everyone could see the smoke. We always wanted to hit DRA columns since they wouldn't

---

Toryalai Hemat was a regiment commander of a mobile force allied with the IUA—Islamic Union of Afghanistan of Sayyaf. He fought in many provinces in Afghanistan. [Map sheet 3185, vic grid 0680].

[3] The Mujahideen acquired a lot of Afghan Army and DRA material. The Afghan infantry battalion had nine Goryunov 7.62mm machine guns and nine 82mm mortars by TO&E.

fight, whereas Soviet columns would. Usually when a column would come, the enemy would establish security forces at suspected ambush sites and occupy them until the column passed or until they were certain that nothing was going to happen. Many times we wouldn't risk taking on the entire column. We would attack the tail since the enemy would not turn back to help the petroleum tankers at the rear. The column would often reach Gardez, but they would have lost a piece of it along the way. Attacking the column from the rear was less risk to us, although sometimes there would be some APCs at the rear of the column.

The enemy reaction when caught in the kill zone was usually ineffective. They normally stopped, dismounted and took cover. They fought back only when assistance arrived. We learned to hit the column and leave. We did not want to fight reinforcements or helicopters because we did not have enough combat power and it was very hard to move our wounded from the area under fire.

Later in the morning, a Soviet security force of armored vehicles moved close to us and occupied a position. Then the column came from the north. The security force rejoined the column before the entire column passed. This left the fuel tankers in the rear of the column for us! We hit them by surprise, and it was effective. We damaged or destroyed one jeep and nine tankers. Mohammad Hashem took out an armored security vehicle with his RPG. We later learned that two Russians fled from the south-bound column when we ambushed it. They were captured by Mujahideen from HIH.

As we were getting ready to leave the ambush site, a Soviet armored column came from the south. My southern security group had already pulled back, so we were caught totally by surprise. They began pouring fire into our ranks. Four helicopters also flew over firing at us. Mohammad Hashem hit one helicopter with his RPG, but the fight was unequal. All of my group, except for Ehsan and myself were wounded—most of them were wounded while we were withdrawing. Most were lightly wounded, but two of them are still paralyzed.

What happened is that as we ambushed the tail of the south-bound column, a north-bound column was traveling on the same section of road. The heavily-armored head of the north-bound column arrived at the kill zone as we were withdrawing. Helicopters were flying air cover for the arriving column as well. Since my southern security group had withdrawn, we did not know of their arrival until they were firing at us.

COMMENTARY: The road runs through a deep gorge three kilometers south of Dehe Naw. The Soviets probably had anticipated problems at this area and leapfrogged the security force there and put the helicopters overhead to deal with this probable ambush site. Security elements should be the last elements to pull out of an ambush—not the first. The southern security element should have been south on the high ground where it could see. Simple hand-held walkie-talkie radios and a security element that performs its mission would have averted disaster for this Mujahideen commander.

The RPG-7 could be an effective anti-helicopter weapon— particularly when several RPGs were fired simultaneously at a hovering helicopter or at a helicopter on the ground.

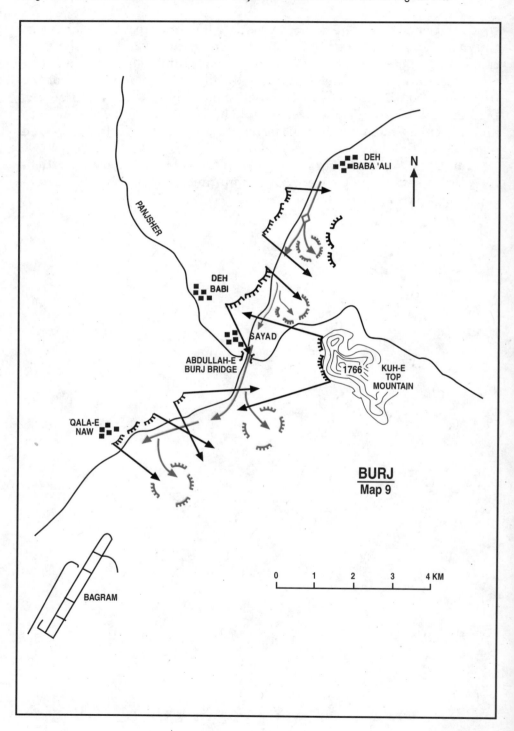

VIGNETTE 8
AMBUSH NEAR ABDULLAH-E BURJ
by Haji Abdul Qader and Haji Qasab

In October 1980, a Soviet column left its base in Bagram to conduct a four-day operation against the Mujahideen in the Nejraw District of Kapisa Province. To get there, they crossed the Abdullah-e Burj bridge over the Panjshir River. The bridge is on the main highway connecting Bagram with the provincial capitals of Mahmoud-e Raqi and Deh Baba'Ali and other major towns including Gulbahar in the north and Sarobi in the south. Since this is the only bridge over the Panjshir River in this region, Mujahideen felt that the Soviet force would return to their base by the same route.

The Mujahideen based around the Abdullah-e Burj decided to ambush the column on its return trip when the troops were tired and more vulnerable. They decided to hit the column while it was crossing over the bridge from Kapisa to Parwan Province. The Soviets would be most vulnerable when half their column had crossed the river and their force was divided by the river (Map 9 - Burj).

Haji Abdul Qader and Haji Qasab jointly planned and executed the ambush. They decided to let the Soviet force move unopposed until the head of the column reached Qala-e Naw, about 3.5 kilometers southwest of the bridge. The Mujahideen had watched the column depart and knew how long the column was. They calculated that when the column reached Qala-e Naw, half of the column would still be on the north of the river with the tail of the column just south of Deh Baba'Ali. Haji Abdul Qader's group (about 150 men) would set up their ambush south of the river along the Bagram-Kapisa road. They would set up in the orchards and hills between Qala-e Naw and Abdullah-e Burj. Haji Qasab, reinforced with local Mujahideen from Commander Shahin's group (about 200 altogether) would ambush north of the river between Abdullah-e Burj and Deh Baba'Ali. The two areas were part of the normal AOs of the two commanders. In both areas, the Mujahideen positioned their RPG-7s close to the road and their heavy machine guns further back on dominant terrain. The Mujahideen also supported the ambushes with a few recoilless rifles and 82mm mortars.

On 5 October, the Mujahideen secretly deployed into their designated positions and prepared covered positions for their anti-tank

---

Haji Abdul Qader was a HIK commander in the Bagram area. Haji Qasab was a JIA commander in the Deh Baba'Ali area. [Map sheets 2886 and 2887].

weapons. The Soviet column returned that afternoon. It moved unopposed across the bridge at Abdullah-e Burj, and the head of the column reached Qala-e Naw around 1600 hours. Then, at Haji Abdul Qader's signal, the ambushes opened fire on the tanks, APCs, and trucks along the entire length of the column. The Soviets were caught by surprise. South of the river, the Soviet forces drove off the road to try to escape to the open plain. However, many vehicles were hit and destroyed by RPG-7 fire. Vehicles were burning and the Soviet infantry which dismounted from the APCs came under heavy machine gun fire.

On the north side of the river, there is little room for vehicles to maneuver in the surrounding green zone of orchards and vineyards. Many soldiers abandoned their vehicles and rushed to try and ford the river.[4] Some soldiers were washed away, while others made it to the other side and headed for Bagram across the open plain. Many Soviet soldiers were in a state of panic, and overall command and control had broken down. Some troops established perimeter defenses around their vehicles to hold on until help came. Others abandoned their vehicles and escaped toward Bagram. Some 20 or 30 vehicles were burning.

Night fell. Soviet artillery pounded Mujahideen positions around Qala-e Naw, but it was not very effective. The Mujahideen moved through the burning and abandoned vehicles removing supplies and scores of weapons. In the morning, the Soviets sent a relief column from Bagram to relieve the trapped column. The Mujahideen withdrew from the battlefield. At 0800 hours, the remnants of the Soviet column moved on to their Bagram base. Mujahideen losses were light. Haji Abdul Qader's group had two KIA and seven WIA. Total enemy casualties are unknown.

COMMENTARY: There were several factors contributing to the Mujahideen success. First, proper selection of the ambush site was key. The Mujahideen caught the Soviet column straddling the river and forced it to fight two separate, unsupported battles. There was little room to maneuver except over the sourthern escape route. Second, the time of the ambush was optimum. The late afternoon arrival gave Mujahideen gunners just enough time to inflict maximum damage, but not enough time for Soviet air power to react. Soviet artillery could cover only a portion of the battlefield and apparently no forward

---

[4] Crossing the Panjshir River, or any of Afghanistan's major rivers, is always very risky. The rivers often appear calm and shallow, but they are treacherous. The Soviet soldiers, who expected to cross the river on a vehicle over the bridge, were probably not briefed as to the danger.

observers were forward to adjust artillery fire during the night. Third, the Mujahideen had surprise. The column had driven out on this road unmolested and expected to return unopposed. The soldiers were cold and tired, and their guard was down. The head of the column could see Bagram airbase when they were hit. Fourth, the simultaneous attack along the entire length of the column stripped the convoy commander of any uncommmited force which he could use as an emergency reserve. The Mujahideen occupied very wide ambush frontages relative to their manpower and this allowed them to attack the entire convoy simultaneously. In retrospect there is little more that the Mujahideen could have done except employ mines and mortar fire on the southern escape route.

The Soviet commander contributed to his own defeat. He had poor intelligence on the area that he was travelling through and did not use reconnaissance forces effectively. He did not use forward detachments to seize dominant terrain and obvious chokepoints, such as the Abdullah-e Burj bridge, in advance of the column. He was highly predictable and used the same route to return that he had left on, yet failed to post security along that route to support his movement. He failed to leap-frog artillery groups along the column so that artillery fire support was immediately available. He apparently did not have helicopter gunships on stand-by to respond to ambush. He appears to have not trained his force in standard counter-ambush drills and procedures. He apparently lost control of the column within the first minute of the ambush.

The Soviet force in Bagram was reluctant to go to the aid of the beleagured column at night. Apparently they were afraid of also being ambushed. This reluctance to leave the relative safety of their base camp at night was to the Mujahideen advantage.

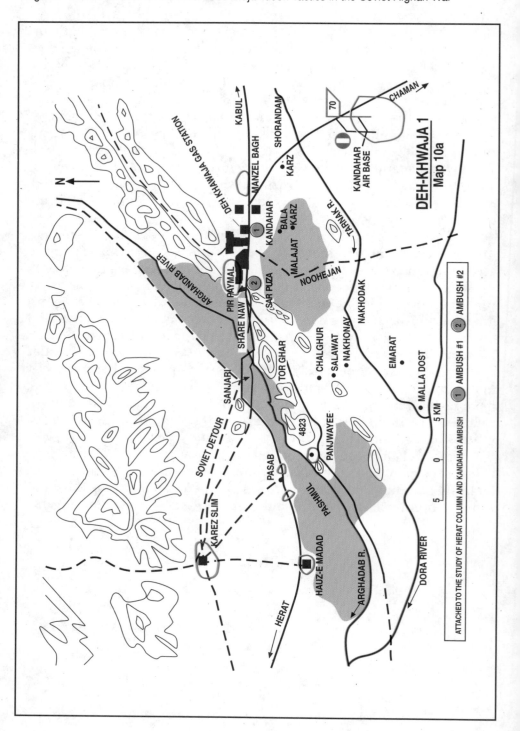

VIGNETTE 9
DEH-KHWAJA AMBUSH
by Commander Mulla Malang

In 1982, the Soviet 70th Separate Motorized Rifle Brigade,[5] supported by DRA forces, launched a block and sweep operation against the Mujahideen forces in the center of Panjwayee District. Panjwayee District is located some 25 kilometers southwest of Kandahar city. Mujahideen sources estimate that hundreds of enemy tanks, APCs, BMPs and other vehicles were involved in the 25-day operation. The Soviet purpose was to punish the Mujahideen groups who constantly harassed Soviet and DRA troop columns and supply convoys on the main Kandahar-Herat highway. The operation was also designed to destroy the resistance bases in the area and widen the security zone around the government-controlled district center.

The Soviet operation in Panjwayee required constant resupply from the main Soviet base located in the Kandahar air base. The supply columns had to travel along the main Chaman-Kandahar road to its junction with the Kabul-Herat highway and then proceed through Deh-Khwaja and Kandahar city to Sarpuza where the Panjwayee access road joins the main highway. (Map 10a - Deh-Khwaja 1)

The Mujahideen groups around Kandahar decided to launch a diversionary action against the enemy in order to relieve the pressure on the resistance in Panjwayee. The Mujahideen realized that the Soviets were weakest and most vulnerable along their supply route and, therefore, decided to strike them there. Although the Mujahideen could conduct small-scale ambushes along the entire stretch of the road, there were only two places suitable for large-scale ambushes. One is a two-kilometer length of road between Manzel Bagh Chawk and Deh-Khwaja. The other is a one-and-a-half kilometer stretch between Shahr-e Naw and Sarpuza.

Mulla Malang was one of the most famous commanders of the Kandahar area. He was an adherent of Mawlawi Mohammed Yunis Khalis-Islamic Party (Hezb-e-Islami-Khalis-HIK). [Map sheet 2180].

[5] The 70th Separate Motorized Rifle Brigade was created using a regiment of the 5th Motorized Rifle Division shortly after the Soviet invasion of Afghanistan. The 70th was designed especially for counterinsurgency and had three motorized rifle battalions, an air assault battalion, an artillery howitzer battalion, a reconnaissance battalion, a tank battalion and support troops. There are also some indications that a MRL battalion might have belonged to this organization.

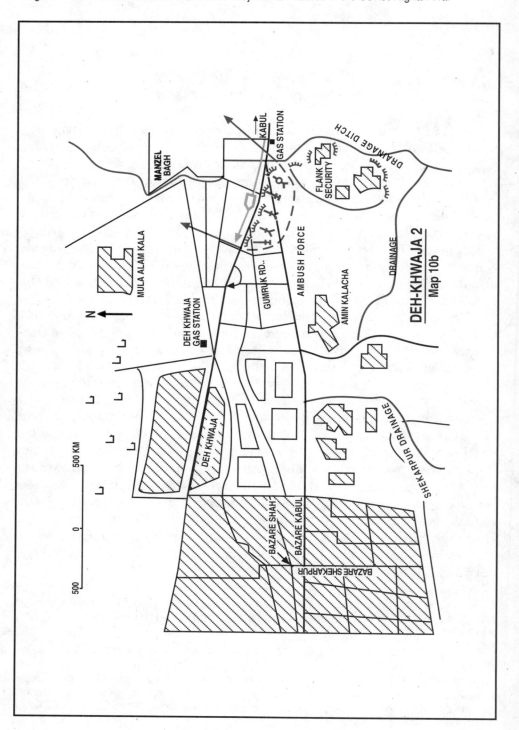

The local Mujahideen groups in the Malajat[6] held a council of war and decided to block the road and conduct a large-scale ambush at each site. In addition to the ambush forces, the Mujahideen also designated support groups for both ambushes to protect the flanks and rear of the blocking/ambush detachments. About 150 Mujahideen, split up into small groups, moved from the Malajat area during the night and took up positions in the orchards, buildings and ditches along the main road between the Manzel Bagh Chawk and Deh-Khwaja gas station. The back-up group for the detachment deployed south of the city. (Map 10b - Deh-Khwaja 2) A similar detachment blocked the road between Shahr-e Naw and Sarpuza.

Early in the morning, a convoy of trucks carrying ammunition, rockets and gasoline moved from the Kandahar air base toward Panjwayee. As the column reached the first roadblock, the Mujahideen opened fire simultaneously with RPG-7s, machine guns, rifles and a recoilless rifle. Taken by surprise, the column stopped while the Soviet security vehicles returned fire. Their fire hit the Deh-Khwaja residential areas and caused much destruction. However, Mujahideen fire finally struck the ammunition trucks. They caught fire and hundreds of rockets and boxes of other ammunition began to explode. The explosions were so powerful that burning tires from APCS were thrown as far away as Bala Karz, some two kilometers from the ambush site. The ambush destroyed about 30 enemy supply trucks and damaged many others. The rest of the Soviet convoy turned back. The Mujahideen roadblock at Shahr-e Naw and Sarpuza had no enemy to attack.

This Mujahideen ambush had a decisive impact on the enemy operation in that it forced the Soviet forces to end their siege of Mujahideen forces in Panjwayee and return to Kandahar. However, in order to prevent future ambushes in the area, the Soviet forces bulldozed Deh-Khwaja homes along the main road out to a distance of 300 meters from the highway.

COMMENTARY: Security of the lines of communication was a constant challenge facing the Soviet forces in Afghanistan. Security of the lines of communication determined the amount of forces which the Soviet could deploy in Afghanistan and also determined the scale and frequency of offensive combat directed against the Afghan resistance forces.

In this example the Soviets had to move supplies to a large group of forces about 50 kilometers away. The road, although an all-season major highway, was vulnerable to Mujahideen ambushes at almost

---

6 The large green zone to the south of Kandahar.

every point. Further, the Soviets and Mujahideen fought for control of Kandahar for the entire war. The Soviets knew that the road was not secure. And yet, the convoy commander did little to ensure the security of the movement along the supply route. A preliminary road-clearing patrol could have preempted the Mujahideen's successful ambush. Instead, their entire operation was disrupted due to their failure to move the supplies to Panjwayee.

Normally, the Soviets spaced APCs throughout the convoy as security vehicles. In case of ambush, the APCs would stop in the kill zone and return fire while the rest of the convoy caught in the kill zone would drive out of it. The portion of the convoy not under attack would stop and wait for the APCs to drive off the ambushers. Then, when the ambushers had been driven off, the convoy would reform and continue. This is why the Mujahideen established two ambush zones. They did not think that they would stop the convoy at the first ambush and so the second ambush was ready to hit the Soviet convoy again.

On the other hand, it took the Mujahideen about three weeks to decide to help the resistance forces in Panjwayee by hitting the Soviets elsewhere. Had they launched their attack earlier, it could have forced their enemy to terminate his operation against Mujahideen groups in Panjwayee earlier.

Vignette 10
Duranay Ambush
by Commander Haji Mohammad Seddiq

In September 1983, my group and I were visiting the area of Maidan. The Maidan Mujahideen had heard about a future convoy going from Kabul to Ghazni and were planning to ambush it. I joined HIH commanders Ghulam Sakhi, Captain Amanullah, Mawlawi Halim and Zabet Wali in setting up an ambush some 30 kilometers southwest of Kabul. Together, we had some 60 Mujahideen armed with AK-47s, 60mm mortars, RPG-7s and an 82mm recoilless rifle. We planned two ambush sites. One group would deploy east of the road between Duranay Bazar and Sur Pul. The other group would deploy west of the road on the forward slope of Duranay mountain close to the road (Map 11 - Duranay). The Mujahideen already had well-prepared positions at both these sites.

We occupied our positions at dawn and waited for the column. At about 0900 hours, the convoy came from Kabul. It was a column of trucks and armored vehicles. A forward security element preceded the convoy. It drove through the ambush area, but failed to detect our forces. Then the convoy entered the ambush area. We let it pass through until the head of the column reached the second ambush site at Duranay mountain. Now, the column was in about a five-kilometer stretch of kill zone. We opened up from all positions along the entire length of the exposed column.

A heavy battle ensued as we fired at all the vehicles in the open. The enemy had a security outpost at Sur Pul which joined in the battle and fired on our positions. Despite this security post fire, and the fire from the armored vehicles, the Soviet response was fairly passive. Our prepared positions protected us, and the Soviets apparently did not have any infantry accompanying the convoy, so they could not dismount and maneuver against us. Our positions were vulnerable to a flank attack through Kashmirian or Ghlo Ghar, but the apparent lack of Soviet infantry support kept their vehicles pinned

Haji Mohammad Seddiq is from No-Burja village in Logar Province. The village is in the Tangi-Wardak area which connects the Saydabad District of Wardak Province to the Baraki Barak District in the Logar Province. Commander Seddiq's village is located on the border between the two provinces. Therefore, his command fought in both provinces in coordination with other Mujahideen. Commander Haji Mohammad Seddiq was affiliated with Hekmatyar's HIH. [Map sheet 2785, vic grid 8494].

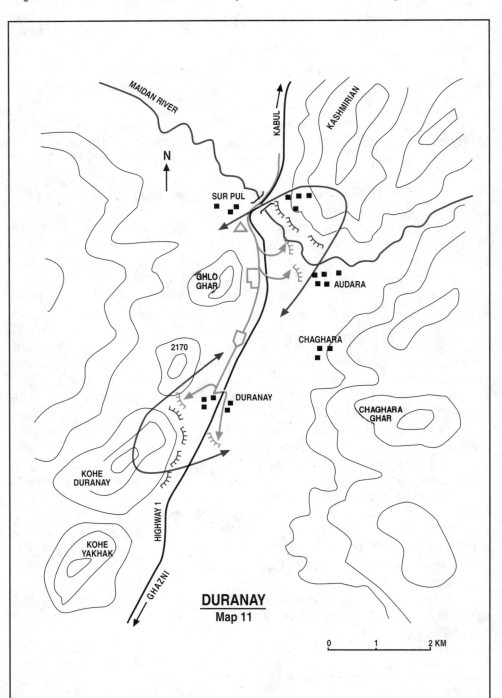

DURANAY
Map 11

down on the lower ground where we continued to shoot them with our anti-tank weapons.

Later in the day, the enemy brought reinforcements to the battle-field and began to pound Mujahideen positions with artillery and air strikes. We began to gradually withdraw our ambush force and by 1500, there were no Mujahideen left in the area. A major Mujahideen commander, Ghulam Sakhi, and several other Mujahideen were killed and many were wounded. We damaged or destroyed 33 armored vehi-cles and 27 trucks. We captured some 40 weapons of different types.

COMMENTARY: The Mujahideen showed good planning and discipline in this ambush, but used prepared positions that they had used before. They also knew that these positions had exposed flanks, but took no precautions. They felt that the Soviets would not dismount to check the known ambush sites and did not expect immediate Soviet counter-actions to turn their flanks. They were right. The Mujahideen were setting a pattern, but the Soviets failed to react to it. The Mujahideen stocked their positions with sufficient ammunition for a fight of sever-al hours duration. They apparently took many of their casualties from artillery and air strikes while moving to the burning vehicles to loot or when pulling back.

The Soviet convoy movement was no secret. The Mujahideen had contacts within the DRA and agents near the assembly areas. The Soviets usually left after first light and therefore arrived in the area between 0830 and 0930. This made it convenient for the Mujahideen who did not have to stay in position all day. The Soviets knew that this was an ambush site, but did not destroy the ambush positions, put security elements on the high ground with helicopters or put a dis-mounted force through the area to check for ambushes. Further, they did not have helicopter gunships flying overhead or on strip alert. They did not carry an immediate reaction force which could get up into the mountains and turn the flanks of the ambush sites. Instead, they relied on the combat power of their armored vehicles and slow-reacting artillery and air support.

The Mujahideen commander had 60 combatants spread over a five kilometers stretch of ambush on both sides of the road. He did not have radio communications with all his people. Instead, the signal to initiate fire was the commander firing the first shot. Other commands were given by messenger or visual signals—mirrors, flares, smoke grenades and waving. Command and control depended greatly on the commander's pre-ambush briefing and SOP actions.

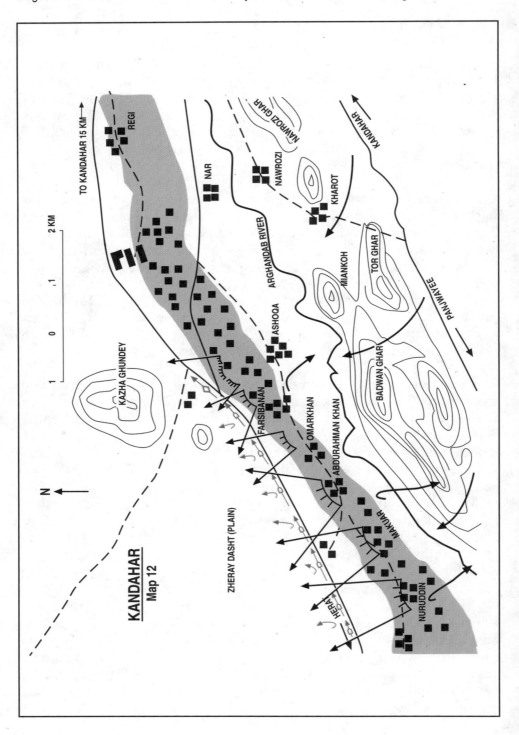

VIGNETTE 11
KANDAHAR AMBUSHES
by Commander Mulla Malang

Despite their best efforts, the Soviets were never able to gain full control of the major Pashtun city of Kandahar. The battle for Kandahar was unusual in that all guerrilla factions cooperated and regularly rotated forces in and out of the battle to maintain pressure on the Soviet and DRA garrisons. The suburbs of Kandahar were one of the major scenes of Mujahideen road blocks and ambushes during the war. Hardly a day would pass without a Mujahideen attack on enemy columns along the main highway connecting the city with Ghazni in the northeast and Girishk in the west.

The enemy columns were most vulnerable on a stretch of the road between the western suburbs of the city and Hauz-e Madad, located about 40 kilometers west of Kandahar. In this area, the Mujahideen were able to hide in the orchards and villages to ambush enemy columns. As the road leaves Sanjari on the Arghandab River, the green zone runs parallel to the highway in the south and an arid plain, that gradually rises toward the mountains, flanks the road to the north. (See Map 10a - Deh-Khwaja 1 in Vignette 9.)

The Herat Column

In one of their early large-scale ambushes, the Mujahideen groups affiliated with different parties planned a series of ambushes along the main highway from Girishk to Kandahar (Map 12 - Kandahar). In September 1984, a Soviet/DRA supply column moved from Torghundi on the Soviet Turkmenistan border through the Shindand air base in western Afghanistan to the Soviet garrison in Kandahar. The column consisted of several hundred trucks escorted by tanks and APCs. Most of the trucks were loaded with gasoline which they

---

Mulla Malang, now 38, is a Pashtun from the northwestern province of Badghisat. He was a student (taleb) at a religious school (madrassa) in Kandahar when the communists came to power in a bloody coup in Kabul in 1978. Mulla Malang joined a resistance cell in the southern suburbs of Kandahar (Malajat) and started fighting the communist regime. He was arrested in the fall of 1979 for spreading anti-government leaflets and later released in general amnesty after the Soviet invasion in January 1980. Mulla Malang immediately fled to Pakistan and joined Mawlawi Mohammad Nabi Muhammadi's Harakat faction. He returned to Kandahar for combat. Mulla Malang later joined HIK and became a major commander of the faction in the province with bases in Arghestan, Malajat, Pashmol and Khakrez. [Map sheet 2180].

brought from Shindand. Shindand was supplied with gasoline from a Soviet-built field pipeline.

Saranwal Abdul Wali of NIFA and I coordinated the Mujahideen plan. We planned to position several interconnected ambushes, manned by small groups of Mujahideen, to surprise and take the entire length of the column under simultaneous fire. This required selection of a favorable stretch of the road that could accommodate all the ambushes required to attack the entire column. We selected a stretch of nearly seven kilometers between a point at the end of Sanjari (the beginning of Ashoqa villages) and a point immediately to the east of Pashmol as the killing zone for the enemy column. We estimated that this stretch of the highway corresponded to the length of the enemy column.

We decided to divide the 250 available Mujahideen into several groups. The groups were armed with RPG-7 antitank grenade launchers and four-to-five 82mm recoilless rifles. All ambushes were sited in the green zone to the south of the road. Each ambush group had an assigned sector of the kill zone. All groups were instructed to open fire simultaneously as the head of the column reaches the Ashoqa villages. It was expected that at that time the tail of the column would have just cleared the Pashmol villages.

At that time, most of the local population still lived in their homes along the road. Few had migrated to Pakistan since no major Soviet military actions had taken place there. The Mujahideen groups coming from Malajat (the southern and southwestern suburbs of Kandahar) and other neighboring bases moved during the night to their designated ambush sites. The ambush plan was kept secret from the local population and local Mujahideen units since resistance groups based in the ambush area were reluctant to participate, fearing retaliation directed at their homes and families still living there.

The ambush groups moved into position during the night and deployed patrols to secure the area. As the day began and locals started moving around, Mujahideen patrols temporarily detained the villagers to ensure secrecy. The Soviet convoy reached the kill zone at 0900 hours. As instructed, the Mujahideen groups opened fire simultaneously, surprising the enemy. The column stopped and many vehicles began moving north onto the open plain. The escorting tanks and APCs fired randomly in panic from on the road without trying to maneuver or close with the ambush sites. Enemy vehicles moving north off the highway soon were out of range of many of the Mujahideen weapons.

In the meantime, several gasoline trucks caught fire and the fire quickly spread to other vehicles. The chain reaction set off several explosions which threw burning debris on both sides of the road. We scored direct hits on about 50 vehicles while many others were damaged in explosions caused by the blown up trucks and gas tankers. The action lasted 30 minutes. We withdrew before enemy aircraft could be scrambled. The enemy did not pursue us.

This ambush marked the beginning of a continuous battle for control of the western road to Kandahar. Until the Soviet withdrawal in 1989, this road was under constant threat by the Mujahideen who would set up road blocks, conduct ambushes, mine long stretches of the road and demolish bridges, underpasses and viaducts using unexploded aerial bombs. Faced with continuous Mujahideen ambushes and attacks on convoys along the highway, the Soviet forces established several security posts and fire bases in the area. They built a major fire base at Kandahar Silo and another at Karez Slim in the northern plain overlooking the Kandahar western highway.

The Soviets set three security outposts at the points where orchards and the green zone stretched to the road providing concealment for Mujahideen in ambush. They were established on both sides of Pasab and at Hauz-e Madad (Map 10a Deh-Khawaja 1 in Vignette 9). The posts were protected by earth berms. The road-side security posts were connected to the main fire base at Karez Slim by communications trenches which allowed safe, rapid reinforcement. The twin Pasab posts were each manned by 10-15 men and each had a tank, a howitzer and a mortar. The security post at Hauz-e Madad was two times as large as the two Pasab posts combined.

The new security arrangement impeded Mujahideen movement in the area. Repeated attempts by the Mujahideen failed to knock out the Soviet outposts. Lala Malang[7] sent for me and asked me to join in a coordinated attack on the Soviet security posts in November 1985. Mujahideen forces lacked the ability to knock out security posts since they had to fight from exposed positions with little cover and they lacked engineering equipment to neutralize mine fields around the enemy positions. Therefore, the Mujahideen could not sustain pressure on the outpost garrison.

We Kandahar Mujahideen decided to first enhance our tactical survivability and then renew attempts to destroy the enemy security

---

[7] Lala Malang was a well-known Mujahideen commander who was based in Pashmol (he was killed during a major Soviet sweep of the Arghandab Valley in 1987).

posts. We began to steadily improve field fortifications areas around Kandahar. We dug trenches with overhead cover overlooking the enemy security posts. We constructed bunkers, underground night shelters and covered access trenches, and stocked ammunition and supplies in these prepared positions. Wherever possible, we built overhead cover using timbers covered with a thick layer of dirt as protection against artillery and aviation. We prepared firing positions for our multi-barrelled rocket launchers. Each of these positions had a pool of water so that the firing crew could splash water on the site before firing to absorb the flames and fumes from the rocket launch.

These positions significantly enhanced Mujahideen field sustainability and enabled them to fire on the enemy outposts around the clock. Enemy attempts to dislodge the Mujahideen with air strikes and artillery fire repeatedly failed. Enemy tanks and motorized rifle forces were also unable to penetrate the green zones to eliminate the positions.

Finally the enemy was forced to abandon his posts at Pasab and Hauz-e Madad and shift his forces to Karez Slim. A local Mujahideen commander, Mulla Nek Mohammad, and some others intensified their daily harassment of enemy movements in the area close to the green zone. Every morning, the Soviets would deploy security patrols from their base at Kandahar Silo to secure the highway from the city to Sanjari area. The Karez Slim fire base covered the area west of Sanjari.

As Mujahideen attacks further threatened the security of the enemy convoys on the highway, the Soviets decided to avoid the stretch of road they could not control. They constructed a detour road to the north of the highway. The bypass road was built in 1985 and connected Sanjari and Karez Slim (See Map10a - Deh-Khwaja 1 in Vignette 9).

COMMENTARY: Soviet lack of adequate reconnaissance cost them dearly. Moving a convoy of supply vehicles in close terrain, without effective security arrangements, often resulted in major tactical setbacks. They further failed to cover the convoy movement with helicopter reconnaissance and helicopter gunships. The Mujahideen had calculated the reaction time for helicopter gunships from Kandahar air base. Timely action by helicopter gunships could have saved the day for the Soviet convoy, but they were apparently not planned for and not on call.

Normally, the Soviets spaced APCs throughout the convoy as security vehicles. In case of ambush, the APCs would stop in the kill zone and return fire while the rest of the convoy caught in the kill zone would drive out of it. The security detail followed this SOP. Instead of aggressive efforts to use their armored strength and fire power to outflank the ambush groups and cut off their withdrawal, the Soviet security vehicles passively remained with the embattled column and fired on suspected Mujahideen positions. They had little effect.

Later on, as the Soviet forces established stationary security posts in the key areas along the highway, they failed to support and sustain them in the face of constant Mujahideen attacks. This later led them to construct a bypass road further to the north away from the dangerous green zone. The Soviet surrendered the initiative in movement control to the Mujahideen and never regained it. Consequently most of the Soviet actions in the area were reactive. In a guerilla war, the loss of initiative becomes decisive in the outcome of tactical combat.

What mostly contributed to Mujahideen success in inflicting heavy losses on the enemy was their elaborate planning, secrecy in movement and coordinated action. This became possible through detailed information about the enemy including the size, direction of movement and estimated time of arrival of the enemy convoy to the ambush site. Simultaneous attack on the enemy column along its entire depth was perhaps the most decisive element in this ambush. In this case, the Mujahideen had approximately 40 combatants to a kilometer of ambush. This was much denser than usual Mujahideen ambushes and reflected that they were fighting from a green zone which could accomodate more combatants.

However, the Mujahideen failed to exploit the initiative they achieved through surprise by moving to the road to complete the destruction of a demoralized and panicked enemy. Instead, they pulled out immediately after their success. This failure to fully exploit an ambush became a hallmark of Mujahideen hit and run tactics throughout the war.

Later fighting confirms the importance of field fortifications and terrain to increase battlefield survivability and sustain combat despite enemy air and artillery superiority. This was a lesson once learned by the Mujahideen that was effectively implemented throughout the war. The Soviets and DRA, on the other hand, did not make a concerted effort to find and destroy these positions.

The parochial nature of the resistance always affected selection of the place and time of tactical actions against the enemy. In areas where the local population remained in their homes and had not emigrated, local resistance units preferred to reserve for themselves the choice of time, place and method of action against the enemy and not let outside Mujahideen groups risk their security and plans by conducting combat in their area without their consent. The decentralized nature of the resistance, factionalism and lack of unified command were both a Mujahideen strength and weakness.

VIGNETTE 12
AMBUSH AT QALA-E HAIDAR
by Asil Khan

As early as 1980, Mujahideen began attacking Soviet columns along the major southwest highway connecting the Afghan capital of Kabul to Ghazni and Kandahar. This 480-kilometer stretch was vulnerable in many areas. The road between Cheltan and Maidan, just outside of Kabul, was continuously attacked by Mujahideen operating out of bases in the suburbs of Kabul, Paghman, Kurugh, Arghandeh and Maidan. Initially, Soviet/DRA forces would establish security outposts at key points along the road every time they moved a column on the highway. According to the DRA security plan, different military units were responsible for sections of road and for manning the security outposts while Soviet or DRA convoys were moving through their area. Later on, as military traffic along the highway increased, units would routinely post security details at the outposts in the morning and pull them out at dusk. One of the outposts was located at the old fort of Qala-e Haidar, some 15 kilometers west of Kabul. This outpost was vulnerable to attacks by Mujahideen who would sneak up on the outpost from neighboring villages which were not under government control (Map 13 - Haidar).

In the beginning of October 1984, the DRA tired of the repeated Mujahideen attacks and did not man the outpost for many days. Asil Khan decided to conduct an ambush at Qala-e Haidar, although he knew that he could not hold the site for more than a few minutes after the ambush, since the DRA could quickly reach the outpost from adjacent outposts. On the night of 18 October 1984, Asil Khan led a 15-man team to Qala-e Haidar. There had been some road repair by the outpost and the road had been scraped down and graded. Asil Khan had his men bury three powerful remote-controlled mines in the road immediately in front of the outpost. They also buried or disguised the wires leading away from the mines to the ambush site. They spent two nights mining the highway and preparing fighting positions in the orchards and in a ditch in front of Qala-e Haider. Lookouts watched the road for approaching columns.

Asil Khan is a famous urban guerrilla who operated in and around Kabul. He belonged to the NIFA faction. Other notes and the DRA security plan consulted for this vignette. [Map sheets 2785, 2786, 2885 and 2886].

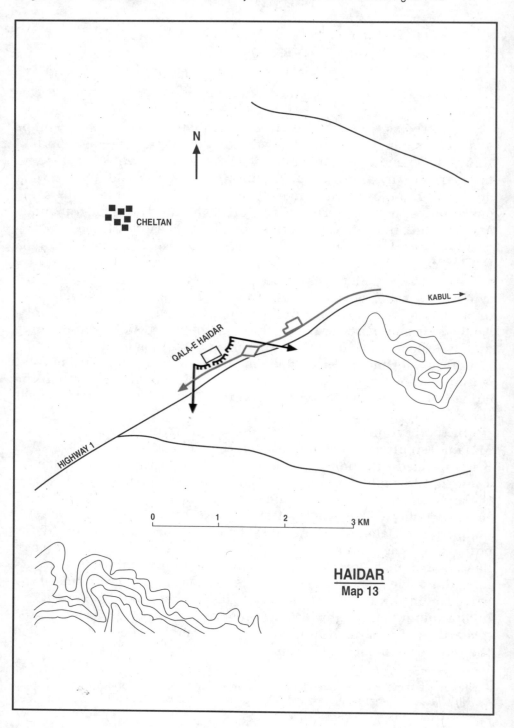

N

CHELTAN

KABUL →

QALA-E HAIDAR

HIGHWAY 1

0   1   2   3 KM

HAIDAR
Map 13

On the morning of 20 October, there were an unusual number of helicopters flying in the area. Asil Khan felt that this indicated that a convoy was leaving Kabul and so he moved his men into the ambush site and waited for the column to arrive. Around 1000 hours, a large supply column, escorted by tanks and APCs, approached the Mujahideen position. Helicopters were flying overhead. As the leading tanks and APCs reached the kill zone, the Mujahideen detonated the mines. One tank blew up and the column came to a sudden halt. The Mujahideen opened fire on the column. But the Mujahideen were so concerned about making a fast getaway, that their fire was not too effective against the vulnerable column. They destroyed just one truck with their RPGs before they broke contact and fled unscathed to friendly territory in the west.

COMMENTARY: The Mujahideen achieved surprise but failed to exploit it fully once the column stopped. The commander's desire to safeguard his force prevented their further damaging the column. Still, a tank and a truck is a good days work for a 15-man ambush. Proper selection of the ambush site is key and this area was very open and offered little protection to the force. Some 12 kilometers further south is the Kotal-e Takht (the Takht pass) which is far more suitable for an ambush. The terrain there also allows surprise and provides better protection and concealed exit routes for the ambushing force. An ambushing force could fight much longer in this area and inflict more damage on a column. However, there are certain limitations in selecting an ambush site in the area. First of all, Mujahideen groups generally operated on their home turf. Acting outside their home turf could have unfavorable political, and support ramifications. Secondly, the Mujahideen wanted to harass their enemy as close to the capital as possible for political and propaganda reasons. Attacks at the gates of Kabul were more significant than attacks further out. Finally, since the area is very open, an ambush here had a good chance at surprise since it is not an obvious ambush site.

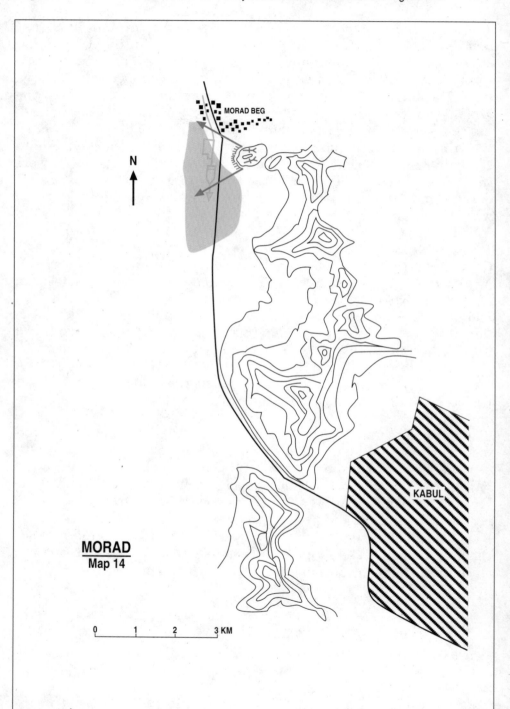

N

MORAD BEG

KABUL

MORAD
Map 14

0   1   2   3 KM

VIGNETTE 13
AMBUSH AT THE SADRE AZAM HILL
by Doctor Mohammad Wakil

It was August 1984. We had information that a Soviet supply column would come to Kabul from the north. There is a small hill on the highway south of Qala-e Morad Beg. (Map 14 - Morad) It is the Sadre Azam hill. It is an excellent site for an ambush and we set up our ambush on the hill to the east of the highway.[8] I had 30 Mujahideen and four RPG-7s. This area was closely watched by the enemy and so we could not spread our force out. Therefore, I concentrated the force on the hill with the rifles forward and the RPGs higher up on the hill. We thought that the convoy would arrive at 1600 hours and were in place before that time. At 1600 hours, the convoy came. It was led by a BMP. Soviet soldiers were sitting on top of the BMP. Usually we would not attack the head of the column, but since the lead vehicle was such a good target, we opened fire on it and destroyed it. We took the column by surprise. The column stopped and the enemy dismounted some soldiers who took up positions and fired back at us. We fired at each other for about an hour until a relief column arrived from nearby Kabul to help the ambushed column. We pulled out. The enemy lost one BMP, four gasoline tankers and probably about ten killed and wounded. We lost Malek Mohammad from Karez-e Mir who was killed.

COMMENTARY: This is typical of the small-scale ambushes that the Mujahideen regularly conducted. The losses on both sides were minor, yet over time they added up. The Soviet soldiers customarily rode on top of their APCs since it is safer if the APC hit a mine. A powerful antitank mine blast might merely hurl the the soldiers off the APC whereas it would almost certainly kill everyone inside. Furthermore, the inside of an APC is crowded, is hard to see out of and, in August, is unbearably warm.

Doctor Mohammad Wakil is from Shakardara District north of Kabul. He graduated from high school before the war. He joined the resistance and received medical training in Pakistan. [Map sheet 2886, vic grid 0734].

[8] Author Ali Jalali has conducted tactical classes on this very terrain while teaching Afghan Army officers at the Higher Education School. It truly is an excellent ambush site.

The convoy was hemmed in by the village of Morad Beg, so the Soviets had difficulty maneuvering armored vehicles forward to fire into the ambush site. Since the object of the ambush was to destroy vehicles, it made sense to hit the head of the convoy. If the object had been to capture weapons, then an attack on the middle or end of the convoy would have been better. Available terrain kept the Mujahideen ambush compact—which is not what they prefer. This is closer to a Western-style ambush. After the initial firing, the ambush turned into a desultory, protracted sniping exercise which was more like an afternoon's recreation for the ambushers than decisive combat.

VIGNETTE 14
AMBUSH AT MAZAR CREEK
by Commander Qazi Guljan Tayeb

East of my base in Baraki Barak is the town of Padkhab-e Shana. It is located one and a half kilometers from the Kabul-Gardez highway. The Soviets had put security posts on the high ground around this town to protect the highway from Mujahideen attacks coming out of Baraki Barak District. I decided to attack these posts in July 1985. By that time I had switched from the Hikmatyar faction to the Sayaf faction.

We moved out from Baraki Barak at dusk. I had some 100 Mujahideen with me. We crossed the highway and entered Padkhab-e Shana town. It is a large town occupying a square kilometer and containing some 1,000 houses. My Mujahideen moved into houses and stayed with the people throughout the next day. That night, using local guides, we set up ambushes on the roads leading into the village. The area around the town is also a green zone with orchards and woods (Map 15 - Mazar). Mazar Creek passes through the town near the bazaar. Mazar Creek begins at a spring and has good water. Soviet soldiers would go to the creek to get water, wash, fish and take a dip. We put an ambush at the creek near the spring. We put another ambush along their supply route which ran to the Soviet security posts from the main road. There was a path that ran from the security posts to the town dwellings. Soviets would often come down this path to the town to steal or extort things. We set our third ambush along this path in an area covered by buildings and orchards where the enemy maneuver would be restricted and constrained. We set our fourth ambush along the path from the creek to Mir Ghyas hill.

In the morning, a few Soviets came to the creek. The Mujahideen at this ambush site opened fire and then left quickly after they saw that they had killed some Soviets. About the same time, a Soviet jeep drove along the supply route. That ambush opened fire and hit the jeep. Soviet tanks came from Pule-e Alam and surrounded the town. We hid our weapons and mixed with populace. Gradually we left the

Commander Qazi Guljan Tayeb was a third year student in Kabul Theological College during the communist takeover in 1978. He joined Hikmatyar and later switched to the Sayef faction in the mid-1980s. He was the Commander of Baraki Barak District of Logar Province. [Map sheet 2884, vic 0657].

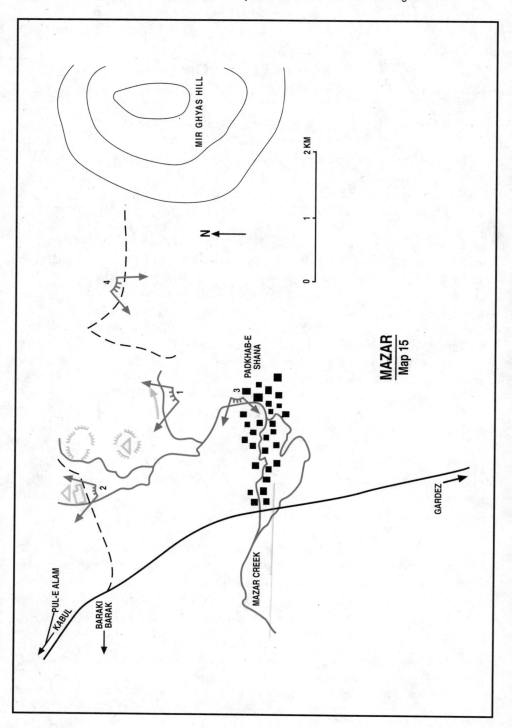

MIR GHYAS HILL

N

2 KM

1

0

4

1

2

3

PADKHAB-E
SHANA

MAZAR
Map 15

KABUL

PUL-E ALAM

BARAKI
BARAK

MAZAR CREEK

GARDEZ

area disguised as civilians and went to the north and west. We had two wounded Mujahideen. We killed 12 Soviets, destroyed one jeep and captured four weapons.

COMMENTARY: The Soviets had set a pattern of behavior which enabled the Mujahideen ambushes. They used the same roads and paths regularly. Their behavior toward the villagers made the villagers willing accomplices in setting the ambushes and hiding the Mujahideen and their weapons. The DRA had traveling propaganda/civil affairs teams which provided entertainment, medical treatment and pro-regime propaganda throughout Afghanistan.[9] Their actions, however, did not offset the effects of poor behaviour by Soviet combat forces.

---

[9] N. I. Pikov, "Vidy spetspropagandistskoy deyatel'nosti Armii Respubliki Afganistan" [Methods of Special Propaganda Activity of the Army of the Republic of Afghanistan], Opyt primeneniya Sovetskikh voysk v Respublike Afganistan [Experience applied by Soviet Forces in the Republic of Afghanistan], Moscow: Institute of Military History, 1990, 151-184 provides a good view of the composition and employment of these teams.

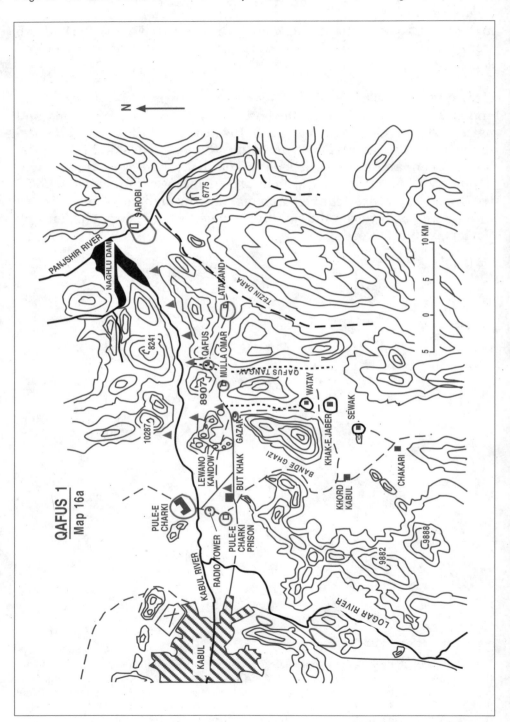

AMBUSH AT QAFUS TANGAY
by Major Sher Aqa Kochay

On August 13, 1985, my 40-man Mujahideen force moved from its base at Sewak (20 kilometers southeast of Kabul) to establish an ambush at the Qafus Tangay (some 25 kilometers east of Kabul). The area was protected by a Sarandoy (Internal Ministry Forces) regiment. This area was previously protected by tribal militia, but exactly one year prior, the local tribal militia of Hasan Khan Karokhel defected to the Mujahideen. Hence, the regiment deployed east of Kabul between Gazak and Sarobi to protect the power lines supplying electricity from Naghlu and Sarobi hydroelectric dams to Kabul. The regiment's headquarters was at Sur Kandow and its forces were deployed along the Butkhak-Sarobi road[10] in security posts. (Map 16a - Qafus 1).

Each day, the regiment sent truck convoys with supplies from headquarters to the battalions. In turn, battalions sent trucks to make deliveries to all their highway outposts. About two kilometers from the DRA Mulla Omar base, the road cuts across the mouth of a narrow valley called Qafus Tangay. Qafus Tangay begins at the Khak-e Jabar pass in the south and stretches north to the Gazak-Sarobi road. The valley offered a concealed approach from the Mujahideen bases in Khord Kabul in the south. The road at the mouth of the valley passes through difficult terrain forcing the traffic to move very slowly. This was a favorable point for an ambush.

I moved my detachment at night reaching the ambush site early in the morning of August 13. My group was armed with four RPG-7 anti-tank grenade launchers, several light machine guns and Kalashnikov automatic rifles. I grouped my men into three teams. I positioned a 10-man party with the four RPG-7s at the bottom of the valley near the road. I positioned two 15-man teams on each of the ridges on the two sides of the valley that dominated the road to the north. Both of the flank groups had PK machine guns. (Map 16b - Qafus 2)

Major Sher Aqa Kochay is a graduate of Afghan Military Academy, Kabul, and received training in commando tactics in the Soviet Union. He served in the 37th Commando Brigade and participated in DRA actions against the Mujahideen in Panjsher Valley. He defected, with a large amount of weapons, to the Mujahideen in 1982 and became a NIFA commander in Kabul. He organized a new Mujahideen base in the Khord Kabul area some 20 kilometers south of the Afghan capital. [Map sheet 2986, vic grid 4919].

10 The southern east-west road on the map.

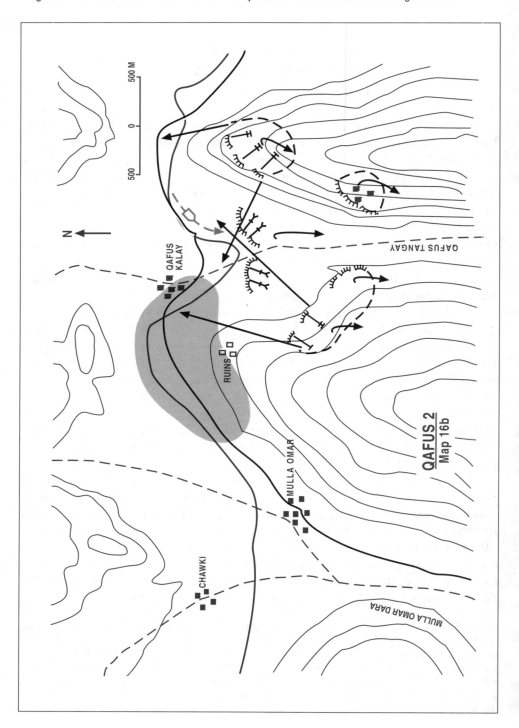

The plan was to wait until the enemy's supply vehicles arrived at the difficult stretch of road directly facing the Qafus Tangay Valley. I planned to assign targets to the RPGs as the trucks moved into the kill zone (for example number one, fire at the lead truck). I hoped to engage four trucks simultaneously, maximizing surprise and fire power. The teams on the ridges were to cover the valley with interlocking fields of fire and to support the withdrawal of the RPG teams while repelling any enemy infantry. They would also seize prisoners and carry off captured weapons and supplies once they had destroyed the enemy convoy.

Finally, the group heard a vehicle approaching from the east. Soon an enemy jeep appeared around a bend in the road. As the jeep slowly moved over the rocky road to the ambush site, a machine gunner on the ridge suddenly opened fire at the vehicle.

I was extremely upset because the ambush had been compromised and ordered one RPG-7 gunner to kill the jeep before it escaped. A few seconds later, the vehicle was in flames and the wounded driver was out of the jeep. He was the sole occupant of the vehicle. He was returning from the battalion headquarters at Lataband where he had driven the regimental political officer. We gave him first aid and released him. He was a conscript soldier from the Panjsher Valley who had recently been press-ganged into the military.

The Sarandoy sent out patrols from the nearby Spina Tana and Nu'manak outposts. Because it was too risky to remain at the ambush site we withdrew through the Qafus Tangay Valley to our base.

COMMENTARY: The Mujahideen ambush failed for lack of fire discipline. The unauthorized initiation of fire compromised a carefully planned and deftly prepared ambush. It was always a challenge for Mujahideen commanders to train and control a volunteer force fighting an organized military power. Further, some Mujahideen commanders ignored certain basic control measures. It is not clear what arrangements Major Aqa made to control the fire of the Mujahideen deployed on the ridges. Had the commander assigned sub-group leaders on each ridge with clear instructions to control the fire of the teams the outcome of the ambush could have been different.

The ambush also lacked sufficient early warning which could communicate the size, composition and activity of approaching convoys. If the commander had early warning and a chain of command, he could have anticipated the arrival of vehicles using something other than sound, determined whether or not to attack the vehicles and gotten his new orders to his men in a timely manner.

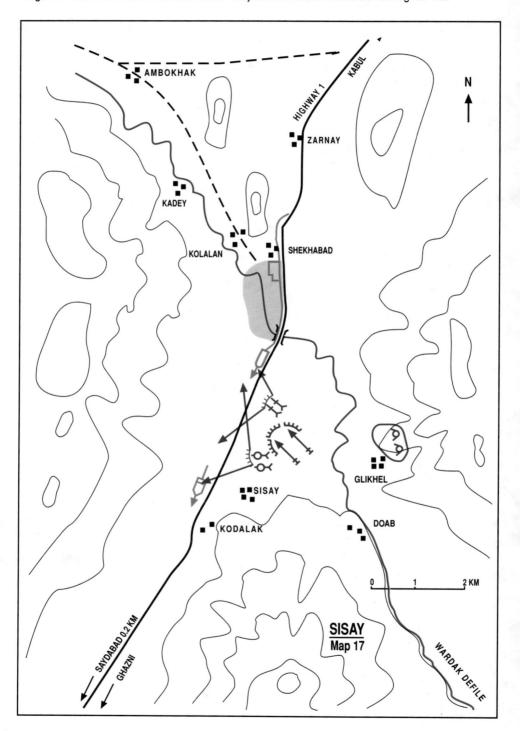

VIGNETTE 16
SISAY AMBUSH
by Commander Haji Mohammad Seddiq

In October 1985, several Mujahideen groups cooperated to establish an ambush at Sisay, some five kilometers north of the Saydabad District Headquarters in Wardak Province. The ambush site is located along the main highway between Kabul and Ghazni. It is located at the mouth of the valley which extends to Logar and offers concealed approach and withdrawal routes for an ambush force. The terrain facilitates the use of all types of weapons by an ambushing force, while restricting maneuver to a force caught in the kill zone.

Mawlawi Faizan, the Wardak provincial leader of HIH, was overall commander of the Sisay combined ambush. He had information from his sources that a large Soviet/DRA column would move from Kabul to Ghazni. Mawlawi Faizan planned the ambush at Sisay and called on several local Mujahideen groups to participate (Map17 - Sisay). He assembled a combined force of 80 Mujahideen armed with four 82mm mortars, six 82mm recoilless rifles, four 60mm mortars,[11] ten RPG-7s and an assortment of Goryunov machine-guns, AK-47 assault rifles and bolt-action Enfield rifles.

I brought my group from Logar Province. It took us three hours to reach the ambush site. Normally, we organized our force into six-man teams, but due to the expected strength of the enemy column, we organized our force into 10-man teams. The ambush had three groups—an assault group, a support group and a heavy weapons group. The assault group had four teams (40 men) armed with the anti-tank weapons. It deployed on Guley hill close to the road. The support group was located behind the assault group. It had three teams (30 men) armed with the machine-guns. It's mission was to support the assault group with machine gun fire, evacuate the wounded and resupply ammunition. The heavy weapons group had one 10-man team

---

Haji Mohammad Seddiq is from No-Burja village in Logar Province. The village is in the Tangi-Wardak area which connects the Saydabad District of Wardak Province to the Baraki Barak District in the Logar Province. Commander Seddiq's village is located on the border between the two provinces. Therefore, his command fought in both provinces in coordination with other Mujahideen. Commander Haji Mohammad Seddiq was affiliated with Hekmatyar's HIH. [Map sheet 2785, vic grid 7666].

[11] The Mujahideen called the 60mm mortar the "guerrilla mortar" (cheriki hawan) due to its light weight and transportability.

armed with the mortars. It established firing positions across the Wardak River. The firing sites were screened from observation by Khadibooch hill.

We occupied our prepared positions in the dark. At about 0900 hours, the forward security element of the Soviet convoy drove into the kill zone from the north. There were two BMPs and another APC in the forward security element. We let them pass. The forward security element just cleared the kill zone and then stopped. They must have assumed that the way was safe, since they then signaled the main body of the convoy to proceed. The forward security element waited while the main body, consisting of GAZ-66 trucks and armored vehicles, moved out of the green zone south of Shekhabad village and into the kill zone. As the column moved into the kill zone, we opened up on the forward security element with our anti-tank weapons. We destroyed both BMPs and the other APC. Then we shifted our fire to the main convoy. The fighting lasted for two hours. The enemy returned fire from his APCs and other armored vehicles, but their fire had limited effect against our well-prepared positions. We punished the enemy severely with our anti-tank fire and mortar fire. The enemy did little to change the situation or to try to gain the initiative. They merely returned fire and those caught in the kill zone died there. I commanded the first team of the assault group. By 1100 hours, we had destroyed all the vehicles in the kill zone and we swarmed into the area to capture whatever weapons and equipment we could carry. Then we withdrew. We left 17 armored vehicles and 45 GAZ-66 trucks and gas tankers burning in the kill zone. We captured four AK-74 assault rifles—the exclusive weapon of the Soviet forces. Mujahideen casualties were 10 KIA and two WIA.

COMMENTARY: Thorough planning, good intelligence, detailed instructions to the combat elements and a simple task organization all contributed to the success of the ambush. The heavily-armed Mujahideen were well-disciplined and controlled. They inflicted maximum losses on the Soviet column before moving forward to loot. This was very effective since it maximized their advantage of fighting from well-protected positions against an enemy caught by surprise and trapped in the open. Perhaps the ambush should have had four elements. The support group had a combat mission (machine gun support to the assault group and a logistics mission of ammunition resupply and medical evacuation). Perhaps these missions should have assigned to different groups. Further, the heavy weapons group needed more men.

Ten men cannot adequately handle four mortars, let alone eight.

The Soviets contributed to their own disaster. The forward security element "cleared" the area by simply driving through it and since they were not fired on, they assumed that it was safe. This was a favorite Mujahideen ambush site complete with well-prepared positions. The Mujahideen had conducted several ambushes from this very site in the past. As a minimum, the Soviets should have sent a force to destroy the positions prior to the convoy departure. Then, the forward security element should have dismounted some troops to search the area for possible ambush and held it until the convoy passed. The forward security element further contributed to the disaster by stopping within anti-tank weapons range (300-800 meters) in an area where the terrain restricted vehicular movement and waiting for the convoy to catch up to it. When the Mujahideen fired on these stationary targets, the forward security element became a burning blockade which trapped the convoy. Had the forward security element moved well ahead of the convoy, it would have allowed part of the convoy to escape south and enabled the forward security element to return to provide fire power to help extricate the trapped vehicles. Had the forward security element moved off the road to the west and taken up covered positions out of anti-tank weapons range, it could have provided considerable immediate firepower to the convoy.

CHAPTER COMMENTARY

The Mujahideen conducted ambushes for harassment or for spoils. Often, harassing ambushes were small-scale ambushes which would only fire a few rounds into the convoy to destroy or damage some vehicles. Then the ambushers would withdraw without attempting to loot the column before the convoy commander could react. Ambushes conducted for spoils (weapons, ammunition, food, clothing and other military supplies) were normally conducted by larger forces who could maintain their positions for up to an hour. Still, the ambush was a short-term action designed to capitalize on surprise and terrain. Road blocks, discussed in a later chapter, were designed to fight the enemy to a standstill and prevent his passage for an extended period of time.

Ambushes for spoils were essential to maintaining the Mujahideen in the field. Mujahideen were unpaid volunteers. Most of them had family responsibilities. Normally all captured heavy weapons and 1/5th of the spoils went to the commander. The other 4/5ths was divided among the Mujahideen combatants. Many Mujahideen would take their captured Kalashnikovs and other trophies to Pakistan where they would sell them and then give the money to their families to live on.

Although the popular concept of the Mujahideen combatant is a hardened warrior clutching a Kalashnikov assault rifle, the most important Mujahideen weapon in the conflict was the RPG-7 anti-tank grenade launcher. This Soviet-manufactured, short-range weapon allowed the Mujahideen to knock out tanks, trucks and, occasionally, helicopters. The RPG was a great equalizer and a great weapon in an ambush. Although the Mujahideen were light infantry, heavier crew-served weapons gave them more range and staying power in a fight. Mortars, rockets, recoilless rifles and heavy machine guns were essential to the force that intended to hold its ground for a time against mechanized Soviet and DRA forces.

The standard Soviet/DRA convoy had a group of armored vehicles at the front of the convoy, more armored vehicles spaced evenly throughout the convoy and another group of armored vehicles constituting a rear guard. The convoy might have a helicopter or ground advance guard or patrol sweep the route prior to movement. Sometimes a mine-detection/clearing force would precede the convoy, although mine-clearing was usually the responsibility of the unit guarding the road and the convoy would not start until the unit had given the "all clear." Sometimes a convoy would have artillery groups move within the column and "leap-frog" to provide rapid, on-call fire support.

When hit, the convoy's standard reaction was to leave armored vehicles inside the kill zone to return fire while the trucks drove out of the kill zone. If the armored vehicles chased the ambushers away, the convoy would continue. If the armored vehicles could not deal with the ambush, helicopter gunships could usually drive the ambushers from their positions. The convoy commander tried to maintain the movement of his convoy and would not usually turn forces around to deal with ambushes. Sometimes this meant that an ambush would split a convoy. The Soviets and DRA seldom dismounted infantry to pursue their ambushers since convoy movement had priority, and they seldom had enough infantry accompanying the convoy to pursue the Mujahideen into their neighborhood and overpower them.

The Mujahideen seldom hit the head of a column unless terrain allowed them to bottle-up the column by doing so. The Mujahideen preferred to hit the middle of the convoy where there were fewer armored vehicles. If possible, they tried to seal off the section of convoy they were attacking if they meant to loot it. Mujahideen usually prepared fighting positions at the ambush site which enabled them to withstand fire from enemy armored vehicles and, sometimes, helicopter gunships.

The most successful Mujahideen ambushes organized the ambush into a heavy weapons support group, flank security groups, an assault group, and a logistics support/spoils removal group. The best ambushes had a well-understood chain of command and radio communications between the groups. Following the ambush, the flank security groups (with an air defense element), covered the withdrawal of the other groups over a secured withdrawal route.

CHAPTER 2
RAIDS

The raid is a surprise attack designed to seize a point, exploit success and then withdraw. It is a temporary measure to capture equipment, destroy installations, bait traps to draw enemy reactions and attack morale. The Mujahideen conducted raids as a primary way to obtain weapons and ammunition—preferably from DRA security posts. They also conducted raids to demonstrate their ability to attack DRA and Soviet installations with relative impunity. Raids generally require fewer supplies than an attack on a strong point since there is no intention of holding the objective for any length of time following a raid.

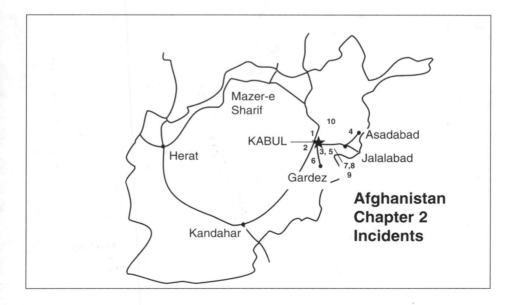

Afghanistan
Chapter 2
Incidents

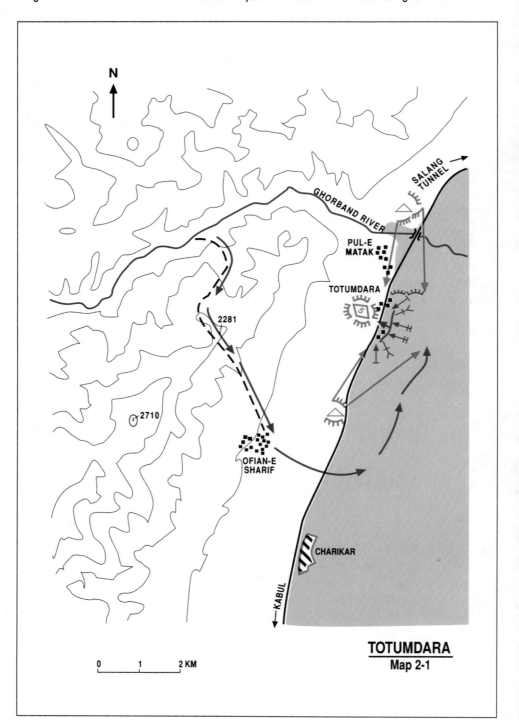

N

GHORBAND RIVER

SALANG TUNNEL

PUL-E MATAK

TOTUMDARA

2281

2710

OFIAN-E SHARIF

CHARIKAR

KABUL

0   1   2 KM

TOTUMDARA
Map 2-1

VIGNETTE 1
RAID ON THE TOTUMDARA SECURITY POST
by Commander Sarshar

The Soviets had a series of security posts protecting the Salang-Kabul highway. They had one at Totumdara which is eight kilometers north of Charikar[1] (Map 2-1 - Totumdara). This post had five armored vehicles. We mounted a raid on the security post in September 1981. My base was in Ghorband Canyon. I had 60 Mujahideen armed with four Goryunov heavy machine guns, two PK medium machine guns, four RPG-7s, and Kalashnikov rifles. The area around my base is very mountainous, but also heavily patrolled, so we had to move at night. We moved from our base over the mountain pass to our staging area at Ofian-e Sharif. Ofian-e Sharif is about three kilometers south of our target and it took us six hours to reach it from Ghorband. We had to carry all our equipment on our backs.

We stayed in Ofian-e Sharif during the day and rested and made our plan. That night we crossed over to the east into the green zone and moved into the villages near the target. I positioned 40 of my Mujahideen to secure our route back into the mountains and to help carry the gear. The other 20 were my raiding party. I divided these 20 men into a 10-man group for immediate security and a 10-man assault group. The assault group had two Goryunov heavy machine guns, two PK medium machine guns, two RPG-7s and some Kalashnikovs. We attacked the post that same night. We destroyed two tanks with our RPGs and terrified their infantry with our Goryunovs. However, the security post was heavily protected by mines so we could not cross the mine fields to get into the post. The Soviet security post at Pul-e Matak and the Project security post (named after the Chinese irrigation project) were on the Totumdara security post flanks. Both of these posts opened fire on us and we

---

Commander Sarshar was a police officer in Parwan who worked clandestinely with the Mujahideen. When his cover was about to be blown, he became a Mujahideen commander in Ghorband. He commanded a mobile group in the Ghorband front near Charikar. [Map sheet 2887, vic grid 1680].

[1] This was part of the Soviet 108th Motorized Rifle Division area of responsibility. At this time, the division's 285th Tank Regiment was stationed in Charikar while the 177th Motorized Rifle Regiment was stationed 13 kilometers north at Jabulassarai. The outpost belonged to one of these two regiments.

were forced to withdraw. We withdrew to our base in Ghorband by the same route we came. We had no casualties.

COMMENTARY: The Soviets employed millions of mines in Afghanistan for installation security, LOC security and area denial. Mine clearing was a major problem for any Mujahideen attack on a prepared site and often prevented Mujahideen success. The Mujahideen needed rugged, light-weight mine detection and clearing gear which would allow them to clear mines quickly under fire. Often the Mujahideen had to resort to heaving large rocks to create a path through a minefield.

Attacking parked vehicles is certainly easier than attacking vehicles which are crewed and moving. Apparently the Soviets had not bothered to create a sandbag wall around their tanks, although an RPG can penetrate the turret armor of older tanks.

The Mujahideen chose a target flanked by two other outposts that could bring fire onto their attacking flanks. The flank security elements were close-in elements that merely guarded the flanks and did nothing to pin the outposts in position. The bridge outpost should have been an easier target with a better chance of success. This attack also could have employed a larger force in two phases. The first phase would be an attack to the flanks to neutralize the flanking fire. The second phase would then be an attack on the Totumdara post. Such an attack would require better coordination and discipline than demonstrated.

VIGNETTE 2
CHAMTALA RAID
by Tsaranwal (Attorney) Sher Habib

In June 1982, Commander Sheragai led a group of ten of my Mujahideen on a successful raid on a DRA outpost on the Chamtala plain near Highway 2, just north of Kabul. Commander Sheragai was a Kochi[2] and a kinsman of a Kochi clan which had its summer quarters in Paghman and in the areas around Kabul. Some of the families of the clan pitched their tents in Chamtala plain. There they tended their flocks of sheep and goats in the grazing lands just north of Kabul. Their grazing lands were close to a DRA security outpost. The DRA outpost hindered Mujahideen movement through the area (Map 2-2 - Chamtala).

We decided to raid the DRA outpost. I selected Commander Sheragai to lead the raid since he could easily gain the full cooperation of his Kochi clansmen in the area. His group was armed with small arms. They left our base at Qala-e Hakim in Paghman and walked to the Chamtala plain. There, Kochi families took the raiding party into their tents and cared for them. The raiding party stayed with the nomads for several days while they studied and evaluated the outpost and prepared for the raid. Commander Sheragai wanted to find an unmined approach to the outpost, so he asked his kinsmen to move their flocks to various spots around the outpost so he could probe the approaches. This went on for three days while Commander Sheragai picked the most secure approach to the outpost where the terrain allowed to Mujahideen to sneak up on the outpost unobserved. They cleared this approach of mines.

On the morning of the raid, the Mujahideen raiders moved to the target within a herd of sheep. Some Mujahideen posed as shepherds, while others crawled along in the middle of the grazing sheep. The herd moved right up to the DRA outpost, but the Mujahideen presence was never detected or suspected by the DRA guards. The raiding group spent the whole day in the middle of the sheep herd and found hiding places. At sunset, the shepherds drove the flock back toward

---

Tsaranwal (Attorney) Sher Habib commanded the Ibrahimkhel Front north of the city of Paghman. His primary AOR extended from Paghman east and northeast to Kabul (some 20 kilometers). [Map sheet 2886, vic grid 2369].

[2] Kochi are nomadic peoples.

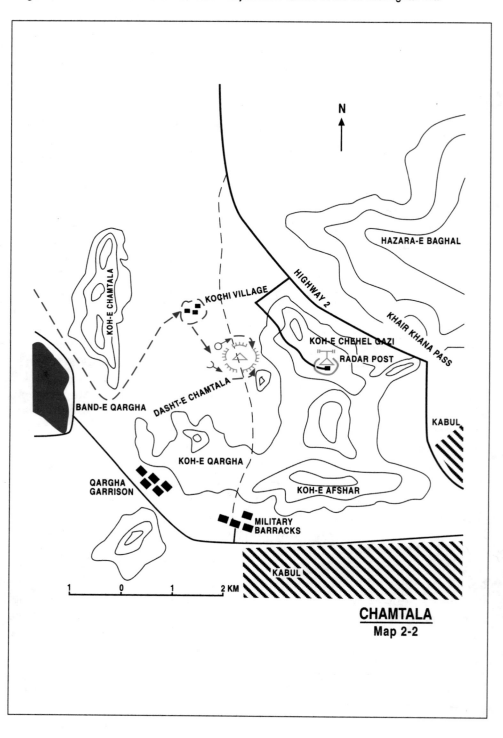

CHAMTALA
Map 2-2

the encampment, while the Mujahideen remained behind in hiding places. One of the things that the Mujahideen had discovered was when the seven-man security outpost had dinner. One guard was left on duty while the rest ate their dinner. As dinner was being served, three Mujahideen crept to the outpost, jumped the guard and disarmed him. One Mujahideen kept his hand on the mouth of the guard to prevent him from screaming. Then the rest of the raiding party swarmed into the outpost. They surprised the rest of the DRA soldiers and captured them all without firing a shot. A DRA lieutenant was among the prisoners. The Mujahideen took whatever they could carry and then left for their base with all their prisoners.

COMMENTARY: Kabul and the surrounding area were heavily guarded. The Soviet 103rd Airborne Division, the 180th and 181st Motorized Rifle Regiments of the Soviet 108th Motorized Rifle Division, the DRA 8th Infantry Division, the DRA 37th Commando Brigade and the DRA 15th Tank Brigade were all garrisoned in Kabul. Careful reconnaissance, strict camouflage discipline and a clever deception plan enabled the Mujahideen to carry off this raid. Local assistance from the Kochi was essential to the plan. The selection of a Kochi commander and his efforts to gain the cooperation of his kinsmen paid off. The Mujahideen relied on the local populace for cover, food and water, intelligence, shelter and early warning. The time and effort spent were essential to the Mujahideen success.

On the other hand, the DRA commander allowed his outpost activities to become routine. The Mujahideen planned the attack when security was relaxed and captured the outpost without firing a shot or alerting neighboring garrisons.

Vignette 3
Raid on Bagrami District Headquarters
by Commander Shahabuddin

In July 1983, local units of all seven major factions united to raid the Bagrami District Headquarters to the southeast of Kabul. (No Map) We assembled about 250 Mujahideen armed with six 82mm mortars, nine recoilless rifles, and eight RPG-7s. We assembled at my base at Yakhdara, made our plans and then spread our forces out in the villages. We assigned 100 Mujahideen to route security and posted them prior to moving our main raiding forces to Bagrami and Qal-e Ahmadkhan. These towns are in the suburbs just outside of Kabul and are part of the inner security belt of Kabul. The Bagrami 40-man assault group had eight RPG-7s, three recoilless rifles and two mortars. They were to attack the district headquarters from three directions. I led the assault group at Qal-e Ahmadkhan. I had 50 men—10 of which I used for flank protection and 40 for the raid. I also attacked from three directions. As we approach Qal-e Ahmadkhan, we were stopped by a small outpost. We overran it. Then we attacked one of the many security outposts in the village. We overran this outpost killing 25 and capturing eight DRA soldiers. We also captured 14 Kalashnikovs and a telephone set. The Bagrami assault group could not get close enough to their target to attack it directly, so they shelled it instead.

COMMENTARY: The DRA and Soviets surrounded Kabul with a series of three security belts composed of outposts, minefields and obstacles. Their purpose was to deny Mujahideen entry into the city and prevent Mujahideen shelling attacks. The Mujahideen often attacked these outposts, but could not hold them. The main benefits of the security belt system to the Mujahideen were these attacks kept a large numbers of troops tied up in passive security roles, the outposts provided a source of weapons and ammunition and these attacks affected the morale of their opponents.

Commander Shahabuddin is from Shewaki Village south of Kabul. There is no map with this vignette. [Map sheets 2885 and 2886].

ATTACK ON THE TSAWKEY SECURITY POSTS
by LTC Haji Mohammad Rahim

Tsawkey is a district of Kunar Province. The DRA established a security post in the Tsawkey High School. This high school security post provided protection for a section of the Jalalabad to Asadabad highway. (Map 2-3 - Tsawkey) It was a usual practice of the DRA to convert public buildings to such uses. I decided to capture this post in October 1983. I had approximately 70 Mujahideen armed with two 82mm mortars, one DShK and some Enfield rifles. We planned our battle in our base in the nearby Babur Gorge. Other Mujahideen joined us from Dawagal. We would attack from three directions—from the north (high ground), along the road from the northeast and from the west. We moved from our base at night, deployed and attacked the target. Our attack lasted 30 minutes. We overran the post but could not hold it. We killed 11 DRA and captured one. We also captured a ZGU-1, a DShK and some Kalashnikovs. We had three Mujahideen KIA and one WIA. We could not hold the security post, so we left it.

There were two DRA security outposts near the Tsawkey District headquarters. One was in the high school and the other was near the bridge. We had a contact inside the second post who was a DRA officer—Musa Khan. In June 1985, he helped us capture his security post. I assembled 50 Mujahideen armed with an RPG-7, Kalashnikovs and Enfields. We came during the night from our base in Babur Valley and followed the road bank to the southwest. We approached the post at dawn from the high ground to the north. Our contact led us inside. Most of the soldiers were asleep and we wanted to capture them. However, some of our Mujahideen were not very quiet and the detail woke up and started fighting us. We killed seven of the security detail and captured one. We also captured one PK medium machine gun, 12 Kalashnikovs and ammunition. The firing alerted the other enemy unit in the Tsawkey high school. They sent a detachment to the outpost, but I had posted a security element on the road. This security element blocked the movement of the detachment and covered our withdrawal. We all withdrew up to our base in the mountains. I had one Mujahideen wounded.

LTC Haji Mohammad Rahim was an officer in the Afghan Army who became a Mujahideen and led a group in Kunar Province. [Map sheet 3186, vic grid 7640].

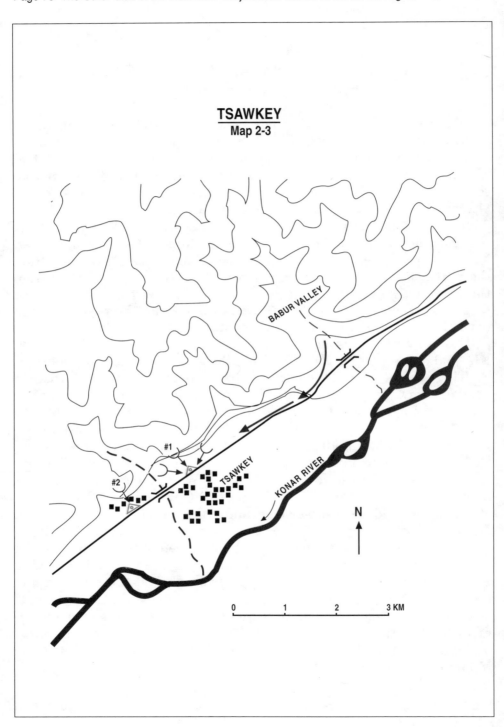

TSAWKEY
Map 2-3

COMMENTARY: Less than 15% of the Mujahideen commanders had previous military experience, yet the impact of the military who joined the Mujahideen was significant. They provided a continuity, an understanding of military planning and issues, a modicum of uniform training and an ability to deal with outside agencies providing aid to the Mujahideen. On the other hand, these were fairly soft targets. The security outposts were situated in existing buildings backed by wooded high ground. The Mujahideen had concealed approaches and exits as well as inside help.

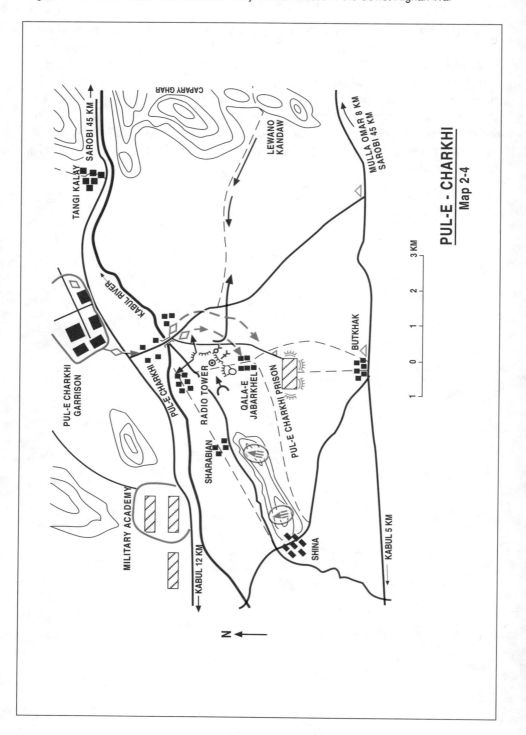

PUL-E - CHARKHI
Map 2-4

VIGNETTE 5
RAID ON PUL-E CHARKHI RADIO TRANSMITTER STATION
by Major Sher Aqa Kochay and others

In June 1984, Provincial NIFA leader Wali Khan issued orders to Major Sher Aqa Kochay, the commander of a NIFA base in Sewak (about 20 kilometers southeast of Kabul). Major Aqa would join two other regional commanders—Haji Hussein Jan of Narey Oba and Sayed Hasan Khan of Khak-e Jabar—in a raid on a radio transmitter station. The transmitter was located near Pul-e Charkhi (20 kilometers east of Kabul city) and the raid would take place on the night of 26 June. The Soviet-backed Afghan government was expanding the transmitter facility which would reach wider audiences inside and outside the country. The station used local broadcasts as well as programs produced in the Soviet Union.[3]

The transmitter station was located in Pul-e Charkhi near a military complex which included the DRA 15th Tank Brigade, DRA 10th field Engineer Regiment and some other units. (see Map 16a - Qafus 1, Chapter 1 and Map 2-4 - Pul-e Charkhi.) Further to the east, between Butkhak and Sarobi, a government-paid militia force patrolled the area and protected the power lines and pylons that supplied electricity from Naghlo Dam through Sarobi to Kabul. The militia was recruited from the local tribe of the Karokhel clan of Ahmadzai Pushtuns. Their chief was Hasan Khan Karokhel. On the surface, Hasan Khan was a government supporter. But he was actually a major Mujahideen collaborator. He provided the Mujahideen with logistic support, sheltered their resistance fighters and even provided medical care to Mujahideen wounded at regime medical institutions.[4]

Principally based on an interview with Major Sher Aqa Kochay in Peshawar on September 14, 1996. Other sources include NIFA documents about the battle, Ali Jalali's discussions with Hasan Khan Karokhel in 1986 in Peshawar, his interviews with the late Wali Khan Karokhel (NIFA's provincial military commander of Kabul) in Peshawar and Islamabad in 1984 and 1986 and interviews with General Abdul Rahim Wardak. [Map sheet 2886, vic grid 3221].

[3] The Soviet Union and their clients in Kabul were also engaged in jamming international broadcasts beamed to Afghanistan. Afghans considered such broadcasts the only source of objective and uncensored news to the country. The jamming was done at other sites.

[4] In fact NIFA's provincial commander, Wali Khan Karokhel, was the brother of Hasan Khan Karokhel. Hasan Khan Karokhel had his headquarters in Mulla Omar, the ancestral home of the Karokhel chiefs.

According to the plan, Mujahideen from the three bases would assemble at Mulla Omar for final instructions prior to the raid. By the afternoon of 26 June, all three groups were in Mulla Omar. Major Sher Aqa and Haji Hussein Jan had each brought 30 men from their bases in Sewak and Narey Oba. Sayed Hasan Khan came with a 50-man unit from Khak-e Jabar.

Wali Khan Karokhel issued the final instructions. Major Sher Aqa was appointed the overall commander of the raiding group. He divided his force into four teams. A 20-man assault team, commanded by Haji Hussein Jan, carried automatic rifles, light machine guns and RPG-7 antitank grenade launchers. Their mission was to attack the transmitter from the southwest, destroy the facility and then withdraw under the cover of the support group.

Major Sher Aqa's 20-man support team would cover the assault team from positions in a ditch immediately to the east of the target. The group had one 82mm mortar, a single barrel 107mm rocket launcher (BM-1), a PK medium machine gun, a few RPG-7s and AK-47 assault rifles. Major Sher Aqa decided to stay with this team since it would be the last to pull-out.

Sayed Hasan Khan commanded a 25 to 30-man containment team. They were armed with small arms and RPG-7s. They would block the Pul-e Charkhi-Butkhak road on the east bank of Kabul River and prevent the enemy forces from reaching the target. The rest of the Mujahideen were assigned as supply and evacuation elements to help the other groups.

Major Aqa decided to launch the assault at midnight. Since it is

---

Hasan Khan later cooperated with the Mujahideen in a major action in 1984. He sheltered, guided and supported a NIFA force which blew up all the electric pylons between Butkhak and Sarobi. This cut off electrical power to Kabul for a long time. "Operation Black-out" marked the end of Hasan Khan's service as the head of the government militia and he, along with his family and 400 followers, migrated to Pakistan and continued his struggle against the Soviet-backed regime from there. Hazhir Teimourian reported on this in *The Times* of London on 31 August 1984.

Wali Khan, Hasan Khan's brother, remained NIFA's provincial leader in Kabul until 1986. Afterwards, he acted independently mostly in the anti Communist political movement outside the country. After the Soviet withdrawal, he joined the Council of Solidarity and Understanding--a movement of Afghan intellectuals campaigning for creation of a moderate government in Afghanistan. The movement, and particularly Wali Khan Karokhel, supported the restoration of the former King of Afghanistan as a person who would serve as a symbol of unity among the fractionalized Afghan Resistance. Wali Khan was assassinated in 1994 on the road between Peshawar and Islamabad by yet unidentified gunmen. Some speculation points to his political enemies among the extremist Islamic groups as the perpetrators of the murder.

about 15 kilometers from Mulla Omar to the site and since the raiding party had to bypass a Soviet unit deployed in Gazak, the departure time was set at dusk (about 2000 hours). The party would move from Mulla Omar through Gazak to reassemble briefly at Lewano Kandow. The Mujahideen force moved out in small groups following each other on the same route all the way to Lewano Kandow. A pair of reconnaissance patrols moved on the flanks and one moved to the front of the column—keeping within voice contact distance.

When the force reached a water spring at the Lewano Kandow, Major Sher Aqa issued the last coordinating instructions and ordered the groups to open fire when he did. This would signal the start of the raid. From their Lewano Kandow assembly area, the different elements of the raiding party moved separately toward their designated areas.

Just before midnight, all groups were in place. Everything was quiet around the transmitter site. At Major Sher Aqa's signal, the assault team opened fire on the site and began the attack. The support team covered their advance. RPG rounds set the wooden buildings on fire and soon fire swept the site. The defenders at the site panicked and failed to put up an organized resistance. The assault team overran the site, killed several soldiers, captured five Kalashnikov assault rifles and demolished the transmitter station.

The DRA quickly responded by moving a tank column from the Pul-e Charkhi garrison to the site. The column crossed the bridge over the Kabul River but then left the main road and bypassed the Mujahideen blocking positions established by the containment (holding) team of Sayed Hasan Khan. The tanks, driving with their headlights off, cut across the plain to the east of the Mujahideen, cutting off their escape route. A young Mujahideen named Babrak hit one tank with an RPG-7 rocket and set it on fire. But the rest of the column moved swiftly to the south-west.

Fearing encirclement, the containment (holding) team and the assault team immediately broke contact and, without notifying Major Sher Aqa, pulled out toward the Lewano Kandow, leaving the support team behind. As Commander Sher Aqa was desperately trying to establish contact with the other teams, he heard tanks moving to the rear of his position. By this time, all electric lights in the area were extinguished, but the transmitter station continued to burn brightly. The Mujahideen and the DRA tank column both used the fire for orientation.

Facing a threatening situation, Major Sher Aqa instructed his men not to panic but to exfiltrate individually through the intervals between the tanks. Using masking terrain, his Mujahideen managed to exfiltrate and move to the designated assembly area at Lewano Kandow. As they straggled in, they found that the assault and containment teams along with supply and evacuation personnel were already waiting there. Major Sher Aqa discovered that all the groups, except his support group, had withdrawn when the enemy tank column arrived. All Mujahideen reached Lewano Kandow by 0200.

Mujahideen casualties were six wounded—one from the supporting team who died on the way back, two from the assault team and three from the containment team. It was not safe for the Mujahideen to move further, since daybreak would be in two hours and the Mujaideen would once again have to bypass the Soviet force at Grazak. The raid on Pul-e Charkhi would clearly have alerted the Soviets to the presence of a Mujahideen force in their area.

Two groups, Haji Hussein Jan's detachment and Sayed Hasan Khan's party, decided to stay during the day in the Lewano Kandow mountain since they could not reach their bases during the remaining hours of the night. Major Sher Aqa's group, along with the wounded, moved forward to Mulla Omar. This was only possible since Hasan Khan Karokhel had sent trucks to Lewano Kandow to carry the wounded and other Mujahideen to safety before daybreak. The trucks, posing as militia patrols trying to hunt down the raiding force, took these Mujahideen to Mulla Omar where they were taken care of and medical personnel were summoned from Kabul who tended to the wounded. The next night, the Mujahideen groups returned to their bases and sent the body of the one dead warrior to his family for burial.

COMMENTARY: The assistance extended by the Karokhel militia contributed markedly to the Mujahideen success. Such assistance was essential for actions conducted around a strongly defended city like Kabul. From 1980 to 1984, the militia helped many Mujahideen infiltrate into Kabul before defecting *en masse* to the resistance. Their assistance was particularly important in suporting the withdrawal of Mujahideen strike groups at the end of an action. Such inside help made it possible for a force of more than 100 to launch a raid right in the heart of the enemy stronghold. Ideally, a much smaller group, like a 15-man team, would have been more appropriate to the task. But the Mujahideen preferred to move in large groups. Large groups could carry heavy loads, provide needed labor in the field and carry and escort the wounded and dead. Many Mujahideen felt more comfortable having their relatives or close friends with them.

Lack of reliable internal communications among the Mujahideen combat teams led to a situation that could have turned disastrous. The containment team did not contain the DRA tanks and pulled out immediately after it saw the tanks bypass its position. The group helped the assault team during the assault, but this was not their assigned mission. Had the group laid anti-tank mines in areas that the enemy tanks had to pass over— particularly in the vicinity of the bridge over the Kabul River and the river fords—it could have delayed the tank column and allowed them to engage it more effectively. This would have prevented the enveloping movement that almost encircled the whole Mujahideen contingent.

Apparently, the DRA had not developed and rehearsed contingency plans to deal with such a raid. This, and luck, helped the Mujahideen escape heavy casualties. A more active reaction by the DRA could easily have jeopardized the concentration of a sizeable Mujahideen force in an area totally controlled by Soviet/DRA forces. Relying on tanks, the enemy failed to deploy infantry with the tanks. Infantry are more effective in the dark against guerrillas and provide protection to the tanks against anti-tank gunners. At the same time, the Mujahideen failed to take advantage of the tank column's vulnerability and use their RPG-7s at close distance against the unprotected tanks. The Mujahideen had the opportunity to kill more than the one tank they actually destroyed.

Fear of being cut off inhibited much of the Mujahideen action after they successfully destroyed the transmitter. However, through good leadership, Major Sher Aqa turned a threatening tactical situation into a more manageable one and succeeded in pulling his men out through the tank cordon.

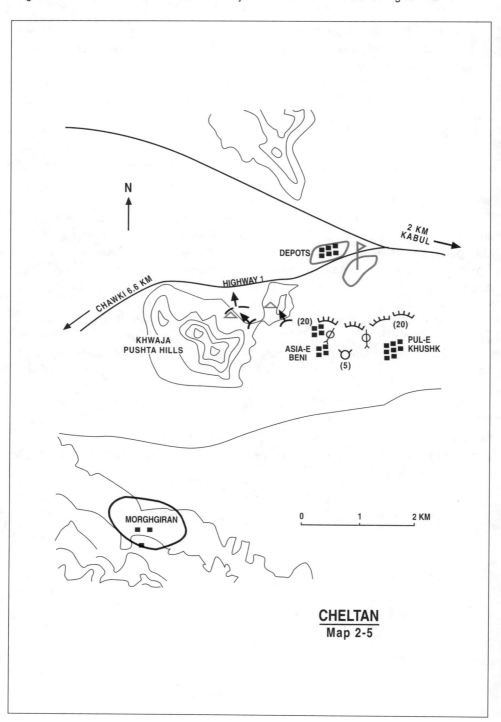

CHELTAN

Map 2-5

VIGNETTE 6
RAID FROM CHELTAN ON OUTPOSTS IN THE KABUL SUBURBS
by Commander Asil Khan

Kabul was surrounded by three security belts made up of security outposts manned by Soviet and DRA forces. A battalion from the DRA 8th Infantry Division garrisoned the old highway construction headquarters, commonly known as "the company," in the western suburbs of Kabul. The battalion also guarded a number of government supply depots located across the highway to the west. The battalion built security outposts on the Khwaja Pushta hills in the south. The battalion protected all its installations with mine fields except for the outposts on the hills. This made all the other installations too difficult to attack in the dark.

I commanded a joint 200 Mujahideen detachment made up from local resistance units affiliated with NIFA, HIK and Etehad-e Islami (IUA). According to our agreed plan, we were to move from our bases around Cheltan and converge on the target area in the dark. We would continually shell the main battalion camp and the depots, while the assault groups would attack the Khwaja Pushta hill outposts (Map 2-5 - Cheltan).

In the late afternoon of 1 June 1985, I led my NIFA Mujahideen from our base at Morghgiran. We arrived near the target after 2000 hours. We deployed for battle according to plan. I established blocking positions at Asia-e Beni and Pul-e Khushk and deployed about 20 Mujahideen at each position. I positioned one 82mm mortar with its five-man crew and two 82mm recoilless rifles (each with a five-man crew) at Asia-e Beni to shell the enemy battalion.

The raid began around 2100 hours and lasted until 2300 hours. Our heavy weapons kept the enemy battalion and the depot forces pinned in place. The enemy responded with artillery fire but made no attempt to counter with infantry or tanks. No enemy helicopters responded throughout the raid. This lack of response left the tactical initiative in my hands. We easily overran the enemy outposts on the Khwaja Pushta hills and captured weapons and a radio set. Most of the DRA soldiers ran away. At one outpost, we killed two enemy soldiers and wounded another. We had no casualties. We pulled out before midnight and the force split up and returned to their bases.

Asil Khan was a NIFA commander and a famed guerrilla commander in the Kabul area. [Map sheets 2885 and 2886].

COMMENTARY: Throughout the war, Soviet and DRA forces were reluctant to respond aggressively to Mujahideen night attacks. Unless the Soviet and DRA forces had planned and rehearsed a counter-attack drill, they rarely left the relative safety of their prepared positions to deal with Mujahideen night attacks. This encouraged the Mujahideen to harass the enemy continuously at night and to attack the weakest points of their defenses. Often, the Mujahideen boldly attacked areas adjacent to large forces. These security posts were out of supporting range of other posts, so the DRA refusal to react to the attack practically handed the outpost to the Mujahideen.

However, the Mujahideen could not fully exploit their enemy's reluctance to fight at night to achieve decisive tactical results. The Mujahideen could not readily penetrate the heavily-mined zones surrounding Soviet and DRA positions. As long as the Soviet/DRA forces felt no serious threat from isolated Mujahideen night attacks, they preferred to respond by artillery fire instead of risking stumbling into an ambush. The Soviet and DRA response came in the form of well-planned major cordon and search operations in those areas where the Mujahideen had gained an upper hand.

In July 1984 three groups of Mujahideen combined to raid Soviet/DRA security outposts on the main Kabul-Jalalabad highway. (Map 2-6 - Mahipar) Highway 1 at Mahipar passes through a deep gorge, with the river flowing immediately to the north of the road and with a steep ridge rising on the south. Other than the highway, the main access to Mahipar is through Mulla Omar Dara, a mountain valley connecting Mulla Omar Village with Highway 1. At that time, the DRA had a militia unit headquartered at Mulla Omar. The DRA militia commander was Hasan Khan Karokhel, the local Ghilzai Pashtun chieftain. Hasan Khan was also a secret collaborator with the Mujahideen. He helped facilitate our movements and combat against Soviet/DRA forces in the area.

My group reached Mulla Omar in the evening after a day march from our base at Tangi Tezin. There, we were joined by two NIFA commanders, Captain Afghan of Deh Sabz, and Sayed Hasan Khan of Khak-e Jabar. All together, we had 80 Mujahideen armed with AK-47s and .303 Enfield rifles, five BM-1s, four 82mm recoilless rifles, four 82mm mortars, two DShKs and 13 RPG-7s. We planned our combined action at Mulla Omar and moved out the next morning toward Mahipar over Lataband mountain. We had packed our heavy weapons on mules. There were three chief components in our combined force—two fire support groups and an assault group. Each fire support group had BM-1s and 82mm mortars. Their mission was to attack and pin down the DRA base on the left flank and the Soviet base on the right flank. The assault group consisted of three teams. Each assault team had a designated outpost to attack. Each assault team had RPGs and recoilless rifles to support their attack.

In order to minimize the daylight available to the enemy's aircraft, we began our attack at 1600. We knew it would take several hours for them to respond. Our heavy weapons pounded the flanking bases to isolate the attack area. The assault teams began to fire on the security posts and slowly move forward. The attack on the security posts was hindered by enemy mines and it took several hours for the

---

Commander Wazir Gul was affiliated with Jamiat-e Islami Afghanistan (JIA) of Burhanuddin Rabbani. His base was in Tezin southwest of Sarobi. He fought in the Sarobi, Lataband and Mahipar areas. [Map sheet 2986, vic grid 4723].

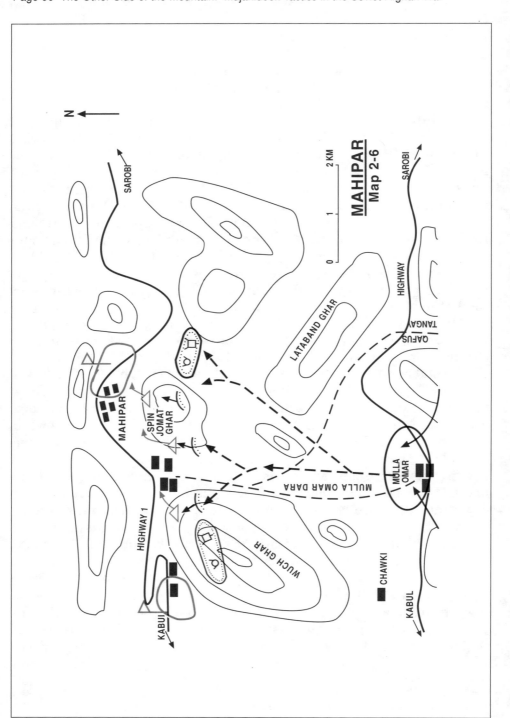

Mujahideen to overrun the outposts after heavy clashes. By 2100, the DRA soldiers manning the outposts were either killed or had escaped. We took one tank crew prisoner.

The Soviet base and outposts further down the road could not support the embattled DRA outposts. But as we pulled out, the Soviet base began heavy fire on the withdrawing Mujahideen groups. Their fire had little effect in the dark. We destroyed two tanks, killed nine enemy soldiers and captured three DShKs, six AK-47 rifles and a large amount of ammunition. Two Mujahideen were wounded in the battle. We spent the night at Mulla Omar and returned to our bases the next day.

COMMENTARY: The terrain here is very restrictive and rugged. The Soviet/DRA bases and outposts were all in the canyon. The Soviets/DRA surrendered the initiative in this area and trusted that the difficulty in crossing the rugged terrain, coupled with their bunkers and field fortifications, would protect these sites from the Mujahideen. There were a series of three security outposts along the road: two on the high ground on both sides of the gorge and the other on the road. The purpose of security outposts was to protect bridges, hydroelectric installations, dams and block the side valleys. The outposts on the high ground were not high enough to interfere with Mujahideen freedom of action. There were a few observation posts on the high peaks but they were not effective, particularly at night. The security outposts on the high ground were mostly manned by DRA or militia which lacked training and were in fact prisoners in their mine-protected enclaves. The Mujahideen could easily bypass them—particularly at night. The Soviets/DRA had mined the main approaches to the gorge, but given the steep nature of the approaches, the mines usually washed away when it rained. The Mujahideen often used such steep areas to descend to the highway.

The Mujahideen, on the other hand, saw this set up as an excellent opportunity to punish their opponent, pick up some weapons and resupply ammunition. The Mujahideen developed a standard pattern for attacking outposts along this road. They would attack late in the afternoon to minimize the effectiveness of air strikes and artillery. They would fire rockets and mortars at the main base camps on both flanks of the target area to seal the area and hold the attention of the base camps so that they would not interfere with the main attack. Then they would launch the attack against the outposts which were mostly manned by ill-trained, poorly-motivated conscript DRA. The

DRA had little stomach for the fight and, once the Mujahideen got through the minefields surrounding the outposts, the Mujahideen would strip the outposts of everything they could carry and disappear into the night. The Mujahideen would usually offer DRA prisoners the opportunity to serve as labor service with the Mujahideen or simply turn them loose. The Mujahideen felt that the conscript DRA soldier had little choice in the fight. DRA officers were kept prisoner until they could be tried by field tribunal. The Mujahideen felt fairly secure from sallies from the base camps at night. Soviet and DRA reaction was mainly limited to area shelling and bombing.

RAID ON LATABAND SECURITY OUTPOSTS
by Commander Wazir Gul

There are two highways between Kabul and Sarobi. The northern highway is the newer one and is part of Highway 1—the main highway of Afghanistan. The older Kabul-Sarobi highway runs roughly parallel to Highway 1, some four-ten kilometers to the south. A series of Soviet and DRA security bases and outposts protected both highways. In September 1985, several Mujahideen groups combined to conduct a raid on the Soviet/DRA security outposts in the Lataband pass east of Kabul (Map 2-7 - Lataband). Lataband is located on the old Kabul-Sarobi highway. The Lataband pass was protected by a Soviet base at Mulla Omar in the west, and a DRA Sarandoy base at Lataband in the east. The area between the two bases was protected by several security outposts manned by DRA military detachments.

My group's base was in Zandeh Kalay which is some 25 kilometers south of the pass. I planned the attack at the base. We left the base at 1500 and moved to the Tezin Valley where we spent the night. We carried our supplies and ammunition on mules. Once we got to the Tezin Valley, I met with the commanders of other groups and we coordinated our attack. The total strength of the combined Mujahideen force was about 150 fighters. We left what we did not need for immediate combat at Tezin and moved out toward our targets. We brought the mules with us. There were three chief components in our combined force—two fire support groups and an assault group. Each fire support group had heavy weapons (three BM-1, four DShK, three 82mm mortars). Their mission was to attack and pin down the Soviet base at Mulla Omar and the Sarandoy base at Lataband. The assault group had twelve RPG-7s and four 82mm recoilless rifles. The assault group was composed of three 20-man teams. Each 20-man team had a designated enemy outpost to attack.

We moved into position. In order to minimize the daylight available to the enemy's aircraft, we decided to start our attack in the late afternoon. We began the attack at 1600 with heavy fire on the bases at Mulla Omar and Lataband. Meanwhile, the assault teams occupy-

---

Commander Wazir Gul was affiliated with Jamiat-e Islami Afghanistan (JIA) of Burhanuddin Rabbani. His base was in Tezin southwest of Sarobi. He fought in the Sarobi, Lataband and Mahipar areas. [Map sheets 2985 and 2986vic grid 5618].

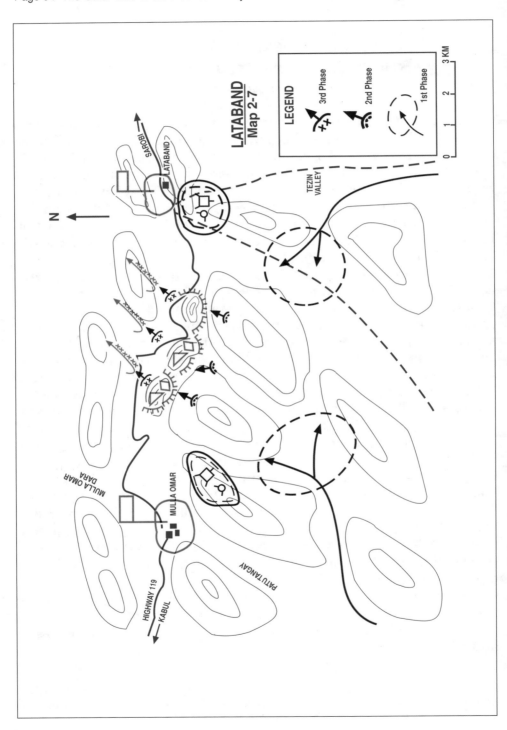

LATABAND
Map 2-7

LEGEND

3rd Phase

2nd Phase

1st Phase

0   1   2   3 KM

ing the high ground south of the Lataband pass began to fire on the enemy outposts below. The shelling confused the enemy as the three teams of the assault group approached their outposts and launched the attack. The battle continued into the evening and the assault teams overran the enemy outposts. As the Mujahideen approached the outposts, most of the DRA soldiers ran away and left behind an enormous amount of ammunition and other equipment. We loaded what we could on our mules and hauled it away. The enemy responded by saturating the area in and around the outposts with artillery fire and air attacks. We lost two mules to artillery fire and so withdrew at 2100. We suffered personnel losses. The losses in my own group were one KIA and six WIA. We captured two DRA soldiers and lots of ammunition and supplies.

COMMENTARY: The isolated highway security posts were extremely vulnerable to attacks by Mujahideen who controlled the surrounding high ground. The Soviets/DRA had insufficient intelligence or surveillance in the immediate region. Furthermore, their contingency plans to reinforce outposts or to react swiftly against Mujahideen attacks were lacking or poorly executed. The forces in the bases seemed to have a severe case of "bunker mentality" and passively sat out the Mujahideen shelling and attack on the outposts. The Soviets and DRA seemed particularly reluctant to move and fight at night. The Mujahideen exploited this reluctance. Air support apparently was slow in coming and was not very accurate at night.

In this example, the Soviet/DRA base forces waited until the outposts were overrun and the Mujahideen were withdrawing before they reacted. They reacted with artillery and air strikes—not maneuver forces. The DRA in the outposts were left to their own devices. The DRA forces were generally ill-trained and had poor morale. Most of the DRA soldiers had been press-ganged into the army and had no desire to fight their countrymen. Therefore, the DRA soldiers were more interested in escaping than in stubborn defense and were quite willing to abandon the ammunition and supplies of the outpost to the attacking Mujahideen. The Mujahideen preferred to attack DRA outposts for this reason.

Mujahideen dependence on these types of raids for weapons and ammunition cost them casualties. The Soviets and DRA reacted with artillery and air strikes when they could, but they did not continue them all night long. This gave the Mujahideen the option of immediately entering the camp to seize what material they could and then leaving to get far away before dawn or waiting for the artillery to sub-side and then leaving with less time until daylight. Both courses entailed risk.

VIGNETTE 9
RAID ON OUTPOSTS AT WRESHMIN GORGE
by Commander Wazir Gul

During October 1985, Mujahideen factions took turns blocking the Kabul-Jalalabad highway at Wreshmin Tangay (gorge) between Dabili and Dargo bridges (Map 2-8 - Wreshmin). My mission was to block the highway for eight days. At that time, I commanded 70 Mujahideen. We were armed with five BM-1s, two BM-12s, four 82mm recoilless rifles, two ZGU-1s, three 82mm mortars and many RPG-7s. In order to block the highway, I had to remove enemy security posts along that stretch of road. I moved my force from Manay in Hisarak to the Tsapar (Capar) mountain where I refined my battle plan. Since there are limited access routes into the area and since the area near the highway was heavily mined, I decided to launch the initial attack against the flanks of the area we were going to block, i.e. against the Dabili bridge in the west and the Dargo bridge in the east. These two places are relatively accessible from the mountains in the south. After destroying the road bridges at these two points, I planned to isolate the area and continue the attack down the highway against the security outposts. The highway approach was best since the highway itself was not mined.

I divided my detachment into two groups and moved them to Dabili and Dargo. I kept a reserve centrally located to the rear between the two attacking groups. The two groups approached the target at night. The next day, they captured the Dabili and Dargo bridges by swift attacks. They immediately destroyed the bridges with explosives. This isolated the area. Then, the two groups attacked down the road (to avoid the DRA minefields) from the opposite directions. They eventually overran 16-17 small Soviet/DRA security outposts located on the road. Then they turned around to consolidate their success and reinforced the defenses at the east and west flanks of the blockade.

During the next eight days, the Soviets and DRA tried to reopen the highway, but failed. Their air strikes and artillery were generally ineffective due to the narrowness of the canyon. The enemy sent a column from Jalalabad to force the road, but we stopped them in the narrow confines around Dargo bridge and they had to withdraw. We spent the

Commander Wazir Gul was affiliated with Jamiat-e Islami Afghanistan (JIA) of Burhanuddin Rabbani. His base was in Tezin southwest of Sarobi. He fought in the Sarobi, Lataband and Mahipar areas. [Map sheets 2985, 2986, vic grid 7617 to 8317].

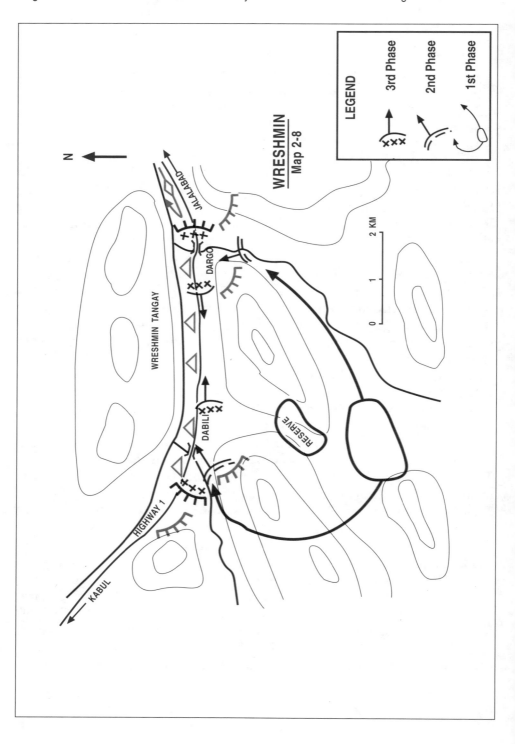

N

WRESHMIN TANGAY

JALALABAD

DARGO

DABILI

RESERVE

HIGHWAY 1

KABUL

WRESHMIN
Map 2-8

0   1   2 KM

LEGEND

3rd Phase

2nd Phase

1st Phase

eight days stripping all the ammunition, weapons and supplies out of the bases and outposts. We hauled the spoils of war into the mountains. We captured about 100 weapons and an enormous amount of ammunition. At the end of our eight days, I withdrew my detachment and we returned to our base. I lost six KIA and 18 WIA or about 30% of my force. Enemy losses were heavier and included some 50 killed or wounded and 24 soldiers captured.

COMMENTARY: The terrain played a major role in shaping the battle. The Soviets/DRA controlled the ribbon of highway running through a narrow gorge, while the Mujahideen controlled the surrounding mountains whenever they wanted to. The Mujahideen had the freedom to choose the time and place to raid dozens of security outposts sprinkled along the treacherous highway snaking through the very narrow canyon in Mahipar and the Wreshmin Tangay. In the Wreshmin Tangay, virtually all Mujahideen groups habitually first attacked the two main bridges i.e. Dabili and Dargo. Then, after destroying the bridges, they would attack the rest of the security posts from both ends. This method proved to be the most effective one given the terrain, minefields, enemy dispositions and Mujahideen capabilities.

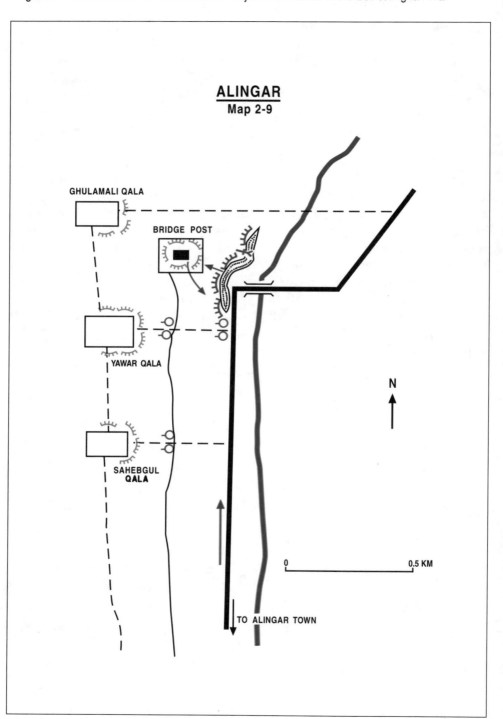

ALINGAR
Map 2-9

GHULAMALI QALA

BRIDGE POST

YAWAR QALA

SAHEBGUL
QALA

N

0   0.5 KM

TO ALINGAR TOWN

VIGNETTE 10
RAID ON THE BRIDGE POST IN ALINGAR
by Doctor Abdul Qudus Alkozai and Commander Haji Sidiqullah

In February 1986, Commander Abdul Qudus Alkozai led a group of 15 Mujahideen on a raid of a government post near the center of the Alingar District in Laghman Province. The post overlooked a bridge on the Alingar River near Barwai Village, some four kilometers north of Alingar. The bridge outpost was located within a walled enclosure and included covered firing positions and parapets. The post included a one-room guard house for the six soldiers who manned the post. The outpost was part of a security belt protecting the district center against Mujahideen attacks. There were several other outposts in the area established in individual houses and fort-like structures. Among them were Ghulamali Qala to the north and Yawar Qala and Sahebgul Qala to the south of the bridge post. They were about 150-200 meters apart (Map 2-9 Alingar).

My guerrilla raiding party left its base in a nearby village at 2200 hours on a dark, cold, rainy winter night. Moving north to the objective, I dropped a two-man observation/security party opposite the Sahebgul Qala outpost. I posted another two-man observation/ security party outside the Yawar Qala outpost and a final two-man observation/security party alongside the road to the bridge. They were to pin down any forces which attempted to come to the aid of the bridge outpost. My eight remaining Mujahideen and I were armed with eight automatic rifles and one RPG-7. We moved to the bridge and deployed in the cover of a roadside ditch. We completely blocked the western approach to the bridge.

My plan was to remain in the ditch until the soldiers at the outpost opened the door of the guard house to relieve the sentry. Then, using the light coming from the opened door to guide on, we would jump over the low (one-meter) outpost enclosure wall, storm the post and kill the occupants.

We waited for two miserable hours in the cold rain, but nothing happened inside the outpost. Finally, I decided to take the initiative.

Haji Sidiqullah was the Provincial Military Commander of the HIH party in Laghman. He joined Hekmatyar in the fight against Daoud--before the communist revolution. He had no formal military education. Dr. Abdul Qudus was a guerrilla commander under Sidiqullah. He doubled as the force medic, since he received medic's training in Pakistan. [Map sheet 3086, vic grid 2455].

I directed three men to move quietly to the post, jump over the wall and attack the sentry. Then, as soon as the other soldiers started to come out of the guard house, we would rush the guard house and demand their surrender.

I positioned the RPG-7 where it could hit the guard house and told the gunner not to fire if he heard his comrades telling the soldiers to surrender (surrender was the code word). I instructed him to open fire if the enemy initiated contact and opened fire on us.

At about 0100, my three-men party approached the outpost. One man covered the team while the other two jumped over the wall. One of these Mujahideen landed squarely on the back of the sleeping enemy sentry. The sentry was wrapped in a blanket and sound asleep, but when my Mujahideen landed on him, he woke up and began to shout. My panicked Mujahideen opened fire and killed the sentry. Anticipating the reaction of the guards, one Mujahideen tossed a hand grenade into the door of the guard room. As it exploded, they rushed into the structure. My RPG gunner heard the commotion, but did not hear his comrades demanding the enemy surrender. Since the code word was not used, my RPG gunner assumed that the enemy had overwhelmed his comrades and therefore opened fire on the guard house.

The RPG-7 rocket ripped through the wall of the guard house, killing two soldiers and seriously injuring one of my Mujahideen standing nearby. This changed the situation drastically. My wounded Mujahideen was calling for help and his comrades stopped to evacuate him. As soon as my other Mujahideen saw their comrades stop to attend to their fallen comrade, they also stopped their attack. I called off the raid and ordered a withdrawal. As we withdrew, my security teams rejoined us and we returned to our base.

COMMENTARY: The Mujahideen timing for the raid was ideal. Inclement weather and night movement covered their approach. The enemy guard was even asleep. This lack of enemy alertness was not unusual. The DRA and Soviets usually failed to deploy foot patrols at night between their outposts. There was also little tactical and fire coordination between outposts. This passivity at night resulted in a bunker mentality among the Soviet/DRA soldiers manning isolated security outposts and allowed the Mujahideen freedom of movement and the chance to own the night and conduct their hit and run raids.

Lack of control of the raiding party at the objective foiled an otherwise skillfully planned action. What went wrong was a combination of Murphy's law, a lack of precombat rehearsals and a lack of a regular chain of command. Landing on a sleeping soldier was bad luck, but dry rehearsals would have exercised the option of an approach being discovered and provided for the continuation of the attack while wounded are being evacuated. Since the force commander did not have communication with his RPG gunner, he needed the firm, positive control that a subordinate leader, located with the RPG gunner, could have provided. Lack of communication, subordinate leadership and fire coordination at the objective cost the Mujahideen a tactical victory.

CHAPTER COMMENTARY

The Mujahideen raid depended on surprise and quick execution. Raids produced needed weapons, ammunition and equipment. They also proved a good way to destroy DRA or Soviet security posts and sites. A well-organized raid had an assault force, a fire support group and a security element. Portable radios were needed to coordinate the raiding elements, but all too often the Mujahideen lacked these radios. The Mujahideen primary obstacle in a raid was to get past the mine fields which the Soviets and DRA emplaced around their security posts and sites. The Mujahideen launched most of their raids at night. They did so to prevent being hit by effective air or artillery strikes and to avoid further contact with DRA or Soviet forces which were reluctant to leave their garrisons at night.

CHAPTER 3
SHELLING ATTACKS

Mujahideen shelling attacks on garrisons, outposts, airfields and cities were a daily event. The Mujahideen usually used mortars, rockets and recoilless rifles in these attacks. Sometimes they used mountain guns and howitzers. The objective was to harrass their foes and destroy war material. Mujahideen gunners learned to construct multiple firing sites and to fire and then quickly displace before DRA or Soviet artillery or aviation could respond effectively. When possible, Mujahideen would keep water near their firing sites to dampen the ground behind the rocket or recoilless rifle. This would help curb the amount of tell tale dust raised by the backblast of the ordnance. The Soviets and DRA tried to curb these attacks with counterbattery fires, rapid reaction forces and ambushes. Due to their routine nature, the Mujahideen did not usually discuss these unless the interviewer probed. The Mujahideen considered these as usually rather dull events that did not bear retelling. The following attacks, however, were hardly dull events.

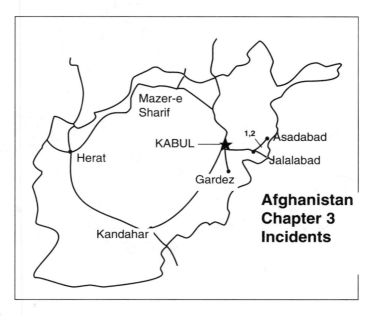

Afghanistan
Chapter 3
Incidents

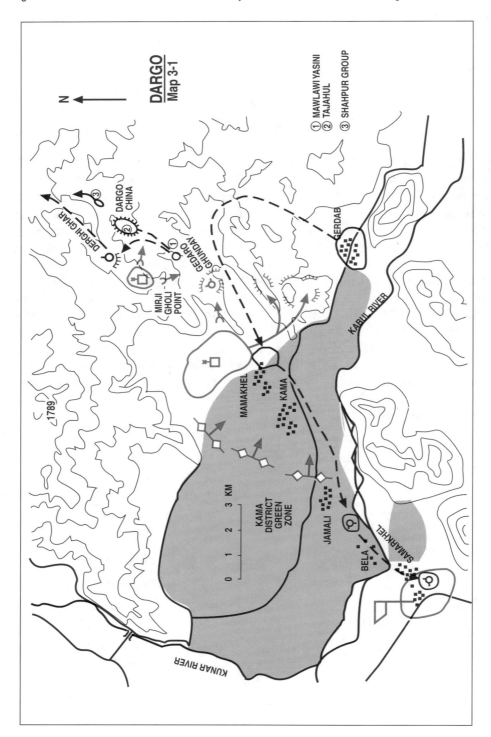

VIGNETTE 1
A SHELLING ATTACK TURNS BAD
by Mawlawi Shukur Yasini

In the spring of 1981, the Soviets and DRA were very active in our area. As a result, we dismantled our permanent bases and changed them to mobile bases scattered throughout the area. I intended to launch a major show of force against the Soviets using my mobile bases. I had two mortars—a 60mm and an 82mm. The problem with the 60mm mortar is that it only has a range of 1,400 meters, so the gunner has to get close to the target to use it. I also had two DShK machine guns, and five RPG-7s. I kept these heavy weapons at my base at Gerdab. My men had small arms which they kept with them.

On 17 April 1981, I launched a shelling attack against the Soviet 66th Separate Motorized Rifle Brigade in Samarkhel. I only took 42 men with me since we were not very well equipped and we were not ready for a major encounter with superior forces. Further, Kama District is right across the river from the 66th Brigade garrison and they kept the area under constant surveillance. I did not want to move a large group of men through the area and alert them. To avoid observation, we went north from Gerdab into the mountains and then west across the mountains and into Mamakhel Village in the Kama area (Map 3-1 - Dargo). We stayed for three nights in Mamakhel and spent the days in the mountains at Dargo China spring—some three kilometers away. From Mamakhel, we went to

---

Mawlawi Shukur Yasini is a prominent religious leader in Nangrahar Province. He is from the village of Gerdab in Kama District northeast of Jalalabad. During the war, he was a major commander of the Khalis group (HIK). Later, he joined NIFA. During the war, he took television journalist Dan Rather to his base in Afghanistan. He also accompanied Congressman Charles Wilson of Texas into Afghanistan several times. During most of the war he was active in his own area, fighting the DRA in Jalalabad and the Soviet 66th Separate Motorized Rifle Brigade at Samarkhel. He became a member of the Nangrahar governing council after collapse of the communist regime—a position he held until the Taliban advance in September 1996. [Map sheet 3185].

One day, three Soviet soldiers from the 66th Brigade crossed the Kabul River for a picnic. They were drinking vodka and cooking shashlik around a campfire when Mawlawi Shukur captured them. One of the Soviets, named Naomov, converted to Islam and fought with the Mujahideen for three years. Author Ali Jalali interviewed Naomov during his visit to Washington,D.C. sponsored by the Freedom House. Naomov spoke Pushtu well by that time. Naomov recommended that "the Mujahideen quit fighting one another and unite against the enemy." Naomov settled in Canada.

Kama Village where some people were still living—although many people had already emigrated to Pakistan.

At Kama, I put my nephew Shahpur in charge and told him to take my two mortars and 38 men and to go shell the 66th's camp.[1] I kept four men with me. The shelling group left Kama at dusk. They positioned the 82mm mortar on the north side of the river at the house of Khan-e Mulla at Jamali Village—since it had the range. Then they crossed the river at Bela and approached the camp through the village of Samarkhel. They occupied positions close to the entrance of the enemy camp. They had the guerrilla mortar (60mm) and the RPGs with them. They opened fire with the RPGs and the 60mm mortar from close range at 2200 hours. The 82mm mortar joined in long-range fires onto the sleeping camp. The shelling attack created chaos. The shelling group fired at intervals over a two-hour period and then broke contact and withdrew. I was in Kama throughout the attack. My men had orders to join me in the mountains at the Dargo China spring the next day. I went to the rendezvous point. I arrived at dawn and they were already there. Two of my men were missing, since they had forgotten the 60mm mortar and a video camera and had gone back to retrieve them.[2]

While I was in Kama, informers told me that the enemy would launch a search and destroy mission in Kama District in five days. I decided that they would now come sooner since we had shelled them. I decided that we had to leave the area. At sunrise, I instructed my men to go deeper into the mountains. I was tired and had a cold, so I decided to go back home to Gerdab. However, as I set out, I saw two helicopters lifting off from the airport and flying low over Kama District. I hit the ground and hid. I was alone except for Haji Shahbaz. Other helicopters followed the first two. At first I thought that the helicopters were enroute to Kunar Province, but then they started landing troops from two helicopters at Mirji Gholi point on Derghi Ghar mountain—about a kilometer away. They also landed

---

[1] The 66th and 70th Separate Motorized Rifle Brigades were forces created for counterinsurgency. They had three motorized rifle battalions, an air assault battalion, an artillery howitzer battalion, a MRL battalion, a reconnaissance battalion, a tank battalion and support troops. The 70th was located in Kandahar. The 2nd battalion of the 66th was located in Asadabad. Each of its motorized rifle companies had four motorized rifle platoons instead of the usual three.

[2] The video camera was an important accessory of this war. Mujahideen used video cameras to record their actions so that they could prove that they expended weapons, ammunition and supplies and achieved results. The video tapes justified the issue of more supplies to the faction.

troops north of Mamakhel on the plain and on Gedaro Ghunday hill. My men saw the helicopters landing and realized that they would be seen if they continued to climb into the mountains. So they turned around in the wide canyon and started back toward me. I was in a ditch between Mirji Gholi and Dargo China and was hidden by the early morning shadow from the mountain. As I raised my head, I could make out some 25 Soviet soldiers along with several people wearing tsadar moving to the southeast from the high ground of Mirji Gholi toward Gedaro Ghunday. I could also see Soviets setting up mortars on top of Gedaro Ghunday. I crawled about 50 meters in the ditch. The Soviets were facing the sun and I was in the shadow, so they couldn't see me. As I crawled, I got rid of heavy things that I had in my pockets—such as pliers and wads of money. I headed north toward the mountain ridge. At that point, Zafar and Noor, carrying the missing 60mm mortar and video camera, walked into the Soviet group setting up at Gedaro Ghunday. They were immediately captured. Noor was my cousin.

I climbed Derghi Ghar Mountain to try and see what was happening. I saw that my men had split. Thirteen were now back in Dargo China. These 13 men were commanded by Tajahul and the rest, commanded by Shahpur, were going back into the mountains. I saw that part of the Soviets were heading toward my 13 men. The Soviets began firing flares at the group of 13 to mark their position. Helicopter gunships then attacked my men with machine gun fire. Other Soviets headed down from Derghi Ghar toward them. After the air attack, the Soviets began attacking my 13-man group. I was midway between the attacking Soviets and my men—about 500 meters away. I looked in my binoculars and saw that another group of Soviets were down in the valley picking up the pliers, first aid packets and money I had discarded. The group examining my things looked different than the others and I thought that they were officers. I decided that when the helicopters made their next strafing run, I would use the noise of their gunfire to hide my fire. When the helicopters made their next gun run, I fired on the group in the valley and hit one. I then took cover, raised my head, fired and got another one. This drew the Soviets attention and they opened up on me. Artillery started to fall all around. I ran from this position to another position about 100 meters away. I had a "20-shooter" [Czechoslovak M26 light machine gun] and some of my men had "20-shooters." As I ran to change positions, I heard firing from "20-shooters" in my group. They were involved in a heavy fire fight.

I then heard noise from the north and I thought that the Soviets were coming from that direction as well. But then I saw Shapur and one of my other men. They were coming for me. Shapur reported that tanks were moving through Kama and had sealed the exits. The enemy were arresting people throughout Kama. We decided to leave to the north. Earlier, Shapur had sent a messenger to my group of 13 telling them to move north. However, they were pinned down by heavy artillery fire and direct fire. They could not break contact and fought to the last man. As we left the area, one of my Mujahideen fired an RPG at a helicopter. The helicopter caught fire and flew off and fell to the ground near Kama—where it exploded. I don't know whether the RPG hit the helicopter or whether other ground fire got it.

We moved to the village of Ghara Mamakhel, some four hours into the mountains, where I met two more of my men. By morning, 12 of my people arrived there. I learned the fate of my group of 13. The Soviets remained in Kama for two days. Then we returned to retrieve the bodies of my men. I found the bodies of my 13 men in a group, plus those of Zafar and Noor and five more of my men. The Soviets had booby-trapped some of the bodies and had sprinkled chemicals on other bodies which caused them to disintegrate. We couldn't evacuate these bodies. So we built graves over them. Their bodies are still there under stones. I do not know what the Soviet casualties were, but I do know that I shot two, we downed a helicopter and the Soviets lost three armored vehicles to our mines during this action.

Throughout the war, I faced the Soviets like this during seven sweeps. I moved the families of the martyrs to refugee camps in Peshawar, Pakistan, since we couldn't support them in the Kama area. I later learned that the Soviets were looking for me personally. They arrested someone who looked like me (the narrator has a prominent nose) while he was harvesting clover. At that time, my beard was shorter. They took him to Jalalabad and paraded him around—"We've caught the son of a b----" they said. Someone finally recognized him, and said that he wasn't me and so he was released. Around that same time, the DRA governor of Kama District was in the Merzakhel Village. The Soviets arrested him and put him into forced labor since they did-n't recognize him. They had him carrying water to their soldiers on the high ground. The Soviets were very careless of Afghan lives. They killed several villagers indiscriminately. They also killed one of my men who was unarmed. I am glad we drove the Soviets out, but the subsequent actions of the Mujahideen tarnish their record of victory. I have written many poems of protest against their current activities.

COMMENTARY: The Mujahideen were able to fire on the garrison over a two-hour period since they periodically shifted firing positions to avoid return fire. The Soviets did not push out any night patrols to find the firing positions but only replied with artillery fire. The artillery fire did no good. Apparently, the garrison commander had not surveyed potential and actual Mujahideen firing positions to counter them.

The Mujahideen rendezvous point was located in one of three escape routes into the mountains from Kama District. Further, it is adjacent to a likely blocking position which the Soviets used during their periodic block and sweep operations. The Mujahideen were caught downhill from the Soviet blocking force and could not escape. As usual, the Mujahideen were severely hampered by the lack of portable, short-range radios which would have allowed them to coordinate their actions.

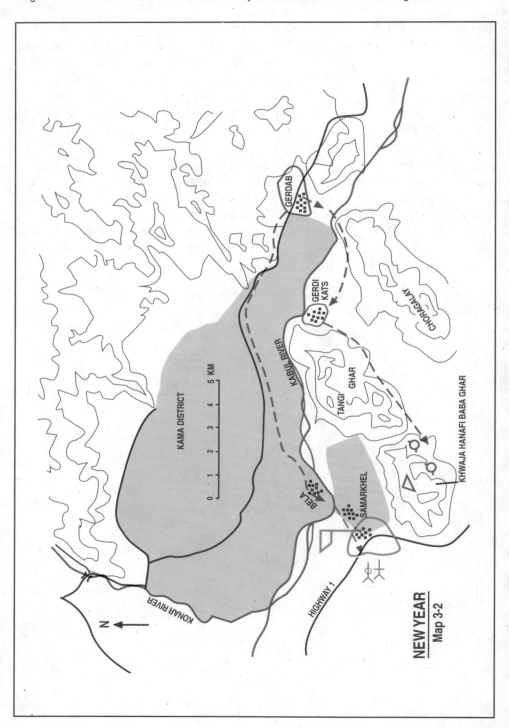

NEW YEAR

Map 3-2

VIGNETTE 2
A NEW YEARS PRESENT FOR THE SOVIETS
by Mawlawi Shukur Yasini

The Soviets invaded Afghanistan on 27 December 1979. I decided that we should give them a combination anniversary and New Years present on 29 December 1983. The present would be a shelling attack on the 66th Separate Motorized Rifle Brigade at Samarkhel. I assembled 150 Mujahideen with two 82mm mortars, two RPG-7s, one recoilless rifle, and five or six antitank mines. We had 250 mortar rounds for the attack. I placed my nephew Shapur in command. He formed four groups: a mortar group commanded by Awozubellah; a mortar group commanded by my son Abdul Basir; an observation post/fire adjustment group commanded by Shapur; and a light group. We started moving the ammunition and supplies on donkeys and mules two days before the attack. We had to move all of it across the Kabul River and stockpile it in the village of Gerdi Kats. From there we had to move it to Khwaja Hanafi Baba Ghar Mountain overlooking Samarkhel (Map 3-2 - New Year).

We moved all the ammunition and supplies to the mountain area undetected during the two days. We set up the mortars behind the mountain and set up the observation post on top. The light group had the recoilless rifle, RPGs and antitank mines. They crossed the river at Bela at night and went through Samarkhel to the west. Local Mujahideen met them, guided them to the objective and helped them plant the mines. They planted the mines in the road near the main gate of the compound near a mosque. Our plan was to start with a quick strike by the light group and then follow on with the mortar attack. The 66th Brigade was garrisoned in barracks and tents, so we hoped that our mortar fire would be effective against them. It was a rainy night with lots of lightning. The light group launched the attack at 2200 by firing the recoilless rifle and RPGs at the main gate of the enemy compound. The enemy reacted with tanks and APCs which came roaring out of the gate. Two of them were destroyed or damaged by the antitank mines. The light group withdrew. At the same time, the mortars went into action. They sent all 250 rounds of hot steel into the enemy compound as our New Year's present to the 66th Brigade. The 66th Brigade responded with BM-21s, artillery and mortars.

Mawlawi Shukur Yasini is the narrator of the previous vignette. [Map sheet 3185].

Round after round of enemy fire slammed into the mountains, while the Mujahideen mortars continued to fire from the valley between the mountains. With the Soviet fire, the Mujahideen mortars and the lightning, the night was practically turned into day. It was a spectacular fireworks display.

I had stayed at Gerdab and had a cow killed and cooked. I planned to welcome my returning heroes with a feast. They were supposed to return at dawn and so all the arrangements for the feast were ready as the eastern sky lightened. But, my men did not return at dawn. They were pinned down by the heavy Soviet return fire. At daybreak, Soviet helicopters and aircraft began flying over the area and firing everywhere. I despaired that anyone would survive. I promised Allah that I would donate a large sum of money to charity if even half of my men would return. At 0800, my body guard, Juma Khan, and I left Gerdab and climbed the mountain overlooking Gerdab. I was using my binoculars, I saw a shepherd running toward me. Everything was now calm. The aircraft had returned to the airfield and the artillery had quit firing. I climbed down to meet the shepherd. He brought me the good news that my Mujahideen had survived and had returned to Gerdab. None of my Mujahideen were even hurt! We had a very good feast.

Due to the heavy Soviet shelling, many other Mujahideen left their areas. Our contacts in the Soviet camp later reported that helicopters evacuated wounded and dead from Samarkhel to Jalalabad airport. The helicopters made 12 trips. Our contacts told me that there were at least 200 killed and wounded. This attack increased Soviet activity and Soviet helicopters were out flying every day looking for Mujahideen.

COMMENTARY: A lot of Mujahideen mortar firing was observed fire from the forward slopes of a mountain with the gunner making firing adjustments. The mortar crews in this attack would not have survived the Soviet return fire if they had tried firing from the forward slopes. Their reverse slope firing positions in the valley made it difficult for Soviet artillery to reach the firing positions. The use of forward observers to adjust fire is a mark of sophistication among Mujahideen forces. However, the Soviet mortar battery commanders should have surveyed these likely firing sites and had them plotted long before the Mujahideen attack. Apparently, they did not. This is a step that fire support commanders should take whenever their forces stop. This was a permanent garrison, so such planning should have been done years before. The figure of 200 dead and wounded seems high, but it was a well-planned and executed attack.

DRA and Soviet intelligence efforts in the Kama area seem inadequate. Commanders, like the narrator, operated from the same area throughout the war and moved freely through populated areas, yet the DRA seemed unable to react in time. The Soviets and DRA knew who the narrator was, what he looked like and where he was from, but they were never able to kill or capture him.

CHAPTER COMMENTARY

The Mujahideen fired from fixed, surveyed sites and from mobile firing bases. The mobile fire base deployed in two phases. During the day, the firing survey party would move into the area, determine weapons positions, map locations, headings, intended positions for the aiming stakes and firing data. At night, the firing party would arrive in a jeep, meet with the survey party, set up their weapons, conduct a quick firing raid and depart.

The Mujahideen also employed unmanned firing bases. Unmanned firing bases were used against targets which were devoid of cover and concealment. The Mujahideen would survey these points in daylight and set up rockets on makeshift or disposable launchers. They would connect these rockets to time-delay firing devices. The Mujahideen would be well away from the area when the Soviet or DRA forces would launch a search for them.

Shelling attacks had mixed results. When launched against military airfields and garrisons, they occasionally destroyed military targets of value. Further, they prevented the DRA or Soviet forces from sleeping and depressed morale. When launched against cities, they frequently killed innocent civilians. This cost the Mujahideen potential supporters. As some civilians expressed it, "the government oppress us during the day and the Mujahideen oppress us at night."

CHAPTER 4
ATTACKING A STRONG POINT

Attacking a strong point is often similar to conducting a raid and many of the same tactical considerations and techniques apply. Attackers quickly abandon their objective after a successful raid, while there is usually an intent to hold a captured strong point for some period of time. Therefore, an attack on a strong point generally involves more supplies and heavier armaments. Most often, the strong points were political centers which the Mujahideen wanted to hold for propaganda value.

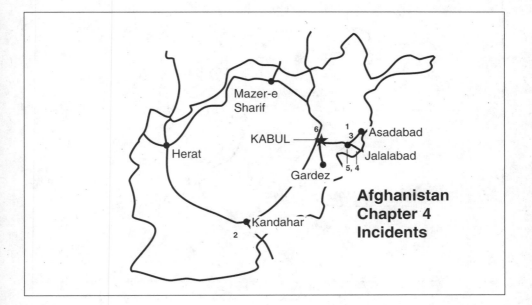

Afghanistan
Chapter 4
Incidents

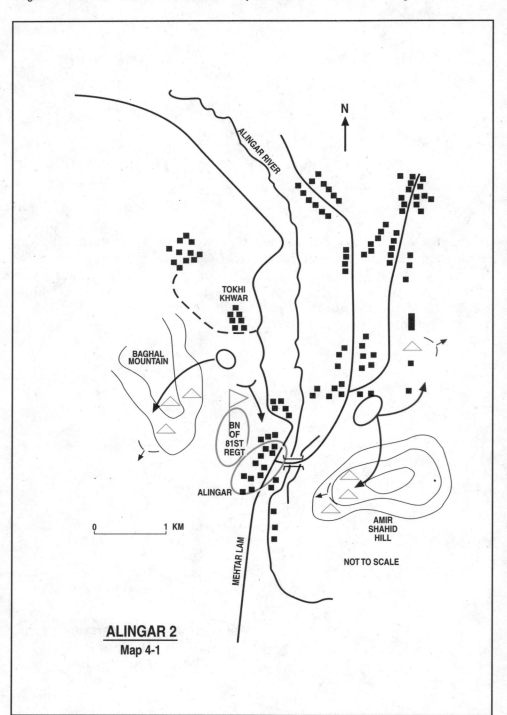

ALINGAR RIVER

N

TOKHI
KHWAR

BAGHAL
MOUNTAIN

BN
OF
81ST
REGT

ALINGAR

0   1 KM

MEHTAR LAM

AMIR
SHAHID
HILL

NOT TO SCALE

ALINGAR 2
Map 4-1

VIGNETTE 1
TAKING ALINGAR DISTRICT CAPITAL
by Nawaz Khan, Doctor Abdul Qudus Alkozai and Haji M. Siddiqullah

In July of 1980, the subdistrict capital of Nengrach was collocated with the Alingar District Capital in the town of Alingar. This is because the Mujahideen had driven the government out of the mountain redoubt of Nengrach. The district government of Nuristan was also there. This was a common practice. The DRA maintained many "governments in exile" for areas they did not control and held "nationwide" congresses using emigrants to represent those uncontrolled areas. The DRA never controlled more than 15% of the countryside. We decided to eliminate all these governments by seizing Alingar town. It proved to be a major victory.

The DRA 81st Regiment had a battalion in Alingar and there were some DRA militia forces as well.[1] (Map 4-1 - Alingar 2) We had two contacts in the DRA garrison. One was Captain Yar Mohammad who had a brother in our Mujahideen group. Captain Mohammad was from nearby Koh-e Safi and routinely provided us information about government plans. We talked to the Captain about capturing Alingar and he agreed to help us. We introduced the Captain to our other contact, Piroz. Piroz was a cook in the DRA garrison. We gave drugs to Piroz. The Captain and Piroz agreed that Piroz would drug the food before our attack and that the captain would signal us when that was done and we could launch our attack. We asked the cook how many Mujahideen we should bring. "Not too many to cause trouble, but not too few to fail" he replied. "Okay, about 70,000" we joked. "No, only about 10,000" he joked back. In any case, the Mujahideen sympathizers in the DRA camp would kill the communist officers. The signal to attack was the firing of a magazine full of tracer ammunition.

Nawaz Khan was a cadet in the Afghanistan Military Academy when he joined the resistance. He was a Mujahideen commander in Mehtar Lam, the Provincial Capital of Laghman Province. Haji Sidiqullah was the Provincial Military Commander of the HIH faction in Laghman. He joined HIH in the fight against Dauod before the communist revolution. Dr. Qudus was a commander under Sidiqullah who doubled as the force medic. [Map sheet 3086, vic grid 2455].

[1] According to Soviet sources, the DRA 71st Infantry Regiment was garrisoned in Mehtar Lam with some forces in the Alingar area. The 81st Mechanized Infantry Regiment was stationed further to the south in Nangrahar Province. General Alexandr Mayorov, Pravda ob Afganskoy voyne [Truth about the war in Afghanistan], Moscow: Prava Chiloveka, 1996, Map set.

There were about 300 total Mujahideen formed in four groups and about 30 subgroups. We called the group commanders together and told them to concentrate their men at night in Tokhi Khwar about one kilometer from the district headquarters. We told them that we had inside contacts but provided no details. We also assigned a group of Mullas with megaphones to begin broadcasting after the attack. They were to persuade the beseiged DRA to surrender. H-hour was midnight.

There were 150 Mujahideen in Nawaz Khan's group. They were armed with three DShK heavy machine guns, two 82mm recoilless rifles, some mortars and Kalashnikov rifles. Dr. Qudus group had one Soviet PPSH submachine gun, some bolt-action rifles and some other weapons. Several Mujahideen were unarmed. The other Mujahideen groups were similarly equipped. The signal to attack was given 10 minutes early. The tracers ripped into the air. Although the drugged food did not have its desired effect, Piroz and 10 other Mujahideen sympathizers had killed their communist officers. The DRA battalion surrendered to us as we stormed inside the battalion compound. The first one in was Doctor Nasar who just this year finished his education in Egypt.

It was the 1st of July 1980. The Mujahideen had deployed forces to the north, south and west of the district center. One group attacked the DRA security posts on Baghal mountain to the northwest. One group attacked along the main road which ran east of the river. One group attacked to seize and cross the bridge. One group attacked the DRA posts on the Amir Shahid hill to the southeast. The DRA military did not want to fight us, however, the local militia units were reluctant to surrender and fought on. The militia were still protecting the government enclaves of Alingar, Nuristan and Nengrach. The military then cooperated with us and turned their guns on the militia. A fierce battle ensued with the Mujahideen and military fighting the militia. During the fighting, the district governor of Alingar and eight or nine aides managed to escape to Mehtar Lam. Still, we captured Alingar and eliminated the DRA governments of Nengrach and Alingar. Thirteen officials from Nuristan made a break, but were cut down in our cross fire. The governor of Nuristan was killed by a Mujahideen whose brother had been killed by this same governor. At one point, Sidiqullah saw Saidagul, the Alingar Communist Party Secretary, being dragged off by a group he did not recognize. Since he had lent his rifle to a friend, Sidiqullah was unarmed and so he struck two stones together to imitate a bolt action rifle action and challenged them. Mawlawi Rahim identified himself and stated that they had captured a DRA soldier. Sidiqullah identified Saidagul and told them that they had a much more important catch. The fighting continued through the night, the Mujahideen moving to cut off the fleeing DRA officials and pursuing them in the dark. The fighting ended in time for morning prayers.

One of the groups involved in the fighting was a group of teenagers from 13 to 18 years old who we called the Khandakiano (bull terriers) group. During the fighting, one 14-year-old was fighting a desperate hand-to-hand combat with a DRA sports captain named Sharif. Fortunately, another Mujahideen killed Sharif during the fight.

We killed 285 DRA officials, police, soldiers, militia and civilians.[2] We captured 80 heavy weapons, two armored vehicles and 1,200 small arms. The heavy weapons included one 76mm mountain gun, one 76mm field gun, some ZGU-1 heavy machine guns, a 107mm mortar, several DShK heavy machine guns, and some 82mm mortars. Many government people also surrendered to us. It was a bonanza. In Nawaz Khan's group, they lost three KIA and seven WIA. In Sidiqullah's group they lost two KIA. We kept the district capital for some time until a joint Soviet/DRA force pushed us out and reestablished DRA government in Alingar.

COMMENTARY: Alingar is about 30 kilometers from the province capital of Mehtar Lam. At this point of the war, the Mujahideen were determined to control political centers so that they could claim to be a legitimate government in Afghanistan. The DRA was equally determined to prevent this.

---

[2] Sidiqullah states 120 DRA casualties.

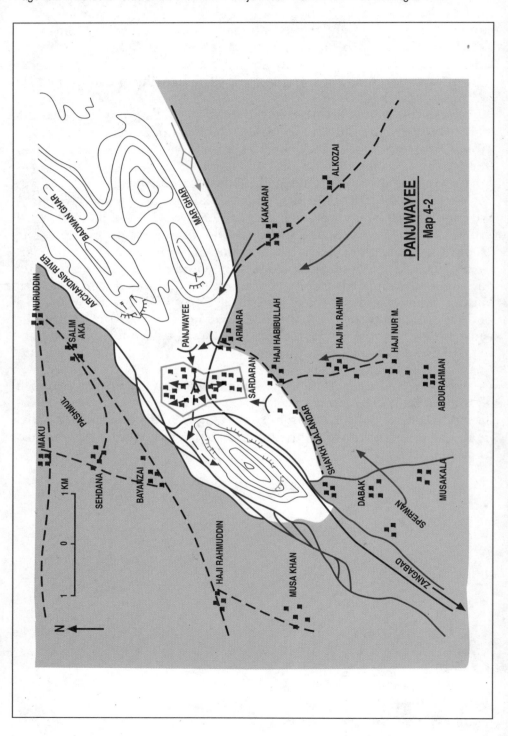

In September 1982, the DRA, backed by Soviet forces, had firm control of Panjwayee, the district capital of Panjwayee District (Map 4-2 - Panjwayee). Panjwayee is located some 25 kilometers southwest of Kandahar. The district was militarily significant to both sides since the town and its surrounding hills provided a favorable base for military action in the green zones which stretch all the way to the city of Kandahar. This area was also the hot bed of resistance in the region. Seizing control of Panjwayee was in the interest of all the local Mujahideen groups based in the area. Therefore, about 1,000 Mujahideen assembled near Panjwayee to take the town. The operation was directed by HIK commander Mulla Malang and others.

The town was defended by up to 300 militia who lived there with their families. The militiamen had turned their houses and all other buildings into fortified positions. They placed bunkers on the roof tops and occupied and fortified the high ground overlooking the town and the approaches to it. The Mujahideen began by surrounding the town and shelling it for two days. The shelling had little effect on the defenders, but the Mujahideen soon found themselves the object of enemy artillery fire and aerial bombardment. Most of the Mujahideen withdrew into the neighboring villages of Sperwan and Zangabad.

On the third day, Commander Mulla Malang decided to penetrate the town with a small group and to seize control of a number of the dominant positions that covered the approaches to the town. At noon, Mulla Malang led a group of 25 Mujahideen to the southern edge of the town. They carried picks and shovels. They quietly dug a hole through the adobe wall and broke into a house. Once inside, they began to advance from house to house by knocking holes into the walls. Their advance was totally unobserved by the militia who were occupying the rooftop positions overlooking the streets of the town. The Mujahideen finally knocked a hole through a wall that opened onto a courtyard. They burst into the courtyard with weapons at the ready. The militiamen were caught by surprise. They assumed that the town

---

Mulla Malang was one of the most famous commanders of the Kandahar area. He was an adherent of Mawlawi Mohammed Yunis Khalis-Islamic Party (Hezb-e-Islami Khalis). [Map sheet 2180, vic grid 4794].

was already captured by the Mujahideen, and fled from the town. Mulla Malang's group established a secure area and signaled the Mujahideen outside the town. Soon, hundreds of other Mujahideen poured into the town and cleared it from the southeast to the north- west, ending on the bank of the Arghandab River. They cleared the town building by building, again avoiding the streets by advancing by knocking holes in the walls. Other Mujahideen immediately climbed to the roof tops and manned the abandoned positions. Only the district headquarters remained under militia control. That night, the Mujahideen consolidated their gains and captured the district head- quarters the next day.

The militia had suffered heavy casualties and retreated to the over- watching high ground of a neighboring hill. The Mujahideen sur- rounded the militia positions. The government forces then opened negotiations with the Mujahideen—apparently to gain time. As they were talking, an armored Soviet/DRA column arrived from Kandahar. The Mujahideen withdrew inside Panjwayee.

The following night, the Soviet and DRA forces attacked Panjwayee and a heavy house-to-house battle ensued. The Mujahi- deen fired from the roof tops at the government forces advancing along the streets. Eventually, the Soviet/DRA combat power made the Mujahideen position untenable. The Mujahideen withdrew in small groups under the cover of darkness. The regime restored the district government in Panjwayee.

COMMENTARY: The Mujahideen gradually learned that overrunning and seizing control of government administrative centers is easy, but retaining them usually resulted in rapid Soviet or DRA retaliation. The Soviets/DRA felt that they had to retain control of local govern- ment agencies and would go to great lengths and take high risks to defend local administrative centers, even when they were tightly besieged by the resistance. Control of a district center symbolized control of the district, though this was seldom the case. In some remote districts, government control was restricted to a few buildings in the center of the district town. The government spared no effort to maintain their presence in these remote district centers despite their insignificant military usefulness and the high costs, in men and mate- rial, of holding them. This policy was promoted by the political impor- tance of maintaining control, albeit nominal, over all provinces, districts and subdistricts in a country which was in revolt against the foreign-installed government.

The battle of Panjwayee is an example of how easily the resistance could seize control of an isolated district center and how vulnerable the resistance became once it was forced to defend the town in the face of overwhelming Soviet/DRA forces. For this reason, it was only toward the end of the Soviet occupation that the Mujahideen again moved to seize control of major district and provincial centers. The source of the resistance power was not the cities and towns but the rural areas and the hundreds of the cross-border supply and infiltration routes which they controlled throughout the war.

Tactically, a 25-man detachment accomplished what a 1,000 man force could not. They did this through surprise and the indirect approach. However, the lack of an overall operational command left the Mujahideen vulnerable. After seizing Panjwayee, the Mujahideen became overconfident and failed to prepare for the enemy counter attack. They confidently parleyed with the militia while the Soviet/DRA force formed and moved. The Mujahideen failed to consolidate their victory and to establish defensive positions on the hills to the east and west of Panjwayee and on the Arghandab River to the north. They failed to post reconnaissance and ambush forces on the likely enemy avenues of approach. Instead of having to fight their way through a series of ambushes and then bumping into outlying Mujahideen fortified positions, the Soviet/DRA relief force moved unopposed to the battlefield and surprised the victorious Mujahideen at Panjwayee.

Tactically, the Mujahideen realized that movement along streets is suicidal in urban combat. However, the spontaneous nature of the unpaid, volunteer Mujahideen made control very difficult. Mujahideen forces joined the battle and left as they wished. Often, they did not bother to let the coordinating commander know.

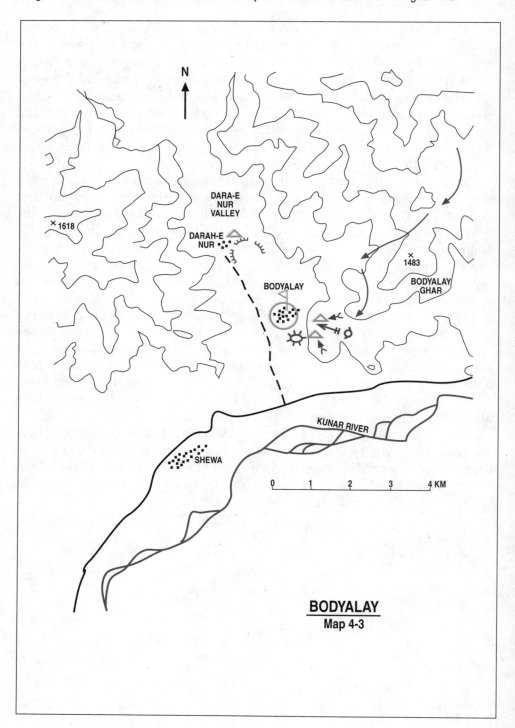

BODYALAY

Map 4-3

ATTACK ON THE BODYALAY GARRISON
by Doctor Mohammad Sadeq

A DRA border guard battalion[3] at Bodyalay near Shewa District had security posts on the high ground commanding the Dara-i-Nur Valley which stretches northward from Bodyalay. We decided to attack the security posts in March 1983 (Map 4-3 Bodyalay). We had 65 Mujahideen armed with one DShK heavy machine gun, one 82mm mortar, four RPG-7s, 22 Kalashnikovs and other small arms. At that time, we did not have a permanent base but moved from village to village in the Dara-i Nur Valley. We came down from the mountains in the north through the side valley that opens onto Ziraybaba about eight kilometers to the east. From that valley, we moved on mountain paths to reach the eastern flank of the main valley at Bodyalay Mountain We positioned the DShK and mortar near the peak of Bodyalay Mountain. I divided our force into four groups. One group deployed against the south side of the battalion garrison to pin them in position and cut off any aid from the south. The second group deployed against the government base at the village of Darah-e Nur to pin them down. The third group deployed against the two battalion outposts on Bodyalay Mountain. The fourth group was the support group which manned the DShK and mortar on the top of Bodyalay Mountain.

We started our attack after midnight. One mortar shell scored a direct hit on a government OP and killed one and wounded five of the enemy defenders. We were fighting for 2 hours and 30 minutes but were unable to overrun either of the outposts. As the day dawned, we had to withdraw since we were surrounded by enemy forces and were about to lose the advantage of night. We withdrew over the same mountain paths. I had two wounded Mujahideen from the attack.

COMMENTARY: The Mujahideen force harassed the DRA battalion, but lacked sufficient combat power to overrun any of its outposts since much of its force was deployed to prevent the DRA forces from moving to reinforce the besieged outposts. Even if the attack succeeded, the attackers would have only had time to grab weapons and other spoils and leave. The Mujahideen force escaped over the same route that

---

Doctor Mohammad Sadeq was a commander with the HIH in Kunar Province. [Map sheet 3186, vic grid 4830].

[3] Probably the 902nd Border Guards Battalion.

they arrived on. If the DRA informer net was effective, the Mujahideen were risking ambush on their return. The Mujahideen had no radios or other rapid communications and so control of the battle was problematic at best.

VIGNETTE 4
ATTACK ON SORUBAY
by Toryalai Hemat

There were a lot of DRA sympathizers in the Nazian Valley. We called this area "Little Moscow", as did the many Arabs in the area who had joined us in *jihad*.[4] The district headquarters of the Nazian Valley is Sorubay. All the residents of Sorubay were communist sympathizers. We decided to seize the district center in July 1985 (Map 4-4 - Sorubay). It was a combined action by the forces of Hikmatyar, Sayyaf, Mohammadi and Khalis (HIH, IUA, IRMA and HIK). There were about 1,000 Mujahideen in various bases in the Maro Mountain stronghold area.

Sorubay District center is 12 kilometers north of the Melava base and Maro Mountains—about a six-hour hike through the mountains. I had 80 men in my command and we were well armed. I had three BM12s, some medium mortars and many heavy machine guns in my group. This was a major attempt by us to seize the Nazian District government and in many respects was closer to conventional war than guerrilla war. For two weeks, Mujahideen supply trains resupplied Melava base, replenished our ammunition and our MRL rockets. We prepared for the attack for an additional week and then moved from Maro Mountain down into the Nazian Valley. Early in the morning, we deployed our first groups against the DRA OPs which sat on the small mountains overlooking Sorubay. There were about 12 security OPs on the mountains surrounding Sorubay, so the attack on the center started with the attack on the security posts. After conducting heavy fire on these posts, we attacked and seized them. We captured Sar Ghar and Tor Ghar security posts by 1000 hours. Then we started shelling the district center and descended on Sorubay. Government officials, DRA soldiers and their families started fleeing. They left in such a hurry that when we entered Sorubay, we discovered that the occupants had left their dinners still cooking and bread dough was waiting to be baked. We captured many impor-

---

Toryalai Hemat was a regiment commander of a mobile force allied with the IUA—Islamic Unity of Afghanistan of Sayyaf. He fought in many provinces in Afghanistan. [Map sheet 3185, vic grid 8299].

[4] *Moscow soghra* is the Arabic. Many Arabs came to Afghanistan for the jihad. The overall Afghan impression of the Arab Mujahideen, gathered from our interviews, is that they were prima donnas who were more interested in taking videos than fighting.

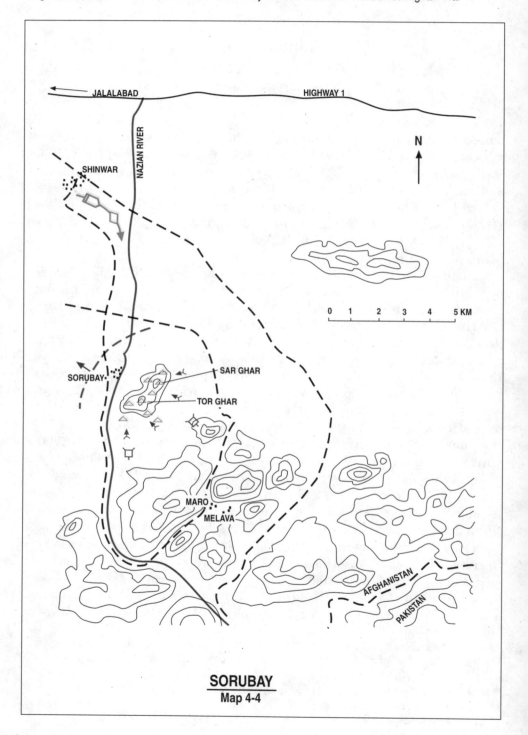

SORUBAY
Map 4-4

tant government documents which we sent to Peshawar. We sent our DRA captives to Landay. I lost seven KIA during the attack. We stayed in Sorubay overnight.

The enemy responded by sending forces from Jalalabad. Heavy enemy artillery fire began to fall on the OPs located on the high ground. Aircraft hit us as enemy armored vehicles neared the district center. We could not hold the district center against the air and artillery and so we vacated the place. During this fighting, we lost many people. I lost another seven KIA in my group. We left one of our dead, Ahmad Said, behind. He used to wear camouflage fatigues. The next day the DRA radio stated that they had identified Chinese mercenaries among our dead. Perhaps this was Ahmad. Two days later, we attacked Sorubay again and I lost yet another seven KIA. I had lost 21 of 80 men in this action. I don't know what the enemy casualties were, but I personally saw 15 bodies when we captured Sorubay. We returned to our bases.

COMMENTARY: There was a political advantage to holding district capitals, as it conferred a degree of legitimacy on the Mujahideen. However, these capitals were usually located on accessible ground and were not sited for defense against modern artillery and air power. In this instance, the Mujahideen moved from guerrilla warfare to a set-piece battle to capture Sorubay and were victorious. However, their attempt to hold the prize resulted in heavy losses and no political advantage.

The outposts overlooking Sorubay appear to have been sited rather haphazardly with little planning for mutual support. The DRA evidently fragmented their force to little advantage.

VIGNETTE 5
STORMING GULA'I
by Haji Malangyar

The Nangrahar agricultural/irrigation project was located in Shinwar District, Nangrahar Province southeast of Jalalabad. The massive irrigation project was built with Soviet help and guarded by several DRA military garrisons. (No Map) A battalion and some militia units protected the irrigation system. The battalion was garrisoned at the main water pump some 1.5 kilometers north of Gula'i. Gula'i is three kilometers northwest of Ghanikhel. A canal runs parallel to the main road north of Ghanikhel and a militia unit guarded a bridge on this road. Another battalion protected a bridge further to the northwest.

Our base at Marochina, was seven kilometers west of Gula'i. There were no people left in Gula'i since everyone had migrated. I had 59 Mujahideen armed with an 82mm mortar and 12 RPG-7s. The 8th of July 1985 was the last day of fasting in Ramadan. The next day would be the Feast of Ramadan (*Eid-al-Fitr*). We felt that many DRA soldiers would celebrate the festival at home making this a good time to attack. As was our custom, we prayed to God and put the Koran inside the cloth *tsadar*. We held the tsadar high and had every Mujahideen pass under it to ask God's blessing on us. We walked to Gula'i and spent the night of July 8th in an abandoned house. I selected four groups of eight-to-ten men each to divert and contain the outposts at the Narai Pul bridge, the Aozhda Ghundai hill, Smats hill, and the Spin Khwar syphon. I had radio communication with all groups. I commanded the 19 men in the main attack. Each containment group had two RPGs and the main attack group had four RPGs. I positioned our mortar near the Congregation Mosque (Eidgah). I started the attack at 1600 hours and three hours later we overran the government post in Gula'i. The containment groups prevented any assistance to the post. After dark, we all gathered at the designated assembly area. We had two WIA. The enemy lost three KIA and two POWs. We also captured 11 Kalashnikovs, 100 boxes of badly needed ammunition and some hand grenades.

Haji Malangyar fought in the heavily contested Shinwar District. There is no map with this vignette.   [Map sheet 3185, vic grid 7910].

COMMENTARY: Radios greatly helped coordinate Mujahideen actions. Evidently, attacking during the Feast of Ramadan also helped. Because the DRA had to protect military, political and economic installations this spread the DRA force thin and inhibited offensive actions. The agricultural project was vital to the economic well-being of the area and, although the Mujahideen attacked the military posts, they did not attack the canals.

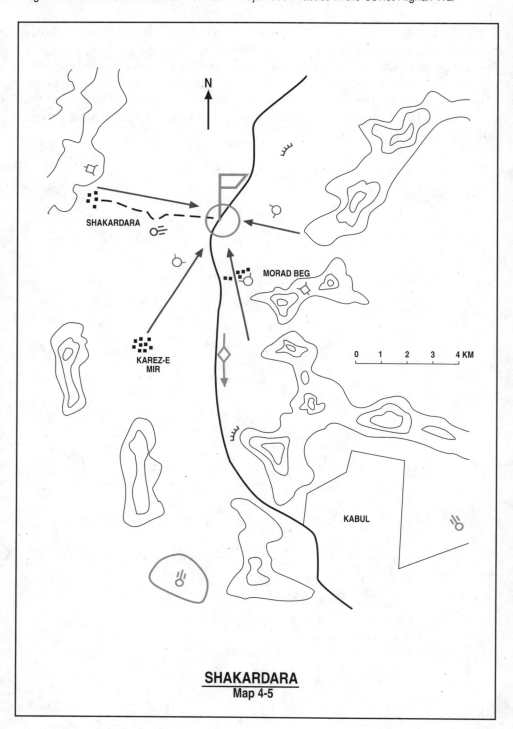

SHAKARDARA
Map 4-5

DESTRUCTION OF THE BAGH-E MUMTAZ BRIGADE
by Doctor Mohammad Wakil

In 1988, the DRA deployed a security brigade north of Kabul to secure the route for the withdrawal of the Soviet 40th Army. It was stationed on the Kabul-Charikar highway near the road junction with the road leading to Shakardara—the district headquarters of Shakardara District. The brigade was stationed in the Mumtaz orchard, so it was called the *Bagh-e Mumtaz* Brigade[5] (Map 4-5 - Shakardara). My brother, the late Commander Wasil, was the overall commander of the many factions involved in this battle. He worked out the plan during several commanders councils at thevarious faction bases. At 0800 hours on 21 June 1988, we would begin our attack on the brigade. The first phase would be the isolation and artillery preparation phase. Mujahideen would block the road from the north and south to isolate the garrison and begin a seven-day artillery preparation with a BM-12, Saqar MRL, 122mm howitzer, 82mm mortars and 82mm recoilless rifles. The artillery preparation would be fired from four directions. The second phase would be the ground offensive. One hundred Mujahideen would attack on each of four axes. The attack from the south would be led by my brother, Commander Wasil, on the southern axis Sehab-e Quli Village—Morad Beg town. Commander Taj Mohammad would lead the attack on the southwest axis from Karez-e Mir Village. Commander Naser would lead the attack on the western axis while Commander Anwar would lead the attack on the eastern axis. Mujahideen armaments included one Saqar, one BM12, one 122mm howitzer, six 82mm mortars, eight 82mm recoilless rifles and approximately 40 RPG-7s. We also had some ZSU-23-2 antiaircraft guns and some Stinger antiaircraft missiles.

The attack started on time, but the garrison did not last for the seven days. The brigade's morale broke and we overran it by 1400 hours on the first day. The brigade's tanks broke out. The brigade commander and some of his deputies were on board the tanks. We tried to stop them with RPG fire, but they escaped to Kabul. I do not know the total Mujahideen casualties, but I do know of four KIA, including my brother. I also know

---

Doctor Mohammad Wakil is from Shakardara District north of Kabul. He graduated from high school before the war. He joined the resistance and received medical training in Pakistan. [Map sheet 2886., vic grid 0737].

[5] Bagh-e means orchard. This was probably the 520th Brigade.

10 of the Mujahideen WIA. We killed around 100 in the brigade and captured some 400-450 DRA soldiers. We also captured some 40 armored vehicles, although not all of them were functioning. We captured 10 trucks and some 600 small arms. The Kabul government was slow in reacting to our attack, since they did not expect that the brigade's resistance would collapse so quickly. After 1400 hours, the artillery of the DRA 8th Infantry Division began firing on the captured garrison from positions in Qargha and the Kabul airport. However, they did not employ any aircraft against us due to the presence of the ZSU-23-2s and Stingers. We did not intend to hold the garrison area and had no desire to remain under artillery fire, so we grabbed what we could and left. The government never reestablished a unit at that garrison site.

COMMENTARY: Planning a seven-day siege within 15 kilometers of the heavily garrisoned capital of Kabul is a high-risk option, but the garrison evidently capitulated as soon as its commander abandoned it and fled in a tank. The Mujahideen southern roadblock was evidently not too effective since the brigade's tanks managed to blast right through it. At this point in the war, the DRA's morale (which was never high) was at a record low. The Soviets had begun their withdrawal on May 15th over this same road and were conducting few offensive actions. The DRA felt like the hapless brigade watching their commander flee. The Soviets were clearly preparing to abandon the DRA.

The Mujahideen, on the other hand, were practically giddy with anticipation of the complete Soviet withdrawal. The Mujahideen had not expected to win the war and now could sense victory. Their actions became more daring. However, after the Soviet withdrawal, the Mujahideen began quarreling among themselves even more than usual and the DRA resolve strengthened. The war went on.

Coordinating an attack by different factions with uncertain communications from four directions is also a high-risk option which chances fratricide. However, audacity prevailed and the Mujahideen quickly destroyed a larger force.

The introduction of the U.S.-manufactured, shoulder-fired Stinger air defense missile caused a change in Soviet aerial tactics. The Soviets would not employ close air support forward of their own forces if Stingers were present. Further, a Mujahideen rocket attack on the Kabul airfield about this same time reportedly destroyed five SU-25 close air support aircraft and damaged three others. Mujahideen air defenses and aircraft availability probably limited the Soviet/DRA response to artillery fire.

CHAPTER COMMENTARY

When the guerrilla force decides to seize and hold a strong point, implied missions are the conduct of regular logistic resupply, the continual manning of the strong point and the ability to withstand artillery and air strikes. None of these are easy for a guerrilla force dependent on part-time guerrillas. Further, it requires the commitment of crew-served weapons and sufficient ammunition—commodities that are hard to remove during a forced withdrawal. The guerrilla is trading his mobility and anonymity for a fixed-piece conventional battle. Quite frequently, the guerrilla is unable to make the transition.

CHAPTER 5
MINE WARFARE

Mine warfare is a favorite technique with the guerrilla. It is a relatively inexpensive way to attack personnel and vehicles. Most Mujahideen mines were anti-tank and anti-vehicular. When the Mujahideen employed anti-personnel mines, they prefered the directional mine (similar to the U.S. claymore mine). Soviet mines were mostly anti-personnel. During the war, the Mujahideen were supplied with many types of foreign anti-tank mines. Often, the Mujahideen would stack three anti-tank mines on top of each other to guarantee a catastrophic kill. Many Afghans are inveterate tinkerers and they preferred to make their own antitank mines from unexploded ordnance and other antitank mines.

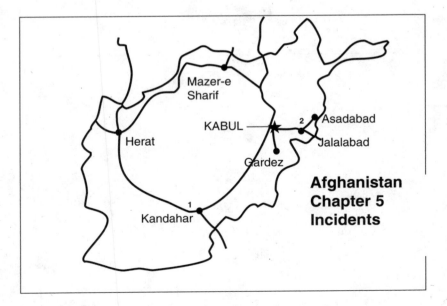

Mazer-e Sharif

KABUL

Herat

Asadabad

Jalalabad

Gardez

Kandahar

**Afghanistan
Chapter 5
Incidents**

DIAGRAM 1 MINE AND BATTERY

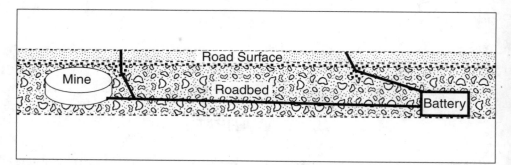

DIAGRAM 2 WATER DETONATOR

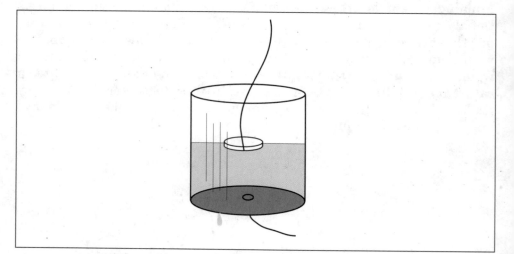

VIGNETTE 1
MUJAHIDEEN DEMOLITION METHODS
by Commander Mulla Malang

The Mujahideen would move heavy unexploded bombs (250-500 kilograms) at night by tractors to the road and bury them under bridges, underpasses and viaducts. The bombs were remotely controlled, usually by home-made detonators, fired some 500 meters from the road. Several such bombs would be detonated under a passing enemy convoy to heavily damage the vehicles. Tanks and other armored escort vehicles were the primary target for remote-controlled bombs.

If remote-control detonation was unfeasible, the Mujahideen used another method to selectively attack the tracked armored vehicles. The Mujahideen would stretch two metal wires across the paved road. The wires were spaced close together and hooked to an electric battery. The rubber tires of civilian and military vehicles would pass over the wires, but the metal tracks of tanks and BMPs would close the electrical circuit and set off the explosion. (See diagram)

Abdul Wali, a Mujahideen from Kandahar, was known for his creative bomb-making. Once in 1986, he sent a floating bomb down the Nosh-e Jan creek (which runs in the western suburbs of Kandahar city from northeast to southwest) to destroy a government outpost at a hotel[1]. Abdul Wali strapped a 250 kilogram bomb onto some truck tire inner tubes. He measured the distance from the outpost to his release point upstream where he would launch his floating bomb. The bomb was hooked to a wire whose length was the length from launch point to outpost. Once the floating bomb stretched out the full length of the wire, it was exactly under the outpost. Abdul Wali remotely-detonated the bomb and destroyed the outpost.

In well-defended enemy areas, the presence of minefields and other obstacles did not allow Mujahideen to raid enemy bases. In this case, delay-fired rockets hit the enemy positions. Kandahar air base, which became a major Soviet military base, was one of these difficult targets. The Mujahideen used delay-firing mechanisms so that they could leave the area before the rocket fired and the Soviet counter-fires began. Initially, only field-expedient delay-firing mechanisms were available.

Mulla Malang was one of the most famous commanders of the Kandahar area. He was an adherent of Maulavi Mohammed Yunis Khalis-Islamic Party (Hezb-e-Islami Khalis).

[1] Gul Sardar Hotel near Sarpuza.

Later in the war, the Mujahideen acquired factory-produced remote control devices to fire their rockets, but they still continued to use field expedient methods to do the job.

One local method was to use a leaking water container. The Mujahidden would punch a hole in the bottom of an empty three-gallon tin can and fill it with water. The trigger wire would be attached to a wooden float. The trigger wire would be inserted into the can. The other end of the wire would be connected to a battery. The battery would not be strong enough to complete the circuit through the water. The tin can would be attached by wire to the rocket. As the water leaked from the can, the floating wire would move lower until it reached the bottom of the can. The contact would complete the electric circuit and set the rocket off (see diagram).

MINING ATTACKS NEAR MEHTAR LAM
by Commander Sher Padshah and Sheragha

After the battle for Alishang District Center, Commander Padshah gathered 30 Mujahideen and moved further south to the village of Mendrawur. Mendrawur is about 11 kilometers south of the provincial capital of Mehtar Lam and about five kilometers north of the Kabul-Jalalabad highway. We received information that an armored column would be moving from Jalalabad to Mehtar Lam toward the end of August 1981 (Map 5-1 - Mehtar). We decided to attack the column with bombs and an ambush. We liked powerful mines, so we usually took the explosives from two Egyptian plastic mines and put these into a single large cooking oil tin container. We also used the explosives from unexploded Soviet ordnance to make our own bombs. We put one bomb under a small bridge and hooked a remote-control device onto it. We strung the detonating wire about 100 meters further south where we established our ambush in an orchard on the east side of the highway. We had two RPG-7s, one PK machine gun and one Bernau light machine gun. There were three Mujahideen in the bomb-firing party.

We saw the Soviet column approach slowly. Dismounted Soviet engineers were walking in front of the column with their mine detectors. They were carefully checking the route. When they came to the small bridge, they discovered the bomb. Several Soviets gathered around the bomb, but instead of disconnecting the wires, they stood around talking about the bomb. The three-man firing party, Sheragha, Matin and another Sheragha, were watching them through binoculars. We saw several Soviets checking the bomb and knew that the ambush was spoiled, so we detonated the bomb killing several Soviets. The Soviet column began firing in every direction. We left the orchard and withdrew through the Bazaar of Mendrawur going north. Some of the villagers were wounded by the Soviet fire.

Three or four days later, we had 40 Mujahideen in our group and were ready to try another ambush. We went to the village of Mashakhel. We buried two of our bombs in the road. We did not have any more remote-control firing devices, so we rigged these bombs with pressure fuses. We put cow manure on the mines to hide them. God bless Matin's soul, he used to always put the manure on the mines. We

---

Commander Sher Padshah and Sheragha are from Laghman Province. [Map sheet 3086].

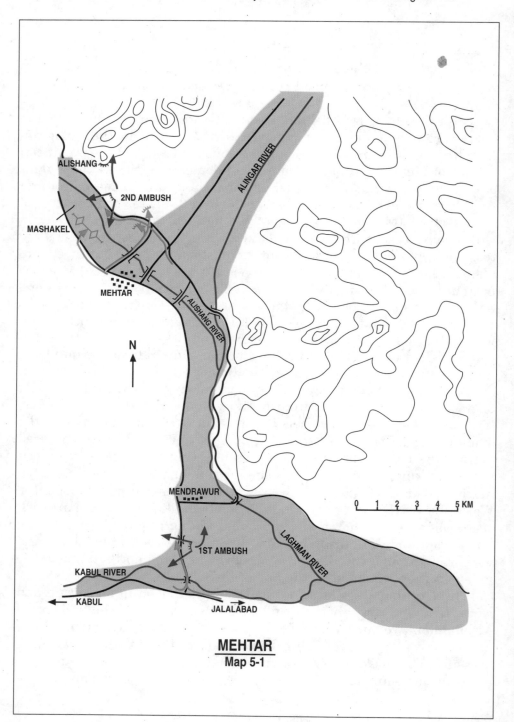

MEHTAR
Map 5-1

set up our ambush covering the mines.

We saw the column approach slowly. Soldiers with mine detecting dogs were walking in front of the column. The dogs were running loose and they promptly found and pointed out our bombs. Sheragha and Shawali moved forward when they saw the dogs. They watched as the dogs stood by the mine. Two soldiers got out of an APC with a long probe. The soldiers started probing the manure piles and they found the mine in the third pile. Four Soviets, including an officer, crowded together looking at the mine. So, Sheragha and Shawali opened fire killing the four Soviets. The remaining Soviets pulled back out of the ambush kill zone.

The Soviets began to return fire. Commander Padshah ordered four Mujahideen to move north onto Tarakhel hill to provide covering fire for the group's withdrawal. To confuse the enemy, he grabbed his megaphone and yelled "Keep your positions. The reinforcements just arrived." A DRA column came from Mehtar Lam and took up defensive positions and started firing at us. Tanks also maneuvered against us on the Mehtar Lam plain west of the road. We withdrew under the cover of night. We know we killed four Soviets and may have killed or wounded up to 18 DRA and Soviets. We destroyed one of their tanks and two trucks.

CHAPTER COMMENTARY

The Mujahideen preference for home-made mines in metal cans made it easier for Soviet mine detectors to find them. The tendency for curious troops to cluster around a newly-discovered mine is not uniquely Soviet, and the Soviets eventually trained their engineers to quit clustering around mines.

The Mujahideen usually combined demolitions and mining with other forms of offensive and defensive action. They usually covered their mines with direct fire weapons. The Mujahideen seldom left their mines unattended if they were located a distance from the border and a ready supply of mines. After an ambush or fight, they would often dig up their unexpended mines and take them with them to the next mission.

CHAPTER 6
BLOCKING ENEMY LINES OF COMMUNICATIONS

The war was a contest by both sides to control the other's logistics. The Soviets used aerial bombing, scatterable mines, crop burnings and assaults on rural villages to drive the rural population into exile or into the cities. Their objective was to deprive the guerrilla of his source of food, shelter and rest.

The Soviet lines of communication (LOC) was a double-lane highway network which wound through the Hindu Kush Mountains—some of the most inhospitable terrain on earth. Mujahideen constantly cut the road and ambushed convoys carrying material from the Soviet Union. The Soviet presence depended on its ability to keep the roads open. Much of the Soviet combat in Afghanistan was a fight for control of the road network. Soviet security of the Eastern LOC required 26 battalions manning 199 outposts, patrolling the LOCs or escorting convoys. The more-open Western LOC required three battalions. More than three-fourths of

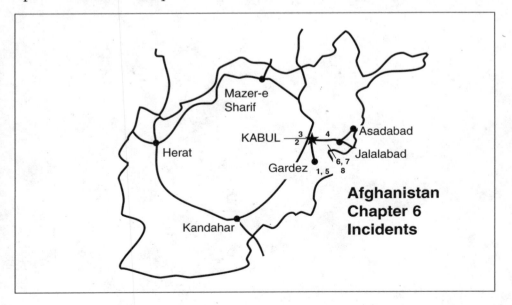

Afghanistan
Chapter 6
Incidents

Soviet combat forces were routinely involved in security missions. DRA forces were also tied down in LOC and area security.

The resistance destroyed over 11,000 Soviet trucks. DRA truck losses were reportedly higher. The Mujahideen ability to interdict the LOC was a constant concern to the Soviets and prevented them from maintaining a larger occupation force in Afghanistan.

VIGNETTE 1
CARVING UP REGIMENTS ON THE APPROACH TO WAZI
by Haji Badshah Khan

In April 1980, I set out to capture the Wazi District Headquarters which sits astride the main road between Gardez and Khowst. I had some 400 Mujahideen who came from the Dari Khel Valley. The Saroti pass is at the northern end of the Dari Khel Valley and offers access from Gardez to Khowst. The Satakandow pass on the main Gardez-Khowst highway was already controlled by the Mujahideen, so the Dari Khel approach was the only possible route for the DRA. In those days, we did not have base camps, but lived in our villages and used whatever weapons were at hand. We had rifles plus some locally manufactured machine guns from Pakistan. I made my plan of attack. During the night, we moved to Wazi which is close to the Dari Khel Valley (Map 6-1 - Wazi). I divided my men in groups and we surrounded the district headquarters on all four sides. I ordered my subordinate group commanders to wait for my signal to attack. In the morning, I intercepted radio communications between the Wazi garrison and their headquarters. The commander was asking for help and stated that he was surrounded by Mujahideen. Shortly after that, two helicopters came, circled the area and returned. The commander of the garrison was Mohammad Hashem. He was from the Jaji tribe and we knew each other. He sent a mediator to me who announced that the garrison was ready to surrender. I told him to disarm his men first and then we would negotiate. He did and then he surrendered the garrison. We captured a lot of weapons. The spoils of this action encouraged other Mujahideen to besiege other posts for their weapons.

The DRA reacted to the fall of Wazi by sending two columns to reestablish government control. The government forces moved on two axes, one from Khowst and the other from Gardez. The column from Khowst reached Said Khel and formed an assembly area there. The column from Gardez approached the Saroti pass. I began to mobilize people against the government forces. I sent harbakai (tribal police or regulators who kept law and order in their areas)

Haji Badshah Khan is from the warrior subtribe of Dari Khel of the Zadran tribe. He lives on the Saroti pass approach to Khost. When the communist coup occurred, he took his family to Pakistan and then returned to build resistance forces in the area. [Map sheets 2883 and 2983].

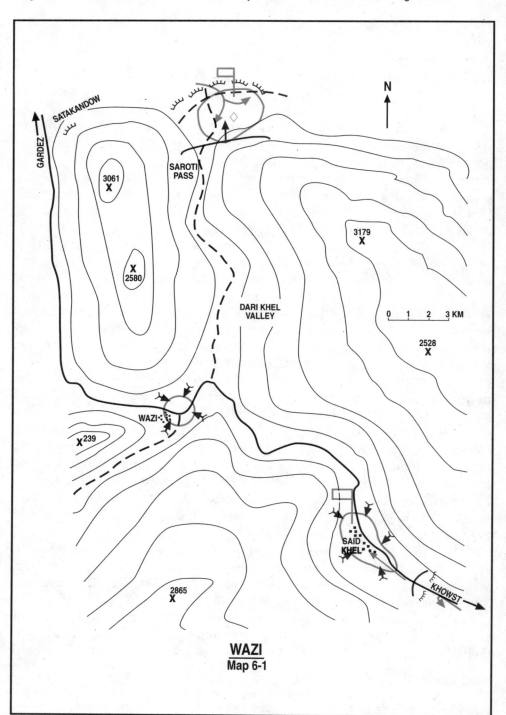

WAZI
Map 6-1

to rally the tribes and the tribes responded since they knew that the DRA would loot the villages if they let them into the area. I assigned two harbakai groups to reinforce the Mujahideen blocking DRA forces at Said Khel. I took the rest of the Mujahideen to the Saroti pass. I arrived at Saroti in the late afternoon and surveyed the area. I determined how many Mujahideen I would need and where I would position the forces. I did not have enough Mujahideen, so I assembled some of the local barbers (Pushtun barbers usually also play drums) to play their drums to gather a *lashkar*.[1] I did this to raise the whole area and to demoralize the enemy. The drummers did a great job. Warriors came from many tribes to Saroti and soon I had a large army. Originally, I had planned to defend the pass, but when I viewed the size of my army, I decided to attack. I promised them the weapons we captured and we attacked the column and captured weapons, trucks and tanks. When we had dealt with the Saroti force, I left a blocking force to deal with any further columns and then took the lashkar to Said Khel.

We cut the road to Khowst behind the DRA regiment which was still assembled at Said Khel. Then we surrounded the regiment. It remained trapped for 20 days. The DRA sent another column out of Khowst to relieve this force, but they could not break through the Mujahideen blockade. After some fighting, the entire force at Said Khel surrendered. There were 1,300 personnel in the column and we captured 1,200. The enemy lost another 100 either KIA or WIA. We captured all the weapons of this regiment including 50-60 trucks and armored vehicles. After the surrender, the DRA air force bombed their own column and destroyed the rest of the vehicles in it, or we would have had even more booty. A few vehicles managed to escape from us. The father of DRA Minister of the Interior Gulabzoi was wounded in the fighting and managed to escape in one of the APCs. His name was Gulab Shah and he was a member of the Zadran tribe, so perhaps some tribesmen helped his escape.

COMMENTARY: Early in the war, the Mujahideen resistance was mostly centered on the tribes. Only later, when the United States, Egypt, Saudi Arabia and other countries began supplying the Mujahideen through the various religious-based factions, did the Mujahideen's primary focus and loyalty shift to the factions. The method of

---

[1] Lashkar in Pushto usage means a tribal army or armed force. A lashkar is usually gathered for a short time.

raising the force and fighting the DRA columns described here is little different from what the British forces experienced fighting these same tribes on the northwest frontier. Once the lashkar assembled, the warriors would chant and sing along with the drums. This occurred here as well.

VIGNETTE 2
BLOCKING THE PAGHMAN HIGHWAY
by Commander Haji Aaquelshah Sahak

I have been in many actions, but one stands out that I won't ever forget, because it was a very trying situation. On 4 or 5 June 1983 we were in Paghman, a district capital (garrisoned by DRA forces),[2] which is some 25 kilometers west of Kabul. We received information one evening that a major Soviet/DRA column would attempt to resupply and reinforce Paghman's garrison and government enclave. There are two parallel highways from Kabul to Paghman. (Map 6-2 - Paghman) The late Commander Habibullah, the late Commander Wahed and others planned to block the convoy. They had some 250 to 300 Mujahideen armed with two mortars, one recoilless rifle, 12 RPG-7s, and some Kalashnikov and Enfield rifles. They assigned sectors of responsibility to different groups. Each group would block the highway with ambushes in its sector. Habibullah (HIK), Commander Aman (IUA) and I (NIFA) were given the sector from Khwajajam to Khwaja Musafer. Khwaja-jam is about a kilometer from the Cheltan road fork. We occupied positions primarily on the south side of the road. Commanders Ajabgul, Wahed, Abduljan and Kochi had the sector from Khwaja Musafer to Pajak. They occupied ambush positions mostly on the southern side of the road. From Pajak to Paghman, Mujahideen occupied ambush positions on both sides of the road.

We occupied our ambush positions at night. The next morning, the column left Kabul. As the leading armored vehicle reached Kwaja Musafer, we opened fire. The ambush turned into a battle as we destroyed 11 armored vehicles and two helicopters. Enemy aircraft and helicopters continually tried to drive us from our positions, but we held and the fighting continued for three days.[3] Even during the fight-

---

Commander Haji Aaquelshah Sahak is from the Chardehi District of Kabul (which is a southern suburb). He was affiliated with NIFA. [Map sheets 2786 and 2886].

[2] Reportedly two companies from the 200th Separate Reconnaissance Battalion.

[3] Zakari, a Mujahideen in Commander Sahak's group, gave the following account of a portion of the battle. "I had an 11-shooter [bolt-action Enfield rifle]. It held 10 rounds in the magazine and one in the chamber. The Russians knew the sound of the 11 shooter and would count off the 11 shots and then charge after the 11th shot while you were trying to reload. I was shooting at this Russian and had fired all 11 shots. He had counted my shots off and charged me. I yelled for help to my friend who had an RPG-7 antitank grenade launcher. 'What, shoot him with this thing?' my friend replied. 'Yes, he'll kill me' I answered. 'Okay" he yelled and fired his RPG-7. It completely disintegrated the Russian."

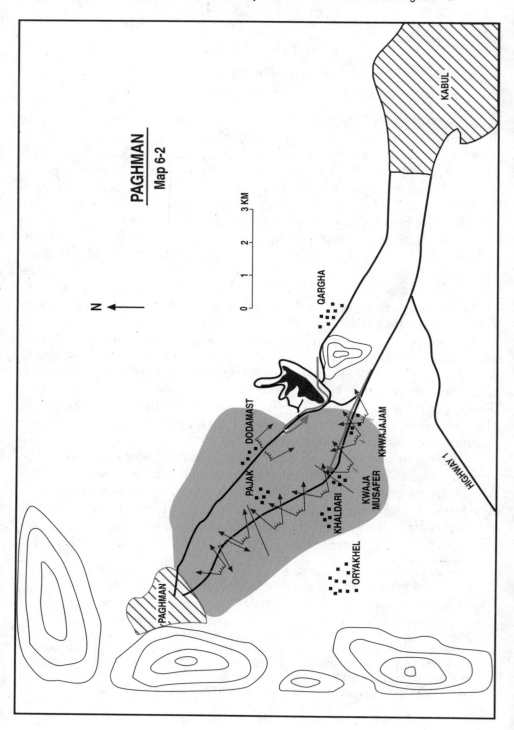

ing, the women from the villages would bring bread and milk forward to our positions. The whole area was actively supporting us. The inhabitants of Paghman, Oryakhel and Khaldari were feeding us. Mujahideen came from outside the area to reinforce us. Modir Zaher of Khaldari took nine wounded Mujahideen into his home. His wife cared for them, nursed them and applied dressings on them. The Soviets tried to bypass our ambush by moving on the northern route to Paghman through Qaragha. Mujahideen stopped this column at Dodamast northwest of Qaragha. The enemy then tried to bypass the Kwaja Musafer ambush by skirting around it, but the bypassing force soon fell into further Mujahideen ambushes. The center of fighting was Kwaja Musafer and we stopped and held the enemy there. After three days of fighting, the enemy broke contact and withdrew to Kabul. In my sector, we lost 13 KIA and many wounded. I personally know of 20 wounded, but there were many more. The enemy lost 14 armored vehicles and trucks in my sector. I know that over 40 DRA soldiers were captured or defected. We captured hundreds of small arms during this battle.

COMMENTARY: This is an example of good Mujahideen field cooperation—not always a feature of the war. The Mujahideen cooperated and their overall formation strengthened as the battle continued since Mujahideen came from all around the area to join in the fight. The British noted that a good fight had almost a magnetic effect on the warrior-tribesmen of Afghanistan and the Soviets learned that this trait had not disappeared over time. The Soviets and DRA broke contact after three days although their lines of communication were intact and the enemy was fixed in known positions. Firepower could not break the Mujahideen and the Soviets and DRA would not commit the necessary infantry to close with the Mujahideen.

The road to Paghman runs through a heavily-populated green zone and the Mujahideen were able to select and fortify good ambush positions along the route. In this summer fighting, the trees and crops provided good concealment for the Mujahideen.

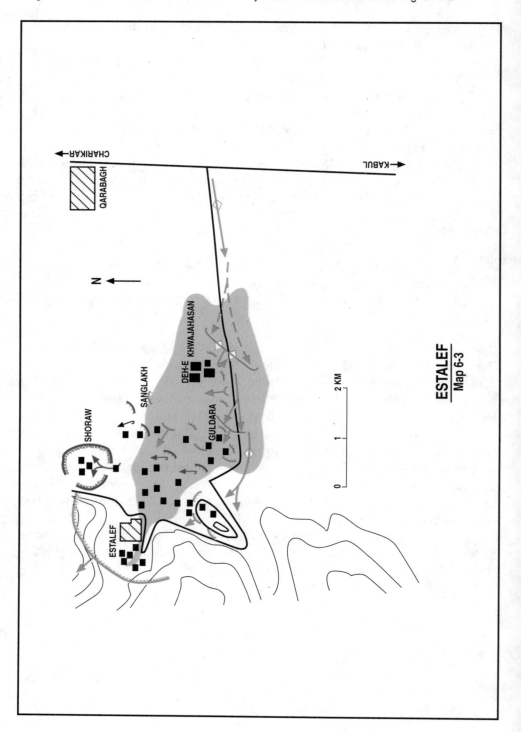

ESTALEF
Map 6-3

VIGNETTE 3
ROAD BLOCK AT ESTALEF
by Commander Sofi Lal Gul

In October 1983, one of my men was injured during a fight with other Mujahideen from the local area. I took a group of 20 of my Mujahideen from my base in Farza and went five kilometers north to Estalef. We were going to meet with local elders in Estalef to settle the dispute with other local commanders. Estalef is a popular summer resort some 40 kilometers north of Kabul.

Informers told the DRA and Soviets about our gathering and the enemy decided to attack us. The Soviet forces came from nearby Bagram and the DRA forces came from Kabul. At night, Mujahideen patrols at the Estalef junction of the Kabul-Charikar highway reported that Soviet and DRA columns have moved from Kabul and Bagram and were heading toward Estalef. The Mujahideen alerted their men at dawn. My 20 men joined a force of nearly 100 commanded by a local commander who was the son of a leading Estalefi chieftain (Wakil Mohammad Amin Khan). We took up positions in the orchards at Deh-e Khwajahasan and Qabr-e Malik (Map 6-3 - Estalef). We planned to block the Estalef road and deny the enemy access to the town which dominated the fertile valley.

The Mujahideen commanders divided their men into small teams of four-five men and deployed them in the orchards along the road in order to ambush the enemy column over a wide stretch. We instructed our men to let the head of the enemy column reach Qabr-e Malik and then everyone should open fire. As the leading vehicles reached Qabr-e Malik, the attack signal was given and relayed through portable megaphones. We hit the lead armored vehicle and a jeep. The battle raged along the length of the column from Qabr-e Malik to Deh-e Khwajahasan. The Soviet infantry dismounted and attacked the Mujahideen positions and heavy fighting ensued. We were scattered throughout the orchards and had plenty of room to maneuver, so it was hard for the Soviet infantry to pin us down. However, we were short of supplies, particularly ammunition. Further, the Soviets/DRA had much more combat power than we did and they

---

Commander Sofi Lal Gul is from Farza village of Mir Bacha Kot District about 25 kilometers north of Kabul. He was affiliated with Mojaddedi's Afghanistan National Liberation Front of Afghanistan (ANLF) during the war with the Soviets. Commander Sofi Lal Gul concentrated his efforts on the Kabul-Charikar highway. [Map sheet 2886, vic grid 0754].

were using helicopter gunships and other aircraft against us. Since we were scattered over a wide area in small groups, Mujahideen command and control over the battle was difficult and sporadic. Coordination of the actions of the many resistance groups became very difficult.

The battle in the orchards continued until 1400 hours. As they ran out of ammunition, the various Mujahideen groups withdrew in different directions and moved their wounded to safe areas. The Soviets consolidated their advance through the green zone, securing the high ground commanding the approaches to Estalef. I pulled my men out to Shoraw, about three kilometers northeast of Estalef. The Soviet/DRA column moved to Estalef and launched an intensive search of homes. The soldiers looted homes, destroyed property and set fire to the houses of suspected Mujahideen. Many people lost their livelihoods due to their actions. The Soviets stayed three days in Estalef and then returned to their bases. Mujahideen casualties in my group were two KIA and 18 WIA. Most of the casualties were from Soviet air strikes.

COMMENTARY: The large Mujahideen concentration in Estalef, close to Soviet/DRA forces, was an extremely imprudent move. If the Mujahideen patrol had not provided early warning, the Mujahideen losses at Estalef might have been much higher. The Mujahideen deserve high marks for their quick reaction and rapid deployment along the road to Estalef. They utilized their familiarity with their home area to quickly select effective fighting positions and they used local terrain and vegetation to conceal themselves from Soviet ground and air power. However, the Mujahideen suffered from lack of effective command and control which prevented the timely coordination of counterattacks and countermeasures. Better command and control might have enabled the Mujahideen to hold the high ground dominating the Estalef approach and to prevent the Soviet entry. But the well-armed and supported Soviet force was able to push its way through. The Mujahideen were reluctant to become decisively engaged in a protracted battle with a much-stronger, better-supplied opponent. They felt that they had to survive to face this opponent over and over again. The Mujahideen lack of a structured, viable supply system hampered their tactical capabilities significantly.

The Soviets and DRA deserve high marks for carrying enough forces for dismounted combat and for using them aggressively. The combination of overwhelming firepower and ground maneuver unhinged the Mujahideen defense and the decisive action taken by the Soviet infantry forced the poorly-supplied Mujahideen to break contact—leaving the dominant terrain and subsequent access to Estalef open. However, the Soviet/DRA forces merely pushed at a more-nimble foe and failed to try to outflank or encircle the Mujahideen force. This kept them from bringing the Mujahideen to decisive combat and allowed the Mujahideen to withdraw without heavy losses.

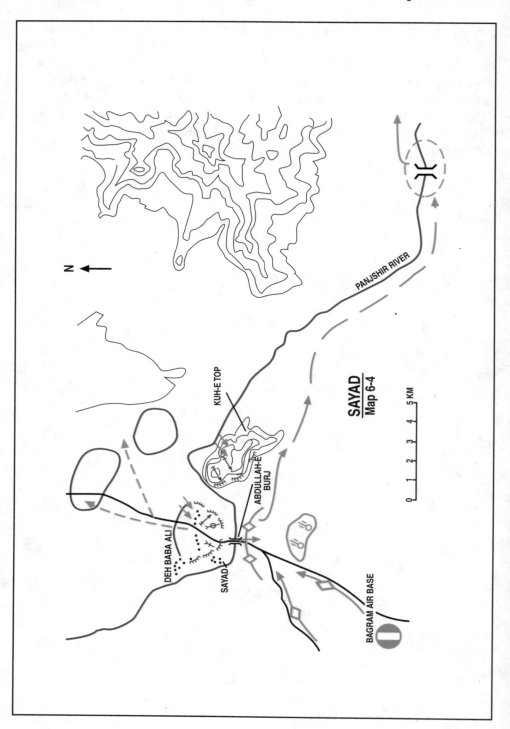

PANJSHIR RIVER

N

KUH-E TOP

ABDULLAH-E BURJ

DEH BABA ALI

SAYAD

BAGRAM AIR BASE

SAYAD
Map 6-4

0 1 2 3 4 5 KM

VIGNETTE 4
DEFENSE OF A RIVER LINE AND ROAD BLOCK AT SAYAD
by Commander Haji Abdul Qader

In late summer and early fall of 1983, the Mujahideen in Nejrao and Tagao Districts of Kapisa Province increased their attacks on government facilities. These districts are located on the east side of the Panjshir River and link Sarobi on the Kabul-Jalalabad highway with key locations in the provinces of Parwan, Kapisa and Laghman. These districts also provided access to several Mujahideen mountain base camps. The only permanent bridge across the Panjshir River (at Abdullah-e Burj) is located in this area and provides direct access to Bagram. We expected Soviet/DRA forces at Bagram to launch a strike through the area. Their purpose would be to protect Sarobi and the main road connecting Sarobi with the Kapisa Province Capital of Mahmoud-e Raqi and Gulbahar located further north at the mouth of the Panjsher Valley.

We decided to block this expected advance with my forces and the forces of Commander Shahin (based around Mahmoud-e Raqi). We prepared defensive positions on the north bank of the Panjshir River around the bridge at Abdullah-e Burj (Map 6-4 - Sayad) We built blocking positions in a deep ditch which passes through upper Sayad village and covers the road as it approaches the bridge. We prepared positions on the high ground south of the river which dominates the approach and both banks of the river. We put in land mines and built shelters with overhead cover to protect our Mujahideen from air and artillery fire. We moved supplies forward to a forward supply base in Deh Babi village immediately northwest of Sayad village. We built covered trenches from the base to the forward positions. The trenches were big enough to allow us to resupply by pack horses, mules and foot porters.

Commander Shahin had approximately 600 men and I had approximately 250. There was not enough space to deploy them all, so one-third of the force occupied fighting positions while the rest were in reserve or given support tasks. Some Mujahideen held flank positions to contain the enemy. Since all of the Mujahideen were locally based, we were able to deploy the blocking force in total

---

Haji Abdul Qader was a Commander for the HIK faction. His forces were based around the vital Bagram area. [Map sheet 2886, 2887, vic grid 2872]

secrecy. This helped surprise the enemy and hit him at a time and place where he was not fully ready to react effectively.

Early on the morning of 31 October 1983, Soviet and DRA forces moved out of their Bagram base along two parallel routes and approached the Abdullah-e Burj bridge. I estimate the strength at several regiments backed by strong artillery support and ample logistics. Tanks and APCs led the column. As the head of the column reached the lower Sayad village on the southern bank, the tail of the column had not cleared their Bagram base some ten kilometers to the southwest. As the enemy tanks and APCs passed through lower Sayad village toward the river, we opened fire and took the enemy by surprise. It took the enemy some time to react and find our positions. We intensified our fire as more vehicles of the enemy column came into anti-tank weapons range. We hit several of their vehicles and they started to burn. Instead of trying to secure the bridge by infantry, the enemy continued to push his tanks and APC's toward the bridge. One tank and two APCs made it to the bridge, but we knocked them out at the bridge site.

The enemy stopped and began pounding suspected Mujahideen positions with artillery fire and air attacks. He also began indiscriminately bombing the area, including the surrounding villages. However, our blocking force was well entrenched and protected against the enemy fire. Most of our Mujahideen moved into the covered shelters for the duration of the enemy fire preparation. As soon as the enemy began to shift his fire so that he could launch an attack, our Mujahideen would reoccupy their fighting positions and engage enemy infantry and tanks with mortars, machine guns, 82mm recoilless rifles and RPG-7s. The news of our defense against the Soviet/DRA forces soon spread throughout the area and reached as far as Kabul, Charikar and Panjsher. Mujahideen from these areas began to move to the fight. This had a demoralizing impact on the enemy as these Mujahideen began probing attacks against his flanks and rear.

In early afternoon, the enemy reinforced his efforts with some DRA troops and launched another attack to clear the roadblock. We drove back the attack and inflicted heavy casualties on the enemy. In the late afternoon, the enemy again conducted heavy artillery and air strikes on our positions. Artillery, jets and helicopter gunships took their turns against us and then a Soviet unit attacked us. We defeated this attack as well. During the night, the enemy tried to attack across the bridge three times. Each time he was unsuccessful. The river could not be forded by vehicles and he did not try using infantry in assault boats to cross at another point to outflank us. Probably the number of Mujahideen who had come to the fight on both sides of the river discouraged the enemy from risking an infantry assault crossing at night.

On the morning of 1 November, the enemy resumed heavy artillery fire and air attacks. At the same time, we detected enemy activity toward the south. Around 1000 hours, the enemy facing the bridge began to break contact. Most of their troops headed south across the plain on the southern bank of the Panjsher river. We later found out that the enemy built an engineer bridge across the river near Shokhi, some 20 kilometers down stream and crossed there to move against Nejrao and Tagao Districts. Seeing the enemy withdraw, we left our positions and collected what the enemy had left behind. The next day, we pushed their disabled tanks and APCs off the bridge into the river.

COMMENTARY: The Soviet/DRA force did not lead with reconnaissance, nor did it use forward detachments to seize potential chokepoints before it moved. The Soviet/DRA force was evidently surprised by the strong resistance they met. Had they detected the Mujahideen road block in advance, they could have dealt with it more effectively than trying to force a crossing through repeated frontal attacks.

The Soviet/DRA force had several options besides frontal attacks. First, they could have moved DRA forces from Jabul-e Seraj and Gulbahar in the north to attack the Mujahideen positions from the flank and rear since these forces were already garrisoned across the river. Second, they could have conducted an infantry assault crossing at an unopposed site and then attacked the Mujahideen position from the flank. Third, if speed was essential, the planners could have selected the option it was later forced to choose after sustaining losses and losing much time at the Abdullah-e Burj bridge.

Once delayed by a strong Mujahideen resistance, the Soviet/DRA columns acted very slowly to try to seize the initiative. Tanks were ineffective in forcing the bridge. The Soviet/DRA force needed to use well-trained infantry to seize the dominant Kuh-e Top Mountain quickly. This mountain was on their side of the river and would facilitate forcing the bridge. By allowing the column to stall in a Mujahideen area, the Soviet/DRA force became vulnerable to flank and rear attacks by local Mujahideen. Quick, decisive action is key to the survival of a stalled, surrounded force.

Mujahideen secrecy while planning and implementing the road block was commendable. The local commanders coordinated their actions and the force fought staunchly. Their well-prepared defensive positions allowed them to survive artillery fire and air bombardment. The Mujahideen had the advantage of fighting on home turf with local support.

Had the Mujahideen developed a more effective system of operational cooperation and coordination, the enemy column might not have succeeded in reaching Nejrao and Tagao. Lack of a viable operational command and control system prevented the Mujahideen at Abdullah-e Burj, Shokhi, Nejrao and Tagao from acting together. A more elaborate operational coordination could have mobilized the Mujahideen forces at Shokhi to prevent the Soviet/DRA troops from crossing the river to Kapisa Province.

VIGNETTE 5

THE DEFENSE AGAINST THE SOVIET OPERATION "MAGISTRAL"

by General Gulzarak Zadran, Lieutenant Omar, Mawlawi Nezamuddin Haqani, and Mawlawi Abdul-Rahman

"We were a very desperate people without much equipment or armaments, but we had the power of our faith, love for our homeland, love of freedom and reliance on the Almighty. We were fighting against very heavy odds."

General Gulzarak Zadran

Sources in the DRA warned us that a combined Soviet/DRA force would launch an offensive to open the road between Gardez and Khowst. We Mujahideen closed the road in March 1979 and the government had supplied their garrison at Khowst by air ever since. The DRA had tried to open the road on many occasions and had two entire regiments annihilated in the process. The road had become a thing of myth—the Mujahideen-held road that no power could open. We watched the enemy mass his forces and supplies in Gardez in November 1987. This was clearly going to be a major 40th Army operation involving forces from several Soviet motorized rifle divisions, the Soviet airborne division, DRA units, Spetsnaz, massed artillery, surface-to-surface missiles, and Soviet air power. At the time, General Zadran analyzed the impending operation to determine its operational significance. He determined two possible goals for the operation: this unprecedented massing of such a major force either meant that the Soviets wanted to escalate the war by threatening Pakistan directly from Paktia; or the Soviets wanted to shatter

General Guzarak Zadran was an officer in the Afghan Army and attended the Afghan Army Higher OfficersTraining Institute where the author, Ali Jalali, was his instructor. He joined the resistance and fought in Paktia Province. He fought in Zhawar 1 and 2 and at the Satakandow pass. He belonged to IUA. After the fall of the DRA, he became the Deputy Minister of Defense in the interim government. Currently he lives near Peshawar. [Map sheets 2883, 2884, 2983].

Lieutenant Omar (Zabit Omar) graduated from the Kabul Military Academy in the 1970s. After the communist coup and the Soviet invasion, Lieutenant Omar joined the Mujahideen of the fundamentalist Islamic Party (HIK) founded by Mawlawi Mohammed Yunis Khalis. He was a close aide to Jalaluddin Haqani and fought with him throughout the war. Haqani ran the Mujahideen effort in the crucial Paktia Province. Lieutenant Omar also served as

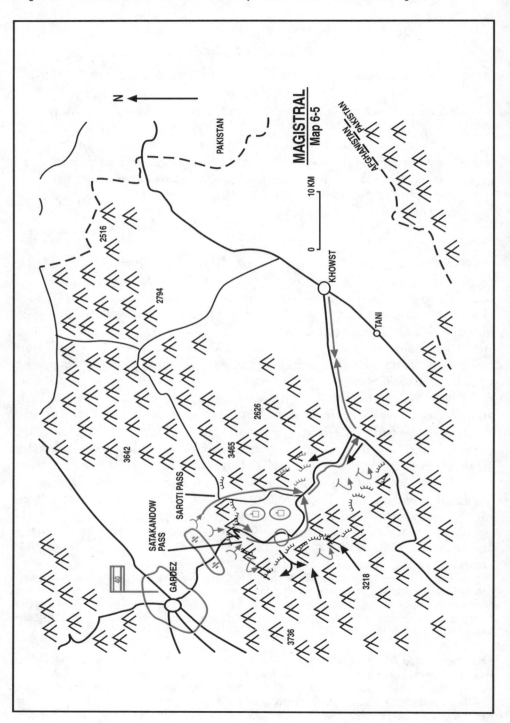

MAGISTRAL
Map 6-5

the myth that the Mujahideen along the Gardez-Khowst highway are invincible by opening the unopenable road. If the Soviet goal was to escalate and to threaten Pakistan, then the Soviets needed to bring more forces to Paktia Province after they opened the road to Khowst. General Zadran thought that this was too dangerous a gamble for the Soviets to take, considering the probable international and regional implications. Instead, General Zadran concluded that the Soviets meant to show their military might to the world by doing the impossible, so that they could then end the Soviet occupation of Afghanistan and withdraw with a solid victory to their credit. In order to accomplish the impossible, the Soviets needed to force the main road from Gardez with at least a division and, having achieved the breakthrough, move toward Khowst to link-up with the DRA 25th Infantry Division which would try to open a corridor to the west. General Zadran's final analysis was that the Soviets needed to flex their muscles by opening the road that had been closed for all those years.

We started to prepare for the Soviet offensive against the Satakandow pass. The shoulders of the pass loom some 400 meters over the road and, once in the pass, the road follows a slow, twisted route packed with hairpin curves. It is an excellent place to defend. We reinforced the minefields along the road. We laid three mine belts on a three kilometer front at the opening of the pass with 300-400 meters between mine belts. We reinforced our positions on the high ground overlooking the road and pass. We had a total of ten BM-12s in the area. We crowned the pass with ZGU-1 air defense machine guns. These are both good positional weapons but are very difficult to displace rapidly when the situation requires. We also had DShK machine guns, 75mm and 82mm recoilless rifles and plenty of RPG-7s. Haji Nawab Khan commanded the

---

Mawlawi Nezamuddin Haqani was a group commander and a deputy to Jalaluddin Haqani. He was a member of the fundamentalist Islamic Party (HIK) led by Mawlawi Mohammed Yunus Khalis. He joined the Mujahideen following the communist coup in 1978 and fought in the Paktia area. Prior to the Soviet invasion, his group had liberated the area surrounding Khowst and only the city of Khowst remained under government control.

Mawlawi Abdul-Rahman of Zadran is the son of Noor Mahmuod from Kandow village. When Soviet forces attacked Satakandow pass, his group of 100-120 local Mujahideen occupied positions at Ghelgoy. They were armed with 82mm recoilless rifles, ZGU-1 machine guns, DShK machine guns, 82mm mortars, MBRL and one Stinger. His group fought a rearguard action through the pass to Sewak before they went into the mountains. He lost ten KIA in the fighting.

Satakandow pass approach. Two kilometers to the west of the Satakandow pass is the Khadai pass—a secondary pass with a dirt trail going through it. We reinforced the defenses here as well. Ismail commanded the Khadai pass approach (Map 6-5 - Magistral).

Most of the Mujahideen in this area were local men who were defending their own villages. Unlike other parts of Afghanistan, the people still lived here and had not been driven out to the refugee camps in Pakistan. The majority of the people in the area belonged to the Zadran tribe, but other tribes and different factions were also involved. The decision to prepare and the decision to fight was not made by the factions, but by the tribal council. This was to be fight for homes and neighborhoods. Our local major commanders were Mawlawi Neza-muddin Haqani, Mula Ibrahim, Mula Abdurrahman, Captain Khan Zamak, Izat Khan, Ghaday, Dool Khan, Ghanamkay, Sadat, Hakem, Jung, Dr. Khiali, Badshah and Alef.

We focused our efforts on the main road where it runs through the Satakandow pass. There is another road some seven kilometers to the east which goes through the Saroti pass and joins the main highway at Lakatega[4]—some 25 kilometers to the south of the Satakandow pass. This is a poor road which passes through the Dari Khel tribe.[5] We did not expect that the Soviets would want to move vehicles along this road, so we did not mine it. However, we did reinforce the local Mujahideen in this area. Each tribe sent harbakai to help and we sent about 300 harbakai as reinforcements to the Saroti pass in the Dari Khel area. Commander Badshah commanded the Saroti approach.

The Soviets established forward bases at Dara and Zawa. They deployed their artillery in Division Artillery Groups (DAGs) near Dara and deployed their Army Artillery Group further back south of Gardez. They moved a maneuver force to Zawa. Suddenly, they launched an attack from Zawa toward Saroti. We were completely taken by surprise. In four to five days of fighting, the Soviets pushed us back on the Saroti approach. Commander Badshah was killed in this fighting. Qader Shah took over command and fought a stubborn withdrawal back through the Saroti pass (Map 6-6 - Phase 1).

Once the Soviets captured the Saroti pass, they launched air assault landings on the high ground located between the main road and the road through the Saroti pass. They now held key terrain

---

[4] Lakatega means erected stone.

[5] The Dari Khel tribe is a subdivision of the Zadran tribe. The Dari Khel have a well deserved reputation as a very military and warlike people.

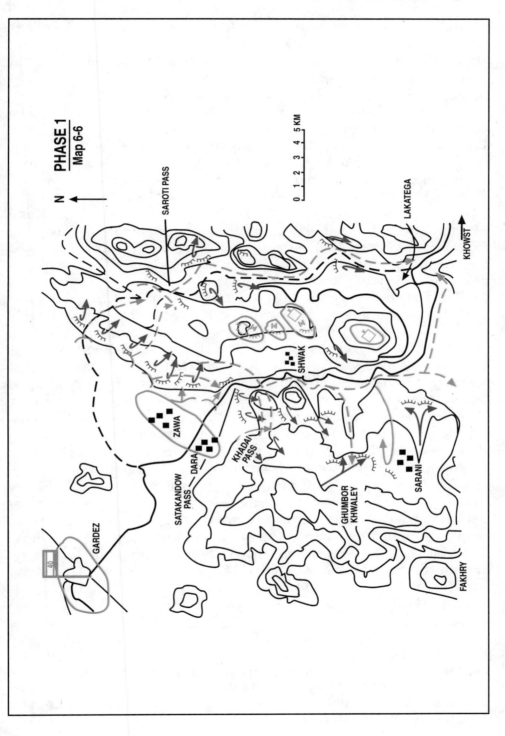

PHASE 1
Map 6-6

controlling both axes with air assault troops and small caliber artillery.[6] From these peaks, they could hit our positions and support their advance through the Satakandow pass on the main road. At the same time, they could support their continued advance along the Saroti approach. Their sudden seizure of the high ground between their two axes gave them a tremendous advantage. The Soviets began bombing the Mujahideen headquarters at Sarani. Command and control suffered greatly from the shelling.

The Soviets on the high ground began directing artillery and rocket fire on the villages in both valleys leading from Satakandow and Saroti. The Zadrans in the villages had not emigrated and the Soviets wanted to displace them. They were successful. Many Mujahideen, concerned about the danger to their families, left the fighting to evacuate their families to Pakistan. This exodus opened the way for the further advance of the Soviet troops. They were now ready for the main attack on the Satakandow axis.

The Soviets opened their operation against the Satakandow pass[7] with heavy air strikes and artillery fire while they moved their maneuver forces to Dara. Then, once their positions were set, they flew an airplane over the pass at high altitude, dropping paratroopers. Reconnaissance aircraft, flying at much higher altitudes, trailed the aircraft that was dropping the paratroopers. We engaged the paratroopers with all our air defense machine guns and whatever other air defense weapons we had. As the paratroopers drifted closer, we realized that we had been duped. The "paratroopers" were dummies and the reconnaissance aircraft had photographed our response and pinpointed our positions.

The Soviets now began firing on our positions in earnest. Heavy artillery strikes followed air strikes, which were followed by more artillery strikes. We were pinned down in our positions by the strikes which continued for hours. Our positions were generally artillery-proof but not bomb-proof and, thanks to their reconnaissance, they were hitting our positions exactly. They then launched their ground attack, but we readily defeated it. The next day, 1 December 1987, they resumed their heavy shelling and bombing.

The overwhelming force of their artillery and airpower took the

---

[6] Possibly the AM 2B9 Vasilyek (Cornflower) 82mm automatic mortar. This weapon can fire direct and indirect fire. Other candidates are the older D-44 85mm gun (which was found in airborne units) or the M-69 76mm mountain gun.

[7] Vignette 17 in *The Bear Went Over the Mountain* describes the battle for the Satakandow pass from a Soviet perspective.

initiative from us. There were no Soviet forces garrisoned in Paktia and we were used to fighting the DRA. The DRA had no artillery larger than 130mm. Now we were getting pounded by heavy artillery including BM21 and BM-27 MRL. In Dara, the Soviets had three, powerful, long-range heavy artillery pieces with four tires each. We saw one of these firing. The firing recoil gases alone flipped a jeep over.[8] Aircraft were dropping cluster bombs on us. We could not survive in these positions, so we left our positions and moved to higher mountains in the west called Ghumbor Khwaley and Fakhry. The Soviets advanced on our positions behind us and, after five days, they seized the Satakandow pass.

We had cut and destroyed sections of the road in the Satakandow pass. As the Soviets tried to repair the road, we started firing on them with our heavy weapons from the high ground. But the Soviet firepower was strong and the Soviets pushed us higher into the mountains. As their converging forces cut our rear, we fell back. They captured Gulzarak Zadran's base at Shwak. The Mujahideen took what equipment they could, but some had to be abandoned to the enemy. The Mujahideen withdrew to the southwest mountains and the Soviets/DRA advanced and established a base camp where they stayed for two days. Then they resumed their advance to Sarani. They destroyed the Mujahideen base camp at Sarani—our first indication that the Soviets/DRA planned to abandon the route instead of trying to maintain a long-term presence there.

The Mujahideen plight was serious and we were suddenly faced with a new problem—the absence of drinking water. The intensity of Soviet shelling was so great, that the chemical residue from the explosions had contaminated the streams. Some of us thought that the Soviets had poisoned the water since one glass of water would choke you up and make you very ill. We had to use snow for drinking water, but the snow was also affected by the chemicals. Our supplies were cut off and food was scarce, but our major problem was thirst. People were suffering from dehydration, but they could not use the local water. We had not made arrangements to haul water into the area since local water had always been adequate for our needs. The roads were blocked so trucks could not enter the area. We had some mules that we could use in some of the area, but

---

[8] This was probably the 2A36 152mm gun, the "Hyacinth". It has a maximum range of 28.5 kilometers and fires 5-6 rounds per minute. The round weighs 46 kilograms and has a muzzle velocity of 942 meters/sec. The piece weighs 9,800 kg and has a 8.197 meter long barrel. *Krasnaya zvezda* [Red star], 16 July 1993, page 2.

we carried in most of our supplies by Mujahideen porters.

The Soviets continued their move south. They preceded their movement by air assault landings to seize high ground on both sides of the road. Their columns would then advance under the protection of these picketing forces. As the Soviets moved forward, they left security OPs behind to secure their lines of communication. The Soviets reached Lakatega and the columns from Satakandow and Saroti linked up. After that, it was smoother for them. The Soviets/DRA left a security detachment at Lakatega and advanced on Khowst. At the same time, a DRA detachment from the 25th Infantry division moved west out of Khowst to link up with the approaching column. After the force secured the road to Khowst, they began moving supply columns along the road to resupply the beleaguered city.

The tide was beginning to turn. The local Mujahideen, who had taken their families to Pakistan, returned. Mawlawi Jalaluddin Haqani and other commanders (Matiullah, Mula Abdul Ghafur, Gulzarak Zadran, Amanullah, Mula Seddiq, Tawakal, Abdur-rah-man, Wakil Wazir Mohammad, Pari, Padshah Khan and Sadat) arrived and moved into the mountains west of the highway. Colonel Imam of the Pakistani ISI arrived and tried to coordinate the Mujahideen action. Haji Amanullah Khan and other commanders arrived. Mujahideen from other areas in Afghanistan arrived. Mujahideen and Taliban arrived from Pakistan. They were all eager for a fight. The Mujahi-deen selected 12 commanders and assigned enemy outposts between Wazi and Satakandow for them to attack. The Soviets had moved into the side valleys, but the 12 commanders forced the Soviets out of the side valleys and confined them to the vicinity of the road. Then they began attacking the road. Jalaluddin Haqani, was at Fakhry. Once again, Jalaluddin Haqani was wounded during battle—this time with shrapnel in his thigh. Although Haqani was wounded, he stayed on for a week. Then he was evacuated on mule back over mountain paths to Miram Shah.

The Soviets/DRA could only keep the road open for 12 days. Then they withdrew. When the Soviet air assault abandoned the heights, they took their weapons, but left all the ammunition behind. The Mujahideen recaptured the road and neither the DRA nor the Soviets could reopen it.

Despite the intensity of battle, Mujahideen casualties were light. There were perhaps some 100 Mujahideen KIA. The villagers suffered greatly and the villages were heavily damaged or destroyed.

Some 80% of the villages in the area were damaged. Soviet/DRA losses are unknown. The Mujahideen shot down one helicopter and three jets. As the Soviets withdrew, we captured two intact Soviet tanks and four trucks. Some 600 DRA soldiers defected or were captured. Most of them defected with their weapons.

COMMENTARY: Gulzarak Zadran's evaluation of the Soviets is not flattering. "I should mention here that the Russian Army is a worthless military institution and that no professional soldier will give them a high mark in discipline or the will to fight. They are useless. I should also note that the Russians relied throughout the action on maximum use of artillery and one Mujahideen would draw the fire of a battery or more for several minutes. The high peaks which they occupied by heliborne troops helped them a lot. Even there, they surrounded themselves with all sorts of mines. And these 'bears' would be sitting around lighted campfires to keep themselves warm in the winter, so the peaks were on fire all night. The Soviet Air Force was not very effective because they flew very high, probably out of fear of our Stingers."

Despite General Zadran's comments, the Soviet planning and execution of this operation was well done. It matches the initial Soviet invasion in tactical surprise, the use of multiple axis, operational tempo and innovation. The fire support and logistics portion of the plan were first rate and the use of dummy paratroopers was a masterstroke. The use of air-assault forces was well-planned and executed. The Soviets needed a "save-face" operation before withdrawal and Magistral was that.

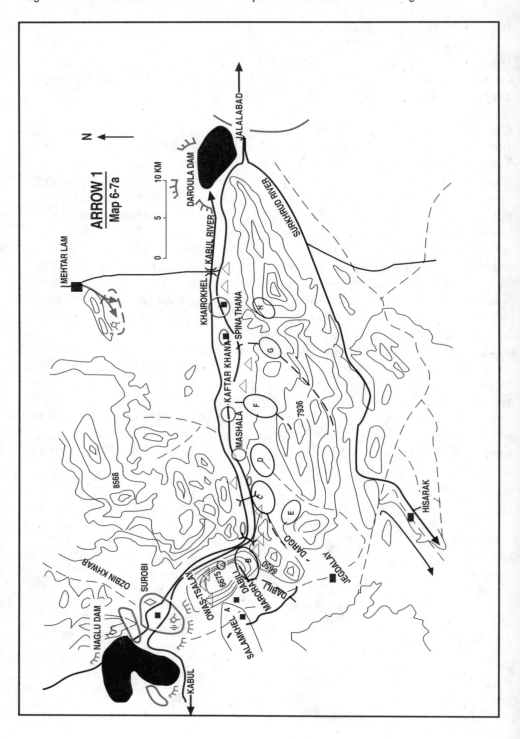

VIGNETTE 6
OPERATION GHASHEY (ARROW IN PUSHTO)
by General Abdul Rahim Wardak

From 23 October to 7 November 1988, a force of some 2,000 Mujahideen from the National Islamic Front of Afghanistan (NIFA) shut down the Kabul-Jalalabad highway along a 70-kilometer stretch between Sarobi and Laghman. I commanded them.

This action was part of a four-party (NIFA, HIK, HIH and JIA) combined operation aimed at closing the eastern supply route to the Afghan capital for a period of two months (October-November). Each party was responsible for deploying its units to keep the highway blocked for 15 days. The operation was planned in the wake of Soviet forces withdrawal from the Nangrahar Province. The Mujahideen intent was to prevent the government from reinforcing the Jalalabad garrison while the Mujahideen prepared to advance on Jalalabad from Torkham.

Elements of the DRA 8th and 18th border guard brigades, the DRA 60th Infantry Division, tank subunits from the 15th Tank Brigade, a Sarandoy battalion and local militia manned the enemy's six bases and nearly 20 outposts along this stretch of road. The DRA hoped to protect the highway against Mujahideen attacks and keep the supply route to Jalalabad open (Map 6-7a - Arrow 1). Each base was manned by at least a platoon reinforced by one or two tanks or APCs, 122mm D30 howitzers plus heavy machine guns and 82mm mortars. The outposts consisted of five to ten men reinforced with machine guns, AGS-17 and mortars.[9]

I assembled my force from Mujahideen groups based across

General Wardak was an officer in the Afghan Army. He trained at US military schools before the war and testified before the United States Congress on several occasions during the war. He was one of the most noted Mujahideen commanders. At the close of the war, he was seriously wounded by a SCUD missile and was treated in the United States for his wounds. He became the first Chief of the General Staff of the Armed Forces of the Islamic Government of Afghanistan in 1992 following the Mujahideen victory and the downfall of the communist regime in Kabul. NIFA records and other interviews conducted by Ali Jalali are used in this vignette. Correspondent Askold Krushelnycky accompanied NIFA forces and filed a report on Operation Gashay in The Sunday times of 6 November 1988. [Map sheets 2985, 2986,3085 and 3086].

[9] A layout and discussion of the security outposts along this stretch of highway are found in LTC Tubeev's article on pages 129-133 of *The Bear Went Over the Mountain: Soviet Combat Tactics in Afghanistan*, edited by Lester W. Grau, Washington: NDU Press, 1996.

several districts in Nangrahar and Kabul Provinces. Some of these groups were based more than 200 kilometers apart. Other groups and a contingent of 70 former Afghan Army officers, who were used to work with combat task forces, came from the NIFA central reserve based in Pakistan.

I organized my force into five strike groups (task forces Bravo, Charlie, Falcon, Gulf and Hurricane), two containment (holding) groups (task forces Alpha and Delta), one reserve (task force Echo) and one rocket launcher group (Saqar Rocket launcher). The force composition follows:

A. **NIFA's Kabul Province Eastern Sector Forces** under the overall command of Dr. Shahrukh Gran

1. **Task Force Alpha**
   AO: Marora and Salamkhel Tangay
   Number of Mujahideen: 350
   Unit commanders: Sadiq Patang, Haji Sangeen, Mir Wali, Khawani, Mirajan, Wrekhmin, Haji Habib, and Mo'alem Karim.

2. **Task Force Bravo**
   AO: Debili
   Number of Mujahideen: 393
   Unit commanders: Janat Gul, Haji Mir, Gulbat, Sakhi Usmankhel, Ghulam Rasoul

3. **Task Force Charlie**
   AO: Kamkay Dargo
   Number of Mujahideen: 276
   Unit commanders: Mohammad Alam, Zaher Khan, Sahak, Sakhi Janikhel, Majnoon

4. **Task Force Delta**
   AO: Ghata Dargo
   Number of Mujahideen: 411
   Unit commanders: Noor Hasan, Sayed Rahman, Captain Zalmay, Afridi, Gulab, Noor Rahman, Ruhullah.

5. **Task Force Echo**
   AO: Dargo
   Number of Mujahideen: 343
   Unit commanders: Hasan Khan Kairokhel, Sartor, Asel Khan, Captain Hashmat, Khalil, Ehsan

6. **Task Force SSM (Saqar)**
   AO: Chakari targeting Kabul Airport
   Number of Mujahideen: 100
   Unit commanders: Captain Sediqullah, Zaher Kahn, Shinwari, Hanan, Ghulam Haider, Umar, Hasan Khan, Momin Khan

B. **NIFA Forces From Nangrahar Province, Southwestern Sector:**

1. **Task Force Falcon**
    AO: Tor Ghar opposite the Kaftarkhana base
    Number of Mujahideen: 250
    Unit commanders: Lt. Wali, Shari'ati, Mohammad Anwar

2. **Task Force Gulf**
    AO: Tor Ghar opposite the Spina Thana base
    Number of Mujahideen: 350
    Unit commanders: Haji Zaman Ghamsharik, Zabit Zaher

3. **Task Force Hurricane**
    AO: Tor Ghar opposite Khairokhel base
    Number of Mujahideen: 130
    Unit commanders: Asef Khan, Qazi Samiullah

While all these groups were assembling to the south of the Kabul River, I ordered a group of about 50 Mujahideen under command of Lieutenant Ali Ahmad and Ghuncha Gul to move from their bases in the north (Ozbin area) and take positions at the northern ridge along the Kabul-Jalalabad highway overlooking the Debili bridge. They were to observe enemy activity and support the operation by fire. This group occupied the designated position but was unable to participate effectively and withdrew after a few days.

While the number of Mujahideen in each group ranged between 100 and 350, I could use only one third of them for combat since the rest were required for logistics and security tasks and occasionally relieving combatants at the front lines.

My force was armed with individual automatic rifles (AK-47), light machine guns (RPK), heavy machine guns (PK), light anti-tank grenade launchers (RPG-7), Milan anti-tank missile launchers, 82mm recoilless rifles, 75mm recoilless rifles, 82mm mortars, 107mm Multiple Barrel (twelve barrel) rocket launchers (BM12), Saqar Rocket Launchers, and Stinger shoulder-fired air defense missiles.

I instructed my five strike groups to attack and seize enemy bases/outposts, establish road blocks and lay ambushes against the enemy columns.

The western containment (holding) group—Task Force Alpha— was positioned in Marora and Salamkhel Tangay area. I ordered them to block enemy columns attempting to enter its AO or attempting to outflank my forces along the old Sarobi-Jalalabad road. This road passes through Jegdalay, one of my main Mujahideen supply bases. I gave Task Force Alpha an "on order" mission to disrupt any enemy concentration in Sarobi by fire. I gave the eastern containment (holding) group—Task Force Delta—a similar mission on the eastern flank of the operation area, i.e. eastern mouth of the Abreshmin Gorge. I gave Task Force Delta an "on order" mission to be prepared to serve as a strike group. I had the Reserve group (Task Force Echo) concentrate in the Dargo area. They were prepared to act against enemy heliborne insertions; to relieve task forces Alpha, Bravo, Charlie, Delta; and to launch a counter-attack if needed.

I had the rocket launcher detachment operate independently. Their mission was to occupy firing positions in the Chakari area (about 80 kilometers away)and hit the Kabul airport to divert attention from the rest of the operation.

Conduct of the Operation

During the late part of September and first three weeks of October 1988, I directed the preparation, resupply and movement of participating Mujahideen forces as they moved to the area of operation and deployed for action. I moved a total of 400 tons of various supplies from Pakistan to the area of operation by mules and other pack animals. Supplies included mines, small arms ammunition, rockets, mortar rounds and anti-tank ammunition.

One major challenge facing me was to covertly move the various Mujahideen groups from widely dispersed locations to the deployment area, avoiding enemy observation and air attack. Further, moving ammunition, supplies and men from Pakistan through the three provinces of Paktia, Logar and Kabul required detailed planning and careful execution.

Mujahideen were all unpaid volunteers who joined the jihad to fight. One leadership challenge was to convince guerrillas to perform the vital, if unglamourous, missions of rear area security and LOC security instead of participating in actual combat. This was always hard since these volunteers wanted to fight.

Another leadership challenge was commanding and controlling a volunteer multi-regional force and integrating them into a single command. In fact, as later transpired, the right flank strike groups (task forces Falcon and Hurricane) left their positions and withdrew unannounced to their permanent bases when their permanent bases came under enemy threat. Further, as our operation continued over a week many Mujahideen became restless and gradually left the battle area unannounced. Mujahideen had developed the habit of what Ali Jalali terms "short hit and long run tactics."

There were several reasons for this. First, the Mujahideen felt that they were fighting a war of "a thousand battles" and no single battle was a decisive one. Therefore, the Mujahideen felt that combat should be limited in terms of time and space in order to increase the Mujahideen's survivability.

Another reason was the absence of an efficient logistic system to provide meals, medical support and other required services. The fighters were issued all available supplies prior to the battle. There was seldom resupply available afterwards. This forced the Mujahideen to carry heavy loads and forage for food. Local food resources were scarce since the Soviets had destroyed the local economy and driven out the population in the rural areas. Consequently, Mujahideen field rations had to be carried from Pakistan and were poor and monotonous (usually bread with tea or boiled rice and dhal (a split chick pea dish).

Mujahideen fought best on their home territory. This area of operation was not the "home turf" for most of my forces. They were not fighting on their home territory but away from their villages where they were better provided for and had a better chance for rest. Given the traditional attachment of the Afghan resistance to its home territory, many Mujahideen did not feel the same enthusiasm they showed in fighting their own villages.

Finally, the long treks in the mountains sometimes lasted for weeks and contributed to fatigue before the battle began. Mujahideen commanders were hard pressed to keep their extremely hungry and tired fighters together for an extended period of time.

Although my operations plan encompassed a wide front from Sarobi to Surkhakan Bridge (70 kilometers), the main action took place on a four-kilometer stretch between Debili and Dargo bases (Map 6-7b - Arrow 2). Combat at other points was either in support of this action (task forces Alpha, Delta and Echo), or were separate actions (such as attacks on Khairokhel Post, Spina Thana Base and Kaftarkhana Base).

The operation began with rocket attacks on the Kabul military airport on October 19. The rocket launcher detachment targeted the airfield and kept it under intermittent fire until a few days after the beginning of the road block when the rocket detachment moved to Jagdalay to fire on an enemy concentration in the Nghlu-Sarobi area.

My operations plan had four phases:

1. Attack to destroy and seize enemy bases and outposts.

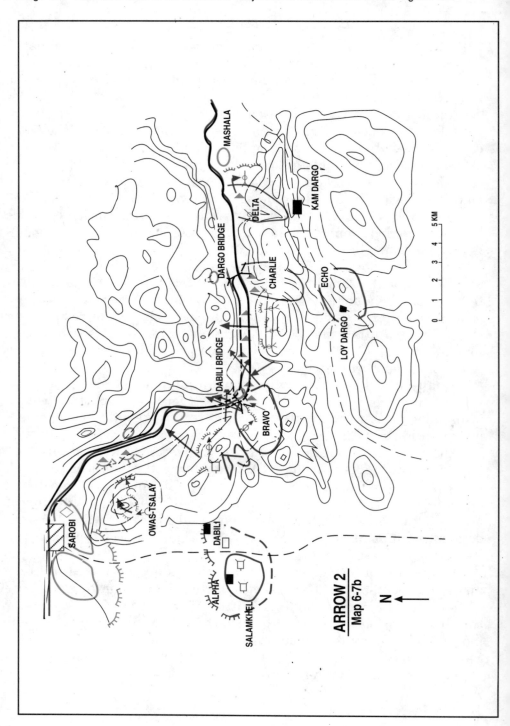

ARROW 2
Map 6-7b

N

0 1 2 3 4 5 KM

2. Block the road by destroying bridges, laying mines and shelling enemy columns attempting to reopen the highway.

3. When the enemy manages to reopen the highway, conduct a large-scale ambush to inflict heavy losses.

4. Break contact and withdraw.

PHASE ONE

The strike groups initiated their attack along the extended front at 1000 hours, October 23. Rocket launchers, mortars, recoilless rifles and heavy machine guns provided supporting fire from the southern high ground overlooking the highway. Since the area was heavily mined by the enemy, my Mujahideen could not descend on the road from all points. Instead, they moved down a limited number of mountain arroyos. These arroyos were safe since minefields could not be maintained in them due to the periodic flash floods which swept through them. These arroyos were mostly in the Debili and Dargo area.

Once my Mujahideen passed through the mined area, they fanned out and attacked the enemy using the paved road as the main approach. Their movement was covered by fire from the high ground dominating the gorge. The assault groups stormed the targeted enemy outposts and bases. After fierce fighting, several posts were overrun and others isolated from their bases and neighboring posts by 1600 hours.

During subsequent attacks through October 25, my force seized 14 outposts and four bases. The occupants were killed, fled or captured. We seized about 100 prisoners, 11 tanks or APCs and 21 other vehicles. We damaged the hydroelectric installations at Sarobi and Nghlu which supply electricity to Kabul and Jalalabad. Our losses were 10 killed and 21 wounded.

Phase Two

As my strike groups secured the highway, they destroyed three highway bridges—Khairokhel bridge, Istehkam (Dargo) bridge and Debili bridge; mined the road; set up road blocks and established firing positions on the southern high ground overlooking the highway, the roadblocks and the destroyed bridges. Four other outposts and the remaining bases, except the Mash ála base, fell to us by October 31.

The DRA's reaction was slow and incremental. The DRA now lacked sufficient observation and security posts on the high ground flanking the highway. The DRA failed to recapture any of his out-posts except the Owa-Tsalay post. The Owa-Tsalay post was located on the highest peak overlooking Sarobi and provided observation of Mujahideen groupings and artillery positions. The Owa-Tsalay out-post changed hands several times, but we finally held it. The DRA held the Mash'ala Base throughout the operation.

Our attack gained control of this stretch of the highway. DRA reaction was very slow and ineffective. DRA forces in Sarobi fired lots of artillery against my attacking force while their aircraft bombed suspected Mujahideen positions on the rocky ridges south and southwest of the gorge. DRA and Soviet helicopter gunships were not very effective since they did not dare fly low through the gorge or fly close to our positions. The DRA made no attempt to outflank NIFA positions from Sarobi or from the eastern mouth of the gorge at Mash'ala base. They also made no attempt to use heliborne troops to cut our supply and withdrawal routes.

From October 25 through the end of the operation, the enemy concentrated its efforts on building up forces at the two entrances of the gorge and continuously tried to demolish our roadblocks and regain control of the gorge section of highway. The DRA launched frontal attacks using infantry supported by tanks moving from   the Mash'ala base in the east and from Sarobi in the west. The DRA reinforced the beleaguered Mash'ala base with elements of the 11th DRA Division which had been operating in Alingar District of Laghman Province.

The DRA build-up from Laghman and Jalalabad was possible because Mujahideen groups from Nangrahar Province (task forces Hurricane, Gulf and Falcon) withdrew a week after overrunning their assigned objectives. The DRA had moved reinforcements and launched attacks in Nanagahar Province and the Mujahideen from that area left to defend their homes. Consequently the DRA was able to push more troops into the gorge from the east in an attempt to break through the main obstacles (between Dargo and Debili). From 25 through 31 October, the DRA launched several unsuccessful attempts to open the road and suffered losses in men and vehicles.

As the task forces Falcon, Gulf and Hurricane withdrew from their sectors, two mechanized columns of DRA moved into the area from two directions. Elements of 8th DRA Division, reinforced with Soviet elements, moved east from Kabul to Sarobi and tried to open the highway. Another column moved west from Jalalabad trying to overrun Mujahideen blocking positions between Dargo and Debili. The pressure of the two-pronged attack on the widely scattered Mujahideen groups and the lack of supplies forced me to narrow my front and concentrate in the four-kilometer stretch between Dargo and Debili between the two highway bridges which his Mujahideen had destroyed earlier.

From 1 to 6 November, the enemy moved bridge-building vehicles supported by tanks and motorized infantry to lay bridges across the Kabul river at Debili and Dargo. We Mujahideen repeatedly disrupted and defeated these attempts by firing from the high ground south of the narrow gorge. We also took DRA columns under cross-fire from well-prepared positions. During these attempts, the DRA lost several tanks, APCs and bridging equipment sets.

PHASE THREE

The third phase of the operation was the conduct a large-scale ambush before withdrawal. I ordered all Mujahideen task forces to observe complete radio silence and cease firing effective 2000 hours on 6 November. I further directed some Mujahideen to physically withdraw as part of the deception. The next morning, the entire front was quiet. The DRA moved freely along the highway and replaced the necessary bridges. At 1530 hours, the DRA started moving large mechanized columns across the Debili bridge toward Dargo, entering our "kill zone." A large number of vehicles entered the kill zone as traffic surged into the gorge from both directions. The two-way lanes were full of vehicles and a traffic bottleneck ensued. The head of the column coming from the east reached the repaired bridge at Debili and the head of the column coming from the west reached the newly-

Enemy Outposts Overrun:

1. Owa-Tselay Post
2. Sherkhan Upper Post
3. Gharray Post
4. Two outposts set between the Pul-e Estehkam bridge and Debili bases.
5. Two outposts around the Pul-e Estehkam Base
6. One outpost set between the Dargo and Pul-e Estehkam Bridge
7. Dargo post
8. Kalima Post
9. Girdabi Post
10. Toot Post
11. Soorey Tiga Post
12. Lakai Post
13. Tekas Post
14. Surkhakan Bridge Post
15. Khairokhel Post
16. Lower Khairokhel Post

Enemy Bases Overrun during the Operation

1. Debili Base
2. Dargo Base
3. Pul-e Estehkam Base
   (Engineer Bridge Base)
4. Tori Zhawari Base
5. Kaftarkhana Base
6. Spina Thana Base

restored bridge at Dargo. The four-kilometer stretch between the two restored bridges was jammed with traffic when I gave the signal to open fire. My Mujahideen opened fire along the entire front, taking the DRA by surprise. Mujahideen firing began at 1600 hours and continued until 1900 hours in the evening. We inflicted heavy losses on the trapped columns. The DRA columns retreated into Sarobi.

PHASE FOUR

My Mujahideen withdrew without DRA interference. They broke contact during the night following the ambush and returned to their bases.

DRA/Soviet Losses

Total losses during the entire operation include:

- Forty-two tanks and APCs, six BMPs, nine artillery pieces, one BM-13 MRL, one bulldozer, two cranes, 65 soft-skin vehicles, two jet aircraft and one helicopter gunship destroyed or damaged. Most vehicle losses were inflicted during the Phase 3 ambush.

- Over 500 soldiers killed or wounded and 212 soldiers and 11 officers captured.

- Four pistols, 261 assault rifles, two flare guns, three light machine guns, four medium (PK) machine guns, three heavy 7.62 machine guns, three 12.7 DShK machine guns, seven ZGU-1 14.5mm heavy machine guns, two AGS-17 automatic grenade launchers, thirteen RPG-7 antitank grenade launchers, seven medium 82mm mortars, and nineteen tactical radio sets captured.

Mujahideen Losses

18 killed and 53 wounded.

COMMENTARY: OPERATION ARROW was one of the few thoroughly-planned and fairly well-coordinated large-scale operations conducted by the Mujahideen. The command and staff and the Mujahideen combatants showed a high level of combat capability and resoluteness during the action. It was a complex, daring undertaking which achieved an ambitious goal. Considering the number of combatants, the time spent for preparation (two-three months according to General Wardak), the complexity of the planning, the amount of supplies needed to be moved to the battle area—mostly all the way from Pakistan across three provinces (Paktia, Logar, Nangrahar)—and the results achieved, it appears that OPERATION ARROW was an expensive and not very cost-effective venture.

OPERATION ARROW was driven more by political than military considerations. The Soviet Union was withdrawing from Afghanistan and, by this time, over half of the Soviet forces had already left. People expected the DRA to rapidly crumble once the Soviets were gone. The various political factions of the Mujahideen were jockeying for position in the post-communist government of Afghanistan. In order to maintain the interest and financial support of their Arab and Western backers, the Mujahideen had to demonstrate their ability to work together militarily—a cooperation that had been lacking (except, to some extent, in the fighting around Kandahar) throughout the war. This need for a show of military/political cooperation was one of the key factors in planning and conducting such a large-scale operation in this guerrilla war. OPERATION ARROW was a success and boosted Mujahideen prestige and particularly promoted the lagging image of the National Islamic Front of Afghanistan (NIFA), which enjoyed the greatest military success during the operation.

Militarily, the resources could have been better used by substituting a series of smaller actions (conducted successively by groups of about 50-70 Mujahideen at a time) at different points along the highway. These actions would each last for a few days over an extended period of time. Such an option, although not very spectacular, would effectively block the highway for a longer period of time than during OPERATION ARROW. The DRA losses would not have been spectacular each time but should have ended with higher over-all losses. While NIFA could afford to launch an "Arrow"-sized operation once a year, it could conduct several similar actions of smaller size with the same or less cost in men, material, time and other resources.

The political requirement to employ the forces of four Mujahideen factions to close the Kabul-Jalalabad highway for two weeks each was an expensive option. It required four separate deployments of forces, four separate plans of operation, three relief operations as one faction took over the task from another and four withdrawals. This inevitably entailed tactical and logistic duplications, unnecessary transportation costs, and the tactical complications involved with relieving one group by another over a wide front. Dividing the area into four sectors, each the responsibility of one faction for a period of eight weeks, would have achieved the same goal with fewer complications, lower costs, better logistic support, and more focused action. However, the lack of a unified political and military leadership and factional differences among the Mujahideen prevented this option.

The combined command and staff of the Mujahideen force showed a high level of professionalism and operational vision in both planning and execution. The movement of a large force from widely dispersed bases to the area of operation and providing for its logistic support using very limited local resources is an extremely challenging task.   The leadership of the force accomplished this with admirable effectiveness. The impact of the operation went far beyond the tactical and operational level, contributing to strategic and political destabilization of the Soviet-backed government in Kabul. The operation panicked the DRA government which committed unnecessarily-large forces into the area and accepted heavy casualties.

But the Mujahideen also paid a political price for the operation. The highway closure caused losses to civilian merchants who, at this time of the year, export pomegranates from Tagao and grapes from Kabul to Pakistan. The fresh fruit and vegetable trade is one of the major sources of income in Afghanistan. During the first week of November, representatives of fruit dealers appealed to the Mujahideen to open the highway, but to no avail. In a guerrilla war, support of the local population is too valuable to be risked by actions that hurt local economy.

Tactically, the DRA committed several errors. Inadequate DRA reconnaissance allowed the Mujahideen to deploy a several-thousand man force within a short distance of DRA positions without detection or interruption. Most of the Mujahideen movement took place at night and employed natural cover and concealment in the mountainous terrain. However, a more active DRA reconnaissance would have disclose the Mujahideen secret deployment and allowed countermeasures to interrupt the Mujahideen preparations for the operation. DRA failure to establish and man observation posts on the higher mountains also let the Mujahideen move into the area and prepare attack positions undetected.

The enemy forces in Sarobi were in a favorable tactical position to launch a flanking attack against the main base of the Mujahideen toward Hisarak. Such a move, supported by air and artillery support, should have foiled the Mujahideen operation and cut off their withdrawal. Such a move, supplemented by heliborne landings behind the Mujahideen lines, could have created chaos and forced the Mujahideen to abort the operation. The DRA reaction, however was reactive and unimaginative. The road-bound DRA forces paid heavily for this leadership failure.

Falling into the final Mujahideen ambush was the worst and the most costly DRA mistake. After the Mujahideen guns fell silent, the DRA did not bother to ensure that the silence really meant that the Mujahideen had withdrawn and was not a "calm before the storm." The DRA then allowed too much traffic to move down the unsecured highway. The DRA traffic jam occurred right in the Mujahideen kill zone.

The two following vignettes describe battles within OPERATION ARROW on the eastern approaches to the gorge.

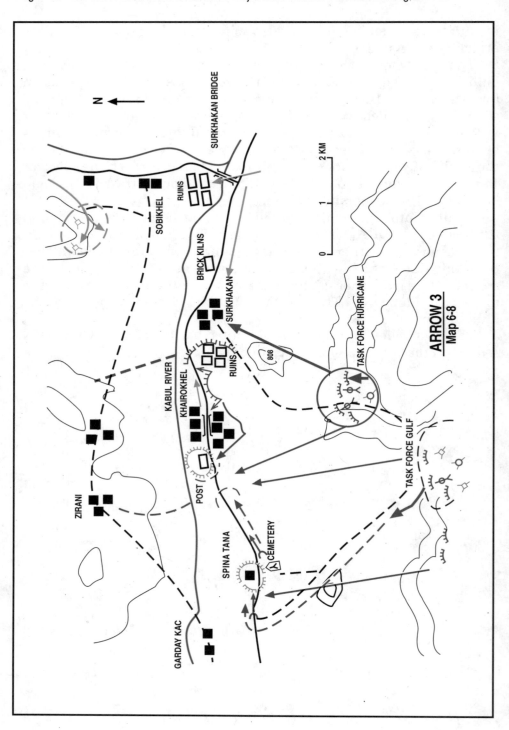

N

SURKHAKAN BRIDGE

RUINS

SOBIKHEL

BRICK KILNS

SURKHAKAN

KABUL RIVER

KHAIROKHEL

RUINS

808

TASK FORCE HURRICANE

POST

ZIRANI

TASK FORCE GULF

SPINA TANA

CEMETERY

GARDAY KAC

2 KM

1

0

ARROW 3
Map 6-8

THE BATTLE FOR THE KHAIROKHEL POST
by Asef Khan

I brought my 130 Mujahideen from our permanent base in Surkhrud District, southwest of Jalalabad to join OPERATION ARROW. My group was designated Task Force Hurricane. My group deployed at night into its attack position located in the folds of the Tor Ghar Mountain. My attack position was about 3 kilometers directly south of my objective—the Khairokhel post (Map 6-8 - Arrow 3).

Khairokhel post was located immediately west of the Khairokhel village. It was manned by a platoon-sized unit supported by two tanks and one APC. They also had mortars and machine guns including DShKs. There was another post connected with the Khairokhel defenses between the village and the Surkhakan Bridge Post to the east. The enemy would detach small teams during the day to patrol the main highway between Khairokhel and the Surkhakan bridge. The patrols would return to their base at night.

Task Force Gulf, commanded by Haji Zaman Ghamsharik, was deployed on the left flank of my group. Its mission was to attack the adjacent enemy base at Spina Thana. Further to the west, Task Force Falcon, commanded by Shari'ati and Lt. Wali, was to attack the Kaftarkhana Base. The right flank of my task force Hurricane was exposed and covered only by mountainous terrain.

I formed my task force into three groups: an assault group, a support group and a service detachment. There were 50 Mujahideen armed with assault rifles and 15 RPG-7 anti-tank grenade launchers in the assault group. The support group manned the heavy weapons including one BM-1, one 75mm gun, and three 82mm recoilless rifles.

At 2200 hours on the night of 22 October 1988, I took a few men down to the Khairokhel village on reconnaissance. I had dinner with the local elders and asked them to talk to the government post commander and convince him to abandon his positions rather than face attack. Following the meal, I completed my reconnaissance and returned to the attack position in the hills overlooking the village. It was so close to the enemy that an American female journalist who was accompanying my group said "If I were the government militia, you would not be able to survive a single night sitting so close to the

---

Asef Khan was the commander of Task Force Hurricane.

government post within range of heavy weapons."

The operational commander, General Rahim Wardak, radioed my adjacent commander, Haji Zaman, and told him that the attack time on the posts would be at 0800 hours, 23 October. When I returned from my reconnaissance, Haji Zaman relayed this information to me. I moved my raiding party into some ruins located one kilometer south of the Kabul-Jalalabad highway in preparation for the next mornings attack. I also set up an ambush near the highway to kill the patrol that left the Khairokhel post and moved toward the Surkhakan bridge every morning. My aim was to keep the area clear for my raid on the Khairokhel Post.

At 0700, a group of about 15 soldiers left the government post and started moving in the direction of Surkhakan bridge to set up security checkpoints. My Mujahideen let them clear the village and, as soon as they reached an open stretch of the road, opened fire from well-concealed positions near the road. My ambush killed six enemy soldiers and wounded a few others.

This action drew a heavy barrage from the enemy bases on either side of Khairokhel. Artillery and tanks were firing from the Spina Thana in the west and from Surkhakan Bridge Post on the east. At this point I radioed a coded message to Haji Zaman saying "get the dogs off my back." He immediately responded with heavy fire against the enemy base at Spina Thana. Haji Zaman's group was ready since it was 0800 hours, the time to start the attack.

Mujahideen fire on Spina Thana took the pressure off my Khairokhel sector. For several hours, Task Force Gulf exchanged fire with the Spina Thana base. Then, some direct hits on fuel drums set the fort ablaze. Task Force Gulf then attacked the enemy base.

As Task Force Gulf launched its attack against Spina Thana, I launched the main part of Task Force Hurricane against the enemy positions around the Khairokhel Post. I kept a security detachment east of the village to block enemy forces trying to enter the engagement area. The coordinated attacks of Task Forces Gulf and Hurricane overran the adjacent Spina Thana base and Khairokhel Post at about 1430 hours. My Mujahideen destroyed the tanks and APCs at the Khairokhel Post and, while part of my group established a perimeter defense around the captured post, the other part moved captured weapons and equipment to my mountain hideout. This continued all day.

During the attack, the enemy was moving communist officials of the Alingar District government to Jalalabad in a military convoy (at this time, due to the ongoing Soviet withdrawal, the communist regime was withdrawing its military and administrative units from those remote areas which could not be easily maintained or defended). This convoy deployed in the Mehtar-e Lam Baba hills north of the Kabul river and began to employ long-range artillery and rocket fire across a wide front stretching from Khairokhel to Kaftarkhana. Their artillery and BM-21 multiple rocket launchers were firing at a range of over 10 kilometers, so their fire was not very accurate or effective. However, later in the day, part of the column moved along the main road toward the battle area and tried to cross the Surkhakan bridge. The enemy base at Kaftarkhana was still alive. However it was under attack by Shari'ati's group and could not spare its fire against the Mujahideen in adjacent areas.

In order to contain the movement of the enemy column, I moved my assault group with all available RPG-7s to positions facing the Surkhakan bridge. I also destroyed the highway bridge at Khairo-khel village with demolition charges that we had brought for this purpose all the way from our home base. The enemy tanks and APCs in his column came under flanking fire from my RPGs. The enemy could not hit my RPG gunners since they were protected by a steep turn in the road. The enemy could not flank my position since the off-road areas were heavily mined and the blown bridge prevented a frontal assault. This significantly boosted my Mujahideen's morale and gave them a sense of improved security. For some reason, enemy air activity was weak despite the fact that the area was open and the fight was going on in broad daylight.

At dusk the enemy column pushed its infantry out front to clear the way for the vehicles, but it did not make any headway. Later, as we moved our spoils and POWs to their mountain positions in the south, I withdrew my security elements from the highway since the enemy was moving yet another motorized column into the area from Jalalabad. By the next day, Task Forces Falcon, Gulf and Hurricane had withdrawn their forces from along the highway. The enemy columns coming from Jalalabad and Laghman moved slowly down the road all the way to Mash'ala Base and reinforced it. The Mujahideen never overran this base and it played a pivotal role in maintaining enemy's presence.

Following this, I limited our action to firing our heavy weapons at enemy targets on the highway. Shortly thereafter, I withdrew my Mujahideen from the operation since DRA forces had moved into my district and were threatening our homes.

COMMENTARY: The confident commander's meal with the village elders certainly helped his reconnaissance, but clearly tipped off the defending DRA commander that the Mujahideen attack might come soon. On the other hand, the Mujahideen had been in the area for some time. Further, the guerrilla commander apparently assumed that all the local inhabitants were favorably disposed to the Mujahideen. His brash behavior succeeded this time, but could have compromised operational security. Apparently, the DRA commander took no action to increase his defenses and may not have even informed his superior.

Apparently, the Mujahideen lacked enough working radios so that each Task Force Commander could have one. General Wardak could not rapidly influence the course of the battle since communications were scarce. Further, General Wardak lacked radio communications with his eastern flank. This seems a serious problem in case the DRA decided to roll up his operation from that flank.

Once the Mujahideen withdrew to the hills, their long-range fires had little apparent effect. Their early departure, however, did create additional problems for General Wardak.

VIGNETTE 6B
THE BATTLE FOR SPINA THANA BASE
based on interviews with Haji Zaman Ghamsharik

I commanded the 200-man Task Force Gulf (See Map 6-8 - Arrow 3). As part of OPERATION ARROW, I launched my attack on the government base at Spina Thana in coordination with attacks on the Khairokhel Post to the east and Kaftarkhana Base to the west. Spina Thana was one of the main military bases providing security for columns moving along the Kabul-Jalalabad highway. It also patrolled against guerrilla incursions across the Kabul River into Laghman Province. A reinforced company supported by tanks, BMPs, APCs, heavy machine gun and guns garrisoned the base. They protected the base with mines and other obstacles. The entire area surrounding the base, except the paved highway running through the base was heavily mined.

Spina Thana would be a tough nut to crack. I could assign up to 150 Mujahideen to the assault group, but using such a large force for the attack carried some risks. I could incur heavy casualties since the group could not effectively deploy due to the mines. I considered a night attack, but this was equally difficult because of the mines, particularly since the enemy habitually mined the exits and entrances to the base at night. I decided on a day-light attack. I intended to move part of my force as close to the base as possible under heavy covering fire. I decided to put my attacking force on the highway outside the mined area and move on the highway in the attack. This was the only route guaranteed free of mines.

I constituted a Task Force support group which manned our BM-12 and BM-1 MRL, 82mm recoilless rifles, ZGU-1 and DShK heavy machine guns and mortars. I positioned it in the terrain folds of Tor Ghar dominating the enemy base on the low ground between the main highway and Kabul river.

I had to begin my planned fires earlier than intended when Task Force Hurricane came under heavy fire from the Spina Thana Base. The enemy responded resolutely to my fires. The fire exchange went

---

Haji Zaman Ghamsharik was the commander of Task Force Gulf. At the start of the war, Ghamsharik controlled Khogiani District. He faked a defection to the DRA and requested that the DRA provide him trained personnel to run the district. The DRA responded by sending him 71 communists—who were promptly executed.

on unabated until my Mujahideen gunners set part of the base on fire with some direct hits. This was the turning point in the battle. As panic spread throughout the defenders, I led a 60-man assault group through a ravine to the west of the base. We got on the highway and attacked east. I instructed my men to stay on the pavement. Two of my Mujahideen who strayed had their legs blown off by mines. We moved quickly to the base entrance. The defenders had little time to mount an organized defense, particularly since some of the defenders had fled from their positions in panic and were rushing to the river to escape the fire. We met little resistance in storming the base. We captured scores of defenders including the base commander, Rahmatullah Spelanay. We destroyed the tanks and APCs and whatever else could not be moved. We continued the attack to the east to help Task Force Hurricane which was locked in battle with the defenders of the Khairokhel Post. As we Mujahideen advanced from two directions, most of the Khairokhel defenders fled toward the river. We captured the rest. The actions for the rest of the day unfolded as detailed in the preceding vignette.

COMMENTARY: One estimate claims that the Soviets left over 13 million landmines behind in Afghanistan. The Soviets and DRA surrounded their outposts and bases with minefields. A major Mujahideen problem in capturing a position was getting through the minefield. Mujahideen minefield clearing methods included:

- probing the ground cautiously in a slow advance;

- driving a flock of sheep through the minefield;

- heaving boulders ahead of an advance to provide stepping stones for the advance;

- firing recoiless rifles into the minefield and creating a path via the recoiless rifle craters;

- limited use of some mineclearing systems provided by western and Arab backers.

CHAPTER COMMENTARY

Control of the highway net was essential to the Soviet/DRA effort, but in some regions, the Mujahideen were able to block the highway for weeks, months and even years. The best blocks were maintained by local Mujahideen who were able to look after their personal interests and yet maintain an effective blockade. The least effective road blocks were those done by mobile guerrillas who lacked the supplies and commitment required to keep the road closed.

CHAPTER 7
SIEGE WARFARE

The Mujahideen besieged several isolated DRA garrisons. If the besieging Mujahideen were local, then the siege went on indefinitely. If outside Mujahideen were involved, the siege usually failed since the Mujahideen could not maintain the supplies necessary for the siege or keep enough of the Mujahideen in place. Since the Mujahideen were unpaid volunteers who also had family responsibilities, they were seldom interested in staying around for uninteresting, lengthy sieges.

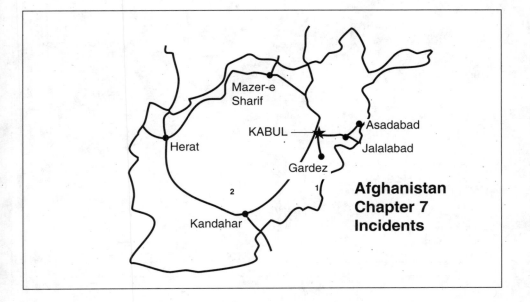

Afghanistan
Chapter 7
Incidents

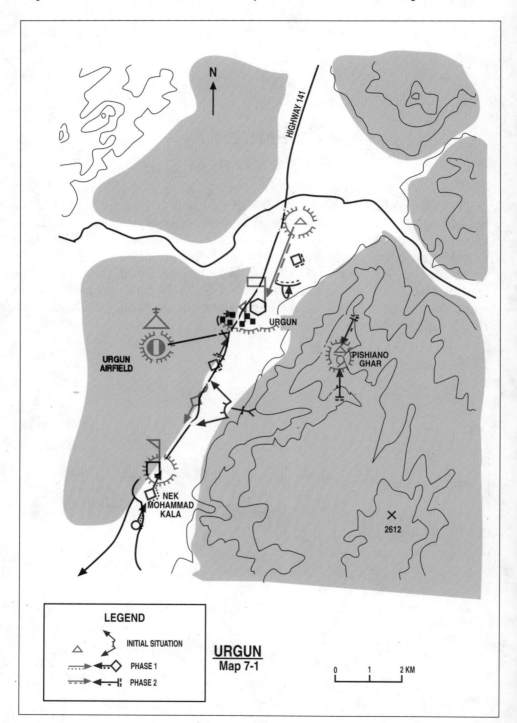

N

HIGHWAY 141

URGUN

URGUN
AIRFIELD

PISHIANO
GHAR

NEK
MOHAMMAD
KALA

✕
2612

LEGEND

INITIAL SITUATION

PHASE 1

PHASE 2

URGUN
Map 7-1

0   1   2 KM

FAILED SIEGE AT URGUN
by General Gulzarak Zadran

Urgun was the home of the DRA's 21st Mountain Regiment. It is located near the Pakistan border and is close to the strategic positions of Khost, Gardez, and Ghazni, as well as Waziristan, Pakistan. Once, after the Mujahideen formed their government in exile, they wanted to make Urgun the symbolic seat of their government. Despite the fact that Urgun is located in an isolated area, its political significance prompted the DRA and Soviet forces to keep it under control at all costs. One of the major Mujahideen actions at Urgun took place in 1983. About 800 Mujahideen from the Wazir, Zadran, and Kharoti tribes took part. Major commanders at the seige included Mawlawi Jalaluddin Haqani, Mawlawi Arsalah, Matiullah, Mawlawi Ahmad Gul and Qauzi Kharoti. The military council for the seige included Captain Abdul Majid, Major Arsala Wazir, Captain Qayum, Captain Sardar, Amanullah, Mawlawi Abdul Ghafur and me. The regiment's main force was located in the old fortress at Urgun which is commonly called the Octagonal Fort (*Hashtrakha Kala*). It had one battalion based in another fort four kilometers south of the regiment at Nek Mohammad Kala. A reinforced company held the airfield to the west of the regimental headquarters. Another company protected the main road to Urgun at a post some 1.5 kilometers to the north. (Map 7-1 - Urgun)

We planned to destroy the regiment in two phases. The first phase would destroy the security around the main headquarters (the southern battalion plus the two outlying companies). The second phase would destroy the regimental headquarters. The first phase began in August 1983. The Mujahideen based in the mountains east of Urgun Valley encircled and besieged the battalion at Nek Mohammad Kala. This enemy battalion was deployed in a fort which had several towers. The fort was surrounded by minefields and heavy ZGU-1 machine

General Gulzarak Zadran was an officer in the Royal Afghan Army. He trained in the United States and attended the Afghan Army Higher Officers Training Institute, where the author, Ali Jalali, was his instructor. He joined the resistance and fought in Paktia Province. He fought in Zhawar one and two and at the Satakandow pass. He belonged to Abdul-Rab Russul Sayyaf's Islamic Union of Afghanistan (IUA). After the fall of the DRA, he became the Deputy Minister of Defense in the interim government. Currently he lives near Peshawar. [Map sheet 2882].

guns were positioned in the towers which made it impossible for the Mujahideen to approach close to the fort. This prevented the Mujahideen from tightening their seige on the fort.

A few days after the seige began, the religious Festival of Sacrifice (*Eid-al-Adha*) occured. It was customary for Mujahideen to go home during the festival and the enemy felt that few Mujahideen would still be around. This time, however, we did not let our people go home but kept them at their bases. Thinking that the Mujahideen were not a threat, the DRA took advantage of the holiday and sent three tanks and a few trucks from the main regimental base to resupply the battalion. We put an ambush force of approximately 70 Mujahideen, commanded by Mawlawi Hasan, in a dry stream bed about halfway between the two forts. Among their weapons were some RPG-7s. When the DRA column entered the kill zone, he sprang the ambush. The ambush destroyed one tank and damaged another. The ambushers killed some DRA soldiers and captured 25. Some others escaped. The DRA abandoned one intact tank, but the Mujahideen could not retrieve it due to heavy machine gun fire from the battalion's fort. The fire forced the Mujahideen force back into a side canyon. When night fell, Mawlawi Hasan and Khan Zamak led a group of Mujahideen back to the intact tank. The Mujahideen group included some former DRA tank crewmen. They drove the tank away to their position.

We planned to attack the battalion fort three days later, using the tank as the main weapon. We formed an 11-man tank protection group and mounted them on the tank. They were armed with some RPGs and small arms. They would ride the tank during a night advance through the antipersonnel minefield that surrounded the fort. In case the tank got stuck, the tank protection group would protect the tank and free it. A 65-man assault force would follow in the tracks of the tank as it passed throught the minefield. The tank crew would blow a hole in the wall of the fort using the main gun of the tank. The 11-man tank protection crew would then dismount and secure the hole opening and the 65-man assault team would enter the fort. Mujahideen communications personnel would also help in the assault by interrupting the communications between the battalion and regiment. When possible, the radio operators would misdirect the artillery.[1]

---

[1] It was common practice for Mujahideen and DRA to enter each others radio nets for deception, harassment or to pass messages. General Gulzarak would often talk to the other side and curse and insult them.

At 2100 hours, the attack started. The Mujahideen tank moved on its designated route with the tank protection crew mounted on top. As it approached the fort and crossed the antipersonnel mine-field, a few antipersonnel mines exploded, but the tank protection crew was unscathed. The tank crew opened fire on the fort's towers with their main gun. The main gun rounds knocked out the heavy machine guns. However, the artillery located with the regimental headquarters began firing into the area. Our Mujahideen communications personnel began screaming into the radio their fire was short and was falling on the battalion. The artillery command post became confused with their demands that the fire be shifted further away. The artillery stopped firing. The Mujahideen tank crew then fired at the wall of the fort. After several rounds, they knocked a hole in the wall. The tank drove to within ten meters of the wall and the tank protection crew signaled the assault group with a flashlight. The tank protection crew immediately dismounted and secured the breach. The assault group followed in the tank's tracks and entered the fort. The enemy was surprised by the sudden breach and offered no resistance. The Mujahideen captured 243 men plus all the weapons and ammunition in the fort. We let those DRA prisoners who wanted to join us. We released the others. We were now four kilometers closer to the main fort.

Pishiano Ghar (the mountain of the cats) overlooks the octagonal fortress. The regiment had a security post with mortars located on the mountain. Our next move was to seize the security post so that the seige would become more effective. A few days later, 70 Mujahideen attacked the security post from the north and south in a night attack. The Mujahideen attack was successful. Once we controlled Pishiano Ghar, the regiment pulled back the company that protected highway 141 to the regimental base. We prepared for phase two. The enemy was now completely beseiged and could not receive supplies by road and had to get supplies by air. The beseiged DRA could only get to the airfield, located some 1.5 kilometers to the west of the fortress, by armored vehicles, since we could take out trucks and jeeps. Our machine guns on Pishiano Ghar prevented DRA resupply by day. We continued to tighten the seige. Mujahideen from Zadran brought their tank to help out.

The DRA brought in an operations group from Kabul. Their job was to help the regiment plan its defense and a linkup with a Soviet unit which was coming from Ghazni to break the seige. DRA General Jamaluddin Omar was in charge of the group. He was my old tactics instructor at the Royal Afghan Military Academy. The DRA spread their 3rd battalion in the south of the city instead of in the fort. They had two companies in the forward defensive line. To the southeast, natural ditches and ravines created barriers to our advance. The airfield lay to the west. One approach to west of the airfield was inadequately mined, so the DRA covered the gap with guards and patrols.

Besides our two tanks, we had two 76mm mountain guns, one 122mm D30 howitzer, one 107mm mountain mortar, other lighter mortars, many RPGs, many DShK and ZGU heavy machine guns and other lighter machine guns. It was January and snow was on the ground. We covered part of our tanks with white cloth to hide them. We recorded the sound of a moving tank. We received some loud-speakers from Peshawar and assigned people to use them on the eastern flank to depict tanks coming from the east. We structured our forces for the assault by creating several groups:

- A tank and tank protection group commanded by Mawlawi Shadam
- Two assault groups—Northern and Southern
- An evacuation group to carry away the spoils.
- A family and dependents protection group to protect the families of DRA officers who were in the garrison
- A truck transport group
- A command and control group

We planned the attack. Following an artillery preparation, a tank would spearhead the assault from the north and the south to clear a path through the antipersonnel minefields. An assault group would follow in the tank's tracks to hit the enemy from two sides simultaneously.

I was with the southern forces. At 2000 hours on a cold January night, our Mujahideen were all in position. We started artillery preparatory fire on the DRA positions. Ten minutes later, our tank moved north toward the city. The tank fired on two city towers and knocked out the machine guns in them. Then we turned on the loud-speakers in the southeast to create tank noises there. The enemy fired at the noises as our tank changed direction and headed west where it could reach the unmined area. Fifteen Mujahideen, including Mawlawi Shadam, Ismail Turkistani and me were on the tank as it entered the city. As we passed through the mined area, we dismounted and moved to the rear of the 3d battalion. Assault group south followed the tank's tracks into the city. They stormed through the city and the 3d battalion resistance collapsed. Battalion person-nnel either surrendered or retreated north. As the Mujahideen continued to advance, we were stopped by the fire of a DShK machine gun some 50 meters to our north. It was now 0300 in morning. We attacked the position and killed the gunner—a Soviet adviser. The rest of the DRA regiment had retreated into the fortress with General Jamaluddin Omar.

At this point, Mawlawi Shadam reported that his tank was out of ammunition. The tank driver, Lt Mohammad Gul Logari, was wound-ed in the arm and the gunner was killed. The enemy resolve was strengthening and showing renewed resistance. Other Mujahideen in the assault group were running low on ammunition. We had failed to plan for ammunition resupply. We instructed Mawlawi Shadam to take the tank and go back to get all types of ammunition and then return to resupply and support our combatants. As the tank moved back, the Mujahideen and the DRA heard it and thought that we were withdrawing. It was cold, early in the morning and our command and control was collapsing. Mujahideen began to fall back. The enemy counterattacked and pushed us out of the city. Daybreak came with the disorganized Mujahideen milling around outside the city. Wave after wave of enemy aircraft appeared and began bombing and straf-fing the Mujahideen caught in the open. They destroyed our tank. We retreated into the mountains.

I later learned that the northern assault group had not moved that night since their tank was stuck in the sand and they could not free it. The entire assault was from the south. This cost us an almost certain victory. We had no other choice but to withdraw into our mountain hideouts in the east. In the following days, as we were preparing to resume the seige, a Soviet regiment arrived in Urgun from Ghazni to resupply and reinforce the Urgun garrison.

COMMENTARY: Ammunition resupply was clearly a problem and the withdrawal of the tank at a critical juncture turned the tide of battle. Communications was as big a problem. The Mujahideen had radios, but they were not able to accompany the assault forces. The northern and southern assault groups were unable to communicate with each other and, presumably, with the command and control group. If both attacks had occured, prevention of fratricide would have been a diffi-cult problem without radio communications. Further, members of the military council were forward with the assault forces rather than directing the battle.

Mujahideen air defense planning was also limited. The natural air approach into Urgun follows highway 141 in a north-south direction. The Mujahideen had heavy machine guns and control of the high ground flanking the approach. Evidently, most of the machine guns were used to fire on DRA ground forces and the air defense posture was degraded at the time of the Soviet air response.

Mine clearance was a continual problem for Mujahideen forces and the use of tanks to clear lanes through antipersonnel minefields and to breach a hole in the fortress walls deserves high marks. The use of a tank protection group, mounted on the tank, was a tactical innovation that worked well. This may not seem a tactical innovation to professional officers who always keep infantry up with their tanks, but it was not a common practice when Mujahideen acquired armor. The presence of professional officers, like General Zadran, was responsible for the formation of the tank protection group.

VIGNETTE 2
DEHRAWUD OFFENSIVE

In the spring and summer of 1984, the Soviet forces stepped up their attacks on Mujahideen hideouts and mobile bases in the three adjoining provinces of Kandahar, Helmand and Uruzgan. The Soviets also intensified their efforts to intercept Mujahideen supply convoys coming through the mountains from Pakistan. In the fall, a number of major Mujahideen commanders in these provinces decided to set up a regional supply base in the Uruzgan Mountains that could support Mujahideen units deployed in the area. Dehrawud District, located in Uruzgan Province, seemed to be a suitable place for the supply base. It is an oasis in the mountains in the upper Helmand Valley. It is easy to defend and it is conveniently located between the three provinces (Map 7-2 - Dehrawud).

The Dehrawud District capital of Dehrawud was garrisoned by some 500 government militia who manned security outposts around the town. They were supplied by air since the town was blockaded by the local Mujahideen who controlled all the roads leading into the town. The Mujahideen council decided to attack the government enclave, dislodge the militia and consolidate control over the entire valley. To do this, however, they first had to negotiate a truce between rival groups in the region to ensure their full cooperation during the upcoming operation. Two months before the action, Mujahideen delegations from Kandahar and Helmand mediated such a truce.

In October, Mujahideen forces from Kandahar under Mulla Malang, Faizullah and other leaders joined a contingent of Helmand Mujahideen commanded by the late Nasim Akhund Zada, the leading resistance figure in Helmand Province. Haji Assadullah and some Mujahideen fighters from Uruzgan and Baghran areas joined the attacking force. This force eventually numbered over 1,000 men. The Mujahideen force moved along different approaches to Dehrawud and surrounded the government positions in the area. A 300-man detachment sealed off the main approach to Dehrawud from the south along the Helmand River. Another 100-man detachment deployed to the southeast to cover the Kotal-e Murcha (the Murcha pass) and mine its

---

Sources for this vignette include Commander Mulla Malang, Akhund Zada Qasem, several Mujahideen from Uruzgan, Kandahar and Helmand Provinces and Mr. Jalali's personal notes and papers.

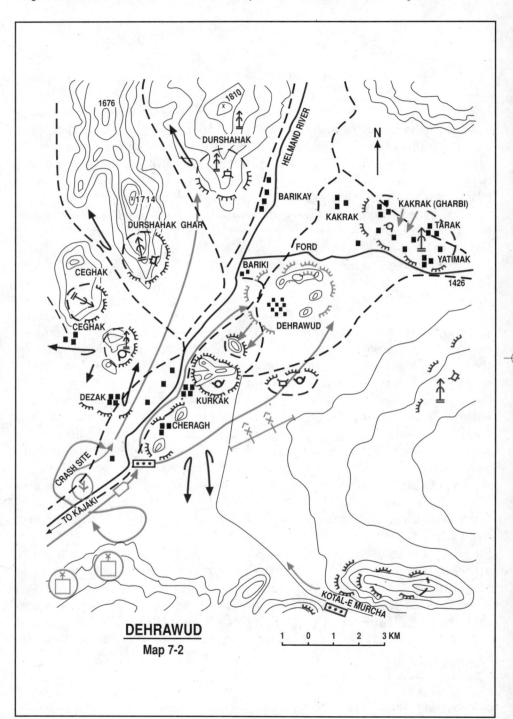

DEHRAWUD

Map 7-2

road. About 500 fighters deployed around the district center, while the rest were engaged in fulltime logistic support.

The siege lasted 45 days while the Mujahideen gradually tightened the noose around the militia positions. The Mujahideen kept only one third of the fighters on the front line at any one time. The rest were either in reserve or involved in logistic service. The front line fighters were relieved every 24 hours.

The Soviets and DRA supported the Dehrawud garrison with daily air strikes on Mujahideen positions to check their advance. They would run two or three attack missions daily using fighter bombers and helicopter gunships. In the meantime, the Soviet/DRA command assembled ground forces from Kandahar and Shindand to relieve the embattled militia at Dehrawud. However, it took the enemy weeks before he was ready to move large columns of infantry and tanks to the mountainous battlefield.

One day, a Mujahideen gun crew on a ZGU-1 anti-aircraft heavy machine gun shot down one of a pair of Soviet fighter-bombers flying over Dehrawud. The plane burst into flames and fell in the Helmand River. The pilot, said to be a high ranking officer,[2] bailed out and landed five to six kilometers from the nearest Mujahideen position. The other fighter circled the area and flew away apparently after pinpointing the crash site of the fallen plane. A seven-man Mujahideen team under Mulla Juma Khan went to capture the pilot. By the time the Mujahideen reached the pilot, he had moved to a position from which he could fire his AK-74 at the advancing resistance fighters. The Mujahideen tried to capture the pilot alive. While they were preparing to try and capture him, a swarm of transport helicopters and helicopter gunships flew over the Kotal-e Murcha pass from Kandahar and began gun runs against the Mujahideen positions. Two helicopters hovered over the crash site. One hovered about 50 meters from the ground and lowered a ladder. The Soviet pilot jumped up from his hideout and started climbing up the ladder. Seeing that the Soviet pilot was escaping, the Mujahideen opened fire and killed the pilot and damaged the helicopter. The helicopter tried to escape but crashed about three kilometers away.

This incident triggered increased Soviet air activity as they tried to soften up the area for the upcoming attack by ground forces moving on two axes to Dehrawud. One column was approaching along the Helmand River from Kajaki dam and the other from Khakrez across the Kotal-e Murcha pass. For three days, Soviet air strikes continued

---

Mulla Malang states that he was a general officer.

uninterrupted from dawn to dusk. However, the Mujahideen suffered fewer casualties than the militiamen, who sustained losses from both collateral damage and "friendly fire."

Following three days of heavy bombardment, a column of enemy infantry and tanks arrived from the Kajaki side. Although the Mujahideen groups assigned to cover this approach had left earlier, the terrain did not support tank movement. A Soviet Movement Support Detachment (MSD) used road construction machines and demolitions to open a way through the rocky approaches to Dehrawud for the tanks and APCs. The Soviets conducted airmobile insertions of soldiers on the heights overlooking the movement route to provide flank security.

By this time, the Mujahideen were too widely dispersed for effective control. The contingents from Kandahar and Helmand were on opposite sides of the Helmand River and could not cross it. Their heavy weapons, such as the ZGU-1, DShK and surface-to-surface rockets were also positioned on both sides of the river. Their fires could not be coordinated. Five days after they killed the Soviet pilot on the Helmand River, the Mujahideen realized that they had lost command and control over the scattered detachments and could not deal with the two-pronged enemy advance. Therefore, the Mujahideen groups withdrew to their separate provincial bases by mountain paths.

The Soviet column from Kajaki reached Dehrawud and recovered the body of the dead pilot. The Mujahideen had removed his documents earlier. As the Mujahideen pulled out, the column from Kandahar stopped at Khakrez and did not proceed to Dehrawud. It conducted a number of search and destroy actions in the area and returned. During the entire 45-day battle, the DRA militia incurred the heaviest losses. Mujahideen casualties were negligible. Mulah Malang states that the Mujahideen shot down a jet fighter and 10 helicopters.

COMMENTARY: This Mujahideen seige was a conventional battle by a guerrilla force. It ended in a tactical setback. Had the Mujahideen established an operational command system in the region, it would have been easier for them to coordinate their action in terms of time and space. Lack of such an arrangement left a sizeable Mujahideen force without operational support by other local groups, especially in blocking the movement of Soviet/DRA reinforcements.

Guerrilla forces are best employed for actions of short duration. Long, extended operations, such as this seige, asks a lot of unpaid volunteers. The Mujahideen did assign detachments to cover the approaches to Dehrawud from the south, but, as the seige continued, many of the fighters found more pressing business to attend to then sitting idly on a mountain. They departed one after another and left the approaches open. Both the Kajaki axis and the Kotal-e Murcha axis were very easy to block with a small detachment of determined fighters. If the Mujahideen had held their positions, they could have stopped the large columns of their enemy and celebrated a Mujahideen victory in Dehrawud. But, once again, the Mujahideen experience demonstrated their tactical and logistical limitations in maintaining control over large forces for an extended period of time. Most of the Mujahideen were not fighting on their home territory and, therefore, were less enthusiastic about remaining in stationary positions for an extended period of time while the Soviet Air Force attacked them.

Air power, while seldom decisive in guerrilla war, played a major role in breaking this seige. Once the Mujahideen assumed static positions, the Soviet Air Force was able to delay the Mujahideen assault and gain the time needed for the ground forces to reach the battlefield.

CHAPTER 8
DEFENDING AGAINST RAIDS

Effective defense against ground raids requires timely intelligence, plans and battle drills, prepared fighting and sheltered positions, a ready reaction force, accessible weapons and ammunition, escape routes, security patrols and sentries and early warning elements posted far enough away to provide adequate early warning. Rehearsal of plans, battle drills, the ready reaction force and escape and withdrawal are essential to effective defense against raids.

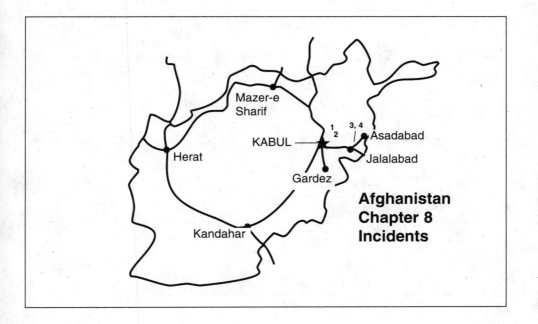

**Afghanistan
Chapter 8
Incidents**

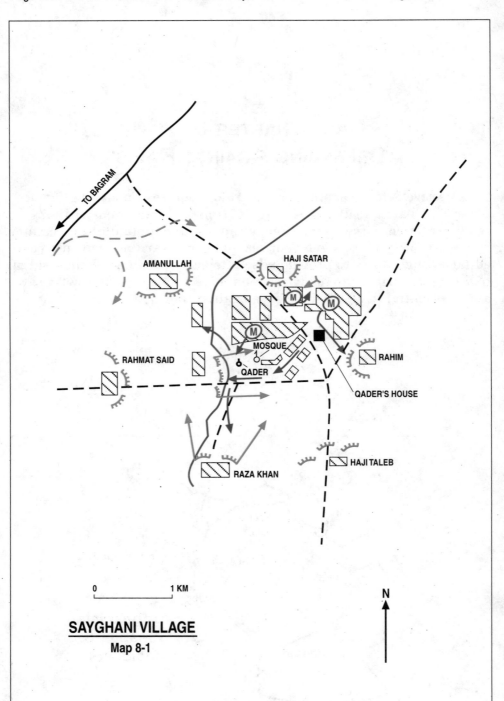

SAYGHANI VILLAGE

Map 8-1

VIGNETTE 1
SOVIET RAID ON MUJAHIDEEN HIDEOUT AT SAYGHANI
by Haji Abdul Qader

On 9 January 1981, a Soviet detachment mounted a raid on my home in Sayghani Village, about six kilometers northeast of Bagram air base. At that time, I commanded a group of some 200 local Mujahideen who were spread among several mobile bases in the area. We would conduct specific missions in Bagram and neighboring districts in Parwan and Kapisa Provinces. I rarely spent the night in my village since it is very close to the Soviet garrison at Bagram[1] and difficult to defend. I would alternate among my mobile bases and would stay at a different location every night. I was usually accompanied by no more than 20 of my men who were disguised as peaceful civilians.

A week before, JIA Commander Mawlawi Zaher of Gujarkhel and I combined forces to ambush a Soviet/DRA column at Sofi Baba along the road from Koh-e Top to Sayad. The column had seven or eight trucks and six APCs. The column was returning from Khanaqa and Niazi in the south where the DRA had conducted a press gang to draft recruits into the DRA army. We ambushed their column at dusk and destroyed two APCs and four trucks with short-range RPG-7 fire. We captured some 70 Kalashnikovs, which we desperately needed. We divided the weapons between our two groups. I believe that the raid on my home was in retaliation for this ambush.

That night I had some guests from Laghman and entertained them until late in the evening in my house in the village. In the late evening, I sent most of my men to other villages and kept about 40 at Sayghani (22 of them were residents of the village).

Sayghani is a village of about 100 homes located off the main road. My home is near the village mosque, protected by several fort-like structures ringing the village (Map 8-1 - Sayghani). I posted two guard details—one at my house and the other at the mosque. The night was very quiet and at midnight the snow began to fall. Early in the morning, I woke up for morning prayer. The guards on my roof reported

---

Haji Abdul Qader was a school teacher who became a Mujahideen commander. He was initially with the HIK faction and later with the IUA faction. [Map sheet 2886, vic grid 2970]. Mr. Anthon Jalali's notes also used in this vignette.

[1] The Soviet 682nd Motorized Rifle Regiment and the 354th Separate Airborne Regiment were garrisoned in Bagram.

that everything was all right. However, when I was half way through ablutions,[2] I noticed signal flares streaking across the cloudy sky. They were coming from the northeast and southeast.

The night may have seemed quiet to my guards, but it was busy for the Soviet raiding detachment. Led by local guides and informants, the raiders had stealthily walked from Bagram to the village during the snowfall and quietly occupied several buildings around the village. By dawn, the enemy had taken up positions at Haji Satar, Rahim, Haji Taleb, Raza Khan, Haji Rahmat Sayed and Amanullah forts.[3]

As soon as I saw the flares, I asked the guards about it. They said that they thought that the enemy was on the road to the village some two kilometers away. I thought that the flares were much closer. I had no time to gather all my men, so I took the 15 men who were staying in my house and we tried to exfiltrate from the village. Shortly after we left my house, I realized that I had forgotten my briefcase full of data about my group. I sent my younger brother to fetch the briefcase and ordered my men to move down the road to the mosque and then on the Rahmat Said fort at the edge of the village. From there, we would take the path to Mujahideen-held areas. I waited for my brother. A few minutes later he joined me and we hurried after the group. We caught up with the group as they approached the stream beyond the mosque. The stream bed was full of Soviet soldiers in ambush. They opened up on my group with AK-74s and killed three of my men on the spot. The rest of my group disappeared in the dark and moved to the southwest, where they were soon trapped in another ambush and killed to the last man. An enemy tracer bullet had set my *tsadar* on fire. My brother warned me that I was on fire. I pulled off my burning *tsadar* and threw it away, but that attracted the attention of the first ambush group who again opened up on us and killed my brother. I had lost contact with my group and so I moved in the opposite direction and slipped out through a house at the edge of the village. The enemy had blocked all streets and escape routes and none of my Mujahideen survived the raid. The enemy killed all 40 Mujahideen and 15 civilians at different locations in the village.

COMMENTARY: Lack of effective security contributed decisively to the Soviet success and led to the destruction of the resistance force. Combat security should protect a unit from surprise attack and

---

[2] Muslims pray five times a day and wash before prayers.

[3] Many of the home in Afghanistan are surrounded by high, thick adobe walls and are actually small forts.

provide sufficient time and space for the main body to prepare and deploy for combat in the most favorable conditions possible. Had the Mujahideen posted security patrols on the approaches to the village, the Soviets probably would have been unable to approach undetected and to surprise the unprepared resistance fighters. The two guard details that Commander Qader deployed inside the village could provide only close-in protection but could not provide early warning or tactical security for the unit.

The secrecy of the Soviet movement to the village and their stealthy deployment at the village played a decisive role in the outcome of the raid. Taken by surprise, the Mujahideen lost control of the situation and were forced to act under conditions dictated by the Soviets.

The Mujahideen could have avoided the disaster by preparing contingency plans with clear-cut instructions to the combatants and group leaders in the event of surprise attack. The plan would determine the location of each combatant and sub-group leader during their overnight stay in the village. Bagram was a major Soviet installation and the overconfidence and bravado of the Mujahideen contributed to their defeat.

Once he discovered the Soviet presence, the Mujahideen commander did little to establish effective command and control over the situation. He said that he did not have time to reach every combatant and sub-group leader. But the commander failed to lead even the small 15-man group that was with him. He waited for his briefcase and told his men to proceed without assigning a group leader in his absence. This group was leaderless as it blundered into the two ambushes.

Local informers and collaborators were also vital to the Soviet success. The Soviet detachment could not have achieved its goal without help from the inside. Such cases of collaboration created a lot of suspicion among the Mujahideen and sometimes resulted in very tragic consequences to innocent people.

Haji Abdul Qader learned a very important lesson at a very high price. As he says, his group never again stayed overnight in Sayghani without posting a strong security detail on approaches to the village at points not less than two kilometers from the place.

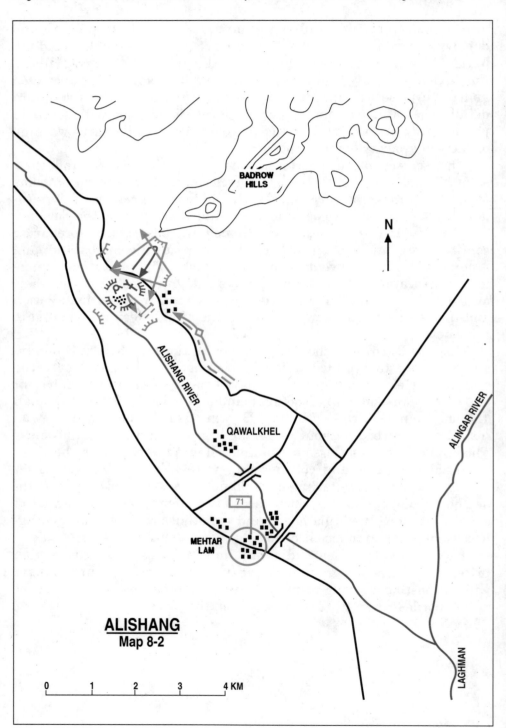

BADROW HILLS

N

ALISHANG RIVER

ALINGAR RIVER

QAWALKHEL

71

MEHTAR LAM

LAGHMAN

ALISHANG
Map 8-2

0   1   2   3   4 KM

VIGNETTE 2
BATTLE FOR ALISHANG DISTRICT CENTER
by Commander Sher Padshah

In August 1981, the Mujahideen controlled the district center of Alishang in Laghman Province. My base was in a remote upper valley near Daulatshah. I brought 29 of my Mujahideen south through the fertile Alishang Valley to Alishang Village. (Map 8-2 - Alishang) This is a trip of over 45 kilometers. When we arrived, we were very tired and the local Mujahideen, who numbered 50, told us to sleep and that they would provide security. In the morning, as we were rising for morning prayers, we heard shots. The guards then realized that we were surrounded. We decided to escape into the mountains. The Badrow hills are about three kilometers northeast of the village and lead to the mountains. As we tried to get out of the village, we came under fire from all directions. Within five minutes, we lost 14 Mujahideen KIA and 50 WIA. Mawlawi Niaz Mohammed, the local Mujahideen commander, was among the dead. Faced with withering fire and heavy losses, we retreated back into the village to conduct a desperate defense.

Our force was down to 15 Mujahideen but our mortars were still in position from where we had set them up the night before. Besides the mortars, we had RPG-7s, PK machine guns, Kalashnikov rifles, and Bernau "20-shooters."[4] We mounted a stubborn defense. We discovered that Soviet forces had surrounded the village. At 0800 hours, a DRA reinforcing column with tanks and infantry came from the provincial capitol of Mehtar Lam. We started firing the mortars at the column. The DRA kept trying to get into the village, but we drove them back. Sometimes the fight degenerated to hand-to-hand combat. We hit one tank with a RPG-7. Around noon, a jeep full of Soviet advisers drove into range. One of my RPG-7 gunners destroyed the jeep. We also captured some of the DRA soldiers who were close to the jeep. We demanded that they surrender and they did. The fighting continued until 1600 hours. Then, as sunset neared, the DRA and Soviets withdrew, leaving the village in our hands. Besides our 14 Mujahideen KIA and 50 WIA, there were many dead and wounded Afghan civilians

---

Commander Sher Padshah is from Laghman Province. [Map sheet 3086, vic grid 0149].

[4] The Bernau is the Czechoslovak M26 light machine gun. The Mujahideen called them "20-shooters."

including women and children. I do not know what the total enemy casualties were.

I am sure that someone from the village had told the government that we were there. Some of the villagers had left the village before the Soviets surrounded it. The villagers that were left actively helped the Mujahideen in the defense. The women provided us with food and showed us where to take cover. They led us from house-to-house as the enemy tightened his noose around us. That evening, after the fighting, we asked the locals for donkeys and mules to haul away our dead. We put our dead on their animals and took the bodies to their villages for burial. We took our wounded to local doctors for treatment. They helped as best they could, including some of the doctors from the government hospital.

The Soviets left some of their dead in the village of Alishang. They moved south to the village of Qawalkhel. They surrounded the village and told the villagers to go to Alishang and recover their dead or they would destroy their village. The Qawalkhel elders came to us and asked for the Soviet dead. We told them that they could recover the Soviet dead after we left.

COMMENTARY: Mujahideen night time security, when sleeping in a village, was usually only a guard or two posted inside the village. The Mujahideen needed to get security out to the key terrain dominating the village to provide timely warning. When the Soviets and DRA had timely intelligence, they were often able to surround sleeping Mujahideen whose guards were within yards of the sleepers. The Soviet forces were probably from the 66th Separate Motorized Rifle Brigade in Jalalabad—some 40 kilometers away. The DRA force was probably from the 71st Infantry Regiment—garrisoned only seven kilometers away in Mehtar Lam. The area is open and easily accessible by road. The local Mujahideen's overconfidence hurt the resistance badly.

VIGNETTE 3
VISION IN THE BAR KOT VALLEY
by Doctor Mohammad Sadeq

It was December 1983. I left my village of Sotan in Dara-i Nur Valley for the nearby valley of Bar Kot. I had five of my Mujahideen with me. In Bar Kot Valley, we stopped at the village of Dud-Reg where we spent the night in a Mujahideen guest house (Map 8-3 - Vision). Dud-Reg is the last village in the valley before the forest begins. In this area, the mountains are all heavily wooded with pine, juniper and sycamore. It was foggy, rainy and very cold. There were other Mujahideen from IRMA staying in the house next door to ours. After supper, everyone but my sentry went to bed. I was asleep and dreaming. In my dream, I saw a man in a white robe who laid his hand on my shoulder and said "You will prevail." Then the man dropped ammunition in my lap and gave me an Enfield rifle. "This is the time to go forward" the man said. I woke up and looked around. I could not find any ammunition or Enfield rifle, but I checked to make sure that my Kalashnikov and pistol were still under my pillow as I was thinking about the dream.

At 0030 hours, I again awoke as I heard a shot fired. I scrambled to my feet and asked the sentry what was going on. "Nothing, everything is all right" Agha Gul replied. I lay back down. Shortly afterward, I heard another shot. I jumped up, pulled on my shoes and grabbed my weapons. The other Mujahideen were also up. I looked outside. The sentry said "The Soviets are here. We are surrounded. I see their signal rockets all around us." The other group of IRMA Mujahideen rushed out into the night and up into the mountains. My five Mujahideen asked me "What should we do?" I replied, "Well, they've come for us, so let's give them a fight." The enemy had us surrounded and had blocked all the exits by this time.

The house that we were in had a large, enclosed courtyard (60 meters x 60 meters). The enemy were firing at us and they knew exactly where we were. I went to the back of the enclosure and crawled over the wall into a narrow meter-wide alley. I asked my Mujahideen to follow me. We moved down the alley and into the open fields. I could see Soviets in the open field. I told my Mujahideen

Doctor Mohammad Sadeq was a commander with the HIH in Kunar Province. [Map sheet 3186, vic grid 4341].

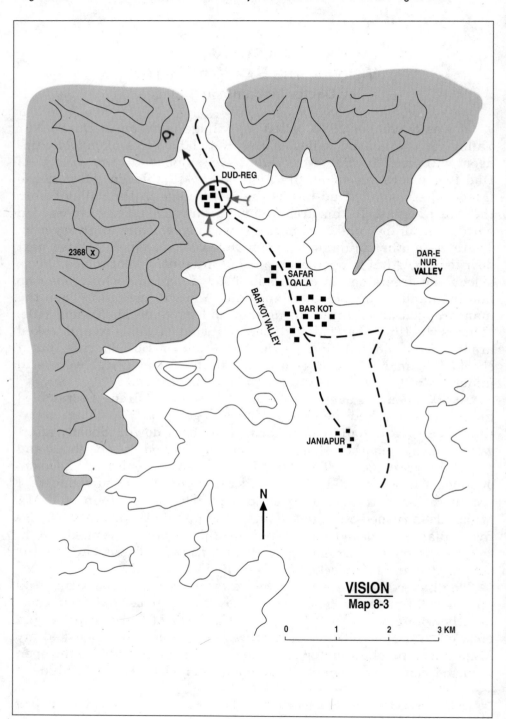

DUD-REG

2368 X

SAFAR
QALA

BAR KOT

BAR KOT VALLEY

DAR-E
NUR
VALLEY

JANIAPUR

N

VISION
Map 8-3

0   1   2   3 KM

that I would lay down a base of fire so that they could cross the field. Once they crossed the field, they were to go to the flank of the field and hold it. Just behind us was the house where the IRMA Mujahideen had stayed. I did not know that they had gone and were worried that they would unintentionally fire into our backs. I fired as my Mujahideen crossed the field, but they came under fire. We all fired back and retreated into the mountains. As we started up the mountains, we bumped into still more Soviets who were positioned in the mountains. As we were taking shelter behind a wall, one of my Mujahideen was hit and killed. We did not know this area very well, so we did not know how to get out. It took us about three hours to find our way safely up into the mountain. As we reached the mountain, we met the IRMA Mujahideen who had escaped earlier. They asked us to use tracer rounds to mark targets for their mortars. I fired at the enclosure that we had started out from with tracer bullets. The IRMA Mujahideen then fired their mortar at the enclosure. As daylight broke the IRMA Mujahideen mortar fire became more effective. In all, they fired 42 mortar rounds. The Soviets did not want to stay around and get mortared, so they withdrew. As I watched the Soviets pull back, I realized that we had prevailed and that my dream had come true. It was now time to go forward.

After the battle, I learned that the IRMA Mujahideen also had one of their group killed by the Soviets. Two Afghan women were also killed near the enclosure. The Soviet force had come from Jalalabad (about 20 kilometers away).[5] They had come at night on their APCs. They were guided by an Afghan named Nader. He was from Shewa. Since the DRA was established in this area, the people were divided in their loyalties and people like Nader worked against us.

COMMENTARY: The Mujahideen were lax about security in this area, despite the known divided loyalties within the populace. The guesthouse that the Mujahideen were staying in was not a private home, but a Mujahideen guesthouse regularly used by Mujahideen passing through the area. All the local villagers knew about its presence and function. The Soviet's guide came from Shewa, which is 15 kilometers away and yet he had no trouble pinpointing its location at night. The Soviets drove through a well-populated area on APCs to conduct their raid, yet the Mujahideen got no advance warning and their sentry was

---

[5] The Soviet force was either from the 66th Separate Motorized Rifle Brigade or the Spetsnaz battalion based in Jalalabad.

surprised. The Mujahideen were complacent about security and set patterns that the Soviets reacted to. Only the presence of the Mujahideen mortar and a large stock of mortar ammunition saved them.

VIGNETTE 4
SURPRISED BY THE SOVIETS IN THE DARA-E NUR
by Doctor Mohammad Sadeq

In March 1984, the DRA and Soviet forces again tried to destroy the Mujahideen forces in the Dara-e Nur Valley. A total of 120 Mujahideen armed with seven RPG-7s, one 82mm mortar, one DShK and many Kalashnikovs blocked their advance at Shokyali Village which is located at the junction of Dara-e Nur and Bar Kot Valleys. (Map 8-4 - Bar Kot) We positioned our forces to block both valleys and the high ground between them. The enemy came and tried to overcome our defenses but failed. Then the government sent a group of the area's elders to talk to us. The elders tried to persuade us not to fight in the area and to leave, but we refused. We held the area for another year before the enemy brought another column against us.

Nader, the DRA police chief for the area, sent us a message also trying to persuade us not to continue to fight in this area. He warned us that, if we did not leave, the Soviets would destroy all the villages in the area. It was now April 1985. At 2030 hours one evening, my group left the village of Sotan. We were armed with an RPG-7 and Kalashnikovs. We were moving to the junction of the two valleys along the foot of the mountains. One of my men stated "I will fire a shot to show our presence and let the people know that we are not cowards. It will show them that we are not intimidated and that we are still here." I tried to talk him out of it, but he finally fired the shot. As soon as he fired, the night lit up with return fire from all the Soviets who we discovered were in the area in force. The Soviets had arrived the previous night and had waited all day for us. We had not reached the junction yet, but were at a place called Kar. The Soviets were firing at us from positions on the mountain to the west and to the east is a steep canyon with a sheer 150 meter wall. We were trapped and surrounded, so we went to ground and fought back through the night and next day. With the day, helicopters came and fired at us. We grimly held our position and waited for the next night when we would try a breakout. But the Soviets had also had enough fighting, and they pulled out at the end of the day. I lost one KIA and one WIA. I do not know if there were any Soviet casualties.

Doctor Mohammed Sadeq was a commander with the HIH in Kunar Province and was also the narrator of the previous vignette. [Map sheet 3186, vic grid 4742.]

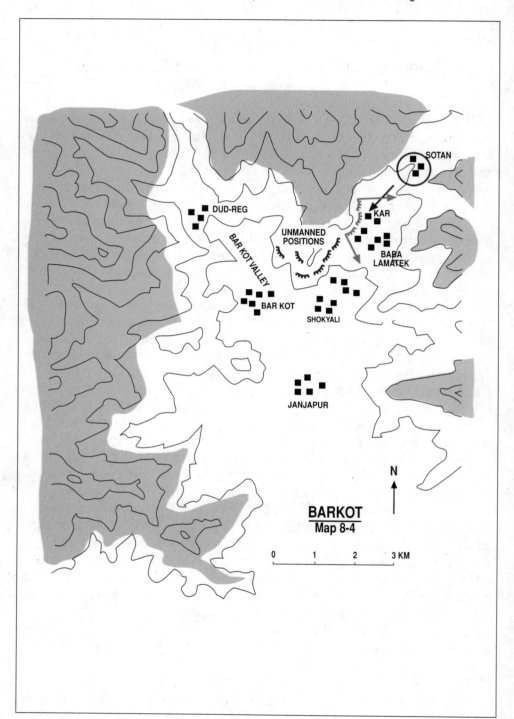

COMMENTARY: The Mujahideen believed in the invulnerability of their defenses and let the routines of positional defense dull their alertness. The Soviets again were able to infiltrate a force deep into the Mujahideen territory and take them by surprise. The lack of Mujahideen discipline triggered the ambush, but apparently triggered the ambush prematurely before the entire force was in the kill zone. Mujahideen leaders led by consensus, force of personality and moral persuasion.

The Mujahideen failed to man their defenses around the clock and the Soviets were able to move through their unmanned positions and surprise the Mujahideen. It is unclear whether the Soviets were in a deliberate ambush or were waiting for night fall to move on Sotan to attack the Mujahideen.

One of the problems that a guerrilla movement has is that the people who suffer the retaliations for guerrilla actions are usually the civilian populace. What starts as a popular cause, supported enthusiastically by the populace, can sour when the local populace has to bear the reprisals with no apparent end in sight. The local populace that remains often just wants to be left alone by all sides. The Mujahideen in this area lost a great deal of local support and, consequently, intelligence information and early warning.

CHAPTER COMMENTARY

Mujahideen local security was often lax in those areas which they controlled or which Soviet/DRA forces had not visited in awhile. Often, Mujahideen local security was even lax in areas adjacent to major Soviet and DRA garrisons. KHAD infiltrators and informers often managed to provide timely information that resulted in successful raids. The Mujahideen often failed to post security at a sufficient distance from their force to provide adequate warning. Instead, they relied on local inhabitants to provide that warning. In areas where the local populace had fled or were tired of the war, the Mujahideen were blind. The factional nature of the Mujahideen also discouraged the distribution of timely intelligence to all Mujahideen forces in an area.

The Mujahideen often failed to plan against raids, constitute a ready reaction force, designate escape routes and assembly areas and rehearse their defense. Aggressive Soviet or DRA raids had a good chance of success against unprepared Mujahideen. The trick was to withdraw before the Mujahideen had a chance to recover and pursue.

CHAPTER 9
FIGHTING HELIBORNE INSERTIONS

Soviet technology often had minimal impact on the Mujahideen guerrilla. Many Mujahideen tactics were virtually unchanged and still effective from their combat with Great Britain in the nineteenth and early twentieth centuries. Soviet high-performance aviation posed a direct threat to the civilian populace of Afghanistan, but the Mujahideen learned how to avoid or misdirect high-performance aircraft. However, the Soviet transport helicopter and helicopter gunship proved to be major concerns to the Mujahideen. Helicopters, and later the SU-25 close air support aircraft, were potent systems in the Soviet arsenal that the Mujahideen respected and feared. Soviet transports could land raiding parties deep in Mujahideen areas while gunships and close support aircraft could attack any opposition. Throughout the war, the Mujahideen had difficulty countering heliborne insertions, but they did learn that planning, drills and air defense ambushes could help alleviate the heliborne threat.

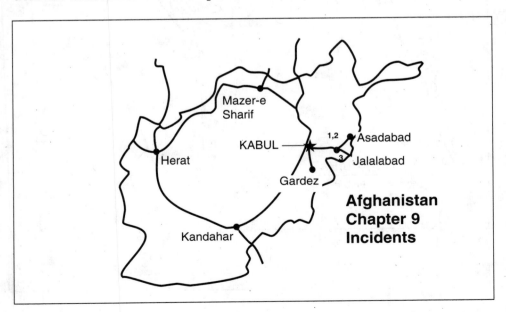

Afghanistan
Chapter 9
Incidents

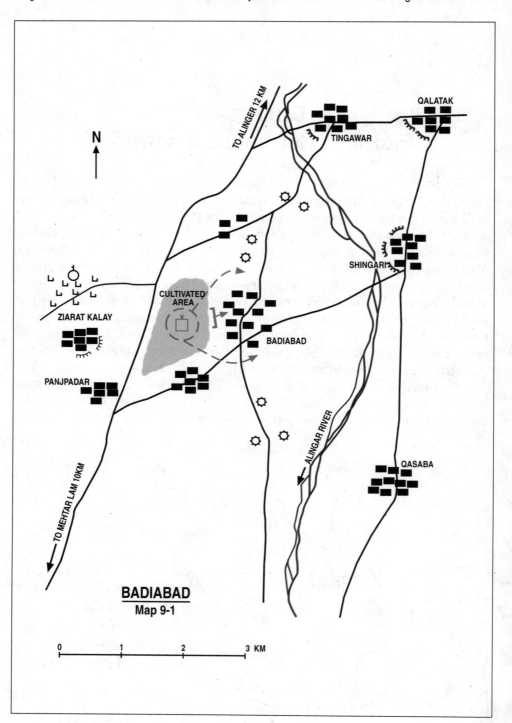

BADIABAD
Map 9-1

VIGNETTE 1
SOVIET HELIBORNE RAID ACHIEVES SURPRISE
by Doctor Abdul Qudus Alkozai and Commander Haji Sidiqullah

In the mid 1980s, Mujahideen forces based in Alingar District of the Laghman Province intensified their attacks on Soviet/DRA columns moving between Alingar and the provincial capital of Mehtar Lam. Mujahideen action included harassing supply columns, blocking traffic and launching raids on security outposts protecting government establishments. These actions were usually conducted by local resistance groups of 30 to 70 men. Most were affiliated with the Hezb-e Islami of Gulbuddin Hekmatyar (HIH).

Mujahideen commanders dispersed their men, weapons and equipment in the villages and hideouts and sometimes even buried their weapons between actions. However, rarely a day would pass in the region without some combat initiated by the Mujahideen or the DRA forces. In response, the Soviet/DRA forces targeted suspected bases or houses (permanent residences or headquarters) of major Mujahideen commanders in the area. Most of the raids were conducted by ground troops. However, after 1984, Soviet special forces launched several heli-borne raids on Mujahideen targets in the region. Their action at Badiabad Village was one of these.

In the summer of 1985, a Soviet heli-borne detachment raided the house of a local Mujahideen commander, Mamur Ghulam Jailani, in the village of Badiabad. The village is located about 15 kilometers northeast of Mehtar Lam on the main road connecting the provincial capital with the Alingar District (Map 9-1 - Badiabad). Commander Jailani commanded 150 Mujahideen located in and around Badiabad. His group was armed with automatic rifles, RPG-7 grenade launchers and a few heavy and light machine guns.

The Soviet raid began around 0900 hours with successive gun runs by pairs of helicopter gunships. Continual heavy helicopter rocket and machine gun raked the village and gave the villagers little opportunity to move into the surrounding hills—a standard practice by women and children to escape the ground force attacks that usually followed

---

Haji Sidiqullah was the Provincial Military Commander of the HIH party in Laghman. He joined Hekmatyar in the fight against Daoud--before the communist revolution. He had no formal military education. Dr. Abdul Qudus was a guerrilla commander under Sidiqullah. He doubled as the force medic, since he received medic's training in Pakistan. [Map sheet 3086, vic grid 1745].

air strikes. That day Commander Jailani was staying two villages away at Mirza Qala, less than one kilometer to the east. His 14-year-old son was alone in the house during the raid. The youngster was wounded, but managed to escape.

The aerial preparation continued about 30 minutes without any Mujahideen reaction or return fire. Four lift helicopters then set down in some corn fields 200-300 meters west of the commander's house. The corn stalks were about 20-30 centimeters high at the time. About 40 commandoes disembarked and immediately split into three groups. Two 10-man groups secured the northern and southern flanks of the village and a 20-man group stormed through the village to the house only to find that it was empty. The commandoes seized (stole) cash and other valuables in the house and destroyed what they could not take away. They searched several neighboring houses and found only women and children. They detained two unarmed Mujahideen who had buried their weapons. They were later released.

Several Mujahideen groups from the surrounding villages moved to Badiabad to fight the Soviets, but none arrived on time. The Soviet detachment withdrew unopposed and flew away in the helicopters that brought it in. The entire action lasted about an hour.

COMMENTARY: Soviet intelligence as to the location of the commander's house was good, probably reflecting the presence of an informer in the area. However, the Soviets did not have current intelligence to pinpoint when the commander would be in his house. This indicates that they were relying on only one intelligence asset and should have directed other assets to supplement their agent's reports. The resulting lack of accurate, current intelligence resulted in a failed mission. On the other hand, the guerrillas did not have an early warning system and had not developed and rehearsed a plan or drills to counter a Soviet-helicopter raid. This lack may have saved the Soviet force.

The guerrillas' lack of an overall village security plan and slow reaction time cost the resistance a good opportunity for inflicting heavy losses on the raiding detachment. A good security plan would concentrate on destroying the lift ships first and then fragmenting and destroying the raiding detachment piecemeal.

Eyewitnesses say that Jailani had left an RPG-7 in his house. As the Soviet gunships started strafing the village, he asked for a volunteer to go to the village and retrieve the valuable weapon. He offered 40,000 Afghanis (about 100 dollars) as a reward. His 17-year-old nephew, Ismail, volunteered, reached the embattled house and retrieved the weapon minutes before the Soviets stormed the place.

Instead of retiring with the RPG-7, the Mujahideen commander could have it used against the raiding force—perhaps to knock out enemy helicopters. There was no lack of brave men among the Mujahideen, like Ismail, who rushed to the village for combat. The Mujahideen, in this case, demonstrated a lot of individual courage but little tactical teamwork, initiative or cohesiveness.

About one month later, the Mujahideen had another chance and reversed the outcome of a similar raid just four kilometers north of Badiabad. This is the subject of the next vignette.

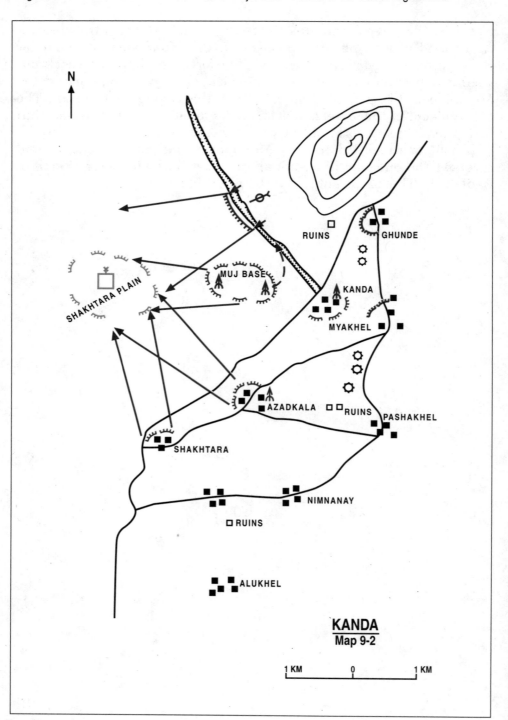

N

RUINS

GHUNDE

MUJ BASE

SHAKHTARA PLAIN

KANDA

MYAKHEL

AZADKALA

RUINS

PASHAKHEL

SHAKHTARA

NIMNANAY

RUINS

ALUKHEL

KANDA
Map 9-2

1 KM   0   1 KM

VIGNETTE 2
SOVIET RAID ON KANDA
by Doctor Abdul Qudus Alkozai and Commander Haji Sidiqullah

In July 1985, about one month after the Soviet raid on the Mujahideen base in the village of Badiabad, the Soviets made a similar attack against the resistance base of Doctor Alkozai at Kanda Warajayee. Kanda Warajayee, commonly called Kanda, is located on the main road between the provincial capital of Mehtar Lam and the Alingar District in the Laghman Province. The village is nearly eight kilometers south of the Alingar District center.

I located my base just outside the village to the west of the main road. I moved all the crew-served weapons from my house in the village to the base since the Soviets had conducted a series of raids on the homes of known Mujahideen commanders. I located my base in a ruin near an intermittent drainage ditch and protected it with security posts and crew-served weapons firing positions.

One day in July 1985, a group of six Soviet helicopters flew into my area. The helicopter group included four gunships which started firing at positions around my house. It seemed to me that the enemy intended to land troops and mount a raid on my house. The Mujahideen in my base opened up with machine gun fire on the enemy helicopters. This forced the Soviets to land at a distance from the village. As the helicopters landed about three kilometers away from Kanda on Shakhatara Dashta (*plain*), six of my Mujahideen carried an 82mm Chinese-manufactured recoilless rifle to a natural drainage ditch which extended from the village to the Prang Ghar Mountain to the west (Map 9-2 - Kanda).

The Soviet soldiers jumped from their helicopters onto the open terrain near a flock of sheep. The Soviets promptly gunned down the unarmed teenage shepherd. The enemy then tried to advance on Kanda under the air cover provided by their gunships. But the intensity of fire from my Mujahideen pinned them down in the open. As the fire fight continued, more of my Mujahideen rushed into the fray. This forced the Soviet troops to withdraw, quickly board their helicopters and fly away. The Soviet raid was a complete failure.

Haji Sidiqullah and Dr. Abdul Qudus are the narrators of the previous vignette. [Map sheet 3086, vic grid 1948].

COMMENTARY: The Mujahideen's prompt reaction to the enemy attack saved the day. The Mujahideen had learned that enemy airmobile assaults in a guerrilla-controlled area have little chance of success when met with coordinated fire from multiple directions. Dr. Alkozai had planned for enemy air assault and positioned weapons to deal with that possibility.

On the other hand, the Soviet forces paid heavily for their attempt to land small units in an area totally dominated by the resistance. A heliborne attack may succeed when it is launched against an enemy caught by surprise and unable to respond swiftly. However, heavy Mujahideen ground fire should have convinced the Soviet commander to abort his mission. Instead, he relied on gunship fire to carry the day and was forced to withdraw from a hot LZ. He was lucky not to lose some lift ships, particularly since his landing zone was so close to the objective.

Soviet intelligence about their target appears to have been good, but the Soviet commander lacked the complete intelligence picture about the strength and location of guerrilla forces. If the Soviet commander had inserted some forces to secure the high ground overlooking Kanda before landing the bulk of his force, he might have been able to suppress guerrilla crew-served weapons and accomplish his raid.

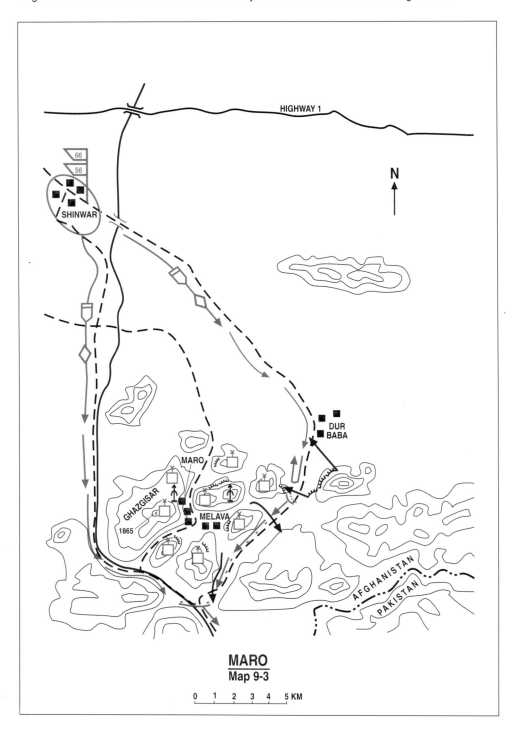

HIGHWAY 1

N

66
56

SHINWAR

DUR
BABA

MARO

GHAZGISAR

MELAVA

1865

AFGHANISTAN

PAKISTAN

MARO
Map 9-3

0 1 2 3 4 5 KM

VIGNETTE 3
AIR ASSAULT ON MARO STRONGHOLD
by Toryalai Hemat

In April 1987, the Soviets and DRA launched a combined strike on the Mujahideen stronghold in Nangrahar Province, Shinwar District near the Nazian Valley. The Nazian Valley was heavily populated, although many of the inhabitants had emigrated to Pakistan to avoid the Soviet bombing attacks. The Mujahideen stronghold that the enemy wanted was at Maro, some 70 kilometers southeast of Jalalabad near the Pakistan border. Several Mujahideen groups from different factions were located around Maro and there were probably some 500 well-armed Mujahideen in the stronghold area. The Soviets called this stronghold the Melava fortified region.[1]

For 18 days prior to the attack, the Soviets hit the area with airstrikes. Then, a mechanized Soviet/DRA column moved east from Jalalabad and, when it reached Shinwar Town, it split in two (Map 9-3 - Maro). One column moved through Shinwar and up the Nazian Valley, while the other column moved further to the east to the subdistrict of Dur Baba and then attacked to the southwest. Commander Saznur and his men defended on the Dur Baba approach. Commander Khaled and I, along with our 10 other Mujahideen, defended Ghazgisar—the highest ground in the area overlooking Maro. The enemy launched heavy air strikes against us. Following the airstrikes, Soviet helicopters landed air assault forces on the high ground between the two axes.[2] Some 40 or 50 helicopter sorties were involved. One of the landing zones was right in front of us. The fighting was fierce. Nine of my group were killed by the bombing or while fighting the air assault force. Only Khaled,

---

Toryalai Hemat was a regiment commander of a mobile force allied with the IUA--Islamic Union of Afghanistan of Sayyaf. He fought in many provinces in Afghanistan. [Map sheet 3185, vic grid 8892].

[1] A Soviet account of this action is contained in vignette 26 of *The Bear Went Over the Mountain.* The Soviet account mistakenly has the action to the northeast of Jalalabad, a mistake that Les Grau made based on a similar name and some vague text.

[2]These were two battalions from the 56th Air Assault Brigade in Gardez. The battalions drove to Jalalabad and then to Shinwar. They staged the air assault from a field site in Shinwar. Why they did not fly to Jalalabad airfield and then stage the air assault from the airfield is a mystery. The ground force was most likely from the Soviet 66th Separate Motorized Rifle Brigade and the DRA 11th Infantry Division.

Abdul Wakil and I survived. The Mujahideen [under Commander Saznur] initially stopped the column from Dur Baba, but the column coming from the Nazian Valley advanced quickly and captured Maro. In my group, we three survivors were caught between two LZs. We snuck out of the area and crossed the border into Pakistan and hiked to the nearby village of Bazar.

When the enemy took Maro, many Mujahideen fled across the border and assembled at Bazar (Tirah Agency in Pakistan). Reinforcements from the HIH and IUA factions poured into the area. Arab volunteers along with Talibs from religious schools also came for the fighting. We launched a counterattack. The fighting for the bases was so fierce that at times it was hand-to-hand combat. I personally was so close to some Russians during the fighting that I would recognize them today. The enemy left many vehicles behind and many dead on the ground. The Soviets did not usually leave their dead, but we counted 75 Soviet KIA. I do not know the total number of Mujahideen casualties, but I do know of 72 Mujahideen killed and wounded. The Soviets only held Maro for three days. They burned and destroyed what they could and mined the area before they withdrew.

COMMENTARY: The Soviet air assault raids on mountain base camps usually lasted for one to three days. As in this instance, the Soviets preferred to have ground forces involved to link up with the air assault forces. They tried to seize the area, destroy as much of the base as possible, lay down mines and depart. And, they tried to avoid getting trapped in the mountains fighting the Mujahideen on their turf. As in Zhawar and Magistral, the Mujahideen initially retreated, regrouped and reinforced and then launched a punishing attack. The close proximity of this base to Pakistan allowed the Mujahideen to do this. The Soviet planning and execution of this action was well done, but they apparently were late in withdrawing and had to fight a running withdrawal.

The Mujahideen distribution of forces on the two axes was uneven and the air assault prevented the Mujahideen from employing a reserve against the threatened axis. Part of the maldistribution is due to the fact that various factions of various strengths were in the area and missions were assigned by faction, not by strength.

CHAPTER COMMENTARY

In the early days of the war, Soviet air assault missions were rather timid and unimaginative. Later, the Soviets became more confident with the air assault concept and struck deeper and more aggressively. Ambush forces were delivered by helicopter, and raiding forces struck deep at Mujahideen supply bases and staging areas and even conducted raids against Mujahideen redoubts such as the one at Maro. The Soviets usually sent a ground element to link up with the air assault element if the air assault element had to remain in the area for any length of time. Soviet air assaults relied on helicopter gunships and SU-25 close air support aircraft for fire support, but frequently brought their artillery with them by helicopter.

The Mujahideen learned to counter air assaults with thorough planning, immediate action drills, an early warning system and air defense ambushes. They learned to mine likely LZs, employ massed RPG fire against hovering or landing helicopters, and to try and overrun a LZ before the air assault forces had an opportunity to get organized and oriented. They also learned to "hug" Soviet forces so that helicopter gunships could not fire at them.

CHAPTER 10
DEFENDING AGAINST A CORDON AND SEARCH

The Soviets preferred large cordon and search operations to deal with large zones of Mujahideen-dominated territory. They would cordon off the area using dominant terrain, roads and rivers as boundaries. Then they would push forces through the area looking for weapons, stores and Mujahideen. The Soviets often used DRA forces to do the actual searching. The DRA usually combined taxation and press-gang conscription with the search. At first, the Mujahideen were vulnerable to these large-scale operations but then they learned to build fortifications throughout the zones, coordinate their defense, constitute a reserve and exact a toll on the searchers.

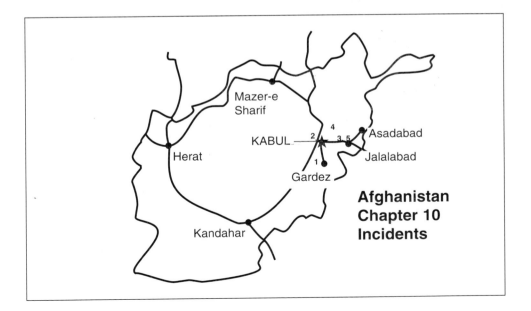

Afghanistan
Chapter 10
Incidents

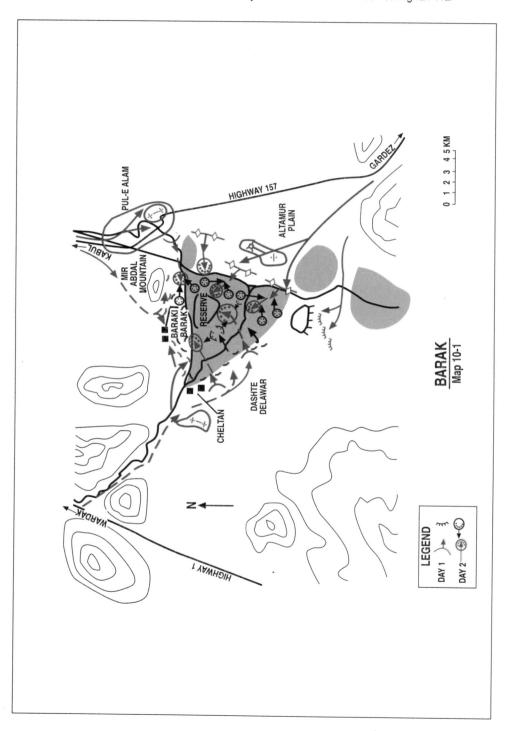

BARAK
Map 10-1

VIGNETTE 1
BATTLE OF BARAKI BARAK
by Commander Qazi Guljan Tayeb

Baraki Barak District is a very fertile oasis and a major green zone located between the two main highways running south and southwest from Kabul. One highway runs from Kabul to Gardez in Paktia Province and the other runs from Kabul to Gazhni and on to Kandahar. The waters of the Wardak River and Wardak Gorge irrigate this fertile area and wheat, corn, and rice fields intersperse with vineyards and orchards. This fertile, well-populated valley provided a natural base from which the Mujahideen could attack both of these main LOCS as well at Muhammad Agha District to the north and Gardez in the south.

In June 1982 there were several Mujahideen bases located in the Baraki Barak District. We had brought a number of heavy antiaircraft machine guns into the area, particularly the ZGU-1 14.5mm single-barreled machine gun. The enemy was concerned about the presence of these air defense weapons. We received information that the enemy was preparing an offensive into our area with three major objectives: first, to seize our air defense weapons that were becoming a hindrance to their air raids in our AO; second, to capture some of the leading Mujahideen commanders who continuously harassed and attacked Soviet and DRA columns traveling on the two highways which bordered our area; and, third, to seize control of the area and restore the district government to the DRA. We had overthrown the DRA district government in 1979.

The Soviets and DRA launched their offensive with more than 20,000 troops involved directly and in support (Map 10-1 - Barak). They sent out three columns, one each from Gardez, Kabul and Wardak.[1] These forces moved to our area, established a cordon

---

Commander Qazi Guljan Tayeb was a third year student in Kabul Theological College during the communist takeover in 1978. He joined Hikmatyar and later switched to the Sayef faction in the mid-1980s. He was the Commander of Baraki Barak District of Logar Province. [Map sheets 2784, 2785, 2884, 2885].

[1] Forces on the Gardez axis were from the Soviet 56th Air Assault Brigade and the DRA 12th Infantry Division. Forces on the Kabul and Wardak axes were probably from the Soviet 103rd Airborne Division and 108th Motorized Rifle Division, while DRA forces were probably from the 8th Infantry Division, 37th Commando Brigade and 15th Tank Brigade.

around it, occupied the high ground and began attacking some of the Mujahideen positions. The column from Kabul occupied Pul-e Alam and from there sent one detachment to the west around Mir Abdal mountain to flank the district from the northwest. The column from Gardez moved west of the road to the Altamur plain and covered the southeastern axis to the district. The column from Wardak occupied positions on the district's western flank. The enemy blocked practically all major axes out of the area. Since we Mujahideen commanders knew of the upcoming offensive, we had gathered earlier to draw up a joint defensive plan. All faction commanders participated and we constituted the southeastern and northwestern defensive sectors and assigned defensive areas within these sectors to different factions and units. We organized our forces into small groups to insure our ability to maneuver and then occupied positions in the perimeter villages of our district. We constituted mobile interior reserves and kept them available to react to enemy actions.

I commanded the southeastern sector. I had approximately 800 Mujahideen, armed and unarmed, under my command. Our weapons included ZGU-1s, DShKs, many RPG-7s, PK machine guns, 82mm mortars, 82mm and 75mm recoilless rifles, machine guns, and a number of .303 bolt-action Enfield rifles. These Enfields were quite effective against dismounted Soviets. They had a maximum effective range of 800 meters compared to 400 meters for the AK assault rifle. Further, the more-powerful .303 round would penetrate Soviet flak jackets while the AK round would not.

The enemy deployed his artillery on the Altamur plain and at Pul-e Alam. His column from Wardak occupied the line Dashte Delawar—Cheltan hill—and the northern villages to the high ground. The enemy initiated their attack with heavy artillery fire and air strikes on the villages and suspected Mujahideen positions. The artillery fire continued for several hours. They hit the positions of the ZGU-1s and set the entire area on fire. The enemy advanced from the southwest between Cheltan and the road and entered our villages and searched them. They also attacked from the other directions against the perimeter villages that they were facing. Our Mujahideen fought them from their forward positions and fell back to back-up positions as the enemy entered the villages. The villages and orchard provided good cover and concealment and, although the enemy had the area surrounded, we were able to move freely within the 10-kilometer-wide area. We began to launch small-group counterattacks with our scattered groups of Mujahideen. We hit the enemy from many directions.

We suffered casualties, but the enemy also got a bloody nose. It was an infantry fight at close quarters. Three Mujahideen in my immediate group were killed during our local counterattack. Soviet forces were encircled and the Soviets launched counter-counterattacks to aid their encircled forces. We also reinforced our forces. Our forces were intermingled and the Soviet artillery was unable to fire into the area of contact for fear of hitting their own troops. Fighting continued until dusk. As night fell, fighting slackened and stopped.

The next morning, the enemy resumed the attack, but this time from the east using tanks and infantry. We Mujahideen had mined the Khalifa Saheb Ziarat[2] approach. The Soviets brought dogs to detect the mines. My group in this area were in well-covered positions with three RPGs. As the enemy cleared the minefield and moved forward, we opened fire with our RPGs on their tanks standing in the open cultivated areas. The enemy responded by moving overwhelming force into the area. The Mujahideen responded by moving out of their positions to move through gaps to attack the enemy on the flanks. Small groups of Mujahideen with RPGs also maneuvered through the concealing terrain folds to engage the enemy. This totally changed the situation, with the enemy stopping and going to ground in defensive pockets. The enemy's momentum was lost as his attack bogged down. The Soviets occupied villages, farm buildings and orchards and turned them into defensive positions as the second night fell. The Soviets were scattered in five or six pockets and the Mujahideen kept them from linking up. We Mujahideen knew the terrain and the local civilians helped us move from position to position. We attacked the Soviets from all sides, but suffered casualties as well. For the next day and night, the situation continued. Both sides were intermingled and the whole area was on fire. We saw guns capable of firing in every direction (D30) and saw a single-barreled grenade launcher (RPG-18). This was the first time we captured AK-74 assault rifles.[3] Flak jackets protected the Soviets from AK fire, but our old .303s penetrated them. After three days and nights, the enemy began to withdraw. Every column returned by the direction it had come.

---

[2] Ziarat means shrine.

[3] The AK-74 Kalashnikov 5.56mm assault rifle was issued only to Soviet troops. DRA troops had the older AK-47 Kalashnikov assault rifle. The Mujahideen called the AK-74 the "Kalakov". One of the Pashtun songs of the time had a line "A mother should not mourn a son killed by a Kalakov" This meant that her son died fighting Soviets.

None of the enemy's three objectives were achieved, but our losses were very heavy with about 250 KIA. The enemy spread rumors that they killed more than 2,000 of us. I don't know what the enemy losses were, but we saw blood trails and blood pools all over the former enemy positions. The enemy had done very hateful things in the villages they occupied. They defecated in the crockery, smashed pots and furniture, and destroyed villagers' food by cutting open sacks of wheat, flour, salt and sugar and pouring it out on the ground. They also pulled down walls, broke doors and ruined houses.

COMMENTARY: The Soviets and DRA throughly planned this operation. The converging movement of three columns from three directions was a desirable operational maneuver since it left the initiative in the Soviets' hands and kept the Mujahideen off balance. However, once the Soviet/DRA force entered the green zone, the terrain and Mujahideen active defense split the communist force into a series of isolated pockets which the Mujahideen were able to contain. The Soviet/DRA force lost the momentum of the attack and were unable to regain it. The initiative passed to the Mujahideen.

The Mujahideen planned their defense throughly. They conducted an active defense which incorporated tactical maneuver. They maintained a central reserve and had the advantage of interior lines. Terrain, well-constructed field fortifications and an aggressive defense enabled the Mujahideen to split the Soviet/DRA forces into isolated groups and stop their advance.

The Soviets and DRA did little to win the hearts and minds of the populace outside of the areas they controlled. On the other hand, Mujahideen activity often endangered the lives and property of the populace. During the course of the war, the Soviets never controlled Baraki Barak, but they bombed and shelled it continually. Farming was disrupted and most of the population migrated to Pakistan or the cities.

VIGNETTE 2
DEFENDING AGAINST AN OFFENSIVE IN PAGHMAN
by Tsaranwal Sher Habib

In August 1982, the Soviet/DRA forces launched a search and destroy operation against Mujahideen bases in Paghman. There were two enemy columns. The main column moved southwest from Kabul and then turned northwest onto the main highway to Paghman. Its mission was to destroy resistance bases in the center, south and southwest of the Paghman area. The other, smaller column moved north from Kabul and then turned northwest. Its mission was to block Mujahideen escape routes along the northeastern edge of Paghman through Ghaza and Zarshakh villages (Map 10-2 - Ghaza).[4]

Initially, the movement of the two columns in opposite directions deceived the Mujahideen as to their enemy's real intention. Nevertheless, when the Mujahideen saw the main column heading toward the city of Paghman and its western and southern suburbs, they quickly occupied prepared defensive positions and readied themselves for battle. However, the Mujahideen lost track of the northernmost column. It came through the town of Karez-e Mir and moved undetected to take up positions on the hills between Somochak and Ghaza. From the hill positions, the enemy column commanded the main road from Paghman to the Shamali plain north of Kabul.

The next morning I dispatched two escorts to take one of my wounded Mujahideen to Shamali for treatment. As they moved through the Somochak Valley, they were ambushed and the escorts were killed. The local Mujahideen from Somochak village went to investigate and discovered that Soviet troops had occupied the ridge overlooking the village. The Somochak Mujahideen attacked the ridge, but the Soviets were too strong to be overrun. Other Mujahideen in the area began to discover the enemy presence. Mujahideen in the village bases of Qala-e Hakim and Isakhel and in the valley base of Dara-e Zargar joined together. I took some 30 or 40 Mujahideen onto

---

Tsaranwal (Attorney) Sher Habib commanded the Ibrahimkhel Front north of the city of Paghman. His primary AO extended from Paghman east and northeast to Kabul (some 20 kilometers). [Map sheet 2786, 2886].

4 The forces on the main axis were probably from the Soviet 108th Motorized Rifle Division, while DRA forces were probably from the 8th Infantry Division, 37th Commando Brigade and 15th Tank Brigade. The forces on the northern axis were probably from the Soviet 103rd Airborne Division.

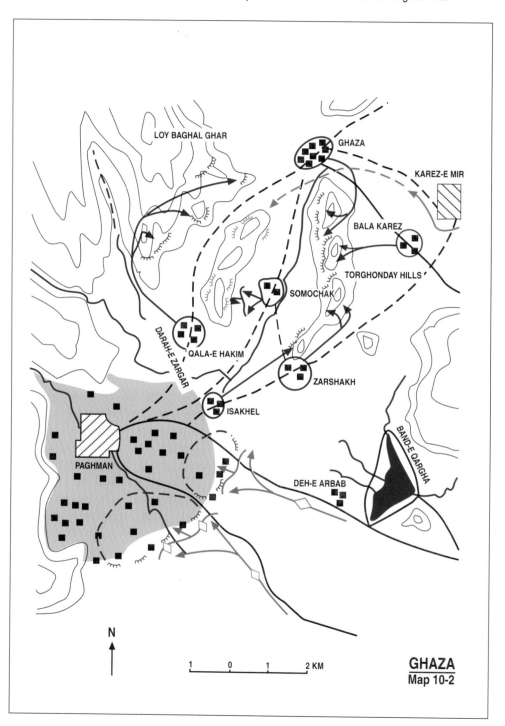

LOY BAGHAL GHAR

GHAZA

KAREZ-E MIR

BALA KAREZ

TORGHONDAY HILLS

SOMOCHAK

DARAH-E ZARGAR

QALA-E HAKIM

ZARSHAKH

ISAKHEL

PAGHMAN

BAND-E QARGHA

DEH-E ARBAB

N

1   0   1   2 KM

GHAZA
Map 10-2

the high ground at Loy Baghal Ghar. The Somochak Mujahideen reinforced their positions near the village. The Zarshakh and Ghaza Mujahideen moved to cut the LOC of the Soviet force east of the Torghonday hills. We had encircled the Soviet force in the northeast sector with about 100 Mujahideen.

The fighting went on against the DRA/Soviet forces throughout Paghman. We kept the northern Soviet blocking force pinned down, exchanging fire with the Soviet troops for two nights and three days. We commanders met and decided to attack and eliminate the Soviet force on the afternoon of the third day. We launched the attack from the west while the eastern Mujahideen contained the enemy. Our progress was slow, however, since we did not have enough support weapons. We had Kalashnikovs, .303 Enfields, a few RPG-7s and some 60mm mortars with a small stock of ammunition. We needed heavy machine guns, 82mm mortars and rockets. As we Mujahideen were closing to the Soviet positions, some 14 Soviet helicopters, including gunships, arrived over the battlefield and began gun runs against us. We sustained heavy casualties and broke off the attack. The transport helicopters landed and began lifting off the Soviet troops and flew them away to Kabul. We had won the fight, but we suffered 23 KIA and many others WIA in the three-day battle.

COMMENTARY: The Soviet/DRA force did an effective job initially in disguising their objective and managing to move their northern column while eluding Mujahideen surveillance. The northern column effectively performed a surprise approach march and quietly occupied necessary terrain. The northern column was organized to block Mujahideen escape routes and so was lightly equipped. It was battalion-sized or smaller. It seized and occupied its initial position, but made no effort to expand that position so that it could achieve its objective of completely blocking Mujahideen escape routes. Further, once it disclosed its presence by firing on the litter party, it made no attempt to seize the initiative, but remained passively in the defense. Coordination between the northern column and the main column was lacking since the main column seemed unable or uninterested in aiding the northern column despite their close proximity.

The Mujahideen reaction was excellent. They quickly took up positions on commanding high ground overlooking the Soviet positions and sealed the area, trapping the Soviet force. However, the Mujahideen lacked long-range heavy weapons, so they could not exploit the advantage that their dominant terrain gave them. The Soviets were in range of the bulk of Mujahideen weapons only during the Mujahideen assault. The Soviet helicopter strike effectively countered this assault. Soviet helicopter gunships were not as effective at night. Perhaps the Mujahideen assault would have had a better chance if the attack were launched at dusk or before dawn.

Mujahideen use of battlefield maneuver was commendable. They offset much of their disadvantage in fire power, took dominant terrain and attack positions, seized the initiative from the Soviets by trapping them and forced the Soviets to stage a rescue by hazarding helicopters. All of this was due to effective Mujahideen maneuver. If the Mujahideen had some anti-aircraft weapons, they could have bloodied the Soviet force badly. As it was, Mujahideen maneuver prevented the success of the Soviet/DRA offensive and decided the outcome of the battle in the Mujahideen's favor.

The Kama area, located northeast of Jalalabad, is approximately 87 square kilometers in area. It is bordered in the west by the Kunar River, in the south by the Kabul River and in the north and east by mountains. It is a large, well-irrigated green zone which was densely populated before the war. The Mujahideen in the area were all locals defending their home turf. In February 1983, I commanded a group of 35 men in my village of Sama Garay (one kilometer east of the town of Kama). We had Enfield and G3[5] bolt-action rifles and a few Kalashnikovs. We lacked the capability to launch major attacks, but conducted hit and run actions. We did not have a base in the mountains, but lived in the village. There were similar units in the other villages in the area. The Kama District Mujahideen were very fragmented and we had no contact with many groups in the area and so we couldn't help each other. The Soviets could deal with us piecemeal. We Mujahideen did not have a common contingency plan to deal with the Soviets when they came in force to kill us all. And even if we had such a plan, at that time our communications were primitive and most communications were done with messengers.

The Soviets were close at hand. The Soviet "Thunder" unit[6] was stationed in Samarkhel to the east of Jalalabad. They crossed the Kunar River and established a base south of the Tirana Ghashe on the plain (Map 10-3 - Kama). Then at dawn on 15 February 1983, 20 to 25 of their helicopters landed troops in the mountains north and northeast of Kama. The helicopters landed at Mashingan Ghar, Spinki

---

Abdul Baqi Balots was a Hezb-e Islami (HIH) commander in the Kama area east of Jalalabad. Before the communist takeover, he was a student in the tenth grade of high school. School authorities were forcing him to join the Communist Youth Organization. His father advised him not to join but to fight. He left school and joined the Mujahideen and fought through to the end. [Map sheets 3085 and 3185].

[5] The US M1917 Springfield Rifle which Springfield Armory produced for the British Army in World War I. The Mujahideen called them the G3 rifle.

[6] The "Thunder" unit was the 66th Separate Motorized Rifle Brigade. The Mujahideen called it the Thunder unit because it was a reinforced unit designed for counterinsurgency. It had three motorized rifle battalions, an air assault battalion, a tank battalion, an artillery howitzer battalion, a MRL battalion, a material support battalion, a reconnaissance company and support troops.

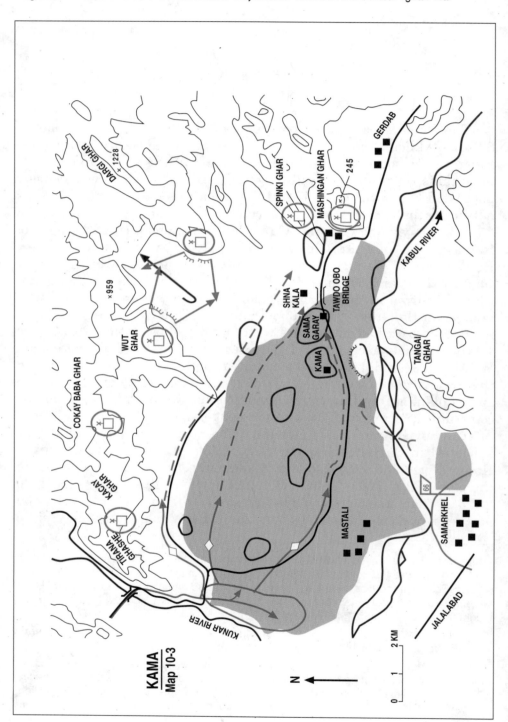

KAMA
Map 10-3

Ghar, Dergi Ghar, Wut Ghar, Cokay Baba Ghar, Kacay Ghar, and Tirana Ghashe. The troops on the high ground sealed off our escape into the mountains. At the same time, a detachment from the Soviet base at Samarkhel crossed the Kabul River to establish the southern part of the cordon. The main Soviet ground sweep started from Tirana Ghar moving to the east.

We woke up to the sounds of helicopters and the lights of flares. We were facing a large force—possibly bigger than a regiment. I was saying my morning prayers when my guard approached and said "Commander, things look different this morning." I told him, "Don't worry, our lives are in the hand of God, not the Russians. We are destined to die on the day that is destined for us. It will not be pushed backward or forward." The helicopters continued to fly over, wave after wave.

I saw a group of Mujahideen from the village of Mastali running away between Wut Ghar and Dergi Ghar. As they moved along the road, the Soviets on the high ground began shooting at them. I saw two of them go down. Gulrang was one and the son of Ghulam Sarwar the driver, was the other. Both were killed. The rest escaped into the mountains.

We were close to the river, so we moved to the south of Kama where there is a bushy area and a mosque. We took refuge and hid ourselves there. Everything was quiet in our area for hours. My Mujahideen came to me and asked what was happening. It was now 1100 hours. I said that the Russians would come when they would come, but we were hungry now. I approached a village for food. Someone came out and told me not leave the hideout since enemy tanks were five minutes from the village. I returned to the hideout. Around 1400 hours, another villager came and told me to leave the bushy area since the Russians were going to set it on fire to flush us out. He said eight tanks and APCs were approaching the area. We moved to the edge of the wooded area where there is a natural berm and took up positions there. We had one RPG-7 with three rounds, two Kalashnikovs, and some Marko Chinese bolt-action rifles.[7] The wooded area was also full of civilians who were hiding from the Soviets, so we felt an obligation to defend them and the wooded area and prevent the Soviets from setting it on fire. I saw BMPs moving toward us. They stopped short of and bypassed the wooded area and turned toward Kama. It was now 1500 hours.

---

[7] Marko is the Chinese copy of the German M-88 Mauser.

When we were scattered throughout the wooded area, I received a message from the rest of my men who described their location and asked me to join them since the air assault troops were moving to Mashingan village. I took my 12 men with me and we moved to join the rest of my men. The Tawdo Obo highway bridge was close to our village. I joined the rest of my men at that bridge which was near the village. We decided that the Soviets coming from the high ground would cross over this bridge, so we took positions on both sides of the road leading to this bridge. As we were taking our positions, a group of Soviets moving toward us opened fire on us.

A bullet hit the butt of the rifle of my cousin, the son of my maternal uncle, and smashed it. "What will I do now?" he asked. "I will find you another," I stated. As I approached the road, I saw my friend Habib Noor some 30 meters to my right shooting at something. I hit the ground and saw that he was shooting at two Soviets. He killed them both. "Get their Kalashnikovs, Commander" he yelled at me. I sprinted across the road and grabbed a Kalashnikov, but the rifle's carrying strap was around the corpse's body and I couldn't get it loose. I saw a lot of Soviets coming at me and they were all firing (they put ten bullet holes through my baggy trousers). Bullets were flying all around me. I kept tugging, but the rifles wouldn't budge, so I abandoned trying to get the Kalashnikovs. I had an RPK-3 anti-tank hand grenade. I wanted to use it, even though there was no tank, to make some noise to distract their attention so I could get away. I threw the grenade. After four seconds, it exploded and made a big noise and I got away to where my friend Habib Noor was. Habib Noor told me that, unless we crossed the stream to the north, we would not be able to engage the Soviets. He told me that since I am short and he is tall, I had a better chance of making it across unobserved and I should cross. I told him " I am your commander, but I am under your command now." I ran across and jumped but landed directly into the stream. "Oh Allah," I cried "you have killed me without dignity." Then I made a big jump, I don't know how since even a tank can't clear it, but I did and got out of the stream. Even today, when I pass that spot, I measure it. I took up a position and fired my Kalashnikov. I killed the Soviet facing Habib Noor. Habib shouted that Soviets were still in the nearby houses of Shna Kala village. I moved down the path from the bridge to get at the Soviets. I approached that position, threw hand grenades at it and fired my Kalashnikov. Everything was quiet after that. I looked back across the road. Habib Noor was standing. I told him to get down. He remained standing, cursing the Soviets and demanding their surrender in Pashtu. At that moment, I saw a light in his stomach. He was hit and fell down. I recrossed the road to get his body. I could see the bodies of Soviets in the stream. When I reached Habib, he died. He had only five rounds left. He was my good friend and was not even from our village. He was from the Ahmadzai tribe, which live away from this area.

Fighting went on all around us. I heard shooting from everywhere, but I only knew what was going on around me. Shaykh Bombar from my unit came up to help. He had the only other Kalashnikov in my group. He had given his Kalashnikov to another guy and taken the RPG and one rocket and moved to my position. As he came, I saw tanks moving toward us through the fields from the Shna Kala village. The sun was setting. The air assault troops had come down from the mountains and were advancing. Tanks were coming from the west. We wanted to carry Habib Noor's body to Rangin Kala village and from there it would be easier to take his body out of the area. I took the RPG and rocket from Shaykh Bombar. We wrapped Habib Noor's body in my *tsadar*—the all-purpose cloth that we all carry and wear. Then I shot the RPG at a tank. The tanks were out of range and so the rocket landed among the infantry. The tanks and infantry promptly stopped, realizing that we had antitank weapons. Their halt enabled us to break contact and take Habib Noor's body out of the area to Gerdab village—about six kilometers further to the east. There, I rented a camel and we took Habib's body to his family at a refugee camp in Pakistan. We buried him in the refugee cemetery in Peshawar, even though his home was in Paktia Province. His family is doing okay now since one of his sons has a job in Saudi Arabia.

COMMENTARY: At this point, the Mujahideen effort was uncoordinated and put the villagers at direct risk. The Mujahideen were poorly trained and their lack of cooperation put the area at risk. Their personal bravery and motivation, however, turned the entire area into a defensive zone that slowed the Soviet effort. Later, as the Mujahideen were better armed, had better communications and began to coordinate their actions, they were more effective against the Soviet and DRA forces. However, by that time most of the civilians were killed or had left the area for refugee camps in Pakistan.

The Soviet effort was well planned and used air assault forces effectively to seal the area. However, their cordon enclosed a large area which they were unable to effectively sweep. They needed to break the cordoned area into manageable segments and sweep those in turn. Instead, their sweep was uncoordinated and large sectors of the green zone were never checked. This green zone is full of villages and fields and requires several days to clear. The Soviets were reluctant to maintain a cordon at night, so they hurried through the sweep and missed the bulk of the disorganized Mujahideen.

VIGNETTE 4
DEFENDING AGAINST A CORDON AND SEARCH OPERATION IN PARWAN
by Commander Haji Abdul Qader

In late January 1984, Soviet forces launched a multi-divisional[8] cordon and search operation in Parwan and Kapisa Provinces. The aim of the operation was to destroy the Mujahideen forces across a wide area stretching from the Charikar-Salang highway in the west, to Mahmoud-e Raqi in the east and Bagram in the south (Map 10-4 - Parwan). This area is covered with villages and cut by irrigation canals to the orchards, vineyards and farms of this fertile area. There were dozens of Mujahideen bases in this area that were affiliated with major resistance factions. Most of the Mujahideen were not in their bases but split up into hundreds of small units living in the villages during the winter.

On 24 January columns of Soviet and DRA tank and motorized rifle forces moved from Kabul, Bagram, Jabal-e Seraj and Gulbahar (at the mouth of the Punjsher Valley) to establish a wide cordon around the green zone on both sides of the Panjsher River. The cordon and sweep operation was backed with extensive air support. The Soviets and DRA hoped to trap the thousands of Mujahideen in this area and to destroy their base camps. The Mujahideen reinforced their defenses along the major roads in the area. The Mujahideen expected enemy advances along these axes of advance and decided to block them to gain time to break out from encirclement.

During the first day, the Soviet/DRA forces deployed and established blocking positions reinforced by tanks, APCs and artillery. At dawn on 25 January, they mounted attacks from several points, including Charikar, Jabal-e Seraj, Gulbahar, Mahmoud-e Raqi, Qala-e Naw and Bagram.

Haji Abdul Qader was a commander in the Bagram area. The authors have consulted other documents to add detail to his account. A former teacher, Abdul Qader hails from the Sayghani village just six kilometers northeast of the Bagram air base. His group was initially affiliated with the HIK faction. He later joined Sayyaf's IUA faction. [Map sheets 2886 and 2887].

8 Most probably the Soviet 103rd Airborne Division and the 108th Motorized Rifle Division and the DRA 8th Infantry Division and 37th Commando Brigade.

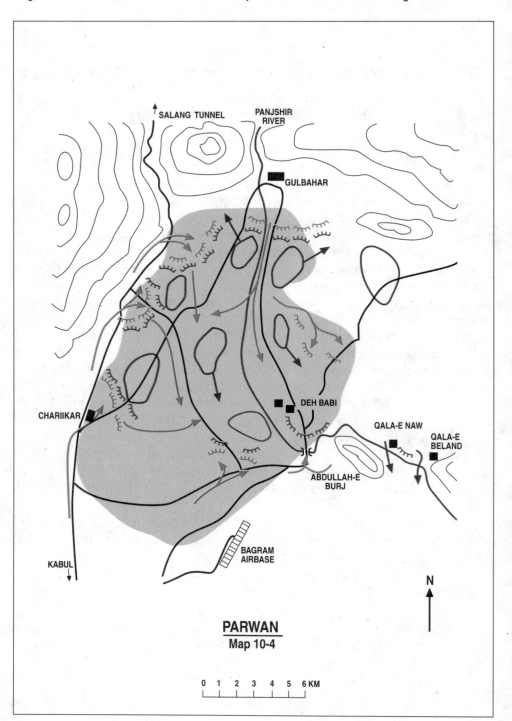

SALANG TUNNEL

PANJSHIR RIVER

GULBAHAR

DEH BABI

CHARIIKAR

QALA-E NAW

QALA-E BELAND

ABDULLAH-E BURJ

BAGRAM AIRBASE

KABUL

N

PARWAN
Map 10-4

0 1 2 3 4 5 6 KM

The Action Near Bagram

At that time, Haji Abdul Qader commanded some 200 Mujahideen in the Bagram District. His permanent base was co-located with a JIA base under Commander Shahin at Deh Babi near Abdullah-e Burj. His other base was at Ashrafi near Charikar. His group was a mobile group and spent most of its time fighting around Bagram or combined with other Mujahideen units in Parwan and Kapisa Provinces.

During the Soviet cordon and search operation in Parwan and Kapisa Provinces, Haji Abdul Qader's unit, along with a 150 strong unit under Commander Sher Mohammad, was to defend a line north of the main Bagram-Mahmoud-e Raqi road between Abdullah-e Burj and Qala-e Beland. To the west, HIH faction Mujahideen were blocking the Bagram-Charikar axis, and on the east flank, JIA units were covering the area on the left bank of Panjsher River (Map 10-4 - Parwan).

The night before the attack, Soviet and DRA artillery pounded Mujahideen positions from fire bases that they established around the area. They attacked swiftly and engaged the Mujahideen on all axes with infantry and armor or pinned them down with heavy artillery and air strikes. Their air force intensified the pressure on the second day as ground attack aircraft and helicopter gunships supported the attacking columns. Mujahideen communications were seriously disrupted and their tactical coordination dropped off dramatically.

Haji Qader ordered his men to occupy prepared blocking positions. They were armed with Kalashnikovs, some 15 RPG-7 anti-tank grenade launchers, three 82mm and one 75mm recoilless rifles, three 82mm mortars, two DShK machine guns and one ZGU-1 heavy machine gun. They also had a few 107mm surface-to-surface rockets. Haji Qader deployed all his anti-tank weapons forward and emplaced his heavy machine guns on the high ground behind the front line. Haji Qader split his force and rotated them in the defensive positions. The Mujahideen who were not manning the positions constituted the reserve and concentrated in Baltukhel and Sayadan, some two to three kilometers to the northwest. Qader's supplies and aid station were also located in this area.

At dawn on January 25, opposing artillery pounded Mujahideen positions for about two hours. The intensity of fire kept the resistance fighters down inside their bunkers. Some Mujahideen took cover in the ruins and terrain folds and ditches. The artillery fire was accompanied by air strikes and gun runs by helicopter gunships. The Mujahideen did not expose themselves during the fire strikes. A little after sunrise, opposing infantry, backed by tanks and BMPs, launched the attack. The attacking columns moved confidently, assuming that the artillery fire and air strikes had destroyed the Mujahideen resistance. However, as they came within range, Mujahideen anti-tank weapons and machine guns opened up. They caught the attackers by surprise and forced the infantry and tanks to fall back. The attackers were not very aggressive, probably as a result of their fear of mines and anti-tank weapons.

During the first two days, the Soviets repeated their attack several times following the same scenario: artillery fire and air strikes would hammer Mujahideen positions. Then the infantry and tanks would advance until they were stopped with withering fire at close quarter. They would then fall back. The tanks that were following the infantry were very slow to advance, particularly when some tanks were hit and the infantry suffered casualties. At the same time, the infantry would lose heart after being hit by withering defensive fire and would fall back to take cover behind the tanks.

As the operation continued, two factors worked against the Mujahideen. First, the enemy penetrated Mujahideen positions to considerable depth on some axes. This raised the fear of being encircled by flanking units. Second, as the Mujahideen began to understand the scope and intent of the enemy operation, they began to escape out of the enemy cordon. This weakened the Mujahideen positions and aided the attacker. Some adjacent units left their forward positions at the Qala-e Belend sector and fell back. This forced Haji Abdul Qader to withdraw his force on the third day to his planned second line of defense on high ground about one kilometer north of the forward defensive positions. For the next three days, the Soviets tried to break through Qader's positions on the high ground. It was even tougher going for them. They used the same method of assault with the infantry leading and the tanks following—and with the same results.

Toward the end of the week, hundreds of Mujahideen used the Qala-e Beland sector as an escape route to their mountain bases in Koh-e Safi in the south. The Mujahideen used a covered irrigation canal to sneak out of the area. Just north of the road near the Qala-e Naw bazaar, there is an east-west irrigation canal. Several north-south feeder canals intersect this main canal. At several points, the canal is bridged and covered to allow vehicles to cross. At these points, the main and feeder canals are covered. In winter, the irrigation system is dry and provided suitable escape passages. During the last nights of the operation, hundreds of Mujahideen escaped through the

canals to Koh-e Safi. The attackers detected this exodus only toward
the end of the operation and opened fire on some escapees. Haji Abdul
Qader's men provided the rear guard and were the last to move out of
the area after blocking the Qala-e Beland sector for one week.

When the Soviets and DRA finally entered the area, thousands of
Mujahideen had escaped. Haji Qader claims that the Soviets only captured about 20 armed Mujahideen and that the Soviet commander in
charge of the operation was reprimanded for his failure. He states that
the Soviets used several divisions, made elaborate plans and fired
thousands of artillery shells and flew hundreds of combat missions
without achieving much. Haji Abdul Qader's group destroyed 11 tanks
and APCs and inflicted dozens of casualties on the enemy. His losses
included seven KIA and 18 WIA. Most of his casualties came from helicopter gunships.

COMMENTARY: Although the Soviet/DRA forces overran many
Mujahideen bases in Parwan and Kapisa Provinces, they failed to
destroy the Mujahideen forces which slipped out of the cordon or went
underground. The Mujahideen enjoyed freedom of movement and
maneuver in a large area until the Soviets and DRA finally penetrated. The Soviet/DRA encirclement was very porous—as was the case
with so many large-scale cordon and search operations of the war—
making it impossible to trap Mujahideen forces. The poor performance
by the Soviet infantry and tanks against a determined enemy cost
them dearly. Instead of mounting coordinated infantry-tank assaults,
the Soviet forces seemed to use each element separately. While a combined action could minimize the vulnerabilities of each element, a dis-
jointed action maximized the vulnerability of both elements in the face
of a resolute defense.

The Mujahideen built a series of covered bunkers near their prepared fighting positions and these bunkers enabled them to survive air
strikes and intense artillery barrages. Most of this massive Soviet fire
destroyed civilians, houses and the agricultural system.

Lack of operational coordination among the Mujahideen groups
cost the resistance some major operational achievements. While the
Soviets failed to capture large numbers of Mujahideen or to destroy a
major Mujahideen grouping, the resistance missed a major opportunity to inflict heavy losses on the Soviets. The Mujahideen focused on
escape, when they had many chances to bloody their enemy by resist-
ing on consecutive defensive positions in the area and by cutting the
Soviet withdrawal routes once they were inside Mujahideen territory.

However, this was not the first nor the last battle for the resistance. They were fighting a war of attrition and refused to become decisively engaged in their home area where the civilians and villages would bear the brunt of the damage. In this area, the civilian population remained in their homes throughout the war.

Tactically, the Mujahideen massed the fires of their light anti-tank weapons at close range. Several anti-tank gunners would fire at the same target simultaneously. This greatly increased their probability of hit, prevented effective counter fires, demoralized vehicle crews, created confusion among their enemy's tank and motorized columns and prevented the employment of accurate, Soviet indirect artillery fire into the area. Heavy machine guns usually backed up the anti-tank gunners to separate the dismounted infantry from the armored vehicles, keep the vehicle crews buttoned up so that their vision was obscured, and provided covering fire should the anti-tank gunners need to leave their positions.

VIGNETTE 5
LAST STAND ON THE ISLANDS OPPOSITE GERDI KATS
by Mawlawi Shukur Yasini

On 24 March 1984, the Soviets sent a large force into Kama District. I was in Peshawar, Pakistan at that time. The Soviet force was not just the 66th Brigade, but also included a force which came from fighting in Laghman Province. The entire force had some 200-300 tanks and APCs in it. I had two groups of Mujahideen in the village of Merzakhel. One group was commanded by Baz Mohammad and the other by my nephew Shapur. Baz Mohammad's group managed to get out of Merzakhel before the Soviets arrived but Shapur's group of 25 was trapped. The Soviets landed troops on the high ground overlooking Merzakhel and their tanks were moving in from the west (Map10-5 - Gerdi). Across the river, Soviet tanks were moving through Gerdi Kats. The Mujahideen moved south from Merzakhel to the low, flat islands of the Kabul River between Gerdi Kats and Merzakhel. These islands are covered with a low-scrub which offers some concealment but not cover. As they reached the islands, the Soviet infantry in Gerdi Kats began to cross the river with inflatable rubber rafts. The Soviets also moved a tank into the river to cross over, but it quickly became stuck. Fairoz, a Mujahideen machine gunner, sunk the rafts with PK machine gun fire. The Soviet infantry sunk into the river and several drowned. The Soviets also had two dogs on the rafts. The dogs swam back to Gerdi Kats. Mujahideen fire from the islands pinned down the Soviets and defeated their crossing attempt.

However, at the same time, the enemy brought pressure on my group from both sides and only a few of my men managed to slip away. They were exposed on the low-scrub islands and I lost 11 KIA, two WIA and two captured. The two captured were Awozubellah and

Mawlawi Shukur Yasini is a prominent religious leader in Nangrahar Province. He is from the village of Gerdab in Kama District northeast of Jalalabad. During the war, he was a major commander of the Khalis group (HIK). Later, he joined NIFA. During the war, he took television journalist Dan Rather to his base in Afghanistan. He also accompanied Congressman Charles Wilson of Texas into Afghanistan several times. During most of the war he was active in his own area fighting the DRA in Jalalabad and the Soviet 66th Separate Motorized Rifle Brigade at Samarkhel. He became a member of the Nangrahar governing council after collapse of the communist regime--a position he held until the Taliban advance in September 1996. [Map sheet 3185].

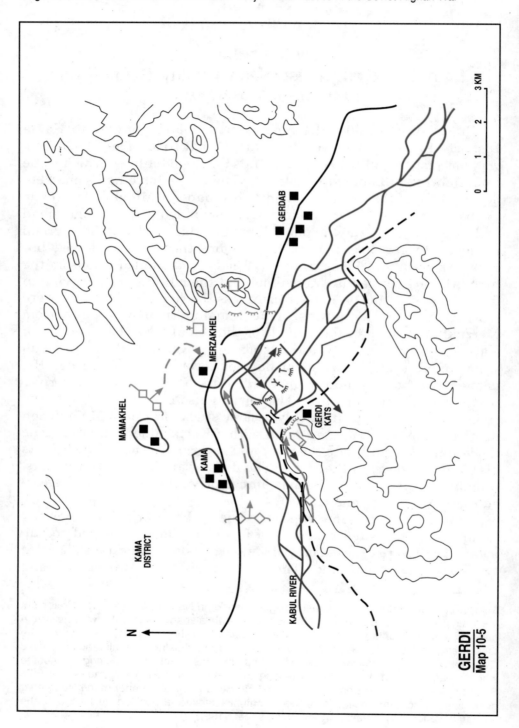

GERDAB

MERZAKHEL

MAMAKHEL

GERDI
KATS

KAMA

KAMA
DISTRICT

KABUL RIVER

N

0   1   2   3 KM

GERDI
Map 10-5

Nazar Mohammad. The Soviets tortured them, but they did not break. They continually claimed that crazy Mawlawi Shukur forced them to fight. Eventually, they were released. Shapur and Fairoz were wounded. Villagers took them to safe houses and kept moving them to hide them from the Soviets, who searched the area for six days. We could not retrieve our Mujahideen dead due to enemy pressure. Many of their remains were torn apart by foxes and jackals. After a week or so, we buried what remains we could find. The Soviets paid a 20,000 Afghanis reward for recovering their dead from the river. When I saw the condition of my dead, I banned Afghans from helping the Soviets recover their dead. "Let the crows of this country have their fair share."

COMMENTARY: The Kama Mujahideen usually tried to avoid the Soviet cordon and search of their district by fleeing into the mountains, but the Soviets habitually used heliborne forces to block their escape routes. This meant that the Kama Mujahideen fought the Soviets within the green zone. However, the Kama green zone had a road network within it and the Soviets could bring their combat vehicles into the green zone where their firepower gave the Soviets a tremendous advantage. The Soviets used the same mountain LZs over and over again, but the Mujahideen made no attempt to mine the LZs or post antiaircraft weapons overlooking these sites on a permanent basis. In this action, the Mujahideen were surprised and unable to escape into the mountains and forced to fight an uneven battle. If they had contested the known LZs, the outcome should have been less costly for the Mujahideen.

Crossing shallow desert rivers looks fairly safe, but can be treacherous. On the 31st of March 1879, the British Army lost 47 men, effectively a squadron of the 10th Hussars, crossing the Kabul River some 35 kilometers to the west of this Soviet crossing attempt. The Kabul River looks shallow and slow-moving, but it has fast, strong undercurrents that can quickly overpower the unwary soldier.

---

9 Colonel H. B. Hanna, *The Second Afghan War, 1878-79-80, Its Causes, Its Conduct, and Its Consequences, Volume II*, Westminister: Archibald Constable and Co., Ltd., 1904, 282-287.

CHAPTER COMMENTARY

The Soviet/DRA cordon and search usually involved a number of forces in a combined arms battle or operation. The Mujahideen who had the best success surviving these did so because their actions were centrally coordinated, they had developed contingency plans to deal with them and they had built redundant field fortifications to slow the Soviet/DRA advance and fragment their efforts. The better-prepared Mujahideen always retained a central reserve and were adept at counterattacking the flanks of the attacker. The Mujahideen who had the most difficulty with cordon and search operations were usually separate groups who had little or no ties to a central Mujahideen planning authority, had worked out no contingency plans and had taken no steps to fortify the area.

CHAPTER 11
DEFENDING BASE CAMPS

Although guerrilla forces would like to retain the initiative and never have to defend, there are times when the guerrilla force must defend. The guerrilla can conduct a mobile defense or a positional defense. Guerrilla mobile defenses are usually rear-guard actions designed to preserve the main force or draw the attacker into a prepared ambush. Guerrilla positional defenses are normally associated with the defense of a pass, bridge, populated area, base camp or supply depot. The odds are stacked against the defending guerrilla. The attacker has the initiative, armored vehicles, air power, the preponderance of artillery and overwhelming firepower. The guerrilla tries to match this through use of terrain and prepared defenses.

In the Soviet-Afghan war, the Mujahideen spent a great deal of time and energy in the defense. Mujahideen defense was associated with Mujahideen logistics. Early in the war, Mujahideen logistics requirements were primarily concerned with ammunition resupply and medical evacuation of the wounded. The rural population willingly provided food and shelter to the Mujahideen, since the Mujahideen were mostly local residents. The Soviets decided to attack Mujahideen logistics by forcing the rural population off of their farms into refugee camps in Pakistan and Iran or into the cities of Afghanistan. They did this by bombing and attacking villages, scattering mines across the countryside, destroying crops, killing livestock, poisoning wells and destroying irrigation systems. The Mujahideen, accustomed to living off the good will of the rural population, were now forced to transport rations as well as ammunition from Pakistan and Iran into Afghanistan. The Mujahideen created a series of supply depots and forward supply points to provision their forces. These depots and supply points had to be defended. The Mujahideen also controlled key passes, which forced the Soviets and DRA to either withdraw cut-off forces or resupply them by air. The Mujahideen defended these key passes zealously.

The rugged terrain of Afghanistan aided Mujahideen defenses. Defensive positions were another key component of the Mujahideen defens. Mujahideen built rugged, roofed bunkers which could withstand artillery and airstrikes. The Mujahideen built elaborate camouflaged defensive shelters and fighting positions connected with interlocking fields of fire, communications trenches, and redundant firing positions. The Mujahideen learned to rotate defensive forces through a position to lessen the effects of combat fatigue and psychological stress.

What follows are examples of successful and unsuccessful Mujahideen base camp defenses against ground attack or a combination of ground and air assault.

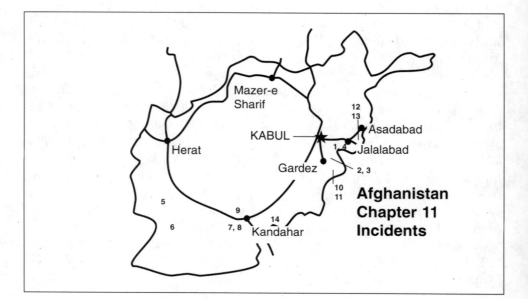

VIGNETTE 1
SOVIET OFFENSIVE THROUGH SURKH RUD
by Commander Mohammad Asef

During 1978-1979, the heavily-populated Surkh Rud District was a hotbed of resistance against the communist regime and a base for Mujahideen actions in Nangrahar Province. Following the Soviet invasion, one of the early major Soviet operations was conducted against Mujahideen bases in Surkh Rud. There are two main roads running northeast to southwest in Surkh Rud Valley (Map 11-1 - Chaharbagh). Highway 134 runs through Chaharbagh, Watapur, Surkh Rud (the district headquarters), Khayrabad, and Fatehabad. The other road runs along the bottom of Tor Ghar mountain. It passes through Darunta, Katapur, Balabagh, and then follows the Surkh Rud River to the west. Most of the Mujahideen bases were located along these two roads and most Mujahideen bases also maintained hideouts in the canyons of the Tor Ghar mountain. My home town of Bazetkhel was located between the two roads, but my base was just to the east of Highway 134.

The Soviet forces concentrated in Jalalabad in May 1980. We were tipped off that the Soviets planned to advance along the two roads, destroying Mujahideen bases as they went. Their southern column would swing north at Fatehabad to seal the pocket. I left my base at Chaharbagh and went to my village at Bazetkhel, where I had 80 men. I took 50 of these men north into a Tor Ghar mountain canyon. We intended to stop the Soviet column on the northern route before they reached the main Mujahideen base at Katapur. We also hoped to buy enough time to allow the civilians to escape into the mountains. When the column approached, my force engaged them and we stopped the column. The Soviets dismounted and began moving aggressively into the mountains. They were a bit too aggressive and our fire cut them down. The Soviets were badly bloodied. The Soviets responded by calling in massive artillery fire on my positions. When night fell, I pulled my force further up the canyon to the mountain ridge and then crossed over into the next canyon to the west. We moved down the canyon and into the town of Katapur.

Mohammad Asef was initially a Hezbi-Islami (HIH) commander until 1984 when he joined NIFA. He was in high school when the communists came to power. He graduated from school and then joined the resistance. He is from Bazetkhel in Surkh Rud District southwest of Jalalabad in Nangrahar Province. [Map sheet 3085].

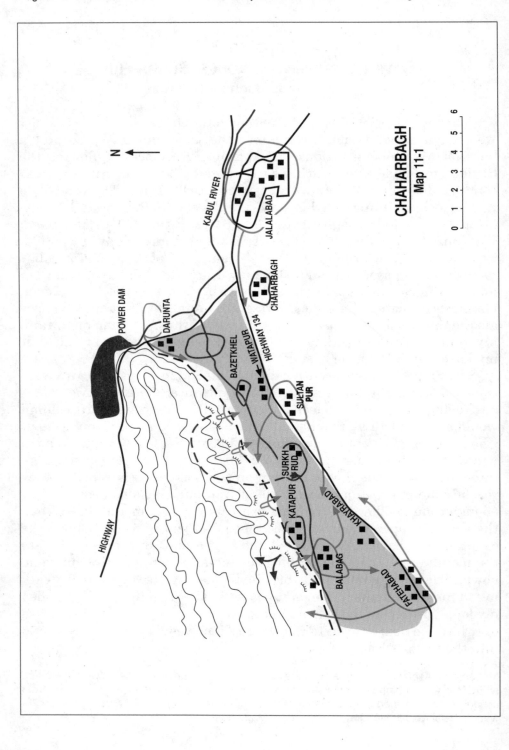

CHAHARBAGH
Map 11-1

At Katapur, the local Mujahideen told us that Soviet troops had chased the civilians into the mountains just north of Katapur and killed many of them. During the fighting near Katapur, the Soviets had left two of their dead behind. The Mujahideen expected that the Soviets would return for their dead. My Mujahideen joined other Mujahideen and we went to defend a canyon to the north of Katapur. We laid an ambush on the high ground. Soon, a Soviet detachment appeared looking for their dead. We opened up on the Soviets and they left seven more dead behind. However, they retaliated on the villagers and massacred civilians and even animals in Balabagh and Katapur and then moved on to Fatehabad. The Soviets could not dislodge the Mujahideen from the mountains and could not find us in the valley, so they killed everything in sight. They established three bases—at Balabagh, Fatehabad and Sultan Pur. The Soviets launched search-and-destroy missions from these bases against the adjacent villages. Many civilians had to flee west while Mujahideen detachments went to their hideouts in the Tor Ghar mountain. Mujahideen commanders calculate that the Soviets massacred some 1,800 people during 12 days in the Surkh Rud. Most of these were innocent civilians. The Soviets expected that they could readily flush out the Mujahideen. Their lack of success led to frustration and the Soviet soldiers ran amok—killing and looting. It was the first Soviet operation in the area. They came looking for U.S. and Chinese mercenaries and instead found frustration and an opportunity to murder and loot.

COMMENTARY: During this stage of the war, the Mujahideen lived in their own houses in the midst of the population. Their food, water and shelter was willingly supplied by the populace. As a result, many civilians died when the Soviets launched their operation. The large number of reported civilian deaths could be a result of lack of officers' control and unit discipline or deliberate policy. The apparent Soviet plan was to separate the guerrilla from the populace by forcing the populace out of the countryside. Later, most of the populace deserted their homes in this area and fled to refugee camps in Pakistan.

This is too large an area to block and sweep as a single action and the Soviets failed to segment the area and clear it a piece at a time. This allowed many of the Mujahideen and civilians to escape the cordon. The Soviet emphasis on the primacy of the large operation instead of the well-executed tactical action worked to the Mujahideen advantage. Mujahideen command and control was fragmented and worked through happenstance and chance encounters. Without advanced warning, the Mujahideen would probably have suffered much more in this sweep.

DEFENDING SURKHAB BASE CAMP
by Haji Sayed Mohammad Hanif

In 1980, the Mujahideen began establishing bases in the mountains near the village of Surkhab in Lowgar Province. There were perhaps 150 Mujahideen in the area belonging to several factions. Mawlawi Mohammad Yusuf of the ANLF, Mawlawi Mohammadin of the IRMA and small groups from JIA and IUA established bases there. My base was in the mountains east of Surkhab in a canyon called Durow. We had 82mm mortars, DShKs and RPG-7s. Early in the morning of the 5th of June 1980, a mixed DRA/Soviet column came from Kabul and exited highway 157 at Pule-e Kandahari heading east. They were coming for us. They deployed their artillery and began shelling our bases. Most of the Mujahideen were in their villages at that time. They came out of their villages and occupied defensive positions while other Mujahideen joined them from their mountain bases.

In order to block the advance of the enemy into our mountain bases, we occupied blocking positions on Spin Ghar mountain overlooking Dara village (Map 11-2 - Surkhab). Other Mujahideen occupied positions south of Durow Canyon on Lakay Ghar mountain. Our original plan was to defend the forward slopes of Spin Ghar and Lakay Ghar. We set an ambush forward of our main defenses. It inflicted casualties but was eventually overwhelmed. After their artillery preparation, enemy tanks and infantry moved along the valley road from Korek and attacked Mujahideen positions at the canyon's western mouth. Fighting was heavy. This was our first experience fighting the Soviets. Their helicopters came in to evacuate their dead and wounded. Our civilians suffered horribly. The people began leaving their homes and fleeing to the mountains. Fighting continued all day long, but the enemy was unable to break through the Mujahideen positions.

On the second day, there were fewer Mujahideen fighting, as some had left the area overnight. The enemy firing kept tremendous pressure on the remaining Mujahideen and many had to withdraw from their fighting positions. There is a covered approach to Spin Ghar mountain from the north using the Tobagi plain. This plain is

---

Haji Sayed Mohammad Hanif is from Logar Province. [Map sheet 2885, vic grid 2577].

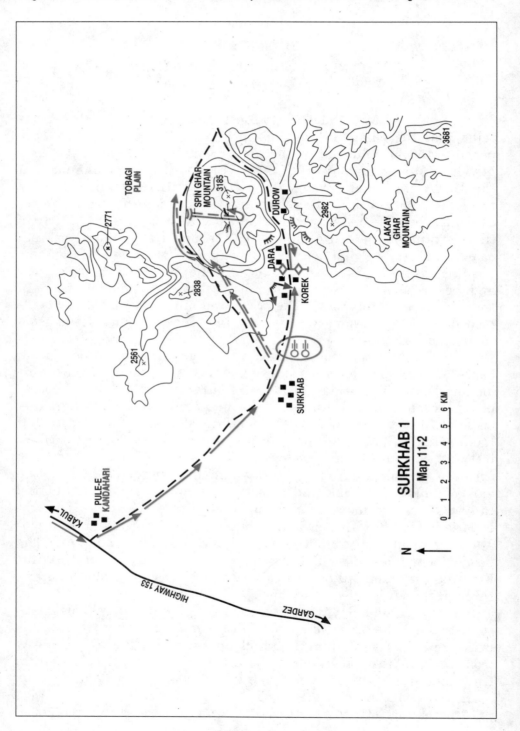

SURKHAB 1

Map 11-2

higher than Surkhab village and it is easier to climb Spin Ghar mountain from the Tobagi plain than from the Surkhab Valley. I was climbing the mountain with two others carrying ammunition. I intended to climb over the mountain to the north face. As we reached halfway up the ridge, enemy aircraft flew over the area. The enemy usually marked their infantry positions for the aircraft by firing smoke or signal rockets. We saw rockets being fired on the other side of the mountain. This meant that enemy infantry were on the other side of the mountain and were trying to encircle the Mujahideen bases by a flanking movement from the Tobagi plain. I had all our spare ammunition with me and at that time ammunition was as precious to me as my faith. We climbed back down the mountain and saw that the other Mujahideen were retreating into their bases. The people of Surkhab came to the Mujahideen and demanded that we move our bases lest Surkhab be invaded everyday. The Mullas had refused to move the bases earlier, but now they were panicked and hiding in caves. The people taunted them with "You told us this was Jihad, but now you are trying to flee." Some of the Mullas came out, but everyone was still panicked. I had all of this ammunition and no one to help me move it. I thought of abandoning the ammunition and saving my skin, but then I thought how vital the ammunition was and what would happen if I was later called to account for my actions.

Finally, a group of us decided to make a suicidal last stand and called for volunteers. Lieutenant Sharab, a DRA deserter, volunteered. We had suspected him earlier, but he proved himself now. Lieutenant Sharab said, "They are not used to mountains. It will take them a long time to climb them and they are afraid of these mountains. If you fire at them from one position, they will stop and return fire for a long time at that position." We fired mortars at the north slope and positioned some Mujahideen on the top of Spin Ghar mountain to draw fire. This was the turning point. All of a sudden, helicopter activity fell off and firing tapered off in the valley. We thought that it was a trick to make us believe that the fighting was over so the Mujahideen would come out of their hideouts and then they would take us from behind. We did not expect that such a powerful enemy would abandon an almost certain victory and retire empty-handed. It was late afternoon when I saw civilians coming from Surkhab. They told us that the enemy had withdrawn. The enemy evidently did not want to have to fight to take the mountain. This was not our doing, but the hand of God. We lost 10 KIA and six WIA in my group. I do not know the casualties in other groups. All the wounded who could walk, walked to Pakistan for treatment. The other wounded were treated by local doctors. Doctors from Kabul hospitals would come to help us also. Dr. Abdur Rahman from a hospital in Kabul would often treat our wounded. I do not know what the enemy losses were, but they must have suffered a lot to quit on the brink of victory.

COMMENTARY: The DRA/Soviets had the opportunity to attack the eastern and western canyon mouths simultaneously. The Mujahideen defenses were oriented to the west. Even on the second day, when the DRA/Soviets tried to envelop the Mujahideen position from the Tobagi plain, they did not hook around the mountain, but tried to go over the mountain. The Mujahideen were used to the mountains, whereas the Soviets were not and their equipment was not designed for climbing in mountains. Later in the war, the Soviets issued better equipment for fighting in the mountains and began training their soldiers at mountain warfare sites. At this point, the non-nimble Soviets and the reluctant DRA were no match for the Mujahideen in mountain maneuver. They should have taken the canyon from both ends. Further, if the DRA or Soviets had covertly moved some artillery spotters onto high ground before the offensive, they could have unhinged the Mujahideen defenses before they were established.

The Soviets had not yet developed their air assault tactics for counterinsurgency. The mountain tops of Spin Ghar and Lakay Ghar can handle heliborne landings and the Mujahideen air defense posture was negligible at this point. A small Soviet force, reinforced with mortars, artillery spotters and forward air controllers and machine guns could have created havoc from the mountain tops.

FALL OF SURKHAB BASE CAMP
by Haji Sayed Mohammad Hanif

In early September 1983, we laid an ambush at Pul-e Khandari on Highway 157, the major road between Kabul and Gardez. At that time, Mujahideen ambushes were hurting the DRA/Soviet efforts to keep Gardez supplied. The enemy convoys always left Kabul in the morning. We would get into position in the morning and wait until afternoon. If no convoys had shown by afternoon, we would quit and go back to base or go take a nap in the villages. The enemy finally figured out that we were reacting to their pattern and changed their pattern. They started moving their convoys in the afternoon on the assumption that we Mujahideen would have abandoned the ambush sites, since it was long past time for the convoy to arrive. As usual, we set up our ambush in the morning and waited. No convoy came. We left the ambush site and, by late afternoon, most of the Mujahideen had left the area. Then the column of some 180 trucks arrived. What Mujahideen were left in the village ran to the road and engaged the supply convoy which was hauling ammunition, fuel and food. We got part of the convoy and divided the booty among the Mujahideen groups that had representatives at the ambush. My group managed to capture some ammunition trucks, which we drove to our base near Surkhab in Durow Canyon.

A few days later, a major enemy force moved against our base camps to retaliate for this attack. They kept the area under siege for eight days. We had a total of about 300 Mujahideen from various groups in the area at this time. Our heavy weapons were DShK machine guns and mortars. We had expected some retaliation, so we had prepared defensive positions on the ridges on both sides of the canyon mouth and laid some antitank mines in the area. We also laid an antitank minefield on the trail to the Tobagi plain (Map 11-3 - Surkhab2). The enemy column came through Pule-e Kandahari. They attacked and lost some Soviet armored vehicles to mines on the northern and southern approaches to the canyon. Mujahideen fighting positions on the high ground overlooked these minefields, so we could fire on the advancing enemy as they tried to

---

Haji Sayed Mohammad Hanif provided the previous vignette. [Mapsheet 2885, vic grid 2577].

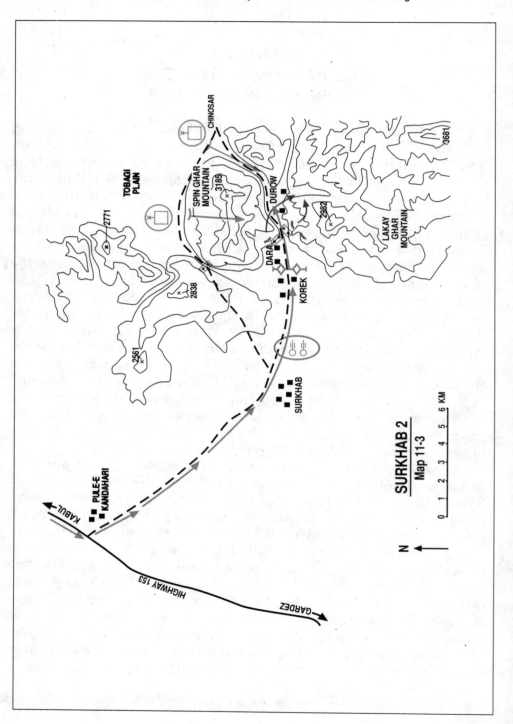

SURKHAB 2

Map 11-3

get through the mines. This slowed the enemy, but we also took losses from their aerial bombardment. We held on and managed to stop the enemy advance. The enemy evacuated their damaged tanks and armored vehicles.

After one week of fighting, the enemy reinforced his effort. Some of the Mujahideen had left since the enemy was stopped and they had to take care of their families. The enemy employed air assault forces, which they landed on the Tobagi plain and at Chinosar at the eastern mouth to our canyon. They had outflanked us. Now the enemy renewed his offensive with an attack against the western and eastern mouths of the canyon and over the Spin Ghar mountain. We could not hold and withdrew from our western positions on Spin Ghar and Lakay Ghar mountains. We torched the trucks that we had captured to prevent their recapture. The enemy reached our canyon village of Durow and found the burnt-out hulks. We moved east into the mountains and harrassed the enemy with mortar fire, but they now controlled our base camps. They destroyed what they could and left. As they left, they scattered mines in some areas.

COMMENTARY: By 1983, the Soviets were using their air assault forces more aggressively, but still not landing them directly on the objective. In this case, Soviet air assault forces landed on Tobagi plain and then climbed to the top of Spin Ghar mountain. By 1986, Soviet air assault forces would be landing directly on the objectives.

The Mujahideen were tied to their bases and had to defend them. This logistic imperative provided some advantages to the DRA and Soviets, who knew that the one way to get the Mujahideen to stay in an area where they could concentrate air power and artillery against them was to locate the Mujahideen logistics base and attack it. Still, the Soviets and DRA seldom did anything to "close the back door" to the base while they attacked it. Consequently, many Mujahideen lived to fight another day. Long range reconnaissance patrols, scatterable mines, helicopter-landed ambush forces and conventional forces in backstop positions are ways to prevent the escape of guerrilla forces.

The Mujahideen appear to have done little to improve their defenses since this same base camp was almost overrun in June of 1980. The DRA and Soviets knew where this base camp was and how it was defended, yet the Mujahideen established no eastern defenses. The Mujahideen's one improvement appears to be mining the approach to the Tobagi plain, but they had no force guarding that minefield. The Soviets flew over that minefield anyway.

VIGNETTE 4
LOSS OF THE TOR GHAR BASE CAMP
by Commander Sher Padshah

Tor Ghar mountain lies eight kilometers northwest of Jalalabad. Adam Khan and Rasul Khan established the Tor Ghar Mujahideen base but were killed in early fighting. In 1980, the overall commander of the base was Qari Alagul. The base held some 200 Mujahideen from four or five factions. I was a subgroup commander under Commander Abdullah at the time. We had bases at both Chaharbagh and Tor Ghar and regularly launched attacks against the Soviets from Tor Ghar. Our contacts in the DRA had told us that the Soviets would soon attack Tor Ghar in retaliation. Late one afternoon in July 1980, our DRA contacts told us that the Soviets were coming that night. I was with my group in Chaharbagh on the southeast side of the mountain. Commander Abdullah was at the Tor Ghar base. We immediately sent him a note to warn him and asked him to bury the ammunition and everything else since the Soviets would come in strength and Abdullah's force could not expect to hold them. Abdullah sent a note back to us. "As long as you hear my 20-shooters,[1] you know that we are holding. We will swear on the Koran not to leave our position." Abdullah had 25 men armed with RPGs, Kalashnikovs, Bernaus and bolt-action rifles.

The Soviets attacked from several directions (Map 11-4 - Tor Ghar) launching advances from Sorkh Rud, Jalalabad and Darunta. I withdrew my group from Chaharbagh. Soviet tanks deployed along the road on the north-west side of the mountain and fired on the base. BM-21s fired from Jalalabad. Artillery and BM-21s fired from multiple artillery sites. Helicopters strafed the area. They set the mountain on fire. Then the Soviets climbed the mountain, reached the base and fought for three days. In places, it was hand-to-hand combat. We could not break into the area to help, since the Soviets had sealed the area. Our Mujahideen fought until their ammunition was gone and died to the last man. The Soviets destroyed the bases and infested that mountain with mines.

COMMENTARY: Mujahideen insistence on holding base camps cost them

---

Commander Sher Padshah is from Laghman Province. Map sheet 3085.

[1] Bernau M26 Czechoslovak light machine guns.

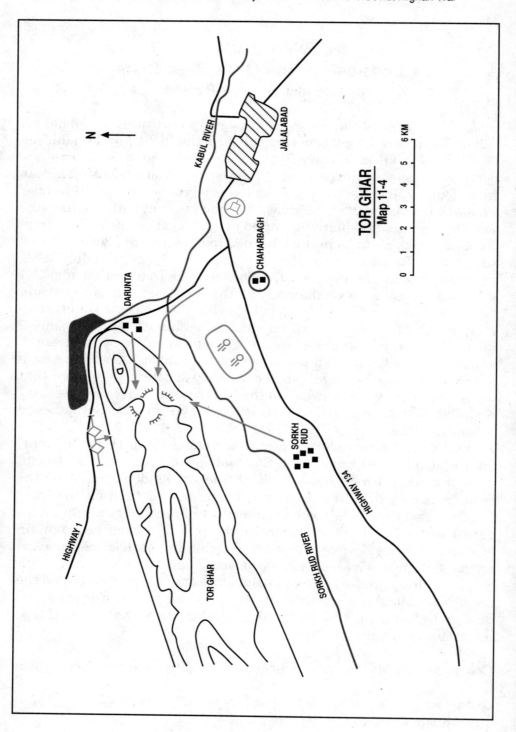

TOR GHAR
Map 11-4

dearly. At this point in the war, base camps were not essential to Mujahideen logistics and Abdullah's base camp was not the only one which the Soviets overran. It was a pointless battle which could have been avoided by the Mujahideen. When the Mujahideen held real estate, it allowed the Soviets to concentrate their superior firepower on the Mujahideen.

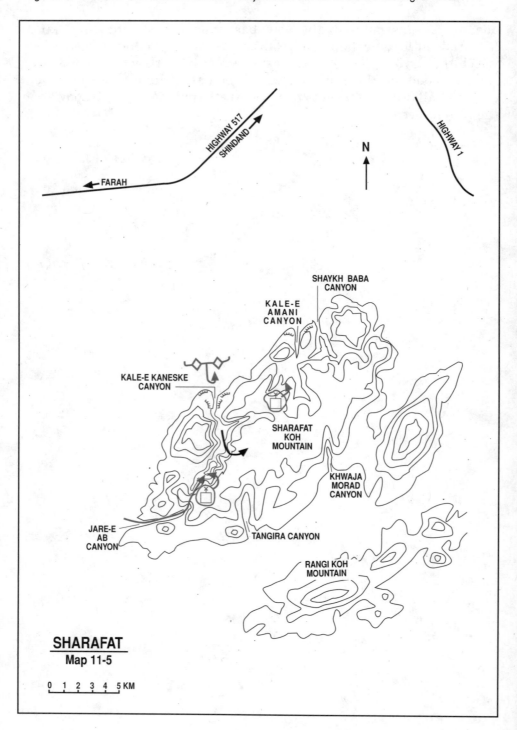

SHARAFAT

Map 11-5

0 1 2 3 4 5 KM

VIGNETTE 5
BATTLES FOR SHARAFAT KOH MOUNTAIN FORTRESS
by Engineer Mohammad Ibrahim

Sharafat Koh is a large mountain southeast of the city of Farah. It is located between the paved road running between Kandahar and Herat (Highway 1) and the Daulatabad-Farah road (Highway 517). The real name of the mountain is Lor Koh, but we Mujahideen renamed it Sharafat Koh (Honor Mountain).[2] The mountain is a roughly rectangular-shaped massif with a plateau on top. It rises some 1,500 meters above the surrounding desert and its sides are steep. It covers over 256 square kilometers and is often snow capped. Many large and small canyons (*kals*) cut into the mountain. On the north side is the Shaykh Razi Baba Canyon (Map 11-5 - Sharafat— red and blue graphics apply to last battle). To the northwest is the Kale-e Amani Canyon. This canyon was populated by ancient peoples and you can see their drawings of hunters with bows and arrows on the rocks. To the west is the Kale-e Kaneske Canyon. The Jare-e Ab Canyon faces southwest and links with the Kal-e Kaneske Canyon at the top. To the south is the Tangira Canyon which had the most water, but which the Mujahideen usually avoided since it was the only canyon wide enough for armored vehicles to enter. Facing south, and further to the east is the Khwaja Morad Canyon near the Khwaja Morad shrine. There is access to all the canyons from the mountain plateau.

The Kal-e Kaneske Canyon was the strongest base at Sharafat Koh. It takes 35-40 minutes to walk from its entrance to the end. The canyon mouth is an opening in solid rock and is only two or three meters wide. When you walk into the canyon, you cannot see the sky above you, but later it widens into a three or four hectare area at the end of the canyon where there are trees. A stream runs intermittently through the canyon. There is even a water fall with

---

Engineer Mohammad Ibrahim is a graduate of Kabul University in the College of Agriculture. He was a group commander in Farah Province and doubled as medical officer and facilitator. Initially he was with Mawlawi Mohammad Shah but left in 1985 when his Barakzai tribe had a falling out with the Achakzai tribe of Mawlawi Mohammad Shah. He then fought for Haji Ghulam Rasul Shiwani. He now works with the UNHCR. [Map sheets 1581 and 1582].

[2] The communists called it Mordar Koh (Filthy Mountain) after the Mujahideen moved their bases there in 1979.

a 40 meter drop. The canyon had a water reservoir, a supply dump and 16 caves holding 60 people. We defended the canyon with DShK machine guns on the high ground on both sides of the canyon.

In the early days of the war, the Mujahideen had very strong bases around the province centers of Farah and Nimruz, but later on Soviet/DRA pressure forced them outward from Farah to Sharafat Koh. The Mujahideen had their first base at Sharafat Koh in the Tangira Canyon in 1979. The Mujahideen were organized into tribal groups and initially the Achakzai, Norzai, Barakzai and Alizai all joined together and moved to a new base in Jare-e Ab Canyon. The Soviets attacked this base in 1980 and the Mujahideen then moved to Kal-e Kaneske Canyon. The Mujahideen had bases within the city of Farah until 1982. As the DRA and Soviets tightened their security around Farah, these Mujahideen moved out and some fell back on Sharafat Koh. After the Mujahideen left Farah, they lost their contact with the city population. The city population was not tribal and looked down on the Mujahideen as rustics. In turn, the Mujahideen looked down on the city dwellers for their easy life.

Sharafat Koh lies about 12 kilometers from Highway 1 and 20 kilometers from Highway 517. We attacked convoys near Karvangah, Charah and Shivan and the Soviets manned posts at Karvangah, Charah and Velamekh to protect the convoys.

SKY WARRIORS STRIKE THE CANYON

In 1982, the Kal-e Kaneske Canyon was our primary base. Our leader was Mawlawi Mohammad Shah from the Achakzai tribe.[3] Mohammad Shah liked to brag about his base and would often escort visitors through the canyon. Once he brought a DRA officer into the canyon and gave him a tour. The DRA officer was also an Achakzai and he told Mohammad Shah that he was stationed in Shindand and wanted to establish secret contact with Mohammad Shah and work with him. Evidently, while the DRA officer was in our canyon, he managed to steal a map showing our base defenses.

At noon in July, about a month after the DRA officer's visit, three Soviet helicopter gunships suddenly flew down the canyon and fired at the caves and structures of our base. Our DShK machine guns were all positioned on the high ground and could not engage aircraft flying below them in the canyon. The gunships were severely damag-

---

[3] Mawlawi Mohammad Shah was one of the famous commanders of the war. He was a member of the Islamic Revolutionary Movement (IRMA) of Mohammad Nabi Mohammadi.

ing our base. Khodai-Rahm was one of the DShK gunners. Physically, he was a weak person, but he took the 34 kilogram (75 pound) weapon off the mount, hoisted it on his shoulder and fired down into the canyon. He hit two of the helicopters, one of them in the rotors. That helicopter gunship climbed to the top of the mountain and then the rotors quit turning. The pilot bailed out, but he was only 50 meters above the mountain and he and the helicopter crashed onto the mountain southern wall near the interior mouth of the canyon. The second damaged helicopter managed to escape, while the third helicopter attacked the Mujahideen DShK gunners. Khodai-Rahm was killed by the third helicopter.

The cheering Mujahideen rushed to the helicopter. There were five dead Soviets—the pilot, two crew members and two passengers. One of the passengers was a woman. One of the Mujahideen cut off the pilot's head and brought it to Mohammad Shah. Suddenly Soviet fighter-bombers flew over our base and began bombing us. Toward late afternoon, Soviet transport helicopters flew in and landed some three kilometers from the canyon mouth. Soviet troops dismounted and took up blocking positions—presumably to prevent us from taking the downed crew out. Early the next morning, Soviet armored vehicles arrived and surrounded the area. (Map 11-6 - Kaneske 1) Soviet infantry pushed forward, supported by armor. The Soviet infantry moved on the high ground along the Tora Para[4] toward the crash site. Some Soviets moved along the canyon floor and the opposite canyon wall, supported by troops on the high ground of Tora Para. As the Soviets advanced, they marked boulders and rocks with numbers for orientation. After seven days of fighting, they reached the helicopter crash site. We retreated to higher ground by the waterfall. On the eighth day, the Soviets left, taking their dead, including the headless torso, with them. They left the hulk of the helicopter behind.

COMMENTARY: One of the more successful Mujahideen air defense ambushes involved digging in heavy machine guns into caves in canyon walls. When the Soviet/DRA helicopters flew down the canyon, the machine guns would fire across the canyon filling the air with bullets. The helicopters could not attack the machine guns and were hard pressed to avoid the bullets. This ambush would have worked well in Kaneske Canyon.

---

[4] Para means ridge.

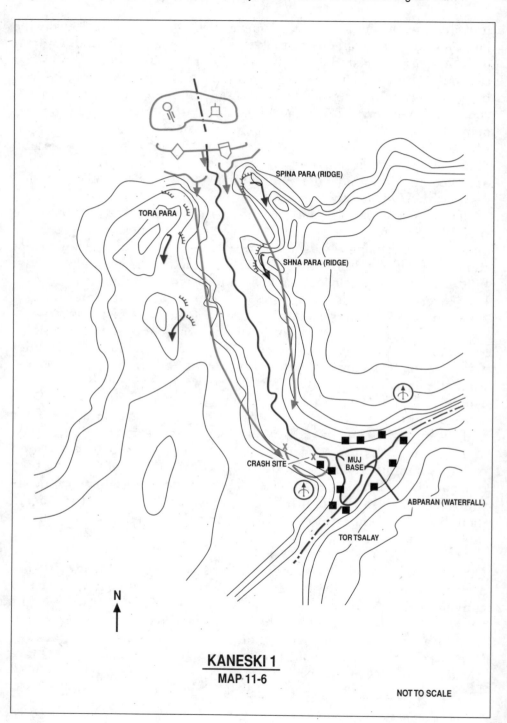

SPINA PARA (RIDGE)

TORA PARA

SHNA PARA (RIDGE)

CRASH SITE

MUJ
BASE

ABPARAN (WATERFALL)

TOR TSALAY

N

KANESKI 1
MAP 11-6

NOT TO SCALE

The Soviets painted numbers on boulders and rocks to provide reference points during their attack. This is a good technique as it aids adjusting air and artillery fire and keeping track of the progress of units as they advance. Still, the Soviet attack was a frontal attack which allowed the Mujahideen to concentrate their fires against the Soviet advance.

A SUCCESSFUL DEFENSE

In March 1983, our group leader, Mawlawi Mohammad Shah, took the bulk of our Mujahideen to Nimruz Province. Iran had supplied him with weapons and encouraged him to join the Mujahideen in Nimruz Province in attacking the DRA 4th Border Guards Brigade at Kang Wolowali (District) near the Iranian border. Along with the Iranian weapons, Mohammad Shah took most of our DShK machine guns. The attack on the border post failed and Mohammad Shah lost 35 men. His own son lost a leg in the fighting. It was a heavy blow to our group and we felt that Iran had conspired in our defeat. At the time, Mohammad Shah was about to form an alliance with the Maoist Gul Mohammad and Parviz Shahriyari. Both were from Harakat (IRMA) and receiving arms from Iran. Under the alliance, we would leave Sharafat Koh and move to Chahar Burjak. This would have strengthened the Mujahideen and Iran wanted to weaken us and make us dependent on Iran. As a result of the disastrous attack, the Sharafat Koh Front was now weakened and we only had 25 men in our base. After the disaster, I was preparing to leave the base and visit my home, but as I moved out I saw that the Soviets were fighting in Shiwan, so I returned to the base where I made radio transmissions supposedly sending 50 men to this ridge and 40 men to that ridge. This radio deception was supposed to keep the Soviets at bay.

I was sleeping at Nizam Qarawol, the gate security post at the mouth of the canyon, when, early in the morning, we heard a helicopter flying over. (Map 11-7 - Kaneske 2) We put our ears to the ground and heard the noise of tanks approaching. We quickly moved through the darkness to our base, pausing only to lay some antitank mines. Mohammad Shah's deputy, Haji Nur Ahmad Khairkhaw, was in charge. We had gathered in the darkness discussing what to do when Malek Ghulam Haidar and his Mujahideen from Shiwan joined us. They had noted the Soviet preparations and guessed that we were the target, so they came across the desert to join us. They

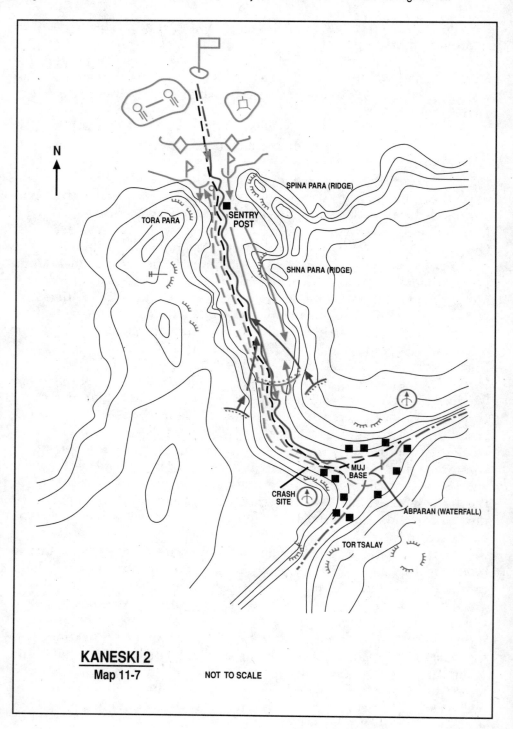

N

SPINA PARA (RIDGE)

TORA PARA

SENTRY
POST

SHNA PARA (RIDGE)

H

MUJ
BASE

CRASH
SITE

ABPARAN (WATERFALL)

TOR TSALAY

KANESKI 2
Map 11-7   NOT TO SCALE

arrived hours before the Soviets. We vowed to resist and to kill anyone who tried to flee. We took up positions on the high ground on
both sides of the canyon on the ridges of Tora Para, Shna Para and
Spina Para. We also put five men on the rear approach to the canyon
and put some men on Tor Tsalay to watch the approach from Jar-e Ab
Canyon. It was raining, but not enough to stop the Soviet aircraft.
Observation aircraft flew over and then fighter-bombers flew over in
groups of three. They made bombing runs on us. We only had two
DShK machine guns left and they were not enough to keep the aircraft away. The enemy intensified his bombing. They also began firing artillery at us and kept it up all night, depriving us of sleep.

Before sunrise on the second day, the enemy ground attack
began. There were probably two battalions in the attack. One battalion attacked Tora Para and the other attacked Spina Para. Tanks
supported the dismounted infantry, who tried to approach the canyon
but failed. During the afternoon of the second day, Malek Ghulam
Haidar was killed deep inside the base area. We had several Afghan
prisoners in our base, who we detained for disputes and crimes
committed in the area controlled by the Mujahideen. A Haji from Zir
Koh was one of our prisoners. He described how a lone Soviet came
into the camp and pointed his rifle at the prisoners. Through sign
language, they indicated that they were prisoners, so the Soviet
herded them into the prison cave and stood outside for awhile. Then
he disappeared. Nabi, who was carrying food to our front lines
returned to the camp and saw the Soviet. Since he was unarmed, he
ran and the Soviet followed him. Nabi ran to the arms depot where
Malek Haidar was. Nabi told him that Soviets had penetrated the
base from the mountain top. Malek took his American G3 rifle and
his Soviet TT pistol and walked out of the depot cave. The Soviet was
waiting behind a rock. He fired two shots and killed Haidar. Then
he took Haidar's G3 and pistol and left. I was sitting at the first aid
station near the front lines when I heard Abdul Hai yell "Who are
you? Who are you? Stop!" at the Soviet. Another Mujahideen was
going to shoot him, but didn't since the Soviet was far away and they
thought that he might be a prisoner carrying supplies to the forward
positions. The Soviet was in uniform, but he was down in the canyon
and we were high above him on the canyon walls and couldn't really
tell. Since the Soviet aircraft were still bombing us, we did not
believe that a single Soviet had snuck into our base and was now
leaving. Timurshah Khan Mu'alim, who was at Shna Para, also
aimed at the Soviet, but Bashar, Mohammad Shah's nephew, talked

him out of it, convinced that the stranger was one of our own. Later, we learned that the Soviets had invited some local elders to the attack site to impress them with their strength. The elders later described how the Soviet soldier came running into the site proudly holding his trophy weapons over his head. The Soviets again fired artillery at us all night.

Early on the morning of the third day, the Soviets again attacked. They figured that we had no forces on the canyon floor, so they fired smoke rounds into the canyon. We thought they were using poison gas and tied handkerchiefs over our faces. The Soviets moved into the canyon under the cover of the smoke. At first, we fired blindly into the smoke from the high ground until we saw them signaling each other with flares. We fired at the flares and then realized, from the flares' positions, that they had penetrated far into the base. The Mujahideen in the base were shouting "The Russians are here!" and firing at close range. We abandoned our positions in the heights and charged down the canyon walls. The fighting was heavy. The Soviets withdrew in the late afternoon, taking their dead and wounded with them. They left blood trails, bloody bandages and many RPG-18s behind. Again, Soviet artillery fired at us all night.

On the fourth day, the Soviets advanced with tanks leading and the infantry sheltering behind the tanks. The infantry was reluctant to leave the shelter of the tanks, but they finally moved into some folds on the canyon wall and sheltered there while the tanks withdrew. The infantry would not move out from the protection of the folds and finally the tanks came forward again and the infantry retreated behind the tanks. At noon, they quit firing and the Soviets broke camp and moved out in the afternoon. We lit bonfires and cheered from the heights. The bonfires were welcome since it had rained throughout the battle and we couldn't light fires earlier as that would have disclosed our positions.

COMMENTARY: Again the Soviets conducted a frontal attack, but this time relied on a smoke screen to aid their advance. The advance was initially successful, but the Soviets failed to clear their flanks as they advanced. Once the Soviets began to take casualties, they withdrew, abandoning ground they would unsuccessfully try to retake the following day. The Mujahideen, who lacked communications, were hard pressed to control the battle.

AN UNSUCCESSFUL DEFENSE

In 1985 we had disputes over leadership and distribution of spoils and the Mujahideen split into tribal units and moved into the various canyons. Haji Abdul Kheleq and his Mujahideen from the Noorzai tribe moved to the Shaykh Razi Baba Canyon. Haji Ghulan Rasul Shiwani Rasul Akhundzada and the Mujahideen from the Alizai and Barakzai tribes moved to the Kale-e Amani Canyon. I went with this group. Mawlawi Mohammad Shah and his Mujahideen from the Achakzai tribe stayed in the Kale-e Kaneske Canyon.

After the groups had moved to the different canyons, the Soviets returned. The Soviets concentrated on Mohammad Shah and his Mujahideen in the Kal-e Kaneske Canyon. He had six DShK machine guns, one ZGU-1 machine gun, three 82mm recoilless rifles, 25 RPG-7s and some medium machine guns. Soviet troop columns with up to 200 tanks and APCs moved from Shindand to Farah and surrounded the area.[5] Soviet aircraft flew from Shindand airbase and bombed the base from high and low altitudes. Soviet artillery moved into position and hammered his positions for several hours with heavy fire (Map 11-8 - Kaneske 3). The Soviets spent the first day with artillery and air preparations. On the second day, they launched an attack against the canyon with infantry supported by tanks. Mohammad Shah's force repulsed the attack. On the third day, the Soviets attacked the canyon mouth again, but they also snuck a force up the Jar-e Ab Canyon and then landed air assault forces on the mountain top. These forces crossed over into the Kal-e Kaneske Canyon and took Mohammad Shah's force from the rear. Mohammad Shah's son was killed while firing his ZGU-1. Mohammad Shah's force was pinned between the two Soviet forces as night fell. Mohammad Shah gathered his force and said "Either we stand and die here to the last man or we take a risk and charge the attackers and try to break out. We should break out as a group. If they see us, we will have enough firepower to fight them. If they don't see us, we will all leave together." All his Mujahideen agreed. Some 70 Mujahideen slipped out between the Soviet forces, up the canyon and into the mountain. Only a few old men remained. The next day, the Soviets continued to pound the canyon with air and

---

5 Troops were from the Soviet 5th Motorized Rifle Division. If the number of tanks and APCs is correct, this was a regiment (probably the 371st Motorized Rifle Regiment) reinforced with air assault forces.

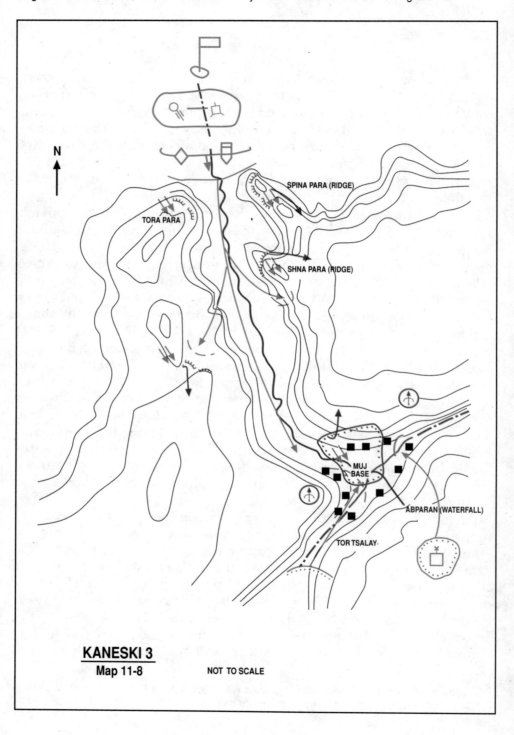

KANESKI 3
Map 11-8

NOT TO SCALE

artillery, not knowing that the Mujahideen had escaped. On the fifth day, they entered the base, mined the caves, looted what they could and left.

The Soviets then turned their attention to Kal-e Amani Canyon. They came across the high ground from Kal-e Kaneske and air assault troops attacked down into the canyon from the high ground. Most of us were unable to escape and we lost some 50 Mujahideen there. The Soviets then turned their attention to Shaykh Razi Baba Canyon, but these Mujahideen had already left. This was the end of the Mujahideen stronghold of Sharafat Koh. We now knew that we could not hold these large bases in Afghanistan indefinitely against the Soviets, so we moved our bases, staging areas and rest areas across the border into Iran.

COMMENTARY: The Mujahideen maintained bases at Sharafat Koh from 1979-1985. It was no secret that they were there and the Soviets and DRA had ample opportunity to work against the base. The Mujahideen were tied to these bases and had to maintain sufficient defenders at Sharafat Koh at all times. This limited the number of Mujahideen who could strike at the Soviets and DRA. Once the Mujahideen split up into several canyons, they lacked communications between the canyons and were unable to provide warning or coordinate actions against the Soviets. The Soviets were able to defeat each group piecemeal.

However, the Soviets were not successful in attacking Sharafat Koh from the desert floor up. It took the Soviets a good deal of time before they would land air assault forces on mountain tops far from link-up forces. Once they started doing so, they were often successful. However, some heliborne forces were isolated and destroyed in the mountains by the Mujahideen. In this case, the Soviets were successful when they used helicopters to land troops on the heights and attack down to link up with ascending forces.

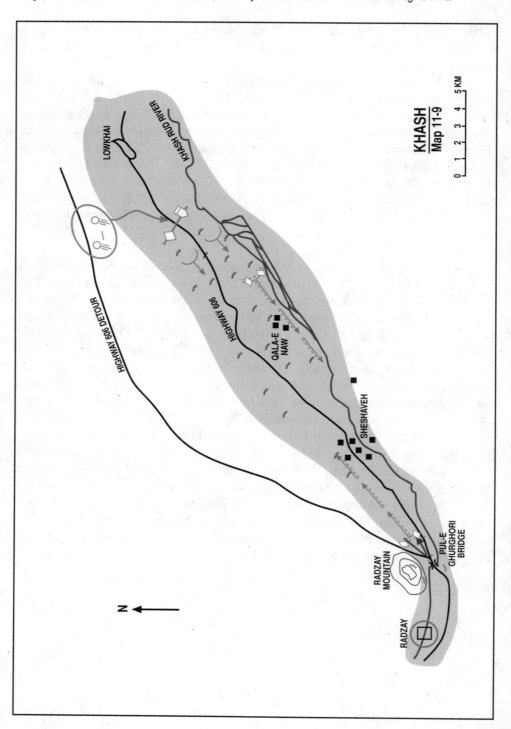

LOWKHAI

KHASH RUD RIVER

HIGHWAY 606 DETOUR

HIGHWAY 606

QALA-E NAW

SHESHAVEH

RADZAY MOUNTAIN

PUL-E GHURGHORI BRIDGE

RADZAY

N

KHASH
Map 11-9

0   1   2   3   4   5 KM

QALA-E NAW BASE CAMP DEFENSE
by Mawlawi Mohayddin Baloch

Nimroz Province lies in the southwest corner of Afghanistan. It is fairly flat, lightly populated and mostly desert. The population lives in the green zones along the river banks. The Khash Rud is one of three rivers which run through the province. It runs northeast to southwest. My base was 10 kilometers southwest of the Lowkhai District capital in Khash Rud District. (Map 11-9 - Khash) It is a wooded area at the village of Qala-e Naw near the banks of the Khash Rud River. Highway 606 runs from Delaram and Zaranj—the provincial capital. It parallels the river and used to run through the green zone. We would often block the highway and intercept convoys traveling on it. Sometimes we would attack the provincial capital. I had about 200 men in my main base at Qala-e Naw and had a forward base at the Pul-e Ghurghori bridge, where the highway crossed over the Khash Rud. I often mined and destroyed that bridge to deny passage to columns going to Zaranj. My main base on the river was split between the southeastern and northwestern banks. During flood stage, it was impossible to cross the river and the Mujahideen on each bank fought in different regions throughout the year. Later in the mid-1980s, when our resistance became very costly to the enemy, they built a detour route on the plain between Zaranj and Delaram. This detour arched about nine kilometers away from my base. When the detour route was built, I could only field reduced groups of 15-20 men against small enemy columns since the area is very arid, very open and water supply is a major problem. We had to let the big convoys pass unmolested. The new road rejoins the old at the village of Radzay. This is about 17 kilometers to the southwest. I started moving our ambushes to the Radzay area. There is a mountain to the east of Radzay with the same name. The road crosses behind the mountain on the southeast side. This is an excellent ambush site since there are also hills which restrict movement to the road as it goes between the hills and the mountain.

Mawlawi Mohayddin Baloch is from Nimroz Province. His base was at Lowkhai, the district capital of Khash Rud District on the Khash Rud River. He was initially with Mawlawi Mohammad Nabi Mohammadi of the Harakat-e Inqelab-e Islami (HAR). Later on he switched to HIK (Khalis). [Map sheet 1579 and 1580].

In the fall of 1984, Khan Mohammad (my deputy) and I were both away from our base at the same time. I was in Iran. Informants told the government that we were both away and so the government attacked our base in our absence. However, the day that the enemy forces attacked our base, Khan Mohammad returned to our base. It was five days before the feast of sacrifice (*Eid-al-Adha*). The enemy moved from Delaram to the plain some 15 kilometers north of us— just north of the main road. They established a base there. Since it is desert, they could move in any direction. They attacked our base the next day. There were only 70 or 80 Mujahideen in base at the time. Our SOP for defense against an attack was to spread the forces over a large area at strong points in some 20 villages. The enemy would usually attack from the northeast to the southwest through the green zone to the base area. He would also send a flanking detachment to the Pul-e Ghurghori bridge and lodge in the Radzay Mountain to encircle my force and pin us in the green zone. My force had to fight in the green zone because the surrounding desert was too flat and exposed for combat. We fought the enemy in the green zone by confronting him with multiple pockets of resistance anchored in fortified fighting positions. When the enemy tried to concentrate against one pocket, Mujahideen from the other pockets would take him in the flanks and rear. The enemy could not fragment his force to deal with all the pockets, but had to stay together for security. We would let the enemy chase us from strongpoint to strongpoint and attack him whenever we could. Eventually, the enemy force would become exhausted. When their water and supplies ran out, they would break contact and go home.

The enemy attack developed as usual and, by the end of the day, the enemy force retired. Unfortunately, my deputy was killed during the fighting. In Iran, I heard about the enemy attack, gathered what Mujahideen were available and started back to our base. The Mujahideen at the base evacuated their casualties to Qala-e Naw, Sheshaveh and Radzay. Informants told the enemy that the base commander was killed. They thought that I was dead and decided that it was the time to destroy all the Mujahideen in the green zone. I arrived on the third day after the opening battle. That night, another enemy column arrived and deployed in the desert north of us. I realized that they were going to attack us. We had one BM-12, one single-barreled 107mm rocket launcher, six 82mm recoilless rifles, five DShKs, three ZGU-1s, and 15 RPG-7s. I now had 120 men. In addition to my Mujahideen, there were HIH Mujahideen in the area and they helped defend the base camp area. I sent 20 of my men to the Ghurghori bridge with four RPG-7s and Kalashnikovs. I told their commander to put 10 men on each bank to block the enemy tanks which would make the encircling sweep. However, that group didn't reach the bridge on time. They stopped short of the bridge to avoid falling into an ambush. The enemy seized control of the bridge at dawn. His other groups deployed at Qala-e Naw, Radzay, Sheshaveh and other points in the area.

The enemy attacked, as usual, from the northeast and southwest. The main attack was from the northeast and involved some 150-200 vehicles. My bridge group attacked the enemy group at the bridge, but the enemy pushed them back and began advancing toward the northeast from Radzay. Six enemy jet aircraft were attacking our positions, while four helicopters adjusted their strikes for them. The helicopters fired smoke rockets to mark the strikes. The fighting continued for two days. Then they broke contact and withdrew. During the fighting, 16 DRA soldiers defected to us. They were soldiers drafted from Farah and Nimroz Provinces. They were from the 21st Mechanized Brigade in Farah and the Sarandoy regiment in Nimroz. There were also DRA deserters from the 4th Border Guards Brigade. Mujahideen casualties were three KIA and several wounded. Enemy losses are unknown except for the 16 deserters.

COMMENTARY: When asked what made him successful Commander Baloch said, "We intended to fight to the last man and they didn't. This is a wide area and we were widely dispersed, which reduced the impact of the enemy air force. Air power was fairly ineffective in this desert. Many of their bombs failed to explode, but buried themselves in the sand. We had covered shelters and covered fighting positions in each village. The enemy was very stylized and never did anything different. We knew from where they would come, how they would act and how long they could stay. Our defensive positions were connected with communications trenches while the enemy was always in the open. We had two kinds of maneuver. One was the dispersal maneuver forcing the enemy to chase all over to find us. The second was internal maneuver within a strong point where we could shift between positions without being observed. We had these positions in all the villages and throughout the area. There are also many canals and ditches in the area, which we improved into fighting positions."

"Once the enemy offered me a deal. 'Don't attack us and we will pay you a toll of 50,000 Afghanis ($250) per vehicle passing through the area.' I turned the deal down with the words 'As long as Soviets are here, we make no deals.' The enemy infantry was the weakest part of their armies—DRA and Soviet. Their sequence of attack was very predictable. They would start with an artillery and air preparation, then they would lay a smoke screen and then their infantry would attack. Their tanks would support the infantry, but as soon as they sustained casualties, they would stop. Their tanks were very wary of antitank weapons. The mere presence of RPGs and recoilless rifles in an area would keep the tanks at bay. We would wait until tanks came within 20 or 30 meters of our antitank weapons before opening fire. I would not allow my people to try long-range shots. They would hold steady in their positions with patience and courage. The tanks could not see us at long range so they couldn't hit us. We could see them and hit them at close range. Most of the time we were fighting an enemy strong in fire power and very weak in the assault. During the two days of fighting, the enemy seldom came within Kalashnikov range. The only innovation that the enemy showed during this attack was that they launched it during the Festival of Sacrifice, when they expected that the Mujahideen would be at home instead of the base. Second, they returned sooner to the area than usual. This broke their pattern. I did not really fight a guerrilla war—I knew the enemy's position and he knew mine. A guerrilla is evasive and attacks from an unexpected direction and time. Here, the enemy kept attacking me at the same place and in the same fashion. Is this guerrilla war?"

"Our ambulance was two sticks and a piece of cloth. Theirs was a helicopter. The secret of our success was that it was a popular cause. Everybody knew that we were hurting the occupiers. This was not a war but an uprising. Therefore, it was not a guerrilla war. We never bothered about the food supply. The locals supplied us with whatever they had. I had two pickup trucks—the enemy had two hundred vehicles. I used the pickups for ammunition and food resupply. We moved them secretly along the river in the wooded area to supply the fighting positions in the evening. Their rations would sustain them until the next night. We basically had a mutton and nan[6] diet that the local populace furnished us free. A normal full day's ration was a portion of cooked mutton wrapped in nan. Water supply was simple since our fighting positions were near the river and my men all had canteens."

---

[6] Nan is flat Afghan unleavened bread. It is oval-shaped and about the thickness and size of a small or medium pizza.

VIGNETTE 7
DEFENDING THE SUBURBS OF KANDAHAR
by Sultan Mohammad of Topkhana

The supporters of the HI faction, mostly Shia, were located primarily in the southwest of Afghanistan. The HI's main base was in the Khakrez southern mountains. This base was near the HIK base of Islam Dara.[7] This was about seven hours on foot from Khakrez, which is some 60 kilometers north of Kandahar. The HI fought in Khakrez, Girishk, Uruzgan and Kandahar. The HI faction had four units in the Kandahar area. We had about 300 Mujahideen. Our overall commander was Ali Yawar who was killed by a mine later in the war. We had two bases in the Kandahar area—Char Dewal in the Malajat suburbs south of Kandahar and Char Bagh in the Arghandab River Valley northwest of Kandahar. I commanded a group at Char Dewal as did Ghulam Shah and Shah Mohammad. Gul Mohammad commanded at Char Bagh. We used to harass convoys and block Highway 1 near the Kandahar prison at Pashtoon Bagh—about a half kilometer from the Sarpooza ridge. Unlike some other areas in Afghanistan, all the Mujahideen factions cooperated with each other in the Kandahar area. Whenever there was any fighting, all the Mujahideen would move to the area to help out. All large Mujahideen operations were combined and were coordinated by the Mujahideen Council.

The Malajat area lies to the south of Kandahar. It is a well-irrigated suburb of the city full of villages, irrigation canals, orchards, farms and vineyards. The Mujahideen moved freely throughout this area despite the best efforts of the DRA and the Soviet forces in the area.[8] Frequently, the DRA and Soviets would throw a cordon around the Malajat area and try to enter it to destroy

---

Sultan Mohammad of Topkhana is a member of the minority Shia religious community in Afghanistan. He belonged to the moderate Harakat-I Islami (HI) faction founded by Ayatollah Asef Muhsini in neighboring Iran. He fought from the communist overthrow of the government until the withdrawal of Soviet forces. [Map sheet 2180].

[7] Islam Dara was the Mujahideen name for their base behind Shawadan mountain. The Soviet 103rd Airborne Division launched an attack on this base in 1985 and this is described in Vignette 25 of *The Bear Went Over the Mountain*. The site location in *The Bear Went Over the Mountain* is wrong.

[8] The Kandahar area was heavily garrisoned by the DRA 2nd Corps Headquarters, the 15th Infantry Division, the 7th Tank Brigade, the 3rd Border Guards Brigade, the 366th Fighter-Bomber Regiment and the 379th Separate Bomber Squadron. Soviet forces included the 70th Separate Motorized Rifle Brigade and a Spetsnaz battalion.

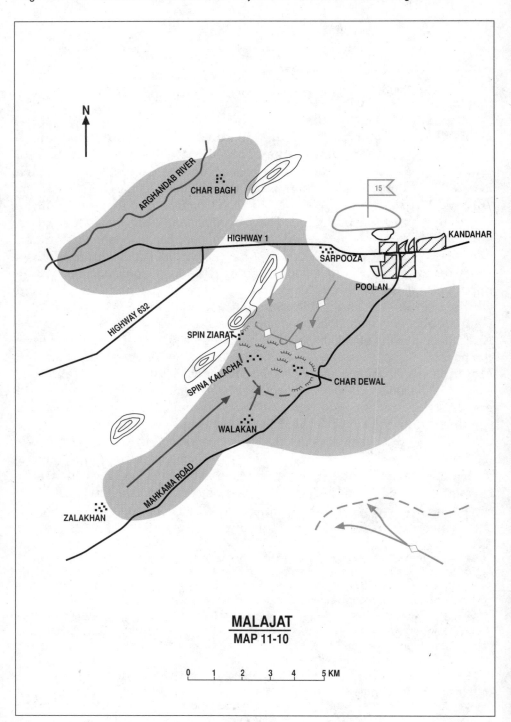

MALAJAT
MAP 11-10

0 1 2 3 4 5 KM

the Mujahideen and their bases. Throughout the war, these efforts never succeeded. There were always at least 1,000-1,500 Mujahideen in Malajat from the various factions. These Mujahideen were all from mobile groups and none were stationed permanently in Malajat. Mujahideen forces would rotate in and out of the Malajat area and thus maintained a high state of readiness. The Malajat mujahideen were well prepared with supply bases and well-fortified bunkers and fighting positions (Map 11-10 - Malajat).

In the fall of 1984, the enemy threw a wide cordon around the Malajat occupying their normal southern positions from Zaker Ghar in the east to Qaitul in the west. Thus they surrounded the Malajat with Kandahar to the north and Highway 4 to the east and a ridge of hills to the west. This encompasses a lot of space and the Mujahideen were still able to maneuver freely within the Malajat area. At 0700 hours, an enemy mechanized column of 30-35 tanks and APCs moved from Sarpooza while another column of 15-16 tanks and APCs moved from the 15th Division headquarters past the Governor's house along the Mahkama road near Poolan toward our defensive position. Our defensive position stretched some three kilometers from Char Dewal to Spin Ziarat and we could always see the enemy defenses from here. We held this position with some 450 Mujahideen from various factions. There were HIK units from Sarkateb, the Gulagha Son of Haji Latif's unit and two of our HI groups. The enemy columns were covered by helicopter gunships who fired at our positions. However, the enemy was unable to advance because we were well-protected by our defensive positions. The enemy would not dismount from his armored vehicles, but deployed his vehicles in a firing line and fired at us for two or three hours. Even the green trees caught on fire. Our defensive positions were three meter by two meter pits which held two-to-three men. They were roofed with heavy wooden beams which had 1.5 meters of dirt and rock tamped down on top of it. During lulls in the enemy firing, our men would pop out of the shelters and fire RPG-7s and recoilless rifles at them. The enemy would promptly start shooting again.

I said that the Soviets surrounded us, but that isn't completely true. Throughout the war, the Soviets always left one side unguarded. At around noon, 100 to 120 Mujahideen reinforcements arrived from Zalakhan and Walakan, which are south and southeast of Spin Zirat. These villages were in the sector that the Soviets left unguarded. The arrival of the reinforcements turned the tide and eventually prompted the Soviets to withdraw about 1800 hours. We destroyed three armored vehicles on the Sarpooza front and two on the Mahkama front.

Sometimes the bombs and artillery fire would block the exits to our bunkers. We would have to go out at night to dig them out. This happened often to our positions near the Panjao Pul bridge. Three times I had to go out at midnight to locate the bunkers and unearth our men. Sometimes they would be trapped in these bunkers from 0500 hours until past midnight, but these bunkers were essential to stopping the enemy in the Malajat.

COMMENTARY: Soviet cordon and search operations usually involved a large force surrounding a large area. The area contained within the cordon was usually large enough to allow the surrounded Mujahideen freedom of maneuver. Once the cordon was established, the Soviets seldom split it up into manageable areas, but pushed through the entire cordoned area if possible. This failure to fragment the area allowed the Mujahideen to move and maneuver against the Soviets. In this case, the Mujahideen were able to reinforce during a hotly contested fight.

Many Soviet combat examples show an unguarded flank in a cordon and search.[9] This might work if an ambush were set along the escape route, but this did not seem to be the case. This might also be a time-honored act to allow their enemy to escape and minimize the casualties on both sides.

Finally, there was an apparent reluctance by the Soviets and DRA to stay in the Malajat area at night. If they would not dismount from their armored vehicles during the day, they would have to dismount at night to secure the vehicles. The arrival of the Mujahideen reinforcements may have kept the Mujahideen in the fight, but may not have been the prime reason that the Soviets withdrew at 1800 hours.

---

[9] As an example, see vignette 5 in *The Bear Went Over the Mountain*.

VIGNETTE 8
DEFENDING THE MALAJAT
by Mohammad Shah Kako and Abdul Ghani

The Malajat, the southern suburb of Kandahar, was a continuous battlefield. The Malajat is a large green zone full of orchards, villages, irrigation canals, and vineyards. The Mujahideen deployed mobile bases throughout it. Many Mujahideen commanders with bases elsewhere would maintain mobile bases in the Malajat as their forward elements in the Kandahar area. Despite belonging to different factions, there was an exemplary cooperation among these mobile groups. The DRA/Soviets tried to force the Mujahideen out by cordon and search operations of the Malajat area. They would occupy the high ground and villages north of the Tarnak River—Shorandam, Zaker-e Sharif, Loy Karazak, Anguryan, and Bala Deh which are north and west of the airfield. Then they would establish the western blocking positions on the Girowal Ghar, Suf Ghar, Zarah Ghar and Chehelzena Ghar mountains (Map 11-11 - Mala). They used the city of Kandahar as the northern blocking position. Kandahar was occupied by DRA forces. Then the Soviets and DRA would push inward into the Malajat area from these blocking positions search for the Mujahideen. They were usually unsuccessful, but they continued to do it over and over again. The blocking positions were also part of the Kandahar security belt, but it was well-penetrated by the Mujahideen. We would fight them initially in the Malajat area and then exit to the south in the Loy Karazak area and Anguryan and in the southwest in the Hendu Kalacha area. The Soviets had trouble controlling these areas.

The Mujahideen prepared blocking positions along major axes and turned this area into an impregnable stronghold. A typical blocking position would be built near a mobile base and include several buildings in a village or orchard, where the mobile group would live. The personnel in the mobile group would be relieved and replaced from time to time from their main bases. Some Mujahideen would stay permanently in the Malajat area. Mobile bases and blocking positions were connected by communications trenches. The blocking positions were dug into the ground and had firing positions for machine guns,

Mohammad Shah Kako initially fought with HIK and then switched to IUA. Abdul Ghani fought with the ANLF. [Map sheet 2180].

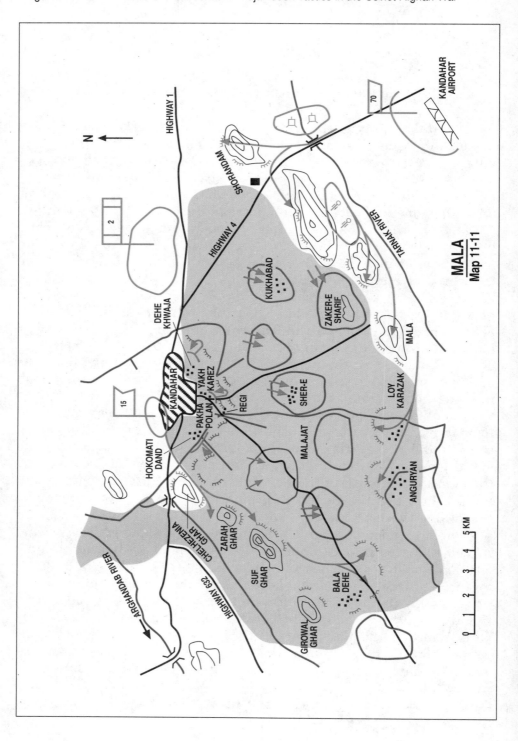

MALA
Map 11-11

recoilless rifles, and RPGs. We covered the fighting positions with berry-tree branches which we then covered with earth and packed it down hard. The bases had covered bunkers to protect our Mujahideen from artillery fire and air strikes. These bunkers were two-three meters in width and six to eight meters long and were covered with timber and a meter-thick layer of well-packed earth which resisted artillery fire and most air strikes. Whenever the enemy would cordon off the Malajat area and launch infantry attacks into the green zone, the Mujahideen would occupy their blocking positions. Most fighting positions were redundant so that the loss of a fighting position would not adversely affect the defense.

In the beginning, the Mujahideen were unprepared and unable to resist beyond two or three days but, after they developed their fortifications, they could withstand and push back the Soviets and DRA. Once the area was cordoned, the Soviets usually launched their attack along the main road from Zaker-e Sharif and further south from Loy Karazak. In the north, the usual line of contact was Hokomati Dand, Pakha Polan, Yakh Karez and Deh Khwaja. This was just outside the built-up area. Later on, the Soviet and DRA forces established permanent, well-fortified and well-protected security outposts. The Soviets had Shorandam hill, Zaker-e Sharif hill and Mala Kala hill. The DRA had Suf Ghar, Zarah Shar Ghar and Chehelzena Ghar mountain sites. Once every two months, the Soviets would launch a major cordon and search against the Malajat area in order to keep it contained.

In November 1987, the Soviets launched an 18-day cordon and search operation. In the cold dawn, the Soviet and DRA troops moved from their garrisons and, by 0800 hours, had occupied their normal blocking positions. Mohammad Shah Kako's base was at Sher-e Surkh where he commanded some 30 men. There were some 350 Mujahideen in the Malajat area from his party. The Mujahideen divided the front line facing western Kandahar into four sectors. Each sector had about 50 men. The northwest sector was a Hizbe-Islami sector. The Pakha Polan area was held by Mujahideen from Sher-e Surkh, Zaker-e Sharif and Kukhabad. This meant that Mohammad Shah Kako's sector had three commanders since there were three factions involved, but cooperation among the commanders was easy since they were all local and knew each other. Regi was the third sector and Abdul Razak commanded this sector. Yakh Karez was the fourth sector and Saranwal commanded it. Ghafur Jan coordinated the four sectors. The DRA attacked from the city, but this time the Soviets did not move from their blocking positions. The DRA infantry were accompanied by troops carrying chain saws. They planned to cut their way through the orchards, destroy them and deny this refuge to the Mujahideen. We had planted mines in front of our positions which deterred the poorly-trained DRA soldiers. We maintained a steady fire from well-situated positions. We kept a reserve of 160-200 men in reserve resting. Every evening, the relief group would move forward, carrying rations and relieve the force who would go back and rest for two days. Then they would rotate forward again. It was usually calm at night when we carried out the relief. In this manner, we kept up the defense for 18 days. We did not resupply during the day, but brought food, water and ammunition forward only at night. The DRA could not break through, but they did cut some trees before we shot them down. It was winter and it was cold. Our positions were good, although resupply was tough. Throughout the fighting, the enemy bombed and shelled all suspected bases in the area. One bomb, intended for our position in Pakha Polan, missed the target and hit the western city gate, killing many civilians. They could not hit us at the front line positions because we were so close to their line and so our front line was safe from air and artillery attack.

COMMENTARY: Throughout the war, the Soviets and DRA were never able to bring Kandahar under complete control. Mujahideen urban groups fought sporadic battles within the city walls and Mujahideen mobile groups maintained control over the suburbs. Unlike other areas of Afghanistan, there was little in-fighting among the factions involved in the fighting around Kandahar and the Mujahideen ran the fight cooperatively through regular meetings of a coordination council. This cooperation provided tactical flexibility to the Mujahideen and their redundant fortifications ensured that Soviet/DRA offensives would never progress far. Most notable is the regular rotation of Mujahideen from the forward positions. A relief in place is a difficult procedure for the best-trained troops. The Mujahideen routinely relieved front-line forces without a loss in combat effectiveness. This is very impressive for any force, and even more so for a force that is in direct contact and is heavily outgunned and poorly supplied.

There was a significant DRA/Soviet force garrisoned in the area. The DRA 2nd Corps, 15th Infantry Division, 7th Tank Brigade, 3rd Border Guard Brigade garrisoned Kandahar city. The Soviet 70th Separate Motorized Rifle Brigade, the DRA 366th Fighter Regiment, the DRA 379th Separate Bombing Squadron and a Soviet Spetsnaz battalion garrisoned the Kandahar international airport. The

DRA/Soviet operations in the Malajat area were very predictable by time and location. They continually tried to penetrate and sweep the entire area instead of cordoning off and sweeping a smaller section thoroughly. Although the combat in the Malajat area was a fight through a fortified area, the DRA/Soviets continued to treat it as a penetration and exploitation rather than a systematic reduction. DRA/Soviet tactical intelligence apparently did not pick up the pattern in Mujahideen resupply and relief activities to exploit it.

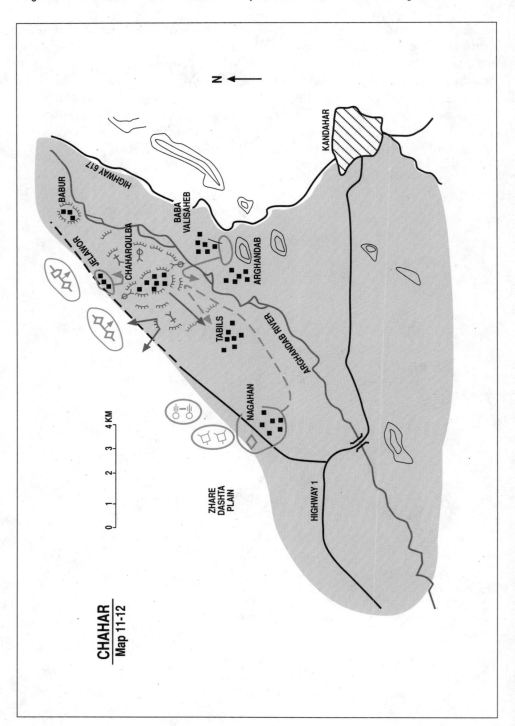

N

KANDAHAR

HIGHWAY 617

BABUR

JELAWOR

CHAHARQULBA

BABA
VALISAHEB

ARGHANDAB

TABILS

ARGHANDAB RIVER

NAGAHAN

ZHARE
DASHTA
PLAIN

HIGHWAY 1

0 1 2 3 4 KM

CHAHAR
Map 11-12

VIGNETTE 9
BATTLE FOR CHAHARQULBA VILLAGE
by Commander Akhtarjhan

During the Soviet occupation, the eastern bank of the Arghandab River near Kandahar city was a safe haven and the Mujahideen would not fight in this area. The west bank was Mujahideen territory. I had my base in Babur village in the orchards of the west bank (later, after the Soviets withdrew, I established east bank bases in Baba Valisaheb village, Pir-e Paymal and in the western suburbs of Kandahar). My senior commander was Mulla Naqib. During the Soviet occupation, he had a remote base in Khakrez mountain, but his main base was in Chaharqulba village. My eldest brother was killed in fighting at this village base. My next oldest brother fought out of the Babur base and became a commander when my oldest brother was killed. Commanders were selected based on the social position of the family, education, and personal leadership talents. Family ties were important. A commander brought his relatives into the group and a prestigious family could raise a large group. Since my brother established the group, it was natural that my brother, and, subsequently, I should succeed to the command. In fundamentalist Mujahideen groups, commanders were picked for ideological commitment and not for family ties. Many teenagers joined the Mujahideen because the DRA would press-gang youth into the army and Mujahideen bases were a good place to avoid the draft.

In June 1987, during the month of Ramadan, the DRA/Soviets launched a major operation in the Arghandab (Map 11-12 - Chahar). During the operation, the enemy concentrated in Nagahan and then moved northeast along the western bank of the Arghandab River. Another column crossed the Arghandab River from Baba Valisaheb. They began with a heavy air attack against suspected Mujahideen bases. We moved to our bunkers. The west bank was actually a Mujahideen fortified zone, which we laced with bunkers, fighting positions and trenches. Further, since the green zone was full of orchards,

---

Commander Akhtarjhan was a Jamiat-I-Islami (JIA) commander in Arghandab District northwest of Kandahar. He was an elementary school student when he joined the Jihad at the age of 12. At the end of the war he was 25 years old and a commander. He joined the Jihad because he had had two brothers in the Jihad and they were both killed. He took their place as family tradition dictated. He served under Mulla Naqib, the most powerful Jamiat commander in the area. [Map sheet 2180].

it was already cut up by irrigation ditches, so there was always a place to fight from. We did not leave the bunkers since we were pinned by all the aviation ordnance. Usually, the Soviets would deploy tanks along the edge of the green zone and, after the heavy artillery bombardment and tank fires, they would send infantry (usually DRA) into the green zone with instructions to collect our weapons since everyone in the impact area would be dead. The infantry would move out confidently and the Mujahideen would come out of their bunkers. The Mujahideen would inflict heavy losses on the infantry and capture many of these ill-trained DRA recruits. We sent the prisoners north through the mountains and then, by circuitous routes, south into Pakistan. We had built a veritable fortress around the base at Chaharqulba. Some Mujahideen would defend the bases, while others would range further afield to provide maneuver and depth to the battlefield. It was very hard to move tanks into the green zone. The Soviets would try to push tanks into the area to get close to the Mujahideen, but the terrain channelized their movement and made them vulnerable.

The Soviets and DRA moved from two directions against the Mujahideen but were met with constant resistance from Mujahideen fighting positions. Soviet tanks came from the Zhare Dashta and stayed on the plain west of the green zone as they crept toward our base at Chaharqulba. It took them a week of fighting to cover the six kilometers to our base. All of their tanks were sandbagged against our RPGs, so we were having difficulty stopping them. Finally, we Mujahideen commanders went to Naqib and said that we are outnumbered and should leave the base. Naqib said that this is their last battle and will decide the contest between them and us. They've tried to conquer the base for years and this is their last throw. If we leave, we will never get in again. If we stop them, then they will not return. We replied that the RPGs were not working against sandbagged tanks. Naqib took an RPG and strode out to the forward positions to kill a tank. We commanders stopped him and promised to fight to the end.

Heavy fighting continued throughout that day, but we stopped the enemy and they withdrew to Ta'bils—some kilometers to the south. We pursued them to Ta'bils, engaging the enemy in the streets, killing many of them. The Mujahideen then withdrew to Chaharqulba before dawn. The following days, the enemy mounted a three-pronged attack from Ta'bils in southwest, from Baba Valisaheb in the southeast and from Jelawor in the northwest. They employed tanks and artillery on the plain of Zhare Dashta in support. Since the orchards were impenetrable to their tanks, their tanks supported their infantry like naval gunfire from ships. Their tanks would wait until their infantry closed with our base and then would edge into the channelized approaches. As soon as their infantry fell back, the tanks would fall back. Tanks are of little value in the green zone and would seldom advance there. APCs, however, would advance in infantry support. However, their movement was also very channelized and they were easy to attack on the flank.

The enemy would precede his attack with heavy air and artillery bombardment. The Mujahideen would stay in their bunkers to survive and only leave a few observers in the fighting positions. As soon as the observers saw the enemy approach, the Mujahideen would come out of their bunkers and man the fighting positions. The enemy infantry would suffer casualties and then fall back. Many of the DRA soldiers defected. We would broadcast over megaphones "We are not your enemy. We are your brothers. Join us." Still, the enemy infantry eventually gathered strength and returned to attack our base from the south and southeast and then closed from Jelawor.

Our defenses were vulnerable in the northwest. After continuous fighting, our Mujahideen were having trouble staying awake. At one fighting position, a DRA patrol penetrated the position and stole a recoilless rifle. The gunner was asleep. Commander Ahmadullah Jan saw them taking the recoilless rifle and followed them. Some 25-30 meters away, two APCs were waiting for the DRA patrol. Before they reached their APCs, Ahmadullah Jan and his men, plus another Mujahideen group, intercepted them and fought a fire fight. They destroyed one APC, recovered the recoilless rifle, captured the patrol and captured the remaining APC. They brought the patrol leader, a DRA lieutenant, to Mulla Naqib. Naqib told him "We don't want to kill you, but tell your fellows that we will not leave and this will mean death for more of you. Stop your attacks and return to your barracks." The lieutenant replied, "I can't do this because my family is in Kabul." We let him go anyway that evening.

The fighting continued for 34 days. During the 34 days, a routine emerged. The enemy would begin the morning with an aircraft and artillery bombardment from the south and southeast. Usually, they would then send eight helicopter gunships to work over the area. Then, they would launch infantry attacks. The Mujahideen would emerge from their bunkers, occupy fighting positions and wait for the approaching infantry. We were hard to see since we had excellent fighting positions and wore garlands of grapevines as camouflage. We let the enemy get closer than ten meters to us before opening fire. We let them get this close for two reasons. First, we wanted to be sure to get them with the first shot. Second, we wanted to prevent their escape. We laid thousands of PMN mines[10] in the area—particularly on the infantry approaches from Jelawor. After DRA attacks failed, they would often run into the mines as they tried to escape. The enemy would retreat and we would go out and collect their weapons, rations and ammunition. If the enemy was not attacking us, we would send out ambush parties to hit his columns on the main road. It was usually quiet at night. Sometimes the enemy would fire artillery and bomb us at night but would never attack at night. They did not know their way around the area in the dark, so they did not attempt any night combat.

The DRA had a district government post and local militia on the east bank. We Mujahideen had our families and R&R[11] facilities on the east bank since the government would not bomb that area. Supplies came from our homes on the other side of the river, but during heavy fighting, they could not supply us and we were on our own. We could not cook since the enemy would shell any smoke they saw. We had plenty of ammunition since the base was well-supplied and we could resupply ammunition to our positions readily. Food, however, was a serious problem although the number of combatants at the Chaharqulba base did not exceed 500 Mujahideen at any time. The intensity of fire sometimes prevented us from eating during the day—and sometimes even during the night. Sometimes we would salvage rations left behind by the Soviets and DRA. The Soviets would leave lots of food behind, particularly bread. Often our sole rations would be Soviet bread soaked in water.

We also had a problem with treating the wounded. We had medics who had graduated from a short course in Pakistan and were qualified to perform basic first aid. We normally evacuated our wounded to Pakistan for treatment and recovery. During the siege, however, we could not send our wounded to Pakistan. We could not remove the shrapnel and so many of our seriously wounded died of their wounds. We had a few Arabs in our base at this time. They were there for Jihad credit and to see the fighting. "If you are Muslims, help us collect the

---

10 The PMN mine is a small, plastic antipersonnel mine manufactured by the Soviet Union. It is pressure activated. The Mujahideen called them Kandani (sugar pots) due to their similarity in size and shape.

11 Rest and relaxation.

wounded," we would tell them. They would refuse.

Except for the Ta'bils offensive and ambushes, we were defending. The Soviets were there in strength, but they stayed on the plain with their tanks and artillery and seldom committed their own infantry. Their tanks and artillery blackened the plain. It seemed that they must have had a thousand of them, but they just stayed there. The DRA infantry was doing most of the attacking and dying. The fight bled the DRA to the point where they could not take any more casualties. Finally, after 34 days of fighting, the enemy forces broke contact at 1100 hours and withdrew. In the past, the enemy had tried to take us, but never had he come in such force or stayed for so long.

We lost up to 60 Mujahideen and commanders KIA in the base and many others in areas around the base. DRA and Soviet casualties are unknown, but we were always catching the enemy in surprise attacks, so his casualties must have been much higher than ours. DRA casualties were definitely higher than Soviet casualties. I feel that the enemy finally quit due to his casualties.[12]

COMMENTARY: The Soviets used the conscript DRA infantry extensively and supported them with artillery and air power. The DRA infantry was poorly trained and equipped and had serious morale problems. The use of DRA forces as "throw-away" infantry did nothing to increase morale. DRA forces had a reputation for passivity on the battlefield and deserting at the first opportunity.

The Mujahideen defenses were relatively weak from the Jelawor direction, but the Soviets apparently did not push hard enough on this axis to discover this. Soviet and DRA tactical intelligence efforts appear inadequate.

The Soviet/DRA willingness to drag combat out for 34 days and then break contact and withdraw is remarkable. Their refusal to push for quicker resolution strengthened the Mujahideen hand and gradually created a qualitative change in the situation to the Mujahideen advantage. On the other hand, the fragmented nature of the Mujahideen resistance meant that the Mujahideen in

---

12 Page 6, Afghanistan Report #40, July 1987, published by the Crisis & Conflict Analysis Team of the Institute of Strategic Studies in Islamabad, Pakistan: "It was reported that over a period of one and a half month (sic) ending June, 1987, the Soviet-Kabul troops had suffered about 250 soldiers killed and 800 injured in Qandahar city and its suburbs. They lost more than 100 vehicles, tanks, and jeeps, besides 13 aircraft/helicopters. About 2,500 Afghan government soldiers joined the Mujahideen during this what seemed to be the longest Soviet-Kabul operation against the Mujahideen for several years. The offensive apparently spilled over into July 1987."

Chaharqulba fought in isolation, bearing the full force of whatever the Soviets and DRA could muster. Outside Mujahideen assistance in the form of ambushes against supply convoys and raids on the forces in Nagahan and on the Zhare Dashte plain would have clearly eased the pressure on the Chaharqulba Mujahideen, but there was little operational and strategic cooperation and coordination among the various Mujahideen factions. The Mujahideen factions in Kandahar cooperated better than elsewhere, but as this vignette shows, this cooperation was still limited.

The Mujahideen were quick to pursue a retreating enemy and their offensive into Ta'bils is a good example. Unless a force has established a strong, cohesive rear guard, it is disorganized during withdrawal and unable to concentrate combat power. This instant transition to pursuit was characteristic of the Afghans when fighting the British earlier this century and last.

VIGNETTE 10
ZHAWAR ONE
by Lieutenant Omar and Mawlawi Nezamuddin Haqani

Zhawar was a Mujahideen base in Paktia Province located some four kilometers from the Pakistan border. A 15-kilometer road goes from Zhawar to the major Pakistani forward supply base at Miram Shah. Zhawar began as a Mujahideen training center and expanded into a major Mujahideen combat base for supply, training and staging. As the base expanded, Mujahideen used bulldozers and explosives to dig at least 11 tunnels into the south-east facing ridge of Sodyaki Ghar Mountain. These huge tunnels stretched to 500 meters and contained a hotel, a mosque, arms depots and repair shops, a garage, a medical point, a radio center and a kitchen. A gasoline generator even provided power to the tunnels and the hotel's video player! This impressive base became a mandatory stop for visiting journalists, congressmen and other "war tourists." Apparently, this construction effort also often interfered with basic construction of fighting positions and field fortifications. The Mujahideen "Zhawar Regiment," some 500 strong, was permanently based there. This regiment was primarily responsible for logistics support of the mobile groups fighting in the area and for supplying the Islamic Party (HIK) groups in other provinces of Afghanistan. Due to the primary logistics function, the regiment was not fully equipped for combat, but was a credible combat force. The regiment was responsible for local defense and for blocking infiltration of Khad and KGB agents between Afghanistan and Pakistan. They manned checkpoints along the road to screen identification papers. The regiment had a Soviet

Lieutenant Omar (Zabit Omar) graduated from the Kabul Military Academy in the 1970s. After the communist coup and the Soviet invasion, Lieutenant Omar joined the Mujahideen of the fundamentalist Islamic Party (HIK) founded by Mawlawi Mohammed Yunis Khalis. He was a close aide to Jalaluddin Haqani and fought with him throughout the war. Haqani ran the Mujahideen effort in the crucial Paktia Province. Lieutenant Omar also served as a group commander in Paktia Province throughout the war. [Map sheet 2983, vic grid 8267].

Mawlawi Nezamuddin Haqani was a group commander and a deputy to Jalaluddin Haqani. He was a member of the fundamentalist Islamic Party (HIK) founded by Mawlawi Mohammed Yunis Khalis. He joined the Mujahideen following the communist coup in 1978 and fought in the Paktia area. Prior to the Soviet invasion, his group had liberated the area surrounding Khost and only the city of Khost remained under government control.

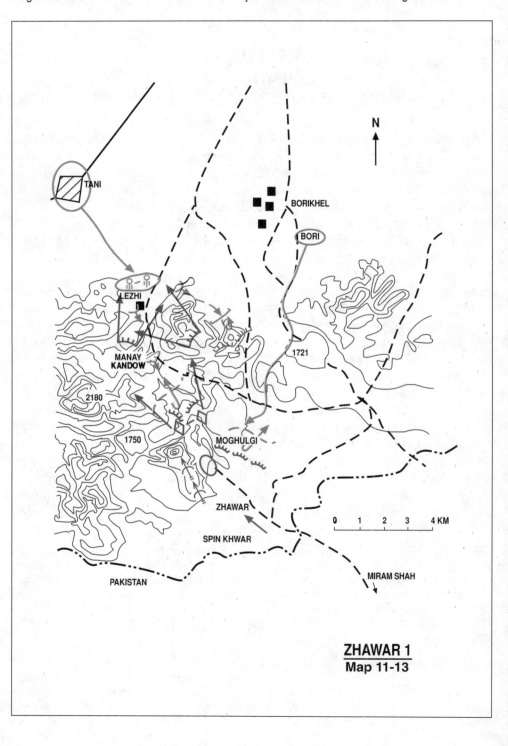

ZHAWAR 1
Map 11-13

D30 122mm howitzer, two tanks (captured from the DRA post at Bari in 1983), some six-barrel Chinese-manufactured BM-12 MRL and some machine guns and small arms. A Mujahideen air defense company also defended Zhawar with five ZPU-1 and four ZPU-2 anti-aircraft heavy machine guns. The air defense machine guns were positioned on high ground around the base. Defense of the approaches to the base was the responsibility of other Mujahideen groups.

In September 1985, the DRA moved elements of the DRA 12th Infantry Division from Gardez, with elements of the 37th and 38th Commando Brigades. They moved from Gardez circuitously through Jaji Maidan to Khost since the direct route through the Satakadow pass had been under Mujahideen control since 1981. This force joined elements of the 25th Infantry Division which was garrisoned in Khost. Shahnawaz Tani[13] commanded this mixed force. The DRA military units had their full complement of weapons and equipment, but desertion, security details and other duties kept their units chronically understrength. Since the DRA could not mobilize sufficient force from one regiment or division, they practiced "tactical cannibalism" and formed composite forces for these missions.

Late one September afternoon, the DRA force began an infantry attack supported by heavy artillery fire and air strikes on Bari, which is northeast of Zhawar (Map 11-13 - Zhawar 1). Zhawar was not prepared for this attack since most of its major commanders, including Haqani, were on the pilgrimage to Mecca (the Haj). The DRA recaptured Bari and drove on to Zhawar. The Mujahideen reacted by positioning an 80-man group to block the ridge on the eastern slope of the Moghulgai mountains which form the eastern wall of the Zhawar base. The DRA force arrived at night and during the night fighting lost two APCs and four trucks. Eventually, the DRA became discouraged, withdrew and returned to Khost.[14] Mujahideen from the nomad Kochi tribe, led by Malang Kochi, Dadmir Kochi and Gorbez Mujahideen, recaptured Bari.

The DRA then launched its next attempt from the town of Tani. They recaptured the town of Lezhi from the Mujahideen and killed Commander Mawlawi Ahmad Gul. The major commanders returned to Pakistan from the Haj on that day (4 September)

---

[13] General Shahnawaz Tani was from the neighboring town of Tani and enjoyed some popular support in the area. He later became DRA Defense Minister. On 6 March 1990, he joined forces with Mujahideen faction leader Gulbuddin Hikmatyar in an attempted coup against communist President Najibullah. When the coup failed, he fled to Pakistan.

[14] Perhaps this was a reconnaissance in force.

and hurried north to Zhawar to take command. The Mujahideen from Lezhi retreated south while a 20-man Mujahideen force blocked the Manay Kandow pass.

The pass is dominated by a high peak which is capped with a thick rock slab. Under the slab was a natural cave which the Mujahideen improved. The cave could accommodate the 20 Mujahideen during artillery and air strikes. The Mujahideen also dug communications trenches so that they could quickly reoccupy their fighting positions once the firing stopped. The firing positions dominated the Tani plain and were well positioned to stop any infantry attack. The DRA repeatedly attacked the pass but could make no headway. The infantry would attack, meet withering Mujahideen fire and stop. Then massed air and artillery would pound the area. The infantry would again try to attack, but would again be stopped immediately. The procedure would then repeat itself, but the DRA made no headway during its 10-day attack. After 10 days, the DRA called in heavy Soviet airstrikes which continuously hit the mountain top. The thick rock slab began to sway and rock. The Mujahideen were afraid that the rock slab might shift and crush their cave, so they finally withdrew. It was 14 September 1985.

As the Mujahideen fell back, the DRA established OPs on high ground and started adjusting air and artillery strikes. This gave the tactical advantage to the DRA and their infantry moved through the pass. The Mujahideen rear guard desperately engaged the DRA infantry with machine gun fire, and aircraft with ZGU machine guns. The DRA continued to advance and seized the high ground of Tor Kamar.

Tor Kamar is within a kilometer of Zhawar base and well within the range of machine gun fire. The DRA thought that the Mujahideen did not have any heavy weapons and became careless and bunched their forces on the high ground. Two Mujahideen, Alam Jam and Muhammad Salim, were former tank commanders in the DRA. In the late afternoon, they moved their tanks out of the caves and swung north into firing positions. They opened fire and their first rounds destroyed a DRA OP sending an artillery OP scope and soldiers flying. The Mujahideen tankers then traversed to the second OP and destroyed it with their next rounds. Then they opened up on the other DRA soldiers.

The mauled DRA force fell back and maneuvered through the

---

[15] Local name for the chalk layers in the rock which mark this saddle.

"bird droppings" saddle[15] to the east side of Tamberi Ghar. The Mujahideen countered with blocking positions which they held for five days. Haji Amanullah Khan and Ismail Khan played major roles in the fighting at this stage.

The DRA Commander, General Tani moved his CP into the Manay Kandow pass and tried to reinvigorate the DRA assault, but the Mujahideen held. During the fighting, the Mujahideen shot down a helicopter, but lost a major commander—Mawlawi Fathullah. Mujahideen reinforcements arrived from Pakistan and as far away as Jalalabad and Urgun. Commander Mawlawi Arsalah arrived. The DRA were getting chronically low on men and supplies and, after 42 days of fighting, General Tani broke contact and conducted a night withdrawal.

Mujahideen casualties were 106 KIA and 321 WIA. DRA and Soviet losses were heavy, but their numbers are unknown because they evacuated their dead and wounded.

COMMENTARY: Zhawar was a symbol of Mujahideen invincibility in the border area and the Soviets and DRA felt that they had to destroy this myth. The Mujahideen were convinced that Zhawar was impregnable and failed to take some basic security precautions. September-October and March-April are historically the best months in Afghanistan for campaigning, since the weather is reasonable and the roads are dry. August-September that year was also the time of the Haj and the senior leadership of the area all made this religious pilgrimage together. Consequently, the senior leadership was absent when the battle started and other Mujahideen commanders had to take command of the battle. Field fortifications around Zhawar were neglected and incomplete. The excellent field fortifications at the mouth of the Manay Kandow pass bought time to improve the other fortifications The complacent attitude almost cost the Mujahideen their base. Only the unexpected appearance of Mujahideen armor at a crucial minute prevented a DRA victory.

The Mujahideen were able to move men and supplies from Miram Shah in Pakistan throughout the battle. The DRA apparently made no attempt to impede access by deploying scatterable mines against the route.

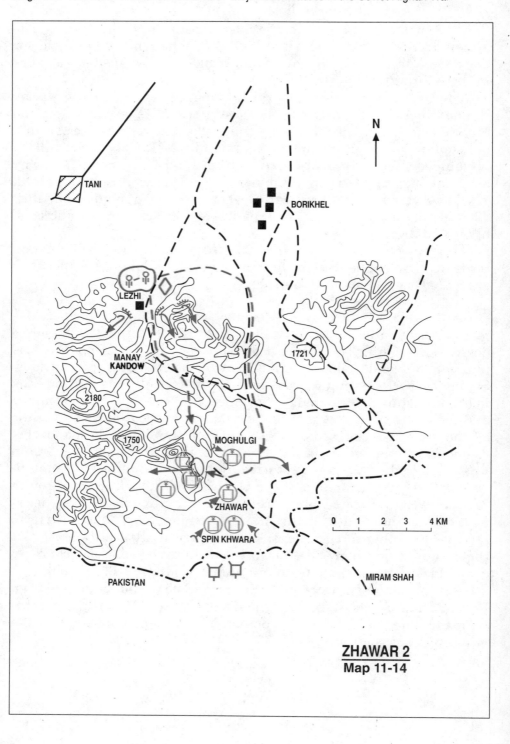

ZHAWAR 2
Map 11-14

VIGNETTE 11
ZHAWAR TWO
by Lieutenant Omar, Mawlawi Nezamuddin Haqani and Mawlawi Abdul-Rahman

On 2 April 1986, Mawlawi Nezamuddin Haqani was in the Zadran area when he saw approximately 20 transport helicopters flying over. He radioed the commanders at Zhawar and warned them. He expected that the helicopters would land at Lezhi or Darakai. After his radio message, he saw another group of helicopters, including some heavy transport helicopters, flying the same direction. These were escorted by jet fighters. He again radioed this information to Zhawar. Zhawar had 700-800 Mujahideen combatants, plus air defense forces, at the time. However Jalaluddin Haqani, the Zhawar Commander, was at Miram Shah. Mawlawi Haqani also radioed this information separately to Jalaluddin Haqani, who set out immediately for Zhawar.

The usual Soviet/DRA pattern for an attack on a Mujahideen base was to pound the area heavily with air strikes and then follow the air strikes with air assault landings, artillery fire and a ground advance to link up with the air assault forces. The air strike gave the Mujahideen commanders warning, reaction time and a solid indicator where the attack would go. In this case, the Mujahideen were caught by surprise. Their intelligence agents within the DRA failed to tip them off and the helicopters landed the DRA 38th Commando Brigade on seven dispersed landing zones around Zhawar. There were 15 helicopters in the first lift which landed at 0700 hours. More lifts followed to get the entire brigade on the ground. The first two helicopters landed on Spin Khwara plain. Some of the landing zones were within a kilometer of the Pakistani border (Map 11-14 - Zhawar 2). Most of the helicopters landed on the high ground to the west of Zhawar. Mujahideen gunners destroyed two helicopters while they were on the ground. Following the air assault, Soviet jet aircraft

---

Lieutenant Omar contributed to the previous vignette.

Mawlawi Nezamuddin Haqani contributed to the previous vignette.

Mawlawi Abdul-Rahman was a group commander from the Zadran tribe in Paktia Province. His brother was killed in this action. Mohammad Yousaf and Mark Adkin, *The Bear Trap*, London: Leo Cooper, 1992, 166-173 and Ijaz S. Gilani and Fazal-Ru-Rahman, *Afghanistan Report*, Islamabad: The Institute of Strategic Studies, Number 25, April 1986, 2-5 also consulted for this vignette.

bombed and strafed Mujahideen positions. Mujahideen air defense was not very effective against these aircraft.

Instead of defending in positions being pounded by fighter-bombers and close-air support aircraft, the Mujahideen went on the offensive and attacked the landing zones. They quickly overran four landing zones and captured many of the DRA commandos. Mujahideen reinforcements moved from Miram Shah in Pakistan to Zhawar and took the commandos from the rear. The commandos were trapped between two forces and were killed or captured. By the end of the day, the Mujahideen captured 530 commandos from the 38th Brigade.[16]

Meanwhile, Soviet aircraft with smart munitions made ordnance runs on the caves. Since the caves faced southeast toward Pakistan, the Soviet aircraft overflew Pakistan in order to turn and fly at the southern face with the smart weapons. Smart missiles hit the first western cave and killed 18 Mujahideen outright. Smart missiles hit the second western cave and collapsed the cave opening trapping some 150 Mujahideen inside. This second cave was 150-meters long and used as the radio transmission bunker. The commander, Jalaluddin Haqani, who had just arrived from Miram Shah, was among those trapped the second cave.

Soviet bombers followed the attack of the aircraft with the smart ordnance. They dropped tons of bombs and, in so doing, blasted away the rubble blocking the cave entrances. The trapped Mujahideen escaped. The battle for the remaining landing zones continued. There was one group of commandos on high ground who held out for three days before they were finally overrun.

The DRA had regarrisoned Lezhi since Zhawar One and had fought for the possession of the Manay Kandow Pass to Zhawar for some 10 days following the air landing. Mujahideen attacked their LOCs and the airfield at Khost while the Mujahideen holding the Manay Kandow checked their advance. In first battle for Zhawar, DRA/Soviet artillery and air strikes stopped at night, but this time they were conducted around the clock. At night, they dropped aerial flares for illumination. This heavy fire support continued for 12 days. Finally, more DRA and Soviet forces came from Khost, through Tani, to reinforce the effort at Lezhi. The Mujahideen fell back from the Lezhi area into the higher mountains and slowly the DRA/Soviet force moved through the Manay Kandow. At the same time, the

---

[16] Following Zhawar Two, the remnants of the 38th Commando Brigade became the base of the newly-formed 2nd Division.

DRA/Soviet force launched a flanking column from the Lezhi area that moved to the east. This column moved toward Moghulgai mountain on the east flank of Zhawar. There, a regiment of HIH Mujahideen waited in defense. However, as the DRA column neared, the HIH regiment withdrew without a fight. At the same time, Jalaluddin Haqani was wounded by attacking aircraft. He had head and facial wounds, but rumors spread among the Mujahideen that Haqani was dead. The Mujahideen evacuated Zhawar and moved high into the surrounding mountains as the two ground columns closed into Zhawar after 12 days of combat.

The DRA held Zhawar for only five hours. Mujahideen had moved MRL up on the Pakistan border and fired on the communists. The DRA hurriedly tried to destroy the caves with explosives and booby-trapped the area. They also planted seismic-detonated mines in the area and sprinkled aerial-delivered butterfly bombs over the area. The DRA took pictures for their propaganda victory and withdrew to their base camps. The Mujahideen returned to Zhawar on the following day. The first Mujahideen to enter the area were killed by seismic mines. The Mujahideen withdrew and fired mortars, BM12 and machine guns into the area to set off the seismic mines. Then they began the slow process of finding the rest of the mines manually. The Mujahideen pushed forward from Zhawar to retake Lezhi and other areas. Since the DRA was only in Zhawar for five hours, the DRA did not manage to destroy the caves, but just collapsed some entrances. Weapons that were stored in the caves were still intact and useable inside. From this experience, the Mujahideen learned to make connecting tunnels between caves. They reopened the caves and built connecting tunnels. The caves were improved and lengthened to 400-500 meters long.[17]

Mujahideen casualties were 281 KIA and 363 WIA. DRA and Soviet losses were unknown, but the Mujahideen destroyed two helicopters on the ground, shot down two jets and captured 530 personnel of the 38th Commando Brigade. The Mujahideen held a field tribunal. Yunis Khalis and others were the judges. They tried and executed Colonel Qalandar Shah, the commander of the Brigade and another colonel who landed with the brigade to adjust artillery fire. There were 78 other officers among the prisoners. They were given a chance to confess to their crimes from different battles and

---

17 Veterans of Zhawar have proposed to Haqani that the caves be restored and kept as a museum so that 200 years from now, people can visit them and reflect on their heritage.

then all the officers were executed. All the soldiers were given amnesty since they were conscripts who were forced to fight. The amnestied soldiers were asked to perform two years of labor service in exchange for the amnesty. They did their service in logistics, were reeducated and released after two years.

COMMENTARY: The withdrawal of the HIH regiment, coupled with the rumors of Haqani's death, greatly aided the DRA victory. Haqani's loss, besides affecting Mujahideen morale, cost the Mujahideen what little command and control they had left at this juncture of the battle. The DRA failed to throw a blocking force on the Miram Shah road, although they knew that Mujahideen reinforcements were moving along this route. As a minimum, they could have employed scatterable mines on the road, but they left the route open.

Pakistan was clearly concerned with the major battle raging on her border and reportedly transported Mujahideen to the border and supplied MRL to the Mujahideen who fired them across the border into Zhawar. The Mujahideen lacked effective air defense against helicopter gunships, and the strafing and bombing attacks of high-performance aircraft. The Mujahideen had some British Blowpipe shoulder-fired air defense missiles, but they were not effective. Pakistan sent some officers into Zhawar during the fighting to take out attacking aircraft with the British Blowpipe shoulder-fired missiles and show the Mujahideen how it was done. After climbing a mountain and firing 13 Blowpipe missiles to no avail, a Pakistani captain and his NCO were severely wounded by the attacking aircraft.[18]

The DRA celebrated the fall of Zhawar as a major victory, but Zhawar was back in full operation within weeks of the attack.

---

[18] Mohammad Yousaf and Mark Adkin, *The Bear Trap*, London: Leo Cooper, 1992, 171.

In late March 1986, the Soviet and DRA forces launched a major offensive against Mujahideen bases at Krer on the Pakistani border (Map 11-15 - Krer 1). Krer is located east of the Sarkani District center in Kunar Province. The Mujahideen maintained two bases in the mountain valley named "Shahid Abdul Latif" and "Fatha." The Mujahideen could reach the Bajuar area in Pakistan from the two bases. The bases served as border supply depots and staging areas for Mujahideen attacks against the Soviet/DRA forces in Kunar Province. My Asama Ben Zaid Regiment manned both of the Krer bases. The regiment's manpower fluctuated depending on the requirements and situation. The proximity of the bases to Mujahideen camps across the border in Pakistan made it easier to reinforce the Krer regiment at short notice. In March 1986, prior to the enemy offensive, my regiment was under-strength. Later in the battle, when reinforcements arrived from Bajuar in Pakistan, the number of Mujahideen reached nearly 400.

We had many indications that the Soviets and DRA were planning an attack, but we did not know when it would be launched. During the last week of March, when the weather was still cold and the mountain tops were still covered with snow, we detected enemy movement from the Sarkani direction across the Nawabad bridge. The enemy made no attempt to conceal or camouflage his action and apparently wanted to draw our attention to his movement. We later found out that the enemy's show of force was part of a deception plan to cover another attack that the enemy launched from Pashad—about 20 kilometers southwest of Sarkani. We did not expect an attack on Krer from Pashad. We prepared for an enemy attacking from

Commander Assadullah is from Charquala village in Narang Subdistrict of Kunar Province. He is the son of Mawlawi Mohammad Amin. He graduated from high school and emigrated to Pakistan in 1978 and later entered the Jamiat Islami faction's (JIA) military academy and completed the year-long course. He became a Mujahideen regimental commander of the Krer-based regiment. This was the Asama Ben Zaid Regiment of Sarkani District (Asama Ben Zaid was a close companion of the Prophet Mohammad and one of the Prophet's military leaders. At one point, Asama ben Zaid fought the Byzantines). The Regiment belonged to the Sayyaf faction (IUA) and so Commander Assadullah switched factions. [Map sheets 3287 and 3387].

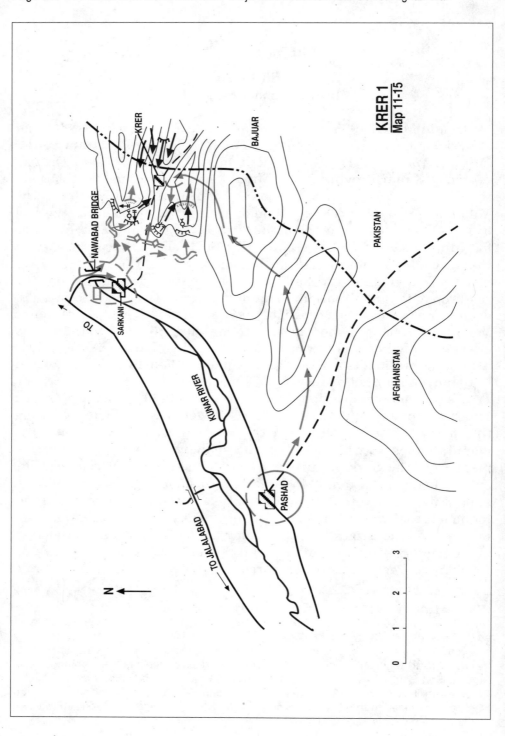

Sarkani and deployed the bulk of the force to the valley entrance facing the Sarkani District center. This was the main avenue of approach to Krer and I expected the enemy to use it.

A mixed Soviet/DRA column, led by local guides, crossed the Kunar River at Nawabad bridge, northeast of Sarkani, and attacked my forward positions in the late afternoon (Map 11-14 - Krer1). This was where I expected them and heavy fighting ensued as enemy infantry and armored vehicles fought with my resistance fighters at the valley entrance. Both sides had heavy losses. While the enemy tied my forces down, he launched another attack from Pashad along the mountain paths to outflank my force. This attacking column consisted of Soviet infantry (possibly a Spetsnaz detachment) and it moved undetected to the rear of my force and seized the undefended high ground on the Spina Tsoka mountains. From there, the Soviet detachment attacked us from the rear and overran both Mujahideen valley bases, including our main supply depot. By next morning, we had lost all our installations and were surrounded by the enemy forces. The enemy was pounding our positions from the high ground to our rear.

I had crossed the border and mobilized a Mujahideen force in the Bajaur camps and, as the enemy fought for Krer, the reinforcing Mujahideen force moved toward Krer to help the embattled defenders. My reinforcements moved early in the morning to the border and infiltrated through concealed approaches to Krer since the enemy dominated the main road from the high ground. Around noon, I was moving with a six-man group when we stumbled on a group of Soviets. Apparently, they were a command group. We attacked the group and after a brief but fierce clash, in which both sides threw hand grenades at each other, we killed a senior Soviet officer. This apparently lead to the withdrawal of the Soviets. With the arrival of the Mujahideen reinforcements, the Soviet position was threatened from the rear. Fragmented fighting broke out in separate areas throughout the valley. The enemy began to pull out in the afternoon and by the evening we Mujahideen recaptured the valley and our bases. The bases were mostly destroyed by the enemy.

We caught a group of Soviet soldiers in one of our supply caves at the depot. We attempted to flush them out and lost several Mujahideen killed and wounded to AK-74 fire. Finally, we fired an RPG into the cave and then threw hand grenades into it silencing the enemy. The next morning we found several dead Soviets in the cave. We buried our dead and evacuated our wounded. I had roughly 25%

casualties (33 KIA and 40 WIA). I think that enemy losses were higher because we captured some 60 enemy small arms.[19]

COMMENTARY: By drawing the bulk of the Mujahideen forces away from their base and attacking the base from the rear, the Soviets achieved a major surprise through deception and good planning. This enabled them to overrun and destroy the Mujahideen bases without facing any resistance. But Soviet failure to block the Mujahideen reinforcement routes resulted in apparent heavy Soviet losses and forced them to withdraw from the areas they had so easily captured. Mujahideen rapid reinforcement changed the course of the battle. Seizing and retaining the initiative is crucial to any tactical scheme. The Mujahideen lost the initiative to the enemy at the beginning of the battle. But, the Soviets failed to retain the initiative and lost it to the Mujahideen maneuver of reserves from the rear. This decided the final outcome of the battle. Guerrilla warfare is no different from conventional warfare in that a reserve can drastically change the situation through quick and effective commitment before the opponent consolidates his tactical success.

---

[19] Pakistani *Strategic Studies Review*, April 1986 notes: "Soviet forces launched air-cum-ground attack on Mujahideen base in Krer area killed 26 Mujahideen destroyed their entire armament and lost 42 men after 15 hours fighting March 26. Mujahideen killed 70 Kabul and 50 Soviet troops and lost 42 men in their bid to break Soviet-Kabul encirclement of Soran base in Krer area of Sarkani District March 28-31. Mujahideen repulsed Soviet attack after hours of occupation of their base in Krer after inflicting heavy losses and capturing three Soviet troops during 48 hours fighting March 30-31."

VIGNETTE 13
KRER TWO
by Commander Assadullah

At the end of 1987, when the Soviet forces were preparing to begin their negotiated withdrawal from Afghanistan, they launched a number of high-visibility offensives, which served their propaganda campaign which claimed that the Soviet Army was able to defeat any Mujahideen force anywhere. To this end, the Soviets conducted operation Magistral in Paktia Province to open the "unopenable" Gardez-Khowst highway. At the same time, the Soviets attacked major Mujahideen border bases. In Kunar Province, the Soviet/DRA forces targeted the Mujahideen bases at Krer for destruction. Apparently, they intended to establish a border security outpost at the Spina Tsoka Mountain on the border with Pakistan to control several infiltration routes connecting the Nawa Pass, Gonjgal and other valleys in Pakistan with the road to Sarkani and the valleys of Shonkray, Shalay, and Olay in Afghanistan.

In late December 1987, I received intelligence reports that a Soviet-led DRA column would attack the Krer bases. The intelligence agents did not know when the attack would come. There were only 170 men in my regiment at that time. I established security posts and conducted reconnaissance along the routes over which I expected the attack. Based on past enemy behavior, I expected him to avoid night combat and night maneuver. I expected him to attack at dawn or later and to use the valley approach. The enemy surprised me. He chose to move and fight at night and, instead of using the valley approach, he moved to the north flank of the mountain and attacked over it. He did this to get behind my forward defenses and unhinge my defense (Map 11-16 - Krer 2).

The enemy moved from Sarkani at night in two columns. One column moved against the Mujahideen "Fatha" base and the other moved deeper in a flanking maneuver to the rear of my defenses and tried to climb the heights of Spina Tsoka mountain. The column heading toward the "Fatha" base climbed the ridge from the east. There was a security outpost there consisting of 10-12 men sleeping in a tent and a small hut. The enemy soldiers silently approached the guard and killed him without making any noise. The other Mujahideen at the

---

Commander Assadullah is the source of the previous vignette.

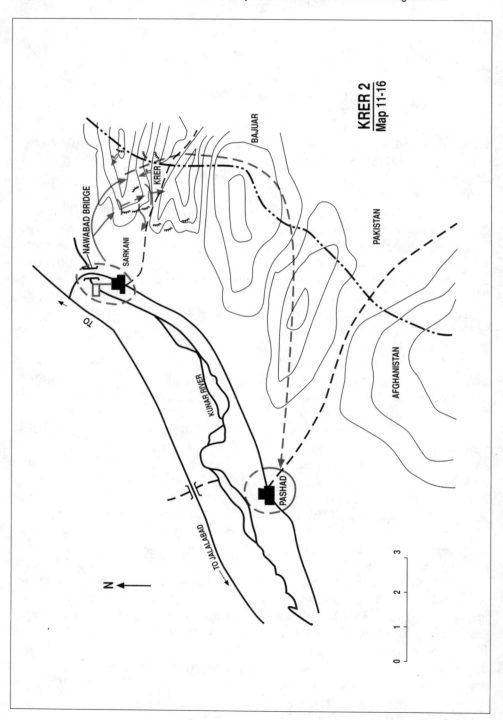

KRER 2
Map 11-16

outpost were fast asleep and were caught by surprise. The enemy was killing them when some of them woke up and a shoot-out ensued. The Mujahideen at "Fatha" died to the last man.

The noise from the gunfire alerted the rest of my Mujahideen. The second enemy column had not yet reached the crest of Spina Tsoka mountain. My Mujahideen occupied fighting positions and met the approaching enemy with heavy fire. A fierce battle continued throughout the night. The enemy column was deep in our positions, but we had cut off his withdrawal routes. We expected to bloody the enemy as he fought to reopen his withdrawal routes. Instead, the enemy column continued over the mountain path all the way to Pashad, some 20 kilometers southwest of Sarkani. We did not expect the enemy to withdraw in that direction.

Meanwhile, my Mujahideen directed heavy fire on the enemy at the "Fatha" base and it began a fighting retreat back to Sarkani. By dawn, the enemy had withdrawn from the Krer base and taken his dead and wounded with him. Mujahideen losses included 18 killed and 20 wounded (again about 25% casualties).

COMMENTARY: The Soviet/DRA commander did a good job on analyzing the pattern set by his forces in the area. Using this stereotype, the DRA commander caught the Mujahideen commander by surprise, even though he had been warned. The Soviet/DRA commander knew that the Mujahideen considered the Soviets and DRA reluctant to move and fight at night and reliant on readily identifiable terrain for night movement. Therefore, he advanced stealthily at night over unexpected approaches. This gave him tactical surprise and allowed him to wipe out a critical Mujahideen outpost virtually without resistance. However, his apparent lack of coordination between the two columns disclosed his attack prematurely and denied victory the second column. Had both columns been in position and launched their attacks simultaneously, they might have achieved better results.

The Mujahideen were asleep despite sufficient warnings because they reacted to a stereotype and pattern. Mujahideen actions, once alerted, were commendable, particularly in cutting off the obvious Soviet/DRA route of withdrawal. Whether the Soviet/DRA commander's original plan included withdrawal over the Pashad mountain route or whether it was a decision that he made on the spot, it clearly saved the force from some heavy casualties. Had the Mujahideen also blocked the Pashad route, the Soviet/DRA force might have been in very serious trouble and faced possible annihilation.

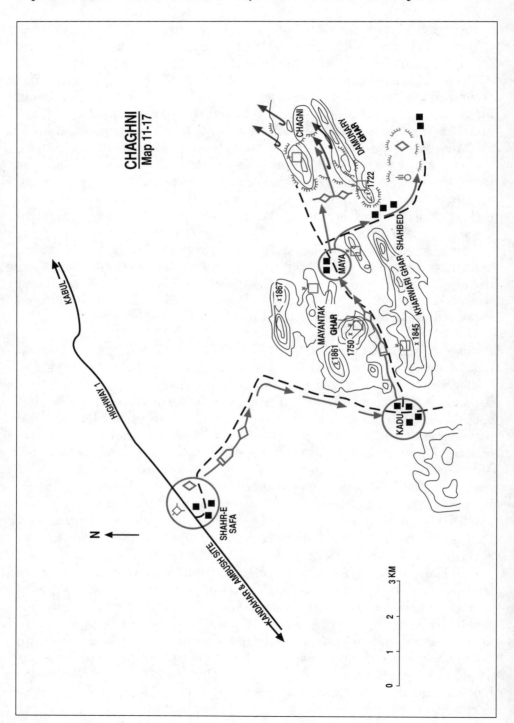

CHAGHNI
Map 11-17

THE FALL OF CHAGHNI BASE CAMP
by Commander Abdul Razek,
Haji Pir Mohammad, and Amir Mohammad

Chaghni base camp is in Shahr-e Safa District about 10 kilometers from Highway 1—the main highway from Kabul to Kandahar. We normally set ambushes on the south side of the road, since the north side is open between Shahr-e Safa and Kalat. There was only one place optimum for ambush—a six-kilometer stretch where a dry river bed parallels the road way. We could hide many Mujahideen in the high ground overlooking the road and escort vehicles could not cross the river bed to get up into our ambush positions, since the dry river banks were like sheer walls. Although no APC or tank could get across, we mined the area between the road and the river bed anyway. The high ground of Sher Alikhan Mountain protected our withdrawal. Further, there were no villages or villagers nearby to provide warning to the enemy. We built permanent fighting positions at this site and we ambushed the enemy at this site continually, but they always seemed surprised. The enemy convoy would usually reach our ambush site in the late afternoon since they left Kabul about 0800. The enemy usually sent tanks, BMPs and APCs to escort their convoys. We normally positioned our heavy weapons on favorable ground higher up and positioned our small arms forward.

At the point that we usually laid our ambushes, there was one road that intersected our area. It had to cross the river bed, but we usually mined that road as well for good measure. The normal reaction of the enemy convoy, when ambushed, was to drive off the road to the north to get out of range of our weapons. They never tried to attack us. Their trucks would be burning and destroyed, everything would be in chaos and everyone was looking to his own survival. There was no coordinated response. Escort tanks and APCs would

---

Abdul Razek was a major commander in the Kandahar area. Several of the current Taliban leaders once worked for him. His command included Shahr-e Safa District northeast of Kandahar. [Map sheet 2280, vic grid 6016].

Haji Pir Mohammad was a subgroup commander for Abdul Razek in the Kandahar area.

Amir Mohammad was a combatant in Abdul Razek's group.

fire at random, but they would never dismount troops and push them forward. Then enemy aircraft would arrive and make strafing runs, but it would be too late because darkness would be falling. Our group and Chaghni base camp was a real thorn in the side of the enemy.

It was in the year of Islam Dara (October 1986) that the Soviets captured our base at Chaghni. Our commander, Abdul Razek, was not at the base but was visiting other Mujahideen in Kandahar and Helmand with a representative of our faction headquartered in Peshawar. At 0400 hours, the enemy dropped illumination flares that lit up the area like it was day. Everybody was sleeping at Chaghni except for the sentries. The enemy followed this with an air and MRL bombardment. Early in the morning, helicopters came and landed troops at four LZs (Map 11-17 - Chaghni). Some 45 helicopters were involved. These four LZs were located on the high ground to secure the flanks for their advancing tanks and infantry. When the air assault forces reported that the way was clear, the tanks and mechanized infantry moved from Shahr-e Safa. The artillery fire and airstrikes were so heavy that they probably assumed that no one was left alive.

The Soviets had moved earlier from Kandahar to Shahr-e Safa. Now, the enemy ground column came from Shahr-e Safa south to Kadu, where they turned east in the canyon between Mayantak Ghar and Kharwari Ghar mountains. Air assault forces on these heights safeguarded their passage. The movement of the enemy was very slow since they waited as the air assault forces moved along the high ground to secure passage for them. They reached Kadu in the morning. It took them from 0800-1600 hours to travel the remaining 11 kilometers from Kadu to our base. At the end of the canyon was the village of Mayu. There, the ground column split. The main body continued east toward the village of Bandaki.

Our base camp was to the east of Bandaki, located in a saddle between the Caki Ghar and Dumunaray Ghar mountains. Again, air assault forces on the heights safeguarded their passage. The other part of their column was a flanking detachment. It turned south at Mayu through the village of Shahbed and then to the south of Dumunaray Ghar mountain to block our escape and to shoot at our base. Their tanks reached our base in the afternoon. As they neared our position, they put in the fifth and sixth LZ to not only secure their advance but also to attack down from the high ground. Haji Pir Mohammad was using a ZGU on hill 1722. Amir Mohammad

engaged a helicopter coming toward them, but missed. The helicopter went over the crest of the hill where Abdul Ghani was waiting
with a RPG. Abdul yelled that the helicopter was landing infantry
and he would get it. He shot it with his RPG. Only four or five personnel had gotten out of the helicopter when he hit it. The remains
of that helicopter were there for more than year.

We had deployed our forces to maximize the fire power of our
seven 82mm recoilless rifles, five ZGU-1 machine guns, six DShK
machine guns and many RPG-7s. We also had some mortars, but we
could not use the mortars very well. A mortar is good against a
stationary target, but is hard to use against a moving target. Most of
the fighting was between their armored vehicles and our recoilless
rifles and RPGs. They were so close that we could hear their Russian
voices. They were also using loudspeakers telling us to surrender
since our plight was hopeless and we would be killed. That language
was Pushto from their Afghans. We answered these broadcasts with
fire and destroyed seven tanks and APCS. We shot down one jet and
they intensified their fire. As they launched their attacks against us,
they would show their location to the supporting aircraft with red
smoke. This kept their own aircraft from attacking them.

Night fell and everything was confused and chaotic as we lost
command and control. No one knew where the Soviets were and where
the Mujahideen were. We Mujahideen fought on until 0200 or 0300
hours in the morning. Then, as we ran out of ammunition, we began
to slip away to the northeast. A close friend of Pir Mohammad's was
standing close to him when he was killed. Pir Mohammad carried his
body to high ground, where he left the body in a safe place and left the
area. There were 220 Mujahideen in the base. We had 22 KIA—21 of
our Mujahideen and one guest who was spending the night at our
base. Most of the 198 survivors escaped to the northeast. The Soviets
now owned the base. They spent 24 hours there, looted it, and
destroyed as much of our installation as they could.

Before Commander Razek had left Chaghni, he had sent groups out
to scout the road.   They reported that the roads from Kandahar and
Arghestan were closed. He sent out scouts again the next night and
they reported that the roads were still blocked.   The next day, toward
late afternoon, he went to Shahr-e Safa by tractor and then north into
the mountains and then turned and followed the Arghandab River
Valley down to Kandahar. The trip took five days. At Kandahar, he
discovered that the airport was very busy as waves of aircraft flew
in and out. He was told that the ground detachment had also left

and was headed northeast. He did not have much communications at that time. In the late afternoon, he learned that the fighting was focused at his base. He went to his other bases in Kandahar and gathered Mujahideen and MRL. He then took the same circuitous route back to his base. As they reached Shahr-e Safa, the Soviets had already gone, so he sent his Kandahar reinforcements back and went on to Chaghni. The survivors were gone and those left were all dead. It was a mess. Everything destroyed or damaged. Booby traps and mines were all over the area. Gradually the surviving Mujahideen returned. Commander Razek decided that this was no longer a safe place for a permanent base and converted it to a mobile base for 50 Mujahideen. Five days after we buried our dead, we packed 150 rockets and went to exact revenge on the Kandahar airport.

One night, some two weeks later, we buried our rockets or put them in hideouts or safe-houses near Khoshab to the north of the airfield. We had to do this very secretly, as we did not want the locals to know. The next night, we set up our 150 rockets with remote-control firing devices aimed at the airfield. The remote control firing devices were essential because it is impossible to stay in the open area after firing. The first salvo of 50 rockets fired at night. After the first salvo, planes took off and hit the area at random. The next salvo fired at sunrise and the third salvo at 0700 hours— about one hour later. After each salvo of 50 rockets, planes would fly over and shoot at random, but there were no Mujahideen in the area. After the third salvo, the enemy sent armored vehicles into the area to search. They encircled the area and sent dismounted infantry into the cordon. They found the spent launchers.

Most of the Soviet aircraft losses were from rocket attacks on planes parked on the ground, not from air defense. This attack reportedly damaged many aircraft. Before Stingers, Soviet and Chinese SA-7s proved very ineffective. We only brought down two aircraft in the Kandahar area with SA-7s.

COMMENTARY: The Soviet advance on Chaghni was slow, but the Soviets were finally learning to dominate the high ground before they moved their ground force. Apparently the Soviets had good intelligence to support this attack. However, the Soviets did not block all escape routes and the bulk of the Mujahideen force escaped.

Mujahideen reconnaissance, on the other hand, was lacking and they were surprised. Still, the Mujahideen had plenty of time to hit the Soviets or evacuate their base during the slow Soviet advance.

They took few precautions and were not aggressive in contesting the Soviet advance. The Mujahideen showed a lack of command and control—reflecting the absence of their leader and a working chain of command. Further, the commander had not trained his mortar crews in engaging moving targets.

CHAPTER COMMENTARY

The Mujahideen safe-havens in Pakistan and Iran were absolutely essential for the survival of their force. Pakistan was particularly important since most of the external aid came through Pakistan. These safe havens allowed the Mujahideen a place to shelter their families, resupply, treat their wounded, train, sell war booty to support their families, rest and exchange tactical information and intelligence. Pakistan provided forward supply depots near the border and the Mujahideen built most of their major supply depots near the Pakistan border. These Mujahideen major supply depots were a constant target of the Soviets and DRA. In some areas, the Mujahideen developed forward supply depots and tried to move most of the supplies forward. In contested areas, the Mujahideen moved their forward supply depots about to avoid capture. The major supply depots, however, were stationary and vulnerable. A dictum of guerrilla warfare is that the guerrilla should not hold ground. Mujahideen logistics forced the Mujahideen to hold ground.

Mujahideen defenses were built around heavy crew-served weapons. The popular image of the guerrilla is a small force carrying an assortment of small arms. Most insurgencies start that way, but successful insurgencies need heavy weapons. The problem with heavy weapons is that they and their ammunition are hard to transport. The Mujahideen became very adept at field fortifications and developed shelters which protected them from intense air and artillery attack. On the other hand, throughout the war, the Mujahideen had difficulty fighting air and artillery systems and had to learn how to survive them—particularly when defending. The introduction of the Stinger man-portable air defense missile in 1986 provided upgraded Mujahideen air defense and forced the Soviets to change their aerial tactics to avoid losing aircraft.

Soviet assaults on Mujahideen defenses were initially hampered by their reluctance to fight at night, their over-reliance on firepower at the expense of maneuver, and their reluctance to operate far from their armored vehicles. As the war progressed, the Soviets developed better light infantry, began conducting more night combat and more-skillfully employed air assault and ground combat tactical elements together. Still, throughout the war, the Soviets were hampered by lack of sufficient infantry forces.

CHAPTER 12
COUNTERAMBUSH

Counterambush is a tedious, time-consuming effort requiring route planning, patrols, timely intelligence, counterambush drills and flank security. Planning should ensure that alternate routes and times of travel are used, that potential ambush sites are cleared and that movement through areas is coordinated with local forces. Movement details need to be safeguarded and deception measures taken to prevent ambush.

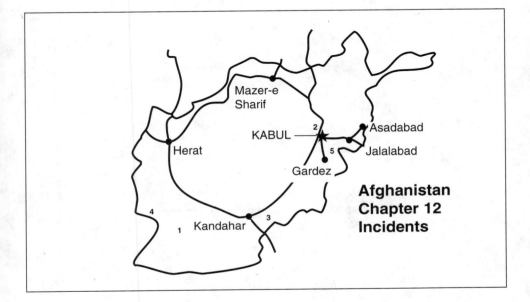

Afghanistan Chapter 12 Incidents

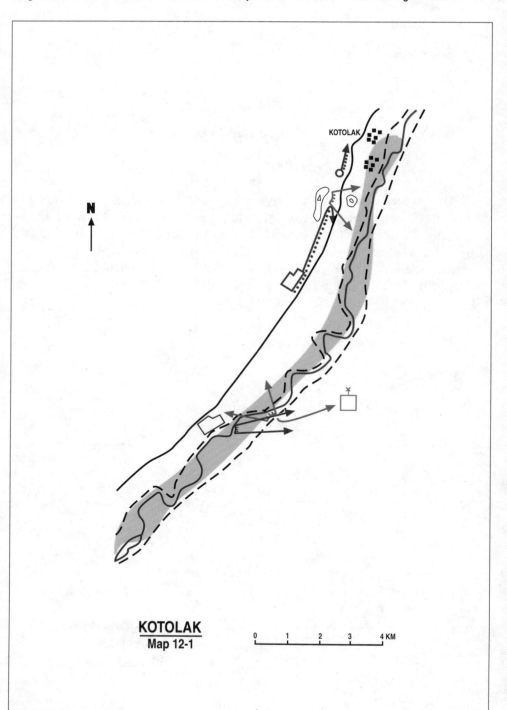

KOTOLAK
Map 12-1

0   1   2   3   4 KM

VIGNETTE 1
CAUGHT IN A SOVIET AMBUSH
by Mawlawi Mohayddin Baloch

In 1983, we had one GMC pickup truck to support my force. We called GMC pickups *ahu* (deer), since they were fleet and nimble. It was the month of Ramadan and we were going from our base in Qala-e Naw to Kotalak to get some gasoline. Soviet soldiers were the main source of our gasoline. We would buy it from them. Our rendezvous point for gasoline was north of Kotolak. We left early in the afternoon and drove along the river avoiding the main roads (Map 12-1 - Kotolak). There was a Kochi[1] in our truck who had visited our base and we were giving him a ride back to his village camp. As we got about 10 kilometers south of Kotolak, we saw the Kochi's camp near the river. We stopped, both to let our passenger off and to wait for dark, since we were now within 50 kilometers of the Soviet base at Delaram and should not travel any further in the day light. We watched as the Kochi entered the woods some 500-600 meters away on his way to his camp. We saw some people attack him and drag him to the side. We didn't know what was going on and thought that it was a fight between Kochis. "What's going on?" we yelled. They did not answer so we fired some shots into the air. The people who grabbed the Kochi realized that they had been seen and started firing at us. We exchanged fire for about a half hour until helicopters landed behind the wooded area. The other group boarded the helicopters and left. It was late afternoon.

We had prematurely and inadvertently triggered a Soviet ambush. We were on the western bank of the Khash Rud river and the ambush force was on the eastern bank. Soviet ambushes were always better planned and prepared than those of the DRA. The Soviets would drop their ambush party by helicopter at night and the party would walk into position so that their ambush could not be detected. This ambush party was probably from Delaram[2] and had

Mawlawi Mohayddin Baloch is from Nimroz province. His base was at Lowkhai, the Khash Rud district capitol on the Khash Rud river. He was initially with Malawi Mohammad Nabi Mohammadi of the Harakat-e Inqelab-i Islami (HAR). Later, on he switched to HIK (Khalis). [Map sheet 1680].

[1] Kochi are nomadic tribesmen of Afghanistan. They live primarily by herding and trading sheep, goats and camels.

[2] More probably, these were Spetsnaz from Lashkar Gah.

probably moved into their wooded position the previous night. The Soviets suffocated the Kochi who had been our passenger and had killed another Kochi earlier in the same fashion. The river was fordable, so after the helicopters left, we forded the river to look at the ambush sight. Villagers found the bodies of the two murdered Kochi. We crossed back to the west side, got in our truck and began driving on the road to Kotolak since it was now night.

About two kilometers south of Kotolak the Soviets had set another ambush in some hills straddling the road. We were moving in enemy territory and I considered the route dangerous so we stopped short of the hills and I had seven of my men dismount and walk the road to the other side of the hills checking for ambushers. If they saw nothing, then we would move the truck forward. This left eight Mujahideen with the truck—three in the cab and five in the pickup bed. My seven walkers walked past the hills, checked for ambush and gave us an all-clear sign—a signal rocket.

The ambush party let my walkers pass through unmolested. When we saw the rocket, we moved out confidently. Suddenly, I thought that someone had set us on fire. We were in an ambush kill zone and bullets were flying all around us. Two men in the truck bed and the man next to me in the cab were killed. The driver was wounded in the shoulder. One tire was hit. The driver slammed the truck into reverse gear and tried to drive out of the kill zone. He drove the truck behind a sheltering hillock and stopped it. I had three KIA and two WIA. We changed the tire and left the area in the dark. My walkers continued to Kotolak. Later on, the walkers returned individually to my base camp. As we were reversing the truck out of the kill zone, the body of one of my dead Mujahideen fell out of the truck bed. The next day when we returned to recover his body, we discovered that it was booby trapped. We had to tie a rope to our dead comrade and drag him for a distance, before it was safe to carry him home for burial.

COMMENTARY: At the first ambush site, the Soviets failed to put out flank observers and consequently were surprised by the Mujahideen in their stationary truck. This failure compromised their ambush.

At the second ambush site, the Mujahideen walkers walked around the hills, not along the military crest where the ambushers should be. The ambushers wisely let the patrol pass to concentrate on the vehicle. However, the Soviets failed to employ directional, command-detonated mines or an RPG to effectively stop the truck in the kill zone. Further, the ambush commander did not know the size of the Mujahideen force and, following the ambush, did not pursue the Mujahideen or push out a patrol to determine the Mujahideen's position and status.

After the first ambush, the Soviets knew that the Mujahideen intended to move north. It was also clear that the Soviets were in the area, yet the Mujahideen did not contact other local Mujahideen groups to check on Soviet and DRA activities in the area. The factionalized nature of the resistance prevented the spread of tactical intelligence which may have saved the Mujahideen from disaster.

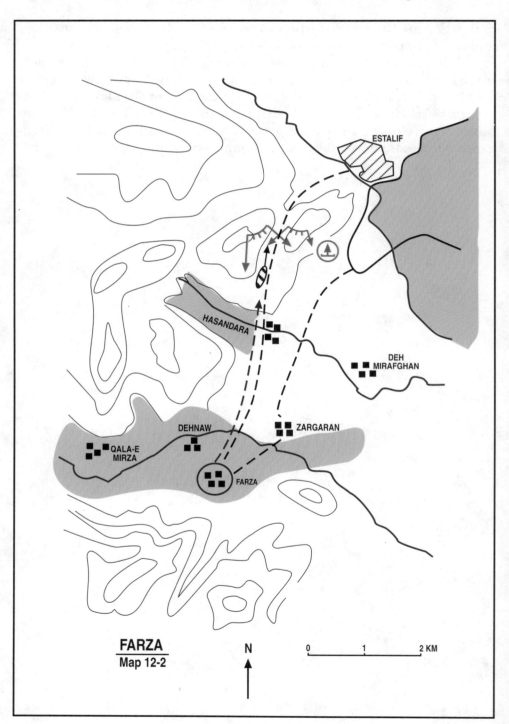

FARZA

Map 12-2

VIGNETTE 2
AMBUSHED AT FARZA
by Commander Sofi Lal Gul

In April 1984, the regional Mujahideen called for a *shura* (local council) to discuss local issues and decide on common approaches. Sofi Rasul and myself were to attend as the local Mujahideen commanders from Farza. The meeting would be held five kilometers to our north in Estalif. We were accompanied by 28 Mujahideen armed with AK47s and two RPG-7s. Someone must have been working for DRA intelligence in our area, since the DRA knew about our plans and set an ambush on the trail near Farza.

We left Farza while it was still dark so that the enemy would not see us. Our route took us between two hills near a DRA air defense battery position (Map 12-2 - Farza). We were about half way to Estalif at a point which we call Wotaq, when the enemy opened fire on us from the surrounding hills. A DRA force had set up the ambush during the night. There is no doubt that they knew the exact route we would take. We went to ground in the kill zone and tried to find good fighting positions. The firing was fierce, we were totally surprised and we did not know the enemy strength and exact positions. Our return fire was ineffective and uncontrolled.

As dawn broke, our situation improved slightly, but we were still in shock. I had no command or control over my men and they acted as individuals trying to break contact and leave the kill zone. Enemy fire was still heavy. During a lull in the fighting, I managed to find a few Mujahideen sheltering in a ditch. I led them to the safety of the mountains in the west. Twelve Mujahideen eventually reached the safety of the terrain folds and mountain valleys in the west. Two others and myself were wounded. We remained hidden in the valley until we saw the ambush force leave that afternoon. Then we returned to the ambush site where we discovered that 18 of our comrades were killed. Some of their bodies were mutilated by the enemy and most had their clothing shredded. Late that afternoon, we moved their bodies for burial. I do not know if there were any enemy casualties, but during

---

Commander Sofi Lal Gul is from Farza village of Mir Bacha Kot District. This is about 25 kilometers north of Kabul. He was affiliated with Mojaddedi's Afghanistan National Liberation Front of Afghanistan (ANLF) during the war with the Soviets. Commander Sofi Lal Gul concentrated his efforts on the Kabul-Charikar highway. [Map sheet 2886, vic grid 0350].

the fighting, I saw helicopters landing and taking off. They may have come to evacuate dead and wounded.

COMMENTARY: This successful DRA ambush inflicted more than 60 percent loss on the Mujahideen force. Soviet/DRA recruitment of local agents and informants gradually expanded their intelligence network in the Afghan rural areas. Often, agent/informant information was not timely, but when it was, the Soviet/DRA planners reacted to it. Intelligence was central to Soviet/DRA ambush planning and attempts to assassinate Mujahideen commanders. The Soviets/DRA usually conducted ambushes based on hard information and seldom placed random ambushes on the hope that a force might stumble into it.

If the Mujahideen felt that they were moving through uncontested territory, they often failed to post route security or send a forward and flanking patrols. This lack of attention to tactical security stemmed from the notion that they completely controlled the countryside and that the DRA/Soviet forces were unable to operate covertly in the countryside for long. This over-confidence cost the Mujahideen dearly. The Soviet/DRA forces exploited this Mujahideen hubris by setting ambushes even in areas located deep inside Mujahideen-controlled territory.

When ambushed, the Mujahideen had difficulty maintaining command and control. This exacerbated the situation and increased their casualties. Mujahideen commanders often failed to train their personnel in drills and counter-ambush procedures. In this example, the commander lost control immediately and failed to regain it. This was a contributing factor to the very-high Mujahideen losses. Further, the middle of a kill zone is no place to establish a defense. If the commander had a counterambush battle drill where his men immediately assaulted into the teeth of the ambush, more of his force might have survived.

VIGNETTE 3
BLASTING OUT OF AN AMBUSH
by Amir Mohammad

It was in 1985. We had a large truck that we were hauling weapons, rockets and ammunition in from Pakistan to our base camp in the Argandab river valley (No map). We were taking a circuitous route. We neared Lora near sunset when we saw a helicopter. There was nowhere to hide since we were on an open plain. The helicopter landed and Soviet soldiers jumped out of it and took up positions all around us. We stopped the truck, jumped out and took up positions all around the truck. We had 13 Mujahideen and there were 10-12 Soviets. The Soviets had the advantage of better weapons, position and fire power. We started firing at each other. The Soviets started to advance on us. The driver was afraid that we would be captured, so he took a jerry can of gasoline, poured the gasoline onto the truck and set it on fire. He yelled at us to take cover. Despite the Soviet small-arms fire, we scurried to new positions for cover. Soon, the fire reached the ammunition and rockets and the truck exploded with a tremendous roar. The rockets and rounds were not stacked neatly, but were stacked in every possible direction. Consequently, the rockets and bullets were exploding and streaking off in every possible direction. It was spectacular. The explosion and flying rounds frightened the Soviets. They ran back to their helicopter and took off. After the helicopter left and things stopped exploding, we walked to a nearby village. Neither side had any casualties, but we lost a good truck and lots of ammunition and we had to walk back to our base camp.

COMMENTARY: The Mujahideen felt that they were in a secure area and were driving during the day. Usually, Mujahideen trucks moved at night. Evidently the Soviets hoped to capture the truck or they would have shot it up and created the same explosion that the Mujahideen did.

Amir Mohammad was a combatant in Abdul Razik's group in the Shahr-e Safa district northeast of Kandahar. There is no map with this vignette.

VIGNETTE 4
CAUGHT IN A DRA AMBUSH
by Mawlawi Mohayddin Baloch

In 1986, we were moving three pickup trucks full of ammunition from Iran to our base. We had two motorcyclists patrolling five kilometers in front of the pickup trucks. We were near the border of Iran at Shand near Helmond lake. There is a point where two hills constrict the road and limit maneuver. The DRA border guard set up an ambush there (No map). Our two motorcyclists rode through the ambush zone and the DRA let them pass. As the motorcyclists cleared the ambush zone, they saw the DRA. They dismounted their motorcycles and took up firing positions on an adjacent hill. Our trucks rolled into the kill zone. The motorcyclists opened fire on the ambushers to warn the pickup trucks and to distract the ambushers. The DRA opened fire and hit the middle truck. The first pickup truck drove out of the kill zone while the Mujahideen in the last truck dismounted and attacked the ambushers. The DRA fled. We lost two Mujahideen KIA and one truck was damaged. There were no known DRA casualties.

COMMENTARY: When Mujahideen felt that they were in a secure area, they would move supplies during the day. The Mujahideen felt secure in this area since they were moving in the daylight. Still, they had a forward patrol checking for ambush. The patrol, however, seems road bound and did not get off the road to check likely ambush sites carefully. The patrol had no communication with the main body, so when the motorcyclists finally detected the ambush, they were unable to immediately contact them. Consequently, two of the three trucks were in the kill zone by the time the motorcyclists opened fire. Still, there was enough spacing between trucks which prevented the entire force from being in the kill zone simultaneously.

The Mujahideen showed aggressive spirit and resolve by immediately assaulting the ambushers and driving them from the scene. The DRA controlled the dominant terrain and had the opportunity to prepare fighting positions. They should have been able to stand, yet they fled in the face of Mujahideen resolve. The immediate assault into the ambush probably saved the Mujahideen convoy.

Mawlawi Mohayddin Baloch is from Nimroz province. His base was at Lowkhai, the capitol of Khash Rud district on the Khash Rud river. He was initially with Mawlawi Mohammad Nabi Mohammadi of the Harakat-e Inqelab-i Islami (HAR). Later, on he switched to HIK (Khalis). There is no map with this vignette.

VIGNETTE 5
AMBUSHED ON THE HIGH PLAIN
by Commander Haji Aaquelshah Sahak

In May 1987, we were moving supplies from Peshawar, Pakistan to our base west of Kabul. We followed the Logar route from Parachinar, Pakistan across the Afghanistan border to Jaji in Paktiya Province. From there, we followed mountain canyons to Dobandi. Past Dobandi, the mountains ended and we had a broad plain to cross before we reached the mountains near our base. We finally reached Dobandi and stayed there for three days (Map 12-3 - Dobandi). We waited there while I made sure that the way was clear because the Soviets would set ambushes to interdict our supplies. I went from Dobandi to Kafar Dara canyon for information on Soviet activity. The Mujahideen at Kafar Dara did not have any information either, so I went on to Sepets where there were several Mujahideen bases belonging to HAR and Hezb-e Islami. These Mujahideen gave us two guides—Akhunzada of HAR and Mulla Nawab. We brought up all our supplies to Sepets in the late afternoon. Including the guides, I had 31 Mujahideen with me. I planned to go forward, clear the route, establish security positions on key terrain and likely ambush sites and then bring the supplies forward. I moved in the middle of the column.

We moved across the open plain from Sepets. There is a place called the Childrens' cemetery where we stopped to offer our late afternoon prayers. Since it was still daylight, we moved well spread out with a distance between every Mujahideen. This was a precaution against air attacks. I told the guide, Mulla Nawab, to stay with us until we passed through this area and reached the Gardez highway. We followed a stream bed through a brush-covered area. We neared the water mill midpoint between Sepets and Khato Kalay at 1920 hours, when I looked at my watch to see if it was time for evening prayer. There was high ground on both sides of us. Suddenly machine-gun fire opened up in front of me. At first, I thought that it was my Mujahideen firing, but then I saw Soviets to the north firing on us. My Mujahideen immediately scattered and crouched behind bushes. The Soviets fired at the bushes, but my Mujahideen held their fire. The Soviets assumed that they had killed all my Mujahideen and jumped

---

Commander Haji Aaquelshah Sahak is from the Chardehi district of Kabul (a southern suburb). He was affiliated with NIFA. [Map sheet 2884, vic grid 3058].

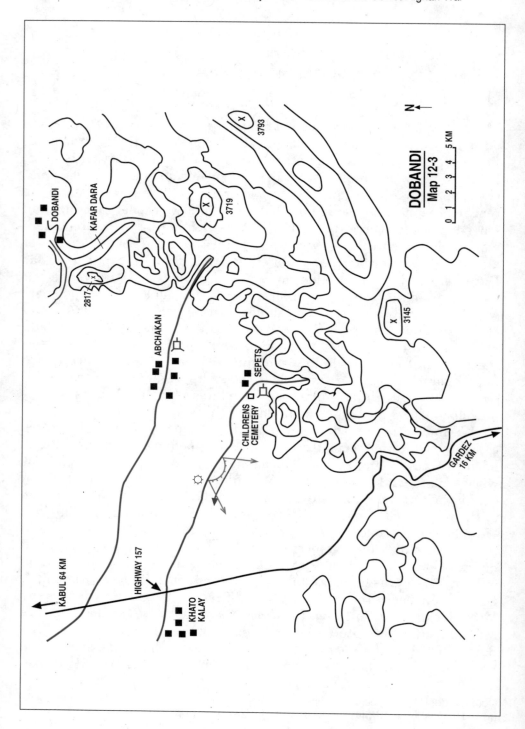

up from their positions. As I saw the Soviets jump up, I yelled "Allah Akbar"(God is the greatest) and we opened fire on them. This led to a prolonged fire fight. My Mujahideen were spread in a single file and I was the 16th person in the column. Dadgul was next to me, but we did not really know exactly where the Soviets were and they did not know exactly where we were. We fired at each other off and on. At approximately 2200 hours, we heard the sound of armored vehicle engines moving toward us. They had come from the northwest at Pul-e Alam. Mamur Abdul Ali began firing rockets in our support from his base in Sepets. One landed close to us and the next went further on. The fifth rocket landed in the enemy column. This slowed down the enemy column. Akhunzada also started firing rockets at the enemy column from his base. I instructed my Mujahideen to fall back to the mountains near Abchakan and then move south of Sepets to the mountain valley where the Mujahideen bases were located. It was 0200 when we reached Akhunzada base. Sixteen of my Mujahideen were missing— those who were in front of me in the column. The next morning at 1000 hours, we went forward and found Mohammaday, who was wounded and my RPG-7 man who was killed. The rest of my Mujahideen had gone on to Logar. I do not know what the Soviet losses were, but there were reports that they had casualties. The Soviets never used that particular ambush site again.

COMMENTARY: The Soviet ambush party probably came from the 108th Motorized Rifle Division or the 103rd Airborne Division. Both were garrisoned in Kabul. The 56th Air Assault Brigade at Gardez was closer to the site, but the relief element came from the Kabul direction. The Soviet ambush site was not well laid out. There was no attempt to seal the kill zone. There were no firing lanes cleared, no aiming stakes emplaced, no directional mines employed and no indirect fire planned on the kill zone. The Soviet ambush was triggered by a lone gunner and not by massed fire directed by the ambush commander. The Soviet commander evidently did not know that he had a strung-out Mujahideen column, which could not mass fires, to his front. Once night fell, the Mujahideen did not break contact and the ambush commander then evidently felt that he was in contact with a large force and called for an armored column to rescue him.

The Mujahideen movement plan was commendable. The commander did not hazard his supplies until he had cleared the route and posted security at key points. He coordinated with other factions to obtain information and tactical intelligence. He moved spread out on open terrain so he did not present an air target and moved in the middle of the column where he could best exert control. He gets low marks for following the guide down a stream bed without sending flankers to sweep the high ground. But, when his force was hit, the commander was able to ascertain that his column was not in immediate danger of annihilation and shut down return fire. This allowed his men to determine where their ambushers were and to draw them out of position. The commander ordered an escape to the northeast and then a move south in the safety of the mountains rather than retracing their route and risking another ambush or drawing the relief column into the Sepets area.

CHAPTER COMMENTARY

Successful counterambush is the result of careful planning, battle drills, rehearsals, information security, patrolling, current tactical intelligence, and deception measures. Movement of supplies needs to vary by route, time and composition of the supply column. Mujahideen supplies were moved on mule, horse, donkey, camel, truck and human porter. While some factions had their own transport, the bulk of Mujahideen supplies were carried by contracted teamsters and muleteers. The cost of transport was high and a group with a reputation of getting ambushed would be hard put to find willing teamsters.

In some areas, the Mujahideen only had to transport ammunition, but in other areas they had to transport food, clothing, and forage as well. Ammunition requirements for a small ambush by a 20-man group armed with Enfields, Kalashnikovs, an RPG-7, a PK medium machine gun, and five antitank mines, might exceed 375 pounds. The weight of required ammunition shoots up dramatically as mortars, recoilless rifles and heavy machineguns are added.[3] Even if the ammunition was furnished free, the cost of getting it to where it was needed was considerable and the wise Mujahideen commander carefully protected his supplies against interdiction.

---

[3] "The Logistics System of the Mujahideen", page 55, unpublished government contract study written in 1987.

Chapter 13
Encirclement

The Soviets developed their encirclement technique to deal with opposing mechanized forces. If enemy soldiers abandoned their vehicles to escape the encirclement, the result was still the same—the mechanized force was defeated. The Mujahideen were not mechanized and they discovered that the Soviet encirclement was usually porous and that the Soviet/DRA force did not have enough dismounted infantry to hold them in the pocket, particularly when it got dark. However, the Soviets and DRA routinely conducted large-scale encirclements, as part of cordon and search operations, and occasional smaller tactical encirclements of marauding bands.

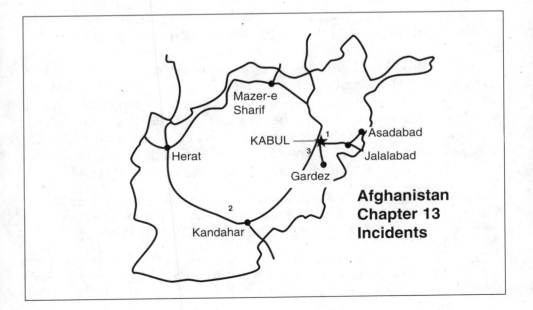

**Afghanistan
Chapter 13
Incidents**

VIGNETTE 1

A TRIP TO THE "GOVERNOR'S HOUSE" GOES BAD

BY COMMANDER SARSHAR

The governor of Parwan Province had his residence in the city of Charikar. It was located next to the Numan High School. There was also a security post in an enclosed house next to the governor's residence and the high school. This post was called the Wali house and there were normally 30 soldiers in it. Everyone called the security post "the Governor's House", although it was not. In January 1983, we planned a raid on this security post (No map). I had about 200 Mujahideen armed with a 76mm mountain gun, five 82mm mortars, two 82mm recoilless rifles, 20 RPG-7s, Goryunov heavy machine guns, PK medium machine guns and Kalashnikov rifles. This was a severe winter and we moved across the mountains at night in the bitter cold. We came to the village of Ofian-e Sharif where we spent the day and planned our raid. I constituted a heavy weapons support team serving the 76mm gun, the mortars and the recoilless rifles. I constituted two security groups—one of which would secure the area to the north behind the heavy weapons support team and one to the south which would secure the approaches to Numan High School. I constituted an assault team to seize the outpost.

At night, we moved from Ofian-e Sharif onto the Ofian plain outside another security post at Qal-e Maqbul, which is just north of the target in Charikar. I launched the attack at night, but right as the assault group was moving forward in the attack, the mortar and recoilless rifle rounds landed in the middle of the assault group. I had 18 KIA and WIA. I aborted the attack and began evacuating the dead and wounded. Coincidently, the enemy had planned a major cordon and search operation which began the next morning. Early the next morning, the enemy moved through the area and cordoned it off with hundreds of tanks and APCs. They encircled hundreds of Mujahideen in the Bagram, Kohistan and Charikar area. We were trapped in our

---

Commander Sarshar was a police officer in Parwan and worked clandestinely with the Mujahideen. When his cover was about to be blown, he became a Mujahideen commander in Ghorband. He commanded a mobile group in the Ghorband front near Charikar. [Map sheet 2887].

[1] There is no map for this vignette. This operation is describe in Chapter 10, Vignette 4; "Defending Against a Cordon and Search Operation in Parwan" by Commander Haji Abdul Qader.

position. As the enemy approached us, we were glad to have the 20 RPGs. We joined the local Mujahideen in the fray. The battle went on for 12 days and we killed 12 armored vehicles during that time. We tried to break out of the encirclement. We moved through the villages to Pul-e Matak at the mouth of the Ghorband Valley. There, we exfiltrated through gaps in the enemy lines to the Ghorband Valley. We had 18 killed and two wounded. We destroyed 12 armored vehicles and four supply trucks. During the 12-15 days that the Soviets and DRA cordoned the area, they succeeded in entering many parts of the area and clearing it. Many Mujahideen managed to escape, but the Soviets and DRA arrested about 800 Mujahideen and civilians in the area.

COMMENTARY: Coordination of fire and maneuver elements is a problem for trained armies. It is a bigger problem for irregular forces. In this case, the Mujahideen fire support fell short of the target with deadly results. Although Mujahideen gunners who conducted regular shelling attacks against fixed targets were able to register their weapons over time, Mujahideen gunners supporting ground attacks seldom had the luxury of registering their weapons prior to the attack. This added greater risk to the assault force.

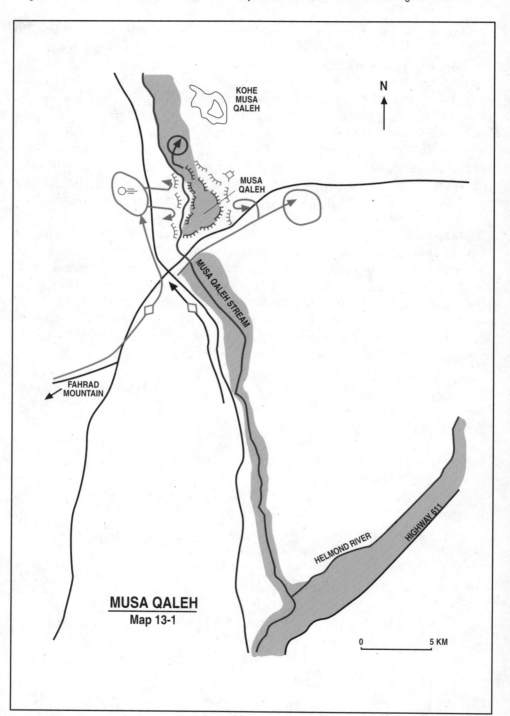

KOHE
MUSA
QALEH

N

MUSA
QALEH

MUSA QALEH STREAM

FAHRAD
MOUNTAIN

HELMOND RIVER

HIGHWAY 611

MUSA QALEH
Map 13-1

0   5 KM

THE BATTLE FOR MUSA QALEH
BY AKHUND ZADA QASEM

We started the resistance using very simple methods. We had few antitank weapons and so our main defenses were antitank ditches and Molotov cocktails that we made in the villages. The people would wait in their antitank ditches with axes to sort it out. I remember one fight where I became so frustrated with our inability to stop armored vehicles that I set my turban on fire and threw it at the tank. However, we eventually received better weapons and set about regaining control of our country. In the summer of 1980, we Mujahideen liberated Musa Qaleh District and established our base there. (Map 13-1 - Qaleh) Musa Qaleh is in a heavily-populated green zone on the Musa Qaleh Stream which empties into the Helmond River. The area around Musa Qaleh is high desert plain.

In June 1983, the Soviets launched an offensive to control Helmond Province. They began with an attack from Girishk moving north toward Nawzad (which is to the west of Musa Qaleh). This column attacked the Mujahideen of HIH at their base in the Farhad Mountain. The Mujahideen of Musa Qaleh sent their MRL to this fight to strike the Soviets. After the Soviets reduced the HIH base, they sent two columns to attack Musa Qaleh. The column that had destroyed the HIH base turned east and moved against us while a second column moved from Girishk along the river roads and approached us from the southwest. The columns met and cordoned Musa Qaleh.

We had established a perimeter defense and we fought the Soviets for seven days in late June and early July 1983. We lost 472 Mujahideen KIA. Civilian deaths were much higher. I was in charge of the hospital at that time and it was overflowing. During the fighting, Soviet tanks arrived from the east and were just 300 meters south

---

Akhund Zada Qasem was a commander with Harakat-e Ingilab-i Islami (HAR) of Mawlawi Nabi Mohammadi. He was also in charge of medical support to the Musa Qaleh Front in Helmond Province. This was a major Mujahideen stronghold under the late Mawlawi Nasim Akhund Zada. Akhund Zada was one of the major Mujahideen regional commanders. After his assassination in 1986, his brother Mawlawi Sediq Akhund Zada took over. This front was in control of much of Helmond Province during the war and was one of the few major unified Mujahideen commands. The front was supported by and became rich from the drug trade. Qasem was in charge of medical support and was a member of the counsel of the command. [Map sheet 1981].

of my hospital. They began shelling the hospital and I had to evacuate the wounded. We managed to move the hospital outside of the cordoned area to the north at night. We carried the wounded on stretchers for about 500 meters where we were met by other Mujahideen from the Baghran front. The Baghran front sent trucks and moved our wounded to safety on the trucks. After I evacuated the wounded, I returned to Musa Qaleh at about 2200 hours. The front council met and we decided to break out of the encirclement. That night, the weather cooperated with the breakout. There was a heavy gusty wind which blew sand around. The noise of the wind and the dust concealed us as we moved between the enemy tanks. There were many Mujahideen in that cordon. There were Mujahideen from two districts and other areas as well. About 2,000 Mujahideen escaped into the night. The dust and wind also helped the civilians exfiltrate and covered their escape. When we got out, the wind died down. Later on, people said that this was the hand of God that got them out. The Mujahideen went to the surrounding mountains. I went to Kohe Musa Qaleh, the small mountain just north of Musa Qaleh.

After this heavy defeat, we decided to keep a presence in Musa Qaleh but to establish a mountain base where we would keep our heavy weapons, ammunition stocks and supplies. We set up our mountain base in Ghulmesh Ghar (mountain) about 30 kilometers northeast of Kajaki dam. The base was in a narrow canyon leading into the mountain. The canyon opened up into a bowl in the mountain. The canyon was about 10 kilometers deep. We protected this base with ZGU-1s and DShKs. We named the base Islamabad (built by Muslims).

The following year, in October 1984, the Soviets attacked Islamabad. They sent a major column from Girishk and again laid siege to Musa Qaleh, while another moved further north and attacked Islamabad. There were few Mujahideen in the mountain base since the majority were in Musa Qaleh. The Soviets landed air assault troops on the high ground and attacked with the ground column to capture the base after three day's fighting. They destroyed the base and left it unusable due to all the mines that they left behind.

We then moved our base and stores to Khanjak Mazar south of Kalata-e Baghni. We distributed our ammunition to different bases and districts so that the capture of our central base would not cripple us completely.

COMMENTARY: The area around Musa Qaleh is open, flat tank country and the Soviets were able to move freely around the perimeter of the green zone. The Mujahideen field fortifications within the green zone enabled them to hold on for seven days, but at a very high price. The Mujahideen wanted to control Musa Qaleh for its political value as a district capital. The political considerations overrode the military and the front still kept the bulk of its force there once they had built a strong mountain base.

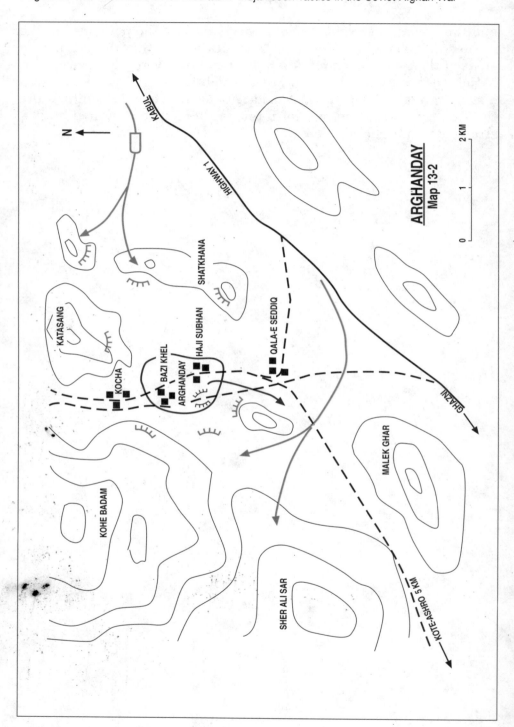

ARGHANDAY
Map 13-2

VIGNETTE 3
ESCAPE FROM THE ARGHANDAY ENCIRCLEMENT
BY COMMANDER HAJI MOHAMMAD SEDDIQ

In July 1986, I took a detachment of 13 Mujahideen to abduct a DRA officer from his house in the western Kot-e Sangi section of Kabul. For several days, we gathered information about the officer—his time of arrival and departure from his house and the road he took to and from his residence. We gathered the information with the help of a contact at the Kot-e Sangi gas station. We discovered that the officer did not stay at his residence overnight, but spent a few hours in the evening at home and then returned to his unit. We decided to abduct him during those hours he was at his house.

We spent the night in the nearby Deh-Bori section of Kabul. The next day, at dusk, we met with our gas station contact who reported that the officer was at his residence. I took three men who were dressed in army uniform with me. I had on traditional clothing. We went to the officer's home which was located between Qala-e Shada security outpost and the Kot-e Sangi Police station. When we reached the house, the uniformed Mujahideen knocked on the door. The officer's daughter answered the door. One of the Mujahideen told her that there was an urgent message for the officer from his unit. A few minutes later, the officer came to the door. As he stepped out, I stepped around from behind the corner and told him to follow us and make no attempt to escape because we would shoot him on the spot. The officer and I knew each other and he recognized me. He was nervous but made no attempt to escape. We escorted him through the streets to Qala-e Shada and from there to the Mujahideen base at Arghanday. At Arghanday, we turned the officer over to a Paghman commander named Zahed. The officer supposedly had killed several Mujahideen from Zahed's group.

We spent the night at the residence/base of Shafeh, a local commander. Early the next morning, at about 0400 hours, we woke up to

---

Haji Mohammad Seddiq is from No-Burja Village in Logar Province. The village is in the Tangi-Wardak area which connects the Saydabad District of Wardak Province to the Baraki Barak District in the Logar Province. Commander Seddiq's village is located on the border between the two provinces. Therefore, his command fought in both provinces in coordination with other Mujahideen. Commander Haji Mohammad Seddiq was affiliated with Hekmatyar's HIH. [Map sheet 2785].

the noise of tanks approaching the village (Map 13-2 - Arghanday). At first, we thought that the noise was from normal military traffic resupplying the security outposts along the Kabul-Ghazni highway. Then Shafeh's father climbed to the roof top and saw that the village was surrounded by tanks and other vehicles. Soviet soldiers and DRA militia men from Rashid Dostum's Militia group occupied the surrounding hills. We were trapped. Shafeh took us to a hideout near the house. It was a cave that they had dug to hide the Mujahideen during the enemy's cordon and search operations. After a while, we heard movement and noticed that the Soviet/DRA search party had posted a guard at the entrance of the cave. The guard called out and asked if there was some one inside. Then he asked for anyone inside to come out. Next, he stooped over to check out the cave. At that point, Alam Gul (who we nicknamed the Uzbek—because he looked like an Uzbek) shot the soldier. The soldier's body fell into the cave. We pulled his body aside and rushed out of the cave. As we came out, we encountered soldiers in the streets. We fought our way to a natural ditch at the edge of the village.

We jumped in the ditch and faced in both directions. We all had AK-47s plus one RPG-7. We fought from this position until 1300 hours. At that time, some Mujahideen units at Kot-e Ashro, about 10 kilometers to the southwest, started shelling the area with BM-12 fire. The rockets' explosions forced the enemy away from the south side of the village. We took advantage of this and slipped out of the encirclement through the southern gap and fled to Kot-e Ashro through the mountains. One of my Mujahideen was wounded.

CHAPTER COMMENTARY

The porous nature of the Soviet and DRA encirclement allowed the Mujahideen to exfiltrate. It helped to have other distracters such as incoming artillery, sand storms and nightfall to escape. The Mujahideen were skilled exfiltrators and often small groups of Soviets or DRA guarding the cordon would allow the Mujahideen to escape rather than risk a fire fight at uneven odds. The Soviets resorted to scatterable mines, ground sensors, parachute flares and other technology to prevent escapes, but Mujahideen groups would exfiltrate singly, or in small groups, and regroup outside the encirclement.

CHAPTER 14:
URBAN COMBAT

Urban guerrillas are surrounded by potential informants and government spies. They must frequently move around unarmed and the government can usually react to their actions much faster than they can in the countryside. For this reason, urban guerrilla groups were usually small and fought back with short-duration actions. Many urban guerrillas lived in the countryside or suburbs and only entered the cities for combat.

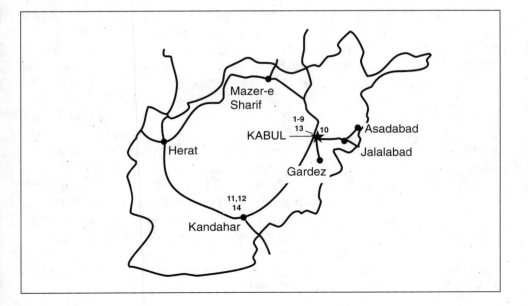

VIGNETTE 1
KIDNAPING A SOVIET ADVISER
by Commander Shahabuddin

We were in contact with an Afghan driver from Paktia Province who drove for a civilian Soviet adviser. The adviser worked with the DRA mining industry. We wanted to kidnap the adviser. The driver had trained for a short time in the USSR and so the adviser trusted him. The driver agreed to help us, but we did not trust the driver and asked him to prove his loyalty. He stated "I will bring my family to stay in a Mujahideen-controlled area as proof of my trustworthiness". The driver came to our camp with his wife and family. I sent his family to my village of Shewaki to stay while we captured the adviser.

One day the driver informed us that the adviser's wife was coming from the Soviet Union to join him. The driver would take the adviser to the airport to meet his wife. We gave the driver a small hand-held radio and told him to contact us if there were any changes. We would contact him within twenty minutes of his call. The driver called us one morning. He reported that the adviser's wife was arriving that day and that no one would accompany the adviser to the airport but the driver. We dressed one of our Mujahideen in a DRA military officer's uniform and put him in a car and sent him to wait at the bridge over the Kabul River at the micro rayon in East Kabul. He got out of the car and waited for the Soviet adviser's car. Soon, the Soviet adviser's car arrived. The driver pointed at our Mujahideen and told the adviser "That's my brother. He's going to the airport. Can we give him a ride?" The adviser agreed and they stopped to pick up "the officer". He got into the back seat behind the adviser and pulled out a pistol. He held the pistol to the adviser's back and ordered the driver to drive to Shewaki. Another car, carrying eight of our Mujahideen armed with pistols with silencers, followed the adviser's car. We had no trouble with the checkpoints since the guards saw the DRA officer's uniform, saluted and waived the car and its "security tail" right through.

We took the adviser to Shewaki and burned his car. The government launched a major search effort, so we moved the adviser again to the Abdara Valley. Government helicopters strafed Shewaki after we left and landed search detachments trying to find the adviser. We kept

---

Commander Shahabuddin is from Shewaki Village south of Kabul. There is no map for this vignette. Kabul map sheets are 2885 and 2886.

the adviser in the Abdara Valley near the Chakari monument (the Buddhist pinnacle) for two days. Then we moved him to Tezin, near Jalalabad, for a few more days. Finally, we took him across the border to Peshawar, Pakistan, where we turned him over to one of the factions. I do not know what happened to him.

VIGNETTE 2
FOUR URBAN BOMB ATTACKS
by Haji Mohammad Yakub

Bombing is a necessary part of being an urban guerrilla. The object is to create fear and take out selected individuals. We got our explosives from Pakistan. Commander Azizuddin and Commander Meskinyar were our contacts in Paghman District who forwarded the explosives and detonators to us. They used elderly people as our go-betweens to carry messages and explosives to us.

[1]   In April 1980, we carried out an attack on the Radio Afghanistan building. This housed the central offices for Afghanistan radio and television broadcasting. Soviet advisers worked at the building where they oversaw radio and television broadcasting and edited and cleared the news before broadcast. The Soviets were our targets. We received a bomb from our contacts and gave it to a woman who worked in the radio station. She smuggled it into the station and armed it. The bomb went off at 1000 hours on a workday. The explosion killed two Afghan Party activists and two Soviets. It also wounded a DRA soldier. For some time after the blast, Afghanistan Radio and TV stopped broadcasting. After this, the security procedures for the building were greatly increased and everyone was carefully searched. Our lady contact later managed to get herself transferred to the payroll office of Kabul University.

[2]   The communist regime converted Kabul University into a center for communist indoctrination. We decided to target the primary Party Organization at Kabul University in January 1981. Bombing seemed to be our best option. By this time, our lady contact at Radio Afghanistan was working in the payroll office at Kabul University. We gave her two bombs. She planted one in the University Administration building and set the timer for 1100. She set the second in the primary Party Organization building and set that timer for 1145. The theory was that, after the first bomb went off, people would mill around the site and then the key party activists would gather in the primary Party Organization building to discuss the bombing. The

---

Haji Mohammad Yakub, whose nickname was Mansur (Victor), was an urban guerrilla in Kabul. He belonged to the HIH faction. There is no map with this vignette.

second bomb would attack this concentration. Our plan worked as we thought it would. Following the blast in the administration building, the party secretaries of all the various communist organizations gathered in the primary Party Organization building. The blast killed a Soviet adviser and several party secretaries. The bombs killed a total of 10 and wounded an unknown number.

[3] On 6 May 1983, we bombed the Ministry of Interior building in Kabul. We had planted 27 kilograms of explosive in a room on the second floor of the building close to the office of the Minister. The bombs were hidden in four large flower pots that had been there for some time. We had a contact who was a gardener for the Ministry of the Interior. He agreed to smuggle in the explosives, plant the bombs and set them for detonation. We trained him how to do the job. He mixed the explosives with limestone and smuggled them in plastic bags over a period of time. We planned to detonate the bombs during the daytime for maximum casualties. However, our HIH headquarters in Peshawar overruled us and told us to set the bombs off at night. HIH wanted to keep Minister of the Interior Gulab Zoy alive since he was a leading member of the Khalq faction and his survival would insure that the friction between the Khalq and Parchim communist party factions continued.

The gardener set all the time pencils for 2300 hours when he went home at 1600 hours. There was no sense setting different times since the building would virtually be deserted. The time bombs went off on time and killed four duty officers and damaged the Minister's office. If we had set off the bombs during the day, we would have killed Gulab Zoy, Ghazi (his body guard), Sheruddin (his aide-de-camp) and perhaps a hundred others. The DRA closed roads around the building for 24 hours and conducted an investigation. However, they thought that the blast was connected to some internal quarrel within the communist leadership and never suspected our gardener.

[4] The Soviets lived in the eastern Micro rayon region of Kabul. We decided to attack the Soviets right where they were living. There was a bus stop in the area where the Soviets would wait for their buses to work. We checked the timing of the buses. There was a daily 0745 morning bus that drew the most Soviets. We needed to establish a pattern so that we could leave a bomb without drawing attention. We got a push cart and loaded it with the best fruits and vegetables that we could get. The produce came from Parwan

Province. We charged reasonable prices. The Soviets and local people got used to seeing us there and buying from us. We kept this up for several days. At night, we would work on the pushcart. We put in a false bottom in the cart so that we could put our bombs in the bottom of the cart and they would be undetected even if the cart were inspected. We attacked on the 2nd of October 1983. We loaded five bombs into the bottom of the cart. We inserted time pencil fuses in the bombs and set them for 0743. Then we put in the false bottom and loaded the cart with produce. Six Mujahideen carried out the attack. None of us carried weapons. We brought the cart to the bus stop as usual. Thirteen Soviets crowded around it to see what was on sale. We slipped away from the cart and mixed with the local people. The bombs went off at 0743 just before the bus arrived. The blast killed 13, wounded 12 and damaged a nearby store. The DRA searched the crowd but made no arrests from our group.

COMMENTARY: Many people find such bombing attacks morally reprehensible, yet have no qualms when much larger bombs are dropped from aircraft. Neither type of bombing attack is surgical and both types kill innocent bystanders. The only real difference is in the size of the bomb and the means of delivery. The Mujahideen lacked an air force but retained a limited bombing option. The Soviets had an air force and conducted large-scale bombing attacks throughout the war.

VIGNETTE 3
INCIDENT AT QALA-E JABAR
by Mohammad Humayun Shahin

During Ramadan (June) of 1981, five Mujahideen were assigned to meet with a Soviet soldier in Qala-e Jabar to buy some Kalashnikov magazines from him. Qala-e Jabar is some three kilometers south of the Darulaman Soviet military base. Our group leader was Alozai, who was known as Sher Khan. Hukum Khan, two others and I made up the group. We went to Qala-e Jabar and met with the Soviet soldier. He said that his name was Hasan and he showed us his merchandise. We agreed to buy the magazines and pulled out a wad of 50 Afghani notes to pay him with. The Soviet soldier was not familiar with the 50 Afghani note. He demanded that we pay in 100s. Since we could not speak Russian, Sher Khan tried to show him that two 50 Afghani notes equaled one 100 Afghani note. He even wrote it on a scrap of paper. The Soviet, however, apparently did not understand and kept demanding 100 Afghani notes. We did not have any 100 Afghani notes.

As we tried to communicate, the Soviet got louder and louder. We were fairly close to the Soviet camp and were beginning to worry that this might be a trap. Hukum Khan grabbed the Soviet in a headlock and wrestled him to the ground while Commander Sher Khan stabbed the Soviet to death. Then we grabbed the rifle magazines, plus the Soviet's AK-74 assault rifle and left the area.

COMMENTARY: There was a regular commerce between the Soviet soldiers and the Afghan populace. Soviet conscripts would sell fuel, ammunition, weapons, batteries and military equipment for hashish, food and Afghan money. They would use the money in the bazaars of Kabul to buy western stereos, music tapes, cigarettes and clothing. Some goods were available in the Soviet PX, but conscripts had little access or cash so they tried to shop locally for items they wanted.

Mohammad Humayun Shahin joined the Mujahideen as a high school student and served as a combatant and commander in the HIH urban guerrillas in the southwestern suburbs of Kabul in the Chardehi District. His high school student identification enabled him to move around Kabul until he graduated in 1981. Then, he was provided with forged documents showing that he had completed military service. This enabled him to stay in the city and avoid being press-ganged into the army. His group often conducted combined actions with the famed Mohseni urban guerrillas. After the collapse of the communist regime, Shahin was appointed regiment commander under the Islamic government and promoted to Brigadier General. There is no map with this vignette.

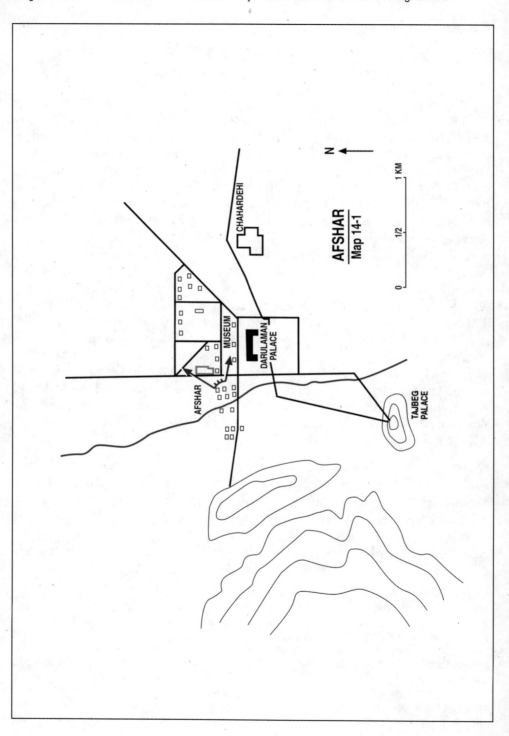

AFSHAR

Map 14-1

N

0   1/2   1 KM

CHAHARDEHI

MUSEUM

DARULAMAN PALACE

AFSHAR

TAJBEG PALACE

VIGNETTE 4
AFSHAR AMBUSH
by Commander Asil Khan

On 28 May 1982, I led a group of four Mujahideen in an ambush at the very gates of the Soviet garrison in Kabul. At that time, elements of the Soviet 103rd Airborne Division and some other units were based in Darulaman about 10 kilometers southwest of downtown Kabul. The headquarters of the Soviet 40th Army was also located there in the Tajbeg Palace. I was a small unit commander in my father's front. My father is Haji Dawlat and the Front's main base was at Morghgiran, 10 kilometers west of Darulaman.

I selected the ambush site after we spent several days in reconnaissance and surveillance of the Soviet traffic around Darulaman. During the reconnaissance, we detected a pattern in Soviet vehicular movement along the road from Kabul to the Soviet headquarters in the Tajbeg palace. Just north of the Soviet Darulaman base is the small village of Afshar. (Map 14-1 - Afshar) It has a typical suburban bazaar with several grocery and fresh fruit stores and stalls. Soviet soldiers frequented this bazaar and would stop their vehicles there to buy cigarettes, food and imported vodka. Afshar looked like a good ambush site. Soviet soldiers felt secure there, there was room enough to set up an ambush, and site entrance and exit were fairly easy. The path to and from the ambush was mostly concealed and we could easily reach Mujahideen bases and safe houses in the Chardehi District using this path.

We spent the day of the ambush in Qala-e Bakhtiar--a village six kilometers to the west of the ambush site. We had four AK-47s and a non-Soviet manufactured light anti-tank grenade launcher. In the early evening, we moved out toward Afshar. It was the Muslim month of Ramadan when Muslims fast during the entire day. Few people were out at sunset since this is the time to break the daily fast. Since our ambush site was in the immediate vicinity of the Soviet base, I decided to conduct a very quick attack on a single Soviet vehicle and to take prisoners if possible.

We moved through a narrow street of Afshar which opened onto the main road north of the Darulaman palace. Around 1930 hours, as

---

Commander Asil Khan was a famed urban guerrilla commander in Kabul. He served the NIFA faction.

my leading riflemen reached the street intersection, a Soviet GAZ-66 truck approached from the east on its way to the military camp. The truck had five passengers—a driver, a soldier in the right front seat and three soldiers in the back. One of the soldiers had a back-packed radio. I told my anti-tank gunner to fire when the vehicle was in the kill zone. He fired, but he narrowly missed the truck. The truck came to a sudden halt and its occupants jumped out of the vehicle, took up positions and started firing at random.

During the brief fire fight, we killed one Soviet soldier. Two soldiers ran away to the southwest toward their camp. One soldier crawled under the truck near the rear tires. The radio-man rushed into an open grocery store and hid there. One of my Mujahideen was close to the shop behind a concrete electric pylon. I told him to follow the Soviet radio-man into the front of the shop while I went into the shop's back door and introduced myself as a "friend". The Soviet soldier was flustered at first, but when he saw the foreign light anti-tank weapon in the hands of my Mujahideen, he uttered "dushman" [enemy]. He kept quiet as we bound his hands and led him out back. I recalled my team and we quickly left the area. The whole action lasted only a few minutes.

Fearing enemy retaliation, we moved out swiftly in the dark, heading to Qala-e Bakhtiar. From there, we went on to Qala-e Bahadur Khan, Qala-e Jabar Khan and Qala-e Qazi until we reached our Front's base at Morghgiran around 2200 hours. We kept our prisoner there for three days and then transferred him to NIFA headquarters in Peshawar, Pakistan.

COMMENTARY: Detailed reconnaissance and knowledge of the enemy's movement and security arrangements contributed to a workable ambush right in the heart of the Soviet garrison area. The Soviets had not posted a vulnerable point adjacent to their garrison--either through overconfidence or negligence on the part of lower-level commanders.

Selection of a small group of fighters with an effective mix of weapons, and good selection of the ambush site played a significant role in the action. However, using a non-standard anti-tank weapon probably caused the gunner to miss a large target at close range. One wonders if the gunner had any training or practice with the weapon before he used it. An RPG-7 and an experienced gunner were needed.

One wonders why the Soviets stopped their truck in the middle of a kill zone once the Mujahideen rocket missed them. Since the

Mujahideen rocket missed the vehicle, there was no need for the truck to stop and the soldiers could have escaped through the small-arms fire before the anti-tank gunner had a chance to reload. The Soviets failed to react effectively. Stopping in the kill zone under small-arms fire was a risky and unwise move that cost the Soviets the life of one soldier while another one was captured.

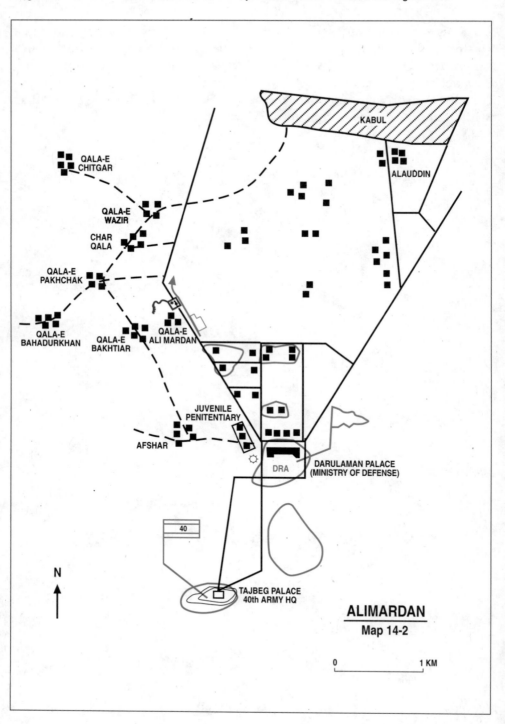

VIGNETTE 5
REMOTE-CONTROL ATTACK ON A CONVOY IN THE SUBURBS
by Mohammad Humayun Shahin

There were some 40 guerrillas in my force. We lived inside Kabul and in the suburbs. Most of the men were ethnic Pashtun, but there were seven Dari speakers from outside Kabul as well. The Pashtu speakers often mingled with the Kochi nomads who would pitch their tents and graze their herds on the outskirts of Kabul. The Dari speakers posed as dairy product buyers when the DRA checked the area.

In October 1982, I was a combatant, not a commander. Our commander was Qarar. He led us on a convoy attack against the Kot-e Sangi--Darulaman road near Qala-e Alimardan (Map Alimardan). It was a combined action involving HIH forces under Commander Didar, Commander Firoz and Commander Qarar, as well as fighters from the Mohseni faction. The combined force numbered 76 men. We expected a convoy from Darulaman to Kabul the next day. We all moved to the area at night and surrounded the area. Our mining teams emplaced seven remote-controlled (*shartaki*) mines. Then they camouflaged them. After positioning two observation posts and designating a detonation team, the Mujahideen withdrew. A Mujahideen known as Sher Bach-e Khala (a Hazara) and I were the detonation team. Commander Qarar was at the Darulaman observation post and another observer was by the mined area. Sher Bach-e Khala and I spent the night in a clover field some 200 meters from the road.

The next morning, Commander Qarar came down the road on his bicycle. He told us that the Soviet convoy was moving from Darulaman. We moved into our detonation position. Commander Qarar then moved to the other observation post. He told the observer to take off his turban and wave it when the first two vehicles had passed the mined stretch of the road. He would do this since we could not see the mined stretch from the detonation position. A moment later, the convoy reached the site and the observer took off his turban, waved it and moved to a safe spot. We operated the detonator and four of the seven mines exploded. The explosion destroyed or damaged one BMP and three trucks. The four-man Mujahideen group safely escaped from the area.

Mohammad Humayun Shahin provided the material for a previous vignette in this chapter.

COMMENTARY: It is always a good idea for a detonation party to be able to see the target area. Mujahideen communications were often primitive and, in this case, depended on one visual signal. The attack, like most urban attacks, was a quick, single strike followed by an immediate withdrawal. Such harassing attacks seldom had any major impact other than on morale. It was a good idea to have a small detonation group, but a 76-man force to secure the area while it was mined seems too large. Kabul was under a night-time curfew and a large group could be detected by patrols along main roads.

VIGNETTE 6
ATTACK ON THE MINISTRY OF DEFENSE
by Mohammad Humayun Shahin

In November 1982, some 60 Mujahideen from HIH and Mohseni's Harakat-e Islami launched a night attack on the DRA Ministry of Defense located in the Darulaman Palace (Map 14-3 - Darulaman). The security in the area was very tight and the area between the Darulaman Palace and the Tajbeg Palace (headquarters of the Soviet 40th Army) was heavily patrolled. We decided to limit the attack to a short-range RPG attack. The HIH group were armed with AK-47 Kalashnikovs, while the Mohseni group had British Sten guns[1] and other weapons. The Mohnseni had the RPG-7 we used in the attack. Both sides provided ammunition for the RPG.

We assembled in the staging area at Char Qala in the late afternoon. Char Qala is about three kilometers north of the target. From there, we moved south in groups to the intermediate villages of Qala-e Pakhchak and Qala-e Bahadur Khan and Qala-e Bakhtiar. Our attack position was a water mill outside the Juvenile Penitentiary close to the Darulaman Palace. As we moved, we dropped off security elements. Most of the men in the group were assigned to provide security during movement to and from the target area. Security elements were positioned at key locations, which facilitated our infiltration and withdrawal. Once our forward security elements secured the firing area, the RPG-7 gunner Saadat (from the Mohseni faction) took his position. He was about 250 meters from the target. He fired two rockets at the building. The enemy response was immediate. Guards from around the palace filled the night with heavy small-arms fire. We did not return their fire. Instead, we immediately began retracing our steps and pulled out along the route held by our security detail. We then scattered into hiding places and safe houses in the villages of Chardehi. Some years later, a prison inmate who was on the DRA side during the night attack told a Mujahideen contact that about 20 people were killed or injured in our attack.

Mohammad Humayun Shahin provided the material for the previous vignette.

[1] The British Sten gun is a 9mm World War II submachine gun. It has a 32 round magazine and a rate of fire of some 540 rounds per minute.

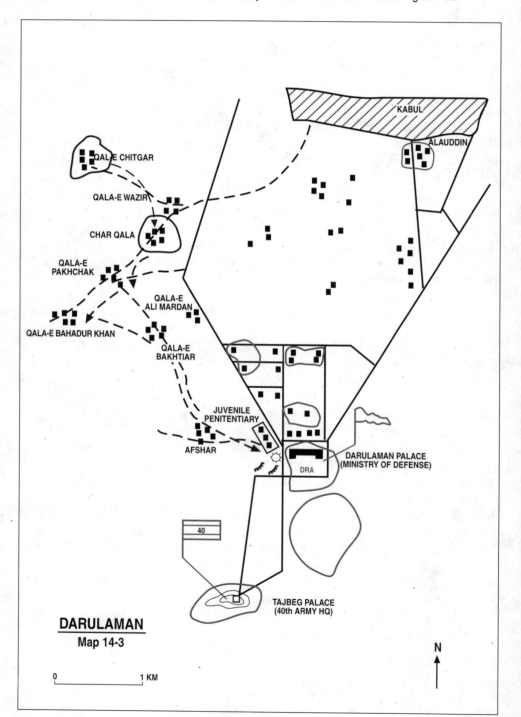

KABUL

ALAUDDIN

QAL E CHITGAR

QALA-E WAZIR

CHAR QALA

QALA-E
PAKHCHAK

QALA-E
ALI MARDAN

QALA-E BAHADUR KHAN

QALA-E
BAKHTIAR

JUVENILE
PENITENTIARY

AFSHAR

DRA

DARULAMAN PALACE
(MINISTRY OF DEFENSE)

40

TAJBEG PALACE
(40th ARMY HQ)

DARULAMAN
Map 14-3

N

0   1 KM

COMMENTARY: The Mujahideen urban warfare tactics were low-level and fairly unsophisticated. Their actions were usually limited to a single strike followed by an immediate withdrawal to avoid decisive engagement with a better-armed and supported regular force. Survival dictated the tactics, but their impact was political and psychological rather than military. The work and risk that the urban guerrillas accepted was great and the results were often minimal or not immediately evident.

Mujahideen success in the urban areas was due primarily to the support of the population and the lack of DRA/Soviet control outside the areas that they physically controlled. The cities were under nighttime curfew, but the patrols enforcing the curfew could hardly move safely off the main city roads. The Mujahideen had great freedom of action outside the main thoroughfares and in the suburbs. However, they could not fully exploit this advantage due to insufficient training, poor organizational structure, a lack of modern weapons and equipment, an ineffective command and control system and a lack of tactical cohesiveness among the various Mujahideen combatant groups. Lack of communications equipment, particularly in the early days of the war, severely hampered the Mujahideen.

VIGNETTE 7
ALCOHOL CAN BE DEADLY
by "The Mountain Man"

The DRA 8th Infantry Division was garrisoned in Kabul. We had a contact who was an officer in that division. Over the years he provided us with lots of good information. His cooperation put him, and his family, at risk. He wanted to defect to the Mujahideen. We helped engineer his defection while hurting the enemy. We told our contact to arrange a party on September 24, 1983. He invited the Political Officer of the 8th Infantry Division with two Soviet advisers who worked with them to his home in Kot-e Sangi. The three accepted his invitation and arrived at night driving their military jeep. Our officer had plenty of Western whiskey and shish kebabs on hand. The Soviets and the Political Officer ate and drank and became totally drunk. They passed out. Then our officer summoned us. We came into his house and carried the unconscious drunks out to their jeep. We drove them to the village of Qala-e Qazi located to the southwest of Kabul. Since we were in their jeep, no one stopped us or challenged us. We took the drunks out and sent the jeep back to the officer. He loaded his family into the jeep and took his family to Pakistan. Then he joined our cause openly.

We carried the drunks to a hideout in the Morghgiran Mountain village.[2] When the drunks sobered up the next day, we offered them the chance to convert to Islam and to choose a righteous path. The Soviets became very angry and began cursing us and insulting us. They stated that "There is no way back from the path chosen. Afghanistan will be communist. We will not accept you or your dirty religion." They refused to cooperate. We could not get them out of the area without some cooperation on their part and we could not shoot them because the shots might draw attention from nearby security outposts. So, we buried them all alive. We kept their clothing and papers which we eventually sent to HIH headquarters in Peshawar. The next day, the Soviets surrounded the area, so we left and went to Parwan and Maidan. While the Soviets were looking for us, they had a clash with Mawlawi Rahmatgul's forces. After the clash, the Soviets found where we had buried the three. They were all dead and their bodies had turned black.

After we interviewed this source, the authors agreed that he should be provided anonymity. There is no map with this vignette.

[2] Morghgiran means "chicken snatchers".

RAID ON BALAHESSAR FORTRESS
by Commander Shahabuddin

A Soviet regiment was garrisoned in the Balahessar Fortress in Kabul. In September or October of 1983, we decided to raid a security outpost south of Balahessar. This outpost formed part of the security belt around the fortress. I had 62 Mujahideen in my group. My armaments included eight RPG-7s and two 82mm recoilless rifles. My base was some ten kilometers south of Kabul at Yakhdara. We planned the raid in our base at Yakhdara, moved in the late afternoon to the village of Shewaki and waited until dark. We moved out at dark. On the way, there were several regime outposts. I detailed a five-man security element against each one as we passed it. The main outpost was at Akhozi and others were at Bagh-e Afzal and Qalacha. The security elements mission was to secure our return trip so that we wouldn't be ambushed by the enemy.

We reached Balahessar fortress which is surrounded by several security posts. I retained a 15-man attack group and posted the rest of my command as security elements guarding the other outposts. I divided my attack group into a five-man support group and a 10-man assault group. We crept up to the outpost, climbed the wall, got up on the roof of the outpost and then attacked it. I led the assault group. We hit the sentry with a RPG and he vaporized. We blew open the doors with RPG rockets and opened fire on the soldiers in the courtyard. We killed 12 of the DRA and captured three of their wounded. The rest escaped through a secret covered passage into Balahessar fortress. I had two KIA. One was Zabet Halim.[3] We took our dead with us. We could not carry the wounded prisoners so we left them there. We captured 16 weapons—Kalashnikovs and machine guns, a mortar and a RPG. As we left, there was a commotion in Balahessar and tanks moved out of the fortress in our direction. One tank came close to us and we destroyed it with an RPG. The other tanks then quit coming toward us—they had lost their taste for a fight. We just wanted to get out of there, so we left for our assembly area. We had a

---

Commander Shahabuddin is from Shewaki Village south of Kabul. There is no map with this vignette.

[3] Zabat Halim was a legendary urban guerrilla who had been an NCO in the Royal Afghan Army. His death was a blow to the Mujahideen.

designated assembly area and, as we approached it, we were challenged and responded with the password. Once I assembled my entire group, we left. My security elements guaranteed a safe return. This raid was on the 10th day of the first month of the Islamic Lunar calendar—the Day of Ashura. This day commemorates the anniversary of the massacre of the Prophet Mohammad's grandson Hussein and his 72 followers at Karbala in Iraq. It is a day of mourning, reflection and solemn thinking for Shia and others. On this Day of Ashura, we thought of our own dead who died defending truth and righteousness. They had died appropriately on the Day of Ashura.

COMMENTARY: Many of the urban guerrilla commanders maintained their main operating base within the suburbs or outlying villages where it was easier to assemble and train a group of men without government observation. The guerrilla commanders maintained a net of informers and supporters who aided their entry and passage through the urban area. Still, guerrilla groups operating within an urban area had to secure their route of entry and withdrawal which took the bulk of their force.

VIGNETTE 9
RAID ON THE KABUL METROPOLITAN
BUS TRANSPORTATION AUTHORITY
by Commander Shabuddin

The Kabul Metropolitan Bus Transportation Authority is located on the eastern side of the city and served as the central bus terminal for 130 buses. In October 1983, I assembled 120 Mujahideen for the raid at our base at Yakhdara. We had 16 RPG-7s, three mortars, three 82mm recoilless rifles and numerous small arms. I divided the force into three 20-man teams to attack the Bagrami textile company, the police station, and our main objective, the city bus transportation authority. Sixty men constituted the security element which would secure our route of advance and withdrawal. A primary consideration of the urban guerrilla is always covering his route of retreat. We moved our force from our base and spread out into the surrounding villages. To preserve mission security, only my subcommanders and I knew the plan. Once we were in position, the commanders would brief their men and tell them what to do. The first group went to the textile mill. The second group, reinforced with a 82mm recoilless rifle, a mortar and some RPG-7s, set out to attack the police station at Kart-e Naw. I commanded the main attack against the bus authority. As we moved, we posted security elements outside all the security outposts in the area. I sent one group of Mujahideen to the Eqbal cinema to attack the security outpost located there so that they would not interfere with our raid. As our Mujahideen were getting ready to attack the outpost, a roving jeep patrol came by. They destroyed the jeep with a rocket. The soldiers in the security outpost saw the burning jeep and ran away. The Mujahideen captured three Kalashnikovs at this site.

I led my group to the large enclosure of the bus transportation authority. When we got there, I posted a few guards to prevent anyone from surprising us. Then we attacked the security detachment at the bus park. We killed eight, captured two and torched 127 buses in the enclosure. Only three buses escaped destruction. We also captured 13-14 Kalashnikovs and 155 bayonets! We withdrew over our escape route to our base camp. I learned that the group

---

Commander Shahabuddin is from Shewaki Village south of Kabul. There is no map with this vignette.

attacking against the textile mill fired their mortar and heavy weapons and inflicted damage on the building. Kabul was without full bus transportation for a good while.

COMMENTARY: The urban guerrilla attacks the credibility of the government by chipping away at morale, attacking notable government targets and disrupting the daily life of the populace. The bus terminal was an optimum target since it clearly demonstrated the reach of the Mujahideen and slowed the life of the capital city considerably.

VIGNETTE 10
WEAPONS RAID IN CHARIKAR
by Commander Sarshar

Charikar, the capital of Parwan Province, has a compact city core, approximately one kilometer by one kilometer, and a large suburb. The northern section of Charikar is called the "new jail" area. The headquarters of the DRA militia forces (self-defense units) was in the "new jail" area. Malek Shah was our contact inside that headquarters. In October 1983, he promised to get us inside the militia compound when the commander of the compound was asleep. I brought 65 Mujahideen from my base camp for this mission. We were armed with two Goryunov heavy machine guns, three PK medium machine guns, four RPG-7s, and Kalashnikov and Enfield rifles. I divided my force into three security groups and an assault group. One security group deployed near the road northeast of the headquarters, while the other deployed to the northwest of the headquarters to cover the other flank. These two security groups protected the assault group. The third security group secured our withdrawal route north to Ofian-e Sharif.

We approached the target in the night at 0200 hours. At 0300 hours, we got a flashlight signal from the headquarters. I climbed the wall and the eight other Mujahideen in the assault group followed me. We were all inside the compound and Malek Shah was just starting to point out the three rooms of the compound building when one of the sleeping militia got up. He saw us and began shouting. We had no time, so we burst into the three rooms firing as we went. I led the group into their commander's room. We killed 20 and I lost one KIA and one WIA. We captured 16 Kalashnikovs and I got their commander's Makarov pistol. Since all the firing was inside the rooms, much of the noise was muffled and the other security outposts did not react. Apparently the other security posts did not know that we had taken this post. We left the post before dawn. We went back to Ofian-e Sharif and the following night returned to our base camp in Ghorband.

COMMENTARY: The side streets of Charikar are narrow and crooked. Security of the flanks and withdrawal route were always a prime

---

Commander Sarshar was a police officer in Parwan and worked clandestinely with the Mujahideen. When his cover was about to be blown, he became a Mujahideen commander in Ghorband. He commanded a mobile group in the Ghorband front near Charikar. There is no map with this vignette. Charikar is found on Map sheet 2887.

consideration and took most of the urban fighters personnel. In this instance, 87% of the force was used for security. It was probably not excessive. One wonders about the effectiveness of Charikar's security system when 20 soldiers are killed with automatic weapons at 0300 hours in the morning—and nobody notices.

VIGNETTE 11
NIGHT RAID ON A CITY OUTPOST
by Ghulam Farouq

I was a high school student in Kandahar. I used my student identification to move freely around the city to support the Mujahideen. I
would try to make contacts with DRA soldiers in the government
outposts during the day and then the Mujahideen would use the
soldiers' information to attack them at night. One day in January
1984, I made contact with a soldier who showed a willingness to cooperate with the Mujahideen in capturing his outpost. This was the
Saray-e Saat-ha security outpost in Kandahar. The post was located
on the second floor of a building in the Bazaar-e Shah section of the
city. This is across from the road junction of Alizai street and Bazaar-
e Shah. The outpost was located there since the Mujahideen used
Alizai street to enter the city and the outpost controlled this path.

I took the soldier with me on my bicycle to Chardewal—some six
kilometers south of the city. There, we met with my commander, Ali
Yawar. We all discussed our plan and then I brought the soldier back
to the city on my bicycle. That night, our group of 30 Mujahideen
assembled. We entered the city on the south side near the Shekarpur
gate (Rangrez-ha street). From there, we moved along Sherali Khan
street near Bazaar-e Herat and from there to Wali Mohammad street.
As we moved along this path, we posted security so we could withdraw
safely. We had agreed with my contact that we would arrive at 2200
hours. We arrived on time and, as we approached the outpost, we
signaled with a flashlight. Our contact answered our signal. We
crossed the paved road and posted our men at the gate. There were
22 Mujahideen now securing the route and gate. The remaining eight
of us entered the gate and climbed to the second floor. Everyone
appeared to be asleep. There was one soldier who just had completed
his turn as sentry and we assumed that he was asleep. He wasn't. He
grabbed his Kalashnikov and fired at us, killing one. The dead
Mujahideen's brother returned fire, killing the soldier and two of his
sleeping comrades. We captured four other DRA soldiers plus nine
Kalashnikovs and a pistol. My contact deserted to us.

Ghulam Farouq was a urban guerrilla in Kandahar. He belonged to the Islamic Movement
(HI-- Harakat-I Islami) of Ayatollah Shaikh Asef Muhseni which is a minority Shia Muslim
faction. His nickname is Gulalai. There is no map with this vignette.

The firing alerted DRA forces and it would be hard to leave the city carrying a body, so we started to take the body to a safe house where we could leave it for the night. As we were moving down the street, one of our four captives escaped. A Mujahideen tried to fire at him, but discovered that he was out of ammunition. We knew that the escaped DRA soldier would report our whereabouts to the authorities and, since he escaped near the safe house, we could not now risk leaving the body there. So we left the body hidden near a bakery. We covered the blood trail with dirt and then withdrew along the same route we entered. We exited the city at 0200 hours.

Since the government knew that we had left our dead behind, they blocked all entrances into the city. We tried to return for our dead the next night but could not get in. On the third night, we tried a different route from the north of town through the Chawnay suburbs. We traveled from Kalacha-e Mirza to Chawnay. We got into the city and we went to the bakery. The government had not found the body, so we retrieved it and took it outside of town for a decent burial. The person who was killed was Hafizullah—a graduate of Kabul university.

COMMENTARY: Movement through a city is high risk unless the route is secured. In this case, over two-thirds of the available force secured the route. This got the force out safely. On the other hand, prisoner security was not too good. Prisoners should be bound, gagged and roped together in small groups for firm control. If possible, they should be blindfolded so that they remain disoriented and unable to give much immediate information should they escape. Finally, a raiding force should be kept small, but the correlation of Mujahideen to DRA was almost one to one. Surprise gave the Mujahideen an advantage, but the non-sleeping soldier offset that advantage.

Vignette 12
Raid on Kandahar Communications Center
by Ghulam Farouq

I continued to use my high school student identification to get around Kandahar. I would deliver messages for the Mujahideen and try to contact DRA soldiers who might give me valuable information or agree to cooperate with the resistance. In August 1984, I again found a DRA soldier who wanted to cooperate. His name was Hanif and he worked in the Kandahar Telephone Exchange Center. He and his friend in the DRA agreed to help us, so I took Hanif to our base south of the city in Chardewal to talk to my commander, Ali Yawar. Ali Yawar said that the exchange was too strong to take in a raid, but Hanif said that he and his friends would help.

Several nights later, Ali Yawar assembled 120 Mujahideen for the raid. We used the northern approach from Kalacha-e Mirza Mohammad Khan to Chawnay suburb. From Chawnay, we went to Topkhana—the Shia section of the city. Then we moved down Bala street. Ali Yawar posted about 100 Mujahideen as security along our route. Finally, we arrived at a point directly across from the outpost which guarded the telephone exchange. We gave our flashlight signal and Hanif answered it. Ali Yawar posted additional security and then we crossed the street one at a time. Twelve of us went inside the walled compound. It had a guard house and other buildings. Hanif took us all into the guard house. We sat there while the roving DRA security patrol passed outside. As usual, the security patrol came from the east and passed by the compound. They did not notice anything unusual. Hanif told us to remain quiet since another roving patrol was due from the west. We waited until they passed. There were three other sentries inside the compound that we had to neutralize. Hanif had held a tea break during the three previous nights. After the two roving patrols passed, the sentries would gather individually in the guard house to talk and drink Hanif's tea and eat his cakes. As the first sentry entered the guard house, we overpowered him, bound and gagged him and took him to the outside security group who took him away. In this fashion, we got rid of the three sentries.

We spent some 35 minutes in the guard room dodging the patrols

---

Ghulam Farouq contributed to the previous vignette. There is no map with this vignette.

and getting rid of the sentries. We exited the guard room carrying our jerry cans of gasoline. We planned to burn down the telephone exchange and surrounding compound. As we entered the main telephone exchange building, the guard who was sleeping inside woke up. As we were climbing the stairs to the second floor, he took his Kalashnikov and began shooting. He killed Mohammad Nabi from Chardewahl and Sherandam. He wounded Ghulam Reza. Things became very chaotic at that point. We were firing in all directions and other people were firing back. No one knew what was going on. We grabbed nine Kalashnikovs and our dead and wounded and left. In our haste, we did not set anything on fire. We retraced our steps and reached Kalacha-e Mirza Mohammad Khan about 0230 in the morning. The next day, we learned that we killed four DRA soldiers plus some of their relatives who were staying there with them.

COMMENTARY: The Mujahideen had a good movement plan through the city, but no plan for action once they were inside the compound. Consequently, there was no rehearsal before the raid. The commander left the critical inside plan to the collaborator—which is not always a good idea. In effect, the commander surrendered his command to an outsider at the critical phase of the raid. The raiding force spent 35 minutes all together inside the guard house. This is very risky. The concentrated raiding force was very vulnerable in case the collaborator had not really turned. Further, sleepers don't always sleep throughout the night and guard houses get a lot of visitors. The raiders needed a covering force inside the compound. Maybe there was no other way to neutralize the other sentries, but this was high risk to the raiding party. The collaborator should have known about the sentry inside the telephone exchange, but apparently made no plan to silence him before the force entered the building. A raiding force needs to get in and out in a hurry. Since the commander had abrogated his command for the critical phase, when things went bad, everyone acted on his own. The Mujahideen evacuation of dead and wounded and their capture of enemy weapons is commendable, but no one took 30 seconds to spill some gasoline and light a match. The main objective was to torch the exchange—and that did not happen.

VIGNETTE 13
ATTACK ON KHAD HEADQUARTERS
by Mohammad Humayun Shahin

On the evening of 13 August 1986, I led a five-man attack on the KHAD headquarters in Kabul. The building of the First Directorate of the KHAD was located near Darulaman at Alla uddin in the south of Kabul. The directorate worked round the clock and was located in a well-protected part of town (Map 14-4 - KHAD). Therefore, we had to use a small group and hit the target and leave. We took an RPG-7 grenade launcher and four AK-47s. Our plan was to sneak up on the building at night, fire a rocket at the building and leave. In the group were my brother, Nurullah, Mamur Abdul, Shah Mohammad and Mohammad Zaher.

I had an underground headquarters in Qala-e Chitgar Village, which is located some 2.5 kilometers from the western edge of Kabul. We kept our weapons there. After each mission, we would clean and lubricate our weapons and then wrap them in cotton cloth and then put them into sealed plastic bags. We would hide the plastic bags in sewer pipes and other out-of-the-way, hidden spots. We prepared for the mission, took out our weapons and waited for dark. We left Qala-e Chitgar in the late evening. The village is some four kilometers west of the target building. When we reached a concealed area outside the KHAD building, I put my security and RPG gunner in position. My regular RPG gunner was absent and so I had to assign another Mujahideen to fire the RPG. Since we were urban guerrillas, we did not have much opportunity for target practice and the gunner had never fired the RPG before. I served as his assistant gunner. I carried his rockets and helped him load the weapon. From the lights in the windows, I judged that the second floor was the most crowded and told him to aim for a second floor window. I did not have any ear protectors for any of us, so I wanted the gunner to keep his mouth open during the firing to equalize the pressure. In order to do this, I told him to loudly chant "Allahu Akbar" [God is the greatest] three times before firing. My new gunner, who was a Shia, smiled and said he would do so but would add "Ya Ali" at the end of the litany.[4]

Mohammad Humayun Shahin contributed to other vignettes in this chapter.

[4] "Ya Ali" is a saying commonly chanted by Shia when asking for heavenly help.

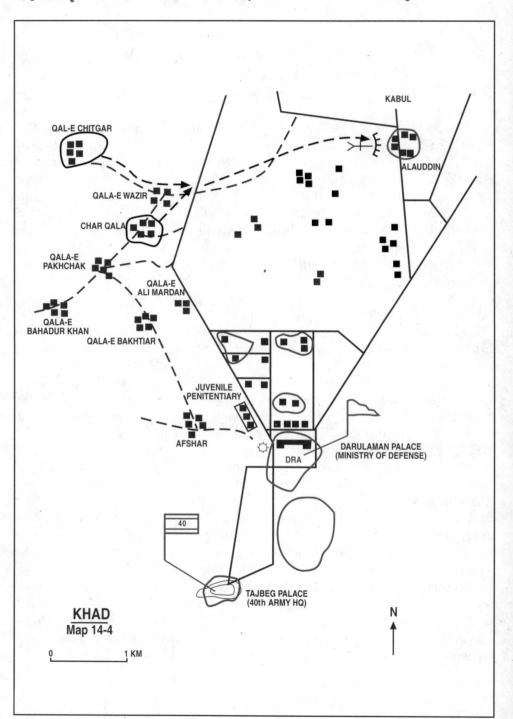

KABUL

QAL-E CHITGAR

ALAUDDIN

QALA-E WAZIR

CHAR QALA

QALA-E
PAKHCHAK

QALA-E
ALI MARDAN

QALA-E
BAHADUR KHAN

QALA-E BAKHTIAR

JUVENILE
PENITENTIARY

AFSHAR

DRA

DARULAMAN PALACE
(MINISTRY OF DEFENSE)

40

TAJBEG PALACE
(40th ARMY HQ)

N

KHAD
Map 14-4

0   1 KM

My gunner aimed, chanted and fired the RPG-7. The rocket flew, but instead of hitting the second floor, it hit the fourth floor. A major commotion ensued, but no one fired at us. We immediately left the area and withdrew to our base. Later on, we were told that more than 20 people had been killed or wounded by our attack.

COMMENTARY: There are better sites for weapons instruction and qualification than in the middle of a mission. In this case, the target was large enough that it was difficult to miss. Still, the gunner was off by two stories. Training to standard was a constant problem for Mujahideen commanders. The best training was conducted in training camps in Pakistan or in mountain bases. Unless urban guerrillas were sent out for training, they had very little live-fire training other than actual combat. Usually, urban guerrillas would detail a large security party to hold the withdrawal route. In this case, the five-man team relied on local contacts to watch the area rather than posting route security.

Vignette 14
Raid on 15 Division Garrison
by Commander Akhtarjhan

The DRA 15th Infantry Division was garrisoned in Kandahar city. We had contacts within the division. In the fall of 1987, our contacts invited us to come and seize the weapons from the division's military police company. We gathered about 100 Mujahideen for the operation. I commanded a group of 15 within the larger group. We crossed the Argandab River from our base camp at Chaharqulba to Baba Walisaheb and, from there, we went through the suburb of Chawnay. Local guerrillas secured our passage through Chawnay. We finally reached the division's main garrison. We waited until the moon set around midnight. The military police company building was at the end of the main compound. We crept to the building and saw that our contacts had placed a ladder against the wall for us. Some 50 of our group took up positions outside the compound while our raiding group of 50 climbed the ladder up onto the roof of the building. Then we climbed down from the roof inside the compound walls.

Some of our contacts were on sentry duty, so we had no troubles. Our contacts met us and led us into the barracks building. We assembled in a large empty room. Our contacts then took us to different rooms where the soldiers were sleeping—five or six soldiers per room. Their weapons were stored in the rooms. We took their weapons. Next to the barracks was a larger arms room. After disarming the sleeping soldiers, we raided the arms room and took hundreds of weapons. We then started carrying all the weapons onto the roof and passing them down to our fellows outside the compound walls. While we were doing this, the company political officer got out of bed and saw us. He started to make a noise, so we killed him with some of the bayonets. We finished getting the weapons out and left for our base camp. Our contacts deserted the DRA and came with us. We had some Arabs who were with us for jihad credit. They had a video camera and all they wanted to do was to take videos. They were of no value to us.

Commander Akhtarjhan was a Jamiat-e-Islami (JIA) commander in Arghandab District northwest of Kandahar. He was an elementary school student when he joined the jihad at the age of twelve. At end of the war, he was 25 years old and a commander. He joined the Jihad since he had two brothers in the Jihad and they were both killed. He took their place as family tradition dictated. He served under Mulla Naqib, the most powerful Jamiat commander in the area. There is no map with this vignette. Kandahar map sheet is 2180.

COMMENTARY: The Mujahideen penetration of the DRA was essential for successful raids like this. Entering a sleeping compound is always a high-risk proposition since someone is always awake, or wakes up, besides the sentries. A secure approach and withdrawal route is essential to urban guerrillas. Having local guerrillas secure the route allowed the force to bring enough people to carry the weapons without worrying about being ambushed on the way out.

CHAPTER COMMENTARY

Urban combat is difficult for the urban guerrilla and the regular force. Throughout the war, the Soviets and DRA were never able to completely control Kandahar and Herat. Finally, the Soviets dealt with the Herat guerrillas by bombing 75% of the city into rubble. That still failed to stop the urban guerrilla. The DRA had more success in controlling Kabul—but still were unable to stop the rocket attacks and guerrilla actions. On the other hand, surviving urban guerrillas are harder to find to interview. The urban guerrilla must be anonymous and ruthless to survive. The Soviets and DRA devoted a great deal of effort to finding and eliminating the urban guerrilla.

CHAPTER 15
CONCLUSION

"As a nation, we believed that history repeats itself. What happened in the 19th Century to the invading British would also be the fate of the Soviet invaders. Philosophically, the Soviets believed that history is unidirectional, progressive and does not repeat itself. History did repeat itself and we did prevail."

General Abdul Rahim Wardak

The Mujahideen understood that guerrilla war is a contest of endurance and national will. Battlefield victory is almost irrelevant, provided that the guerrilla survives to fight the next of a thousand battles before passing the torch to his children. The Mujahideen did not necessarily expect to win this war but fought because it was the right thing to do—it was a religious and national obligation. They accepted an asymmetry of casualties which eventually, but unexpectedly, led to the Soviet withdrawal.

In many respects, the tactics of the Anglo-Afghan Wars (1839 1842, 1878-1880, 1919) still applied. Technology has added range and accuracy, but the terrain still dictates tactics and the Mujahideen were quite comfortable applying their time-honored tactics against a modern foe. Much more innovation was required from the Soviet forces. Two modern systems, the helicopter and the antipersonnel mine, created severe tactical problems which were outside the Mujahideen historical experience. Tactical innovation occurs only where tactical innovation is required and the Mujahideen eventually found ways to work around the problem technology. Where innovation was not required, the Mujahideen stayed with the tried and true. Thus the basic Mujahideen ambush and pursuit were little changed from last century whereas their actions against an air assault or a fortified security post were quickly developed out of necessity.

Technology

Technology can provide advantages but is not decisive in this type of war. Soviet smart bombs had a decided impact when an appropriate target set could be identified. U.S.-supplied, shoulder fired Stinger air defense missiles, in the hands of the Mujahideen, created a great deal of consternation and led to a dramatic change in Soviet air tactics. Neither system, however, was a war winner. The Soviet equipment was designed for a different war on different terrain. It failed to function optimally in the mountains and deserts of Afghanistan. The Kalashnikov assault rifle was not always better than the World War I-designed British bolt-action Enfield rifle. The Enfield shot further accurately and would penetrate flak jackets designed to stop Kalashnikov bullets.

The RPG-7 antitank grenade launcher was the Mujahideen weapon of choice. It is a light-weight technology killer that destroys tanks, armored personnel carriers, trucks and helicopters. The Soviets and DRA tried to stay at least 300 meters away from the Mujahideen—out of Kalashnikov and RPG-7 range. This tactical timidity led to Mujahideen acquisition of crew-served weapons. Over time, heavy machine guns, recoilless rifles, mortars and portable multiple rocket launcher systems became an essential part of the Mujahideen arsenal which the Mujahideen used to pin their enemy in place in order to get close enough to use their Kalashnikovs and RPGs. Crew-served weapons also limited guerrilla mobility.

Soviet high performance jet fighters and bombers played a significant strategic role, but not a tactically significant one. The Soviets used their air forces to devastate the countryside and force the populace to leave in order to deny food to the Mujahideen. The Soviet air force destroyed farms, crops, animal herds, orchards and irrigation systems and forced millions of people to flee. The Mujahideen were then forced to carry their rations along with the other impedimenta of war. However, the Mujahideen seldom presented a target set that the Soviet air force or artillery could fully exploit to influence the tactical fight.

Technology did serve the Soviets as a force multiplier. Besieged garrisons could be maintained indefinitely by aerial resupply. Carpet bombing could stave off immediate disaster. Helicopter medical evacuation could save personnel who could later be returned to duty. Sensors could provide reconnaissance data in isolated areas.

Disunity of Command

The Mujahideen were nominally divided into seven main factions, but the disunity was much greater. There were factions within the factions. Old disputes and disagreements were not always put aside for the duration of the war. There were frequent armed clashes between Mujahideen of different factions. The reputation of certain factions was that they were more interested in fighting other Mujahideen than Soviets. Still, the ISI struggled to coordinate the actions of the various factions into some comprehensive plan. In some combat zones, such as Kandahar, the Mujahideen of different factions cooperated readily despite the politics of their factions.

In the Vietnam War, the North Vietnamese and Viet Cong were controlled by a strict chain of command in a clear hierarchy. This was considered a strength of the communist forces and the United States spent a lot of effort trying to find and decapitate the central leadership. The Mujahideen structure would be difficult to fit into a line-and-block chart and there was never a central leadership that was critical to the cause. Yet this inefficient disunity may have been a strength of the Mujahideen. No matter which commanders or leaders were killed, the Mujahideen effort would continue and the Soviets would never be short of enemies.

On the tactical level, the Mujahideen were prepared for a long war. Their goal was to hit, survive and fight again. Thus, the Mujahideen could not exploit success. After a victory, they went home. Group leaders, let alone loose coalitions, could not hold a force together for long after a fight. As was earlier noted by the British fighting the hill tribes, the mountain warriors could not stay together in victory or defeat. Thus, tactical victory could not be converted into operational gain.

Role of Military Professionals

Not more than 15% of the Mujahideen tactical leaders were professional military officers. However, the Afghan military officer corps played a major role in stalemating or defeating the Soviet invasion. The most important role of the Afghan military officers who stayed in uniform was their lack of cooperation with the government and their subversion directed against the communist regime and its Soviet backers. In 1978 and 1979, Afghan military officers staged numerous, spontaneous uprisings against the regime in Herat, Paktia, Asmar, Bala-hessar (in Kabul) and many others sites. Many Afghan military officers passed information to the Mujahideen. In the mid-1980s, the entire leadership of the Intelligence Directorate of the Ministry of Defense, including the head of the directorate (General Khalil—who was later executed by the regime), was arrested for its secret collaboration with the Mujahideen. Most of the serving Afghan officers refused communist party membership. Many of those who were forced to join the party were not loyal to the regime. Many of them secretly carried membership cards in one of the Mujahideen factions. Such lack of cooperation foiled all efforts by the Soviet Union to create a viable, indigenous military power in Afghanistan. Consequently the Soviet Union was forced to use mostly its own soldiers to carry the fight to the Mujahideen.

Afghan military officers who openly joined the Mujahideen faced many obstacles in integrating fully into the resistance hierarchy, based in Pakistan. Some faction leaders saw these former military officers as a challenge to their leadership and their factional interests and tried to sideline the professionals. Factions with a fundamentalist Islamic orientation were generally more opposed to accepting those military officers who had trained in and served under the old regimes. Therefore, many well-trained military officers who could bring effective leadership and organization to the ranks of the resistance forces, were sidelined by the factional politics of the jihad. Nevertheless, the former officers proved to be the most effective tactical and operational leaders that the Mujahideen had during the long years of war with the Soviet forces.

Logistics

Initially, the Mujahideen lived in the villages they defended and the villagers provided their food and shelter. Ammunition, weapons and other material came from the local bazaar or from Iran or Pakistan. The Soviets decided to break this link between the populace and the guerrilla by driving the populace out of the countryside. Soviet air and artillery attacked villages, standing crops, orchards, animal herds, granaries, water mills and irrigation systems. Eventually the populace was driven out of many rural areas and the Mujahideen could no longer readily subsist in these areas. With the agricultural system destroyed, the Mujahideen had to transport their own food and forage. The Mujahideen factions responded to this crisis by establishing fixed supply bases within Afghanistan. The larger supply bases were located in the mountains near the Pakistan border. Smaller supply bases were caches hidden outside the towns and villages. The Soviets then concentrated on finding and destroying the large and small supply bases. The Mujahideen dependence on the large fixed supply bases meant that they had to defend them. This provided a viable target set for Soviet air and artillery.

Although weapons and material were furnished free to the Mujahideen in the essential safe haven of Pakistan, there were significant costs to the Mujahideen in getting it to where it was needed. Often, the issued material was not what the commander needed in his area. So the material had to be traded or sold for what he needed. Then, the material had to be transported. Transportation was usually by commercial teamsters using donkeys, mules, camels or pickup trucks.[1] Commanders and faction leaders who established their own transportation systems discovered that it was cheaper and easier to stay with the established teamsters and muleteers. Once the materials were loaded and in transit, there were still taxes and fees to be paid. Every time the supplies crossed into a different tribe or faction area, there was a tax or tariff—often 10% of the goods. Mujahideen groups located well within Afghanistan were at the end of the pipeline and found that perhaps 40% of their material had gone to other Mujahideen groups between issue and final receipt. Western nations preferred to distribute aid in goods. Mujahideen leaders, particularly in the interior, preferred cash. They could always buy the needed mines, ammunition, food and material in the local bazaar. Saudi Arabia usually provided cash as aid.[2] Often, the Mujahideen needed more material than they were receiving through the factions and raised their own funds to buy it. Gem stones and narcotics, two traditional exports, provided some of these funds.

As the Mujahideen acquired more crew-served weapons, the ammunition tonnages required rose dramatically. At the same time, Soviet airstrikes on animal herds and their widespread use of scatterable mines along trails and mountain passes killed many of the transport animals. There was more demand for transport and fewer animals to transport the goods. The United States tried to solve the 'mule-gap" by providing Missouri mules. Unfortunately

---

[1] Animal carrying capabilities are: **mule**—250 to 335 pounds [H. W. Daly, *Manual of Pack Transportation,* Washington: Government Printing Office, 1917, page 18]; **camel**—400 to 600 pounds [Lewis Burt Lesley, *Uncle Sam's Camels: The Journal of May Humphreys Stacey Supplemented by the Report of Edward Fitzgerald Beale (1857-1858),* Cambridge: Harvard University Press, 1929, page 9]; and **central Asian horse**—215 pounds [William H. Carter, *Horses Saddles and Bridles,* Baltimore: The Lord Baltimore Press, 1902, pages 262-263]. Donkey figures unavailable.

[2] "The Logistics System of the Mujahideen", unpublished government contract study written in 1987.

these required more food, carried less and died more quickly than the local variety.

Medical care and medical evacuation was a Mujahideen weakness. There were few Mujahideen doctors, although established Afghan doctors frequently treated Mujahideen casualties at great personal risk. Some Mujahideen groups had a medic who had graduated from a eight-month to a year course in Pakistan or other countries. Most groups were lucky to have a graduate of a six-week first aid course. Some French doctors worked inside Afghanistan while many other western doctors worked in the border areas of Pakistan. If the wounded Mujahideen managed to survive the harrowing trip to Pakistan, he probably survived. However, a seriously wounded Mujahideen inside Afghanistan usually died.

Tactics

Guerrilla warfare demands quantities of quality light infantry on both sides. The Soviets never fielded enough. The Mujahideen were natural light infantry. They were hardy, tough, courageous and local. They had high morale, the warrior spirit and excellent tactical intelligence. They were naturals at the ambush and pursuit. They were raised from childhood with weapons, but they lacked unit training and discipline. Training varied from valley to valley and force to force. The Pakistani ISI provided some training courses and the former military officers from the Afghan Army who joined the Mujahideen tried to train the Mujahideen to a standard. Still, the Mujahideen were not trained to a standard and the quality of the individual groups was a function of their leadership.

The Mujahideen had warrior spirit and their focus was on battle, not easy LOC targets. They wanted noise, excitement, personal glory and the spoils of war. The Pakistani ISI cajoled and threatened, but it was difficult to persuade the Mujahideen to attack the lucrative and easy oil pipelines when security outposts were available.[3] The Mujahideen had some distinct tactical faults. If they were in their own area, they tended to ignore local security and could be surprised. They were very predictable in their selection of ambush sites and shelling sites. The Soviets, however, seemed unaware of this predictability. The Mujahideen would habitually reuse the same sites, but there is little evidence of the Soviets exploiting this pattern with aggressive foot patrols, site raids, mining or plotting artillery fire on these sites.

---

[3] Mohammad Yousaf and Mark Adkin, *The Bear Trap: Afghanistan's Untold Story*, London: Leo Cooper, 1992, 36.

The overall Mujahideen air defense posture was weak. The intro-duction of the Stinger shoulder-fired air defense missile toward the end of the war helped, but the Soviets countered the new system with a change in tactics. The tactical threat to Mujahideen were Su-25 close air support aircraft, helicopter gunships and helicopter lift ships carrying air assault forces. The Mujahideen developed the air defense ambush as an answer to the threat of these aircraft. There are several variations of the ambush, but basically the Mujahideen would position air defense weapons in optimum firing positions and then bait the ambush to draw aircraft into the kill zone. The most popular firing positions were caves dug into canyon walls where heavy machine guns could fire horizontally across the narrow canyon. The bait would lure the aircraft into the canyon where multiple machine guns would open up on its flight path. Other aircraft would be unable to engage these machine guns since they could not get an approach shot at the caves. The Mujahideen also learned to identify likely helicopter landing zones and mine them. They would position machine guns and RPG-7 gunners around the landing zone. As the helicopter landed, massed RPG and machine gun fire would tear into the aircraft. The Mujahideen also liked to hit aircraft parked on airfields and would stage shelling attacks for the purpose of killing aircraft on the ground. A large percentage of total Mujahideen aircraft kills was from mortar and multiple rocket launcher attacks on airfields.

Antipersonnel mines were a major problem for the Mujahi-deen. The Soviets employed millions of mines in Afghanistan. They surrounded installations, garrisons, security posts and government facilities with minefields. They mined the road banks along critical stretches of road. They dispersed scatterable mines over trails, mountain passes, cropland and grazing pasture. Most of the mines' components were nonmetallic and hard to detect. These antiperson-nel mines were designed to maim, not kill. Thus, the mine would rip off a Mujahideen's leg and the Mujahideen's comrades would then have to transport the crippled combatant back to Pakistan. Should he survive the slow, painful trip, he would probably never fight again, but the trip back would involve six or eight Mujahideen who could have been fighting. Mine detectors were in short supply and not too effective against plastic mines. Mujahideen would breach minefields with captured vehicles, flocks of sheep, by firing consecutive recoil-less rifles rounds to create a path, or by hurling large rocks across the minefield to create a path. None of these methods were too effective.

Although disinclined to dig in the hard, rocky soil of Afghanistan, the Mujahideen soon learned the value of field fortifications against Soviet artillery, armored vehicles and airstrikes. Field fortifications came to play a dominant role in the war as the Mujahideen learned to build sturdy, redundant, camouflaged bunkers and fighting positions which ensured their survivability.

Finally, the Mujahideen were a tactical force with a tactical focus, but, when the occasion demanded, they were capable of operational-level actions. Such actions as operation Gashay, Zhawar II and the defense against operation Magistral demonstrated this capability. Such actions were usually under the planning or leadership of former officers of the Afghan Army. What the Mujahideen were not capable of was transitioning quickly into a conventional force. After the Soviets withdrew, the Mujahideen tried and failed to take Jalalabad and Kabul by a conventional attack. These efforts ended in disorganized chaos as the DRA found heart and battled on successfully. It would be years before the DRA collapsed and the Mujahideen tried to unite to rebuild Afghanistan.

GLOSSARY

Afghanistan National Liberation Front (ANLF)—Jebh-e-Nejat-i-Melli Afghanistan}) founded by Sebqhatullah Mojadeddi. The party is moderate.

AGS-17—A Soviet-manufactured, tripod-mounted automatic grenade launcher which fires 30mm grenades from a thirty round drum magazine. The maximum range of the AGS-17 is 1,700 meters.

Air assault—Helicopter borne assault into an area.

ANLF—Afghanistan National Liberation Front of Mojadeddi.

AO—Area of operations.

APC—Armored personnel carrier, any of the wheeled or tracked Soviet-manufactured combat vehicles used to transport soldiers.

Bernau—Czechoslovak M26 light machine gun which fires from a top-loading 20-round magazine. This excellent 7.9mm weapon was developed between World War I and II and was sold abroad as the M30 to China, Yugoslavia and Romania. The British Bren gun is based on the M26 design. The Mujahideen called them 20-shooters.

BM-1—Single barrel 107mm rocket launcher.

BM-12—An obsolete Soviet multiple rocket launcher. The Chinese improved and manufactured it as the Type 63. Most Mujahideen BM-12s were actually Chinese Type 63s. It is ground-mounted, has twelve barrels and fires 107mm rockets to a distance of 8,500 meters. It weighs 611 kilograms.

BM-21—A truck-mounted, 40-tube multiple rocket launcher which fires 122mm rockets to a distance of 20.5 kilometers. The Mujahideen mostly called this the BM-40.

BM-22—A truck-mounted, 16-tube multiple rocket launcher which fires 220mm rockets to a distance of 40 kilometers. The type of rocket warheads include high-explosive fragmentation, chemical, incendiary and remotely delivery mines. The Soviet nickname for this lethal system is Uragan (Hurricane). Western analysts initially identified this system as the BM27.

BMP—A Soviet tracked infantry fighting vehicle that carries a three-man crew and a squad of eight soldiers. The BMP-1 mounts a 73mm cannon, a 7.62mm machine gun and an antitank missile. The BMP-2 carries a 30mm automatic gun and a different anti-tank missile and launcher.

BRDM—A Soviet four-wheeled armored car used primarily for reconnaissance. It has two auxiliary wheels for extra mobility. In its various configurations, it carries either a 12.7mm machine gun, a 7.62mm machine gun or both.

BMD—A Soviet air-dropable, armored personnel carrier that carries up to nine men (usually a maximum of seven). It has the same turret as the BMP, so the BMD-1 has the 73mm cannon of the BMP-1 and the BMD-2 has the 30mm automatic gun of the BMP-2. They were widely used by Soviet airborne and air assault force. The Mujahideen called them "commando tanks".

BTR—A Soviet eight-wheeled armored personnel carrier that can carry up to an 11-man squad. It mounts 14.5mm and 7.62mm machine guns and can carry antitank weapons as well. The BTR and BMP were the most common infantry carriers of the Soviet Forces.

Commander—During the war against the Soviets, the Mujahideen had no rank structure, so the term commander applied to all military commanders whether they led 10 men or 1,000.

Dari—Afghan Farsi or Persian spoken by about 50% of the population.

DRA—Democratic Republic of Afghanistan. The communist government of Afghanistan.

DShK—Soviet-manufactured 12.7mm heavy machine gun. It is a primary armament on Soviet-manufactured armored vehicles and is effective against ground and air targets. It has a wheeled carriage, tripod and mountain mount for ground and air defense firing. It has rate of fire of 540-600 rounds per minute with a maximum range of 7000 meters and an effective range of 1500 meters against ground targets and 1000 meters against air targets.

Enfield—British-manufactured .303 bolt-action rifle which was the standard British infantry weapon from 1895 through the

Korean War. It saw wide service on the North-West Frontier and its long range and powerful cartridge made it a favorite in India and Afghanistan. It has a maximum range of 2550 meters and an effective range of 800 meters. It has a 10-round magazine and can carry an additional round in the chamber, so the Mujahideen called them 11-shooters.

Etehad-e Islami (EIA)—Mujahideen faction led by Abdurab Rasul Sayaf.

Ghar—Pushto term for mountain.

Green zone—Agricultural region of gardens, orchards, fields and vineyards bisected by a network of irrigation ditches. They normally border rivers and some sections of highway and most are practically impassible for vehicles.

Goryunov—The heavy machine gun SGM *Stankovy Goryunov Modernizovanniy* M-49 was adopted by the Soviet Army during World War II and modernized versions are in service with the Russian Army today. It is a gas-operated, air-cooled, company-level, 7.62mm weapon that has vehicle and ground mounts. It has a rate of fire of 650 round per minute and a maximum range of 2,500 meters and an effective range of 1,000 meters.

Haji—The title of a person who has made the pilgrimage to Mecca.

Harbakai—Pashtu tribal policemen or regulators.

HI—Islamic Movement of Ayatollah Shaikh Asef Muhsini.

HIH—Islamic Party of Gulbuddin Hikmatyar.

HIK—Islamic Party of Mawlawi Yunus Khalis.

Inter-Services Intelligence (ISI)—Pakistan's intelligence service for internal and external security, political and military intelligence and counterintelligence. The ISI was responsible for funneling aid to the Mujahideen and providing training to Mujahideen combatants and support personnel.

IRMA—Islamic Revolutionary Movement of Afghanistan of Mawlawi Mohammad Nabi Mohammadi.

Islamic Party (HIH)— (Hezb-e-Islami-Gulbuddin) founded in 1974 to fight the Daoud government. It later split as cofounders Rabanni and Khalis founded their own factions. Its leader, Gulbuddin Hikmatyar is a fundamentalist internationalist. Hikmatyar's party received more outside aid from Pakistan, the United States and Saudi Arabia than any other party.

Islamic Party (HIK)—(Hezb-e-Islami-Khalis) was founded by Mawlawi Mohammed Yunis Khalis who left Afghanistan for Pakistan in 1973 after the Daoud coup.   Khalis is from Nangahar Province.   His most famous commanders include Abdul Haq in Kabul and Jalladuddin Hagani of Paktia Province. The party is fundamentalist.

Islamic Revolutionary Movement (IRMA)—(Harakat-e-Inqilab-i-Islami) was founded by Mohammad Nabi Mohammadi.   The party is moderate (traditional Islamist).

Islamic Movement (HI)—(Harakat-i Islami) was founded by Ayatollah Asef Muhsini in Iran as a minority Shia faction. The party has a traditional Islamic orientation.

Islamic Society (JIA)—(Jamiat-i-Islami) was founded by Burhanud-din Rabbani who fled to Pakistan in 1974. His most famous commanders are Ahmd Shah Masood and Ismail Khan. The party is primarily fundamentalist and dominated by ethnic Tadjiks.

Islamic Union for the Liberation of Afghanistan (IUA)—(Itttihad-i-Islami) was founded by Abd Al-Rab Abdul-Rassul Sayyaf. This used to be called the EIA until 1981. The faction is fundamentalist. In the mid-1980s, they again changed the name to the Islamic Union of Afghanistan.

JIA—Islamic Society of Rabbani.

Jihad—Holy war conducted for preservation of the faith.

Kal—Local term in Farah Province for canyon

Kalashnikov—Soviet automatic assault rifle. The AK-47 and AKM Kalashnikovs fire a 7.62mm round while the AK-74 fires a 5.45mm round.

Kandow—Pushto term for mountain pass.

Karez—An Afghanistan system of underground tunnels used for the collection of ground water and for carrying water for surface irrigation. The Mujahideen used them for shelter and ambush.

KHAD—The secret police of the Afghan government responsible for detecting and eradicating domestic political opposition, subverting the mujahideen, penetrating opposition groups abroad and providing military intelligence to the armed forces through its military wing. The KHAD was patterned after the Soviet KGB and GRU and apparently reported to the KGB.

Khalq—(Farsi for masses or people). One of the two communist factions of the PDPA.

KIA—Killed in action.

Kochi—Kochi are nomadic tribesmen of Afghanistan. They live primarily by herding and trading sheep, goats and camels.

Koh—Dari term for mountain.

Lashkar—A Pushto term for tribal armed force.

LOC—Lines of communication.

LZ—Landing zone.

Madrassa—Arabic term for an Islamic religious school.

Markaz—Mujahideen base.

Mawlawi—Islamic religious scholar.

MIA—Missing in Action.

Model 1938 Mortar—The Soviet Model 1938 107mm mortar was originally the standard regimental mortar for mountain units. It is a reduced size version of the 120mm mortar suitable for transport on a pack animal. It can fire 15 rounds per minute and has a maximum range of 5150 meters firing the heavy round and 6300 meters firing the light round.

Mulla—Islamic religious leader or Imam.

Mosin-Nagant—The Model M1891/30 is a Russian/Soviet bolt-action rifle or carbine which fires the 7.62x54 cartridge. It was used in the Russo-Japanese War, World War I and World War II. Many models come with a folding bayonet. The rifle has a maximum range of 2000 meters and an effective range of 400 meters. The Mujahideen called them five-shooters.

MRL (Multiple rocket launcher)—A ground-mounted or truck-mounted rocket artillery system capable of firing a salvo of rockets at a target.

Mujahideen (holy warrior)—A member of the Afghan resistance.

National Islamic Front of Afghanistan (NIFA)—(Mahaz-e-Melli Islami}). Founded by Pir Sayed Ahmad Gailani, this moderate party attracted a number of former officers from the Afghan Army and moderate technocrats.

NIFA—National Islamic Front of Afghanistan of Gailani.

OP—Observation Post.

Parcham—(Farsi for flag) Faction of the communist PDPA.

PDPA—Peoples Democratic Party of Afghanistan—the communist party of Afghanistan.

Pir—Title designating sainthood and leader in the Sufi orders.

PK—Soviet 7.62mm company machine gun which replaced the Goryunov machine gun. It weighs 16.5 kilograms and has an effective range of 1000 meters. The Mujahideen call them 100-shooters since they fire out of a 100 round box of linked ammunition.

POL—Petroleum, oil and lubricants.

Pushtun—The dominant ethnic group (nearly 50%) of Afghanistan who speak Pashtu. The British historically referred to these people as Pathans.

Qawm—The basic subnational Afghan identify based on kinship, residence and sometimes occupation.

Ramadan—The Islamic holy month of fasting.

RDM—Remotely delivered mines. Mines which can be emplaced by aviation, artillery or MRL fire.

RPG-7—Soviet manufactured shoulder-fired antitank weapon which fires a shaped-charge rocket. It has an effective range of 300 meters.

RPG-18—Soviet manufactured single-shot, shoulder-fired antitank weapon which fires a 66mm shaped-charge rocket. The rocket is stored in an extendable storage tube which also functions as a launcher. The launcher is thrown away after use. It has an effective range of 135 meters and is a copy of the USM72A2 LAW.

Saqar—Egyptian 107mm or 122mm MRL. It has one, two, three and four-barrel light-weight launchers. The 107mm (Saqar 20) has a maximum range of 8000 meters and the 122mm (Saqar 30) has a maximum range of 10,800 meters. The 107mm model was more common in Afghanistan. Some Mujahideen state that they had special rounds which enabled the Saqar to reach 20 kilometers and the Saqar 30 to reach 30 kilometers. Saqar means "eagle" in Egyptian.

Sarandoy—DRA Ministry of the Interior armed forces, a heavily armed police force. They were organized into six brigades or regiments (numbering about 60,000 men) and were based in Kandahar, Badakhstan, Baghlan and Paravan provinces plus two in Kabul. The Sarandoy had an additional estimated 6,000 men in operational and mountain battalions.

Shaheed—Martyr. The plural is shaheedan or shuhada..

Shia—The minority Islamic community in Afghanistan following the Imami Shiism (the dominant faith in neighboring Iran) or Ismaili Shiism.

SKS—(Samozaryadiy karabin Simonova}) gas-operated semi-automatic Soviet carbine with a folding bayonet. It has a ten-shot magazine and fires the 7.62x39 cartridge to a maximum range of 1000 meters with a 400 meter effective range. The first models were fielded in 1931 and it was a standard weapon of the Soviet Army during World War II through the early 1950s. The Mujahideen simply called them carbines.

SOP—Standard operating procedures.

Spetsnaz—Soviet forces trained for long-range reconnaissance, commando and special forces type combat.

Sufi—A mystic branch of Islam with considerable influence in Afghanistan. Sufis are more widespread among Sunnis.

Sunni—The majority Islamic community in Afghanistan. Over two-thirds of the populace are Sunnis, followers of the Hanafi School.

Tadjik—Ethnic Afghans from the northeastern regions of Afghanistan who make up about 25% of the population.

Tsadar—All purpose cloth that Afghans carry and wear. It serves as a ground cloth, sleeping bag, camouflage covering, bundle wrap and shroud.

Uzbek—Ethnic Afghans primarily in the north central part of Afghanistan who make up 10% of the population and speak Turkic.

WIA—Wounded in Action.

ZGU—(Zenitnaya gornaya ustanovka}) Mountain air defense weapons mount. Any Soviet air defense weapon that can disassembled for transport into the mountains by pack animals or porters. Usually this means that the weapons mount or pedestal has no wheels.

ZGU-1—A ZPU-1 mounted on a ZGU mount.

ZPU-1—A Soviet 14.5mm ground-mounted antiaircraft machine gun which is towed on a light, two-wheeled carriage. The system is built around a single-barreled KPV heavy machine gun which has a cyclic rate of fire of 600 rounds per minute and a practical rate of fire of 150 rounds per minute. The belt-fed machine gun feeds from a 150 round box and has a maximum horizontal range of 7000 meters and a maximum effective antiaircraft range of 1400 meters. It weighs 581 kilograms.

ZPU-2—A twin-barrel version of the ZPU-1.

ZSU-23-4—A Soviet self-propelled air defense weapon which fires four 23mm machine guns simultaneously. The Soviets used this weapon for counter ambushes and in the destruction of ground targets.

SYMBOLS LIBRARY
Red = Soviet or DRA Forces
Blue = Mujahideen

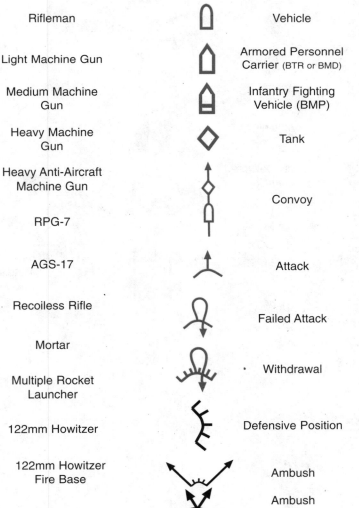

○	Rifleman		Vehicle
↑	Light Machine Gun		Armored Personnel Carrier (BTR or BMD)
↑	Medium Machine Gun		Infantry Fighting Vehicle (BMP)
↑	Heavy Machine Gun	◇	Tank
	Heavy Anti-Aircraft Machine Gun		Convoy
	RPG-7		Attack
	AGS-17		Failed Attack
	Recoiless Rifle		Withdrawal
	Mortar		Defensive Position
	Multiple Rocket Launcher		Ambush
	122mm Howitzer		Ambush
	122mm Howitzer Fire Base		
	Truck		

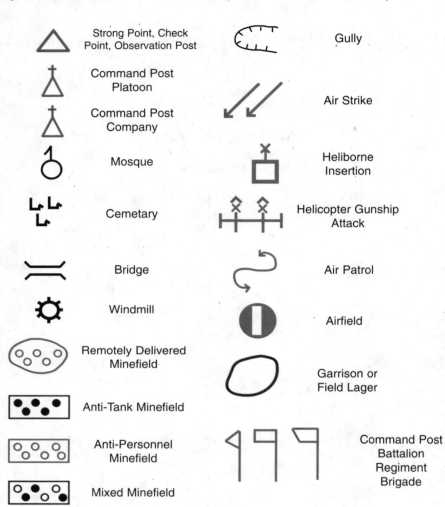

△	Strong Point, Check Point, Observation Post
⟁	Command Post Platoon
⟁	Command Post Company
♀	Mosque
⌐⌐	Cemetary
⊐⊏	Bridge
✿	Windmill
⬭	Remotely Delivered Minefield
▪	Anti-Tank Minefield
○	Anti-Personnel Minefield
◉	Mixed Minefield
⊂⟋	Gully
↙↙	Air Strike
⊡	Heliborne Insertion
⊥⊥	Helicopter Gunship Attack
↺	Air Patrol
◐	Airfield
⬭	Garrison or Field Lager
⊲⊓	Command Post Battalion Regiment Brigade

INDEX

ABOUT THE AUTHORS

Ali Ahmad. Jalali is a former Afghan Army Colonel. A distinguished graduate of the Military University in Kabul, he has also attended the Infantry Officers Advanced Course in Fort Benning, Georgia; the British Army Staff College in Camberley; the U.S. Naval Postgraduate School in Monterey, California; the Frunze Academy in Moscow and the Institute of World Politics in Washington, DC. He taught in the Military Academy and advanced military schools in Kabul. He joined the Mujahideen in 1980 and served as the top military planner on the directing staff of the Islamic Unity of Afghan Mujahideen (an alliance of three moderate Mujahideen factions) during the early 1980s before he joined Voice of America (VOA). As a journalist, he has covered Central Asia and Afghanistan over the past 15 years. He is the author of several books including works on the Soviet Military, works on Central Asia and a three-volume Military History of Afghanistan.

Lester W. Grau is a retired U.S. Army Lieutenant Colonel. He served as an infantry officer and a Soviet Foreign Area Officer (FAO) throughout his career. He fought in Vietnam. In 1981, he completed one year of Russian language training at the Defense Language Institute at Monterey, California and then graduated from the U.S. Army Russian Institute (USARI) in Garmisch-Partenkirchen, Germany in 1983. USARI was a two-year post-graduate school which dealt with all aspects of the then Soviet Union and all classes were taught in Russian. He has served in Moscow and traveled extensively in the former Warsaw Pact and former Soviet Union and continues that travel today. Since 1983, his work has focused on Russian and Soviet tactics and operations. He has written a book on Soviet tactics in Afghanistan. Mr. Grau currently works at the Foreign Military Studies Office (FMSO) at Fort Leavenworth where he continues to work on operational and tactical issues.

The Other Side of the Mountain:
Mujahideen Tactics in the Soviet-Afghan War

Text in New Century Schoolbook 11 point type
Book Editing and Design by Jonathan W. Pierce
Cover Design and Final Map Graphics by Emily Pierce
Initial Map Graphics by Rhonda Gross